BICENTENNIAL
1807
WILEY
2007
BICENTENNIAL

THE WILEY BICENTENNIAL—KNOWLEDGE FOR GENERATIONS

*E*ach generation has its unique needs and aspirations. When Charles Wiley first opened his small printing shop in lower Manhattan in 1807, it was a generation of boundless potential searching for an identity. And we were there, helping to define a new American literary tradition. Over half a century later, in the midst of the Second Industrial Revolution, it was a generation focused on building the future. Once again, we were there, supplying the critical scientific, technical, and engineering knowledge that helped frame the world. Throughout the 20th Century, and into the new millennium, nations began to reach out beyond their own borders and a new international community was born. Wiley was there, expanding its operations around the world to enable a global exchange of ideas, opinions, and know-how.

For 200 years, Wiley has been an integral part of each generation's journey, enabling the flow of information and understanding necessary to meet their needs and fulfill their aspirations. Today, bold new technologies are changing the way we live and learn. Wiley will be there, providing you the must-have knowledge you need to imagine new worlds, new possibilities, and new opportunities.

Generations come and go, but you can always count on Wiley to provide you the knowledge you need, when and where you need it!

WILLIAM J. PESCE
PRESIDENT AND CHIEF EXECUTIVE OFFICER

PETER BOOTH WILEY
CHAIRMAN OF THE BOARD

Introduction to Google® SketchUp®

Aidan Chopra
with Laura Town

BICENTENNIAL
1807
WILEY
2007
BICENTENNIAL

Credits

PUBLISHER
Anne Smith

PROJECT EDITOR
Brian B. Baker

MARKETING MANAGER
Jennifer Slomack

SENIOR EDITORIAL ASSISTANT
Tiara Kelly

PRODUCTION MANAGER
Kelly Tavares

PRODUCTION EDITOR
Kerry Weinstein

CREATIVE DIRECTOR
Harry Nolan

COVER DESIGNER
Hope Miller

COVER IMAGE
By Aidan Chopra

COPYEDITOR
Camelot Editorial Services

Wiley 200th Anniversary Logo designed by: Richard J. Pacifico

This book was set in Times New Roman by Aptara, Inc., and printed and bound by R. R. Donnelley. The cover was printed by R. R. Donnelley.

Microsoft product screenshot(s) reprinted with permission from Microsoft Corporation.

To order books or for customer service, please call 1-800-CALL WILEY (225-5945).

ISBN 978-0-470-17565-1

Printed in the United States of America

10 9 8 7 6 5 4 3 2 1

ABOUT THE AUTHOR

Aidan Chopra is the Product Evangelist at Google for SketchUp and Google Earth. He writes and lectures about how SketchUp is used in design, and writes the *SketchUpdate*, a monthly email newsletter that reaches SketchUp users worldwide. He holds a Master of Architecture degree from Rice University, and has taught architecture at the university level and, at Google, works on ways to mediate between power and usability.

Laura Town has been a professional writer and editor for over ten years, working on topics that range from technology to finance. She is the owner of the editorial services firm WilliamsTown Communications in Indianapolis (www .willtown.com).

College classrooms bring together learners from many backgrounds with a variety of aspirations. Although the students are in the same course, they are not necessarily on the same path. This diversity, coupled with the reality that these learners often have jobs, families, and other commitments, requires a flexibility that our nation's higher education system is addressing. Distance learning, shorter course terms, new disciplines, evening courses, and certification programs are some of the approaches that colleges employ to reach as many students as possible and help them clarify and achieve their goals.

Wiley Pathways books, a new line of texts from John Wiley & Sons, Inc., are designed to help you address this diversity and the need for flexibility. These books focus on the fundamentals, identify core competencies and skills, and promote independent learning. Their focus on the fundamentals helps students grasp the subject, bringing them all to the same basic understanding. These books use clear, everyday language and are presented in an uncluttered format, making the reading experience more pleasurable. The core competencies and skills help students succeed in the classroom and beyond, whether in another course or in a professional setting. A variety of built-in learning resources promote independent learning and help instructors and students gauge students' understanding of the content. These resources enable students to think critically about their new knowledge and apply their skills in any situation.

Our goal with Wiley Pathways books—with their brief, inviting format, clear language, and core competencies and skills focus—is to celebrate the many students in your courses, respect their needs, and help you guide them on their way.

CASE Learning System

To meet the needs of working college students, Wiley Pathways Introduction to Google SketchUp uses a four-part process called the CASE Learning System:

▲ C: Content
▲ A: Analysis
▲ S: Synthesis
▲ E: Evaluation

Based on Bloom's taxonomy of learning, CASE presents key topics related to Google SketchUp in easy-to-follow chapters. The text then prompts analysis, synthesis, and evaluation with a variety of learning aids and assessment tools.

Students move efficiently from reviewing what they have learned, to acquiring new information and skills, to applying their new knowledge and skills to real-life scenarios.

Using the CASE Learning System, students not only achieve academic mastery of Google SketchUp *topics,* but they master real-world *skills* related to that content. The CASE Learning System also helps students become independent learners, giving them a distinct advantage in the field, whether they are just starting out or seeking to advance in their careers.

Organization, Depth, and Breadth of the Text

Modular Format

Research on college students shows that they access information from textbooks in a non-linear way. Instructors also often want to reorder textbook content to suit the needs of a particular class. Therefore, although *Wiley Pathways Introduction to Google SketchUp* proceeds logically from the basics to increasingly more challenging material, chapters are further organized into sections that are self-contained for maximum teaching and learning flexibility.

Numeric System of Headings

Wiley Pathways Introduction to Google SketchUp uses a numeric system for headings (e.g., 2.3.4 identifies the fourth subsection of Section 3 of Chapter 2). With this system, students and teachers can quickly and easily pinpoint topics in the table of contents and the text, keeping class time and study sessions focused.

Core Content

The topics in *Wiley Pathways Introduction to Google SketchUp* are organized into 16 chapters.

Chapter 1, Meeting Google SketchUp, provides a basic introduction to the SketchUp software. Students evaluate the program's limitations and capabilities, as well as learn how SketchUp compares to other available 3D modeling software. The last part of the chapter provides a quick tour of the program, which helps prepare users to create their own models.

Chapter 2, Establishing the Modeling Mindset, explores the basic concepts related to modeling using Google SketchUp. Edges and faces, which are the central components of all SketchUp models, are explained. The chapter then examines the major differences between modeling in 2D and 3D. Finally, it closes with a look at some of the tools within SketchUp that allow users to carry out essential tasks such as navigating around a model, drawing lines, selecting objects, and working with accurate measurements.

Chapter 3, Building Simple Models, walks students through the entire process of creating a basic 3D model—in this case, one of a doghouse. Here, students not only learn how to create and view their model, but they also discover how to alter that model by changing its color, texture, and style and by adding shadows.

In Chapter 4, Modeling Buildings, readers take these fundamentals even further by discovering how to draft a floor plan of a simple, rectilinear building and convert this 2D plan to a 3D model. The chapter then explains how to add elements such as stairs, doors, windows, and a roof to the resulting model.

Chapter 5, Keeping Your Model Organized, describes SketchUp's four main methods for organizing a model: groups, components, the Outliner, and layers. The chapter ends with a detailed example of how all four methods can be used together to make modeling easier.

Chapter 6, Creating Everyday Objects, explores SketchUp's capabilities for creating forms other than buildings. Tools, techniques, and tips for making "rounder" objects are explored. Readers also learn how to create symmetrical models and extrude various 2D shapes into 3D objects.

Chapter 7, Modeling with Photographs, describes several methods for incorporating digital photos into SketchUp models. Specifically, the chapter explains how to paint the faces in a model with photographs, how to model on top of photo-textured faces, and how to build a model from scratch using a tool called Photo Match.

Chapter 8, Changing Your Model's Appearance, provides a complete rundown of styles, which are groups of settings that allow users to easily adjust the appearance of their faces and edges. Readers learn how to prepare a model that incorporates SketchUp's built-in styles, as well as how to make changes to various elements of these pre-made styles. The chapter also discusses how to create new styles, save styles, construct styles libraries, and share styles with other SketchUp users.

Chapter 9, Working with Light and Shadow, examines the two main reasons why most users opt to include shadows in SketchUp: to make their models more realistic, and to study the effects of the sun on an object in a specific geographic location. The chapter starts with a brief description of how the light and shadow controls work, moves on to show how users can make their shadows more realistic, and closes with a look at how to animate shadows to see how they change over time.

Chapter 10, Presenting Your Model Inside SketchUp, explains three methods for displaying a model without ever leaving SketchUp. First, it shows how to "walk" around and through models of 3D buildings. Next, it describes how to create animated slide shows by setting up scenes with different camera views, times of day, and even visual styles. Last, it explores how to show what's inside a model by cutting sections through it without taking it apart.

Chapter 11, Working with Google Earth and the 3D Warehouse, focuses on making SketchUp models that anyone can see on Google Earth. Students learn how to navigate in Google Earth and how to build a model in SketchUp for Google Earth. Readers also discover how they can contribute to the 3D Warehouse, a large online repository of free 3D models that anyone can add to or borrow from.

Chapter 12, Printing Your Work, explains how to print views of a SketchUp model; methods for printing using both the Windows and Mac versions of the software are described. The final portion of the chapter is devoted to the topic of scaled printing, which is somewhat difficult in SketchUp, but still much easier than drawing things by hand.

Chapter 13, Exporting Images and Animations, focuses on the export file formats that are common to both the Windows and Mac versions of Google SketchUp. Various 2D formats, such as TIFFS, JPEGS, and PNGs, are explored, as is the process of exporting animations as movie files that anyone can open and view.

Chapter 14, Exporting to CAD, Illustration, and Other Modeling Software, applies to features that are only available in the Pro (for purchase) version of SketchUp. The first half of the chapter talks about how to use SketchUp Pro to generate 2D files for CAD and illustration software. The second half describes how to export a model to a number of different 3D modeling programs.

Chapter 15, Creating Presentation Documents with LayOut, also pertains to a feature that is only available in SketchUp Pro: a separate piece of software called Google SketchUp LayOut. This is a program that lets users create documents for presenting 3D models both on paper and on-screen. In the chapter, readers learn about the different tasks LayOut can accomplish, how to navigate the LayOut user interface, and how to create a simple presentation drawing set from a SketchUp model.

Finally, Chapter 16, Troubleshooting and Using Additional Resources, closes out the book by describing some actions that may be helpful when SketchUp is slow or crashes, as well as when faces, colors, and edges are not working the way they should. The chapter also discusses a number of plugins that can enhance the SketchUp experience, and it concludes with a list of resources that can help users take their SketchUp skills to the next level.

Pre-reading Learning Aids

Each chapter of *Wiley Pathways Introduction to Google SketchUp* features a number of learning and study aids, described in the following sections, to activate students' prior knowledge of the topics and orient them to the material.

Pre-test

This pre-reading assessment tool in multiple-choice format not only introduces chapter material, but it also helps students anticipate the chapter's learning outcomes. By focusing students' attention on what they do not know, the self-test provides students with a benchmark against which they can measure their own progress. The pre-test is available online at www.wiley.com/college/chopra.

What You'll Learn in This Chapter

This bulleted list focuses on the *subject matter* that will be taught. It tells students what they will be learning in this chapter and why it is significant for their careers. It also helps students understand why the chapter is important and how it relates to other chapters in the text.

After Studying This Chapter, You'll Be Able To

This list emphasizes *capabilities and skills* students will learn as a result of reading the chapter. It prepares students to synthesize and evaluate the chapter material and relate it to the real world.

Within-Text Learning Aids

The following learning aids are designed to encourage analysis and synthesis of the material, support the learning process, and ensure success during the evaluation phase.

Introduction

This section orients the student by introducing the chapter and explaining its practical value and relevance to the book as a whole. Short summaries of chapter sections preview the topics to follow.

"For Example" Boxes

Found within most sections, these boxes serve multiple purposes. Some tie section content to real-world scenarios and applications. Others provide readers with hints and tips for using SketchUp more effectively.

Figures and Tables

Line art and photos have been carefully chosen to be truly instructional rather than filler. Tables distill and present information in a way that is easy to identify, access, and understand, enhancing the focus of the text on essential ideas.

Self-Check

Related to the "What You'll Learn" bullets and found at the end of each section, this battery of short-answer, multiple-choice, and true/false questions emphasizes student understanding of concepts and mastery of section content. Although the questions may be either discussed in class or studied by students outside of class, students should not go on before they can answer all questions correctly.

Key Terms and Glossary

To help students develop a professional vocabulary, key terms are bolded when they first appear in the chapter. A complete list of key terms with brief definitions appears at the end of each chapter and again in a glossary at the end of the book. Knowledge of key terms is assessed by all assessment tools (discussed later in this preface).

Summary

Each chapter concludes with a summary paragraph that reviews the major concepts in the chapter and links back to the "What You'll Learn" list.

Evaluation and Assessment Tools

The evaluation phase of the CASE Learning System consists of a variety of within-chapter and end-of-chapter assessment tools that test how well students have learned the material. These tools also encourage students to extend their learning into different scenarios and higher levels of understanding and thinking. The following assessment tools appear in every chapter of *Wiley Pathways Introduction to Google SketchUp*.

Summary Questions

These exercises help students summarize the chapter's main points by asking a series of multiple-choice and true/false questions that emphasize student understanding of concepts and mastery of chapter content. Students should be able to answer all of the Summary Questions correctly before moving on.

Applying This Chapter Questions

These questions drive home key ideas by asking students to synthesize and apply chapter concepts to new, real-life situations and scenarios.

You Try It Questions

Found at the end of each chapter, You Try It Questions are designed to extend students' thinking and are thus ideal for discussion or writing assignments. Using an open-ended format and sometimes based on web sources, they encourage students to draw conclusions using chapter material applied to real-world situations, which fosters both mastery and independent learning.

Post-test

The post-test should be taken after students have completed the chapter. It includes all of the questions in the pre-test so that students can see how their learning has progressed and improved.

Online Resources

Like all books in the series, *Wiley Pathways Introduction to Google SketchUp* is accompanied by a variety of online elements, including pre-tests, post-tests, and other supplemental materials. These resources are available to instructors and students through the text's Book Companion Website, www.wiley.com/college/chopra.

In addition, Google offers SketchUp users numerous other computer-based tools, including the following:

▲ **Video tutorials:** Google has created several video tutorials to facilitate learning of SketchUp. These tutorials are available for free and can be accessed by anyone with an Internet connection.

▲ **Self-paced tutorials:** In addition to the video tutorials, a number of self-paced online tutorials are also available for free through the Google SketchUp website.

▲ **Online help center:** SketchUp's extensive online help center offers a list of frequently asked questions (FAQs), as well as a knowledge base of technical support issues and solutions.

▲ **Quick reference card:** Through both the SketchUp website and the program's Help menu, users can access a quick reference card that lists all of SketchUp's toolbars, tools, and modifier keys.

▲ **Component libraries:** SketchUp features extensive component libraries that allow users to easily add detail to their models by inserting any number of pre-drawn objects. Specific libraries exist for a variety of fields, including architecture, construction, film and stage design, landscape architecture, mechanical design, and transportation.

Instructor and Student Package

Wiley Pathways Introduction to Google SketchUp is also available with the following teaching and learning supplements. All supplements are available online at the text's Book Companion Website, located at www.wiley.com/college/chopra.

Instructor's Resource Guide

The Instructor's Resource Guide provides the following aids and supplements for teaching an introduction to SketchUp course:

▲ **Sample syllabus:** This syllabus serves as a convenient template that instructors may use for creating their own course syllabi.

▲ **Teaching suggestions:** For each chapter, these include a chapter summary, learning objectives, definitions of key terms, lecture notes, answers to select text question sets, and at least three suggestions for classroom activities, such as ideas for speakers to invite, videos to show, and other projects.

PowerPoints

Key information is summarized in 10 to 15 PowerPoints per chapter. Instructors may use these in class or choose to share them with students for class presentations or to provide additional study support.

Test Bank

The test bank features one test per chapter, as well as a mid-term and two finals—one cumulative and one non-cumulative. Each includes true/false, multiple-choice, and open-ended questions. Answers and section references are provided for the true/false and multiple-choice questions, and section references are given for the open-ended questions. Tests are available in Microsoft Word and computerized formats.

ACKNOWLEDGMENTS

Taken together, the content, pedagogy, and assessment elements of *Wiley Pathways Introduction to Google SketchUp* offer the career-oriented student exposure to the most important aspects of SketchUp, as well as ways to develop the skills and capabilities that current and future employers seek in the individuals they hire and promote. Instructors will appreciate the book's practical focus, conciseness, and real-world emphasis.

We would like to thank the following reviewers for their feedback and suggestions during the text's development. Their advice on how to shape *Wiley Pathways Introduction to Google SketchUp* into a solid learning tool that meets both their needs and those of their busy students is deeply appreciated:

▲ Terri Laurenceau, Art Institute of Pittsburgh
▲ Diego Matho, Boston Architectural College
▲ Jorge Paricio, Art Institute of Pittsburgh

BRIEF CONTENTS

CONTENTS

━ ━

1

MEETING GOOGLE SKETCHUP
A Brief Overview

Starting Point

Go to www.wiley.com/college/chopra to assess your knowledge of SketchUp basics.
Determine where you need to concentrate your effort.

What You'll Learn in This Chapter

▲ The relationship between SketchUp and Google
▲ How SketchUp is different from other 3D software
▲ The capabilities of SketchUp
▲ How to navigate the SketchUp software

After Studying This Chapter, You'll Be Able To

▲ Assess the basics of SketchUp and install the program
▲ Compare and contrast SketchUp with other 3D software
▲ Evaluate the capabilities and limitations of SketchUp
▲ Assess the role of the five main parts of SketchUp in constructing models

INTRODUCTION

Years ago, software for building three-dimensional (3D) models of things like buildings, cars, and other objects was hard to use—people went to school for years to learn it! And if that wasn't bad enough, 3D modeling software was expensive. It was so expensive that the only people who could use it were professionals and software pirates. Then along came SketchUp.

Operating under the assumption that lots of people might want and need to make 3D models, the people who invented SketchUp decided to design a program that worked more intuitively. Instead of making users think about 3D models as complex mathematical constructs (the way computers think), they created an interface that lets users build models using elements they're already familiar with: lines and shapes.

So, do you need to know how to draw to use SketchUp? If you use the latest version of the software, not really. Traditional drawing is about *translating* what you see onto a flat piece of paper—or going from 3D to 2D, which is hard for most people. In SketchUp, however, you're always in 3D, so no translation is involved—you just *build,* and SketchUp takes care of features like perspective and shading for you.

This first chapter is about putting SketchUp in context. In this chapter, you will assess the basics of SketchUp. You will evaluate its limitations and capabilities. You will also assess why Google offers SketchUp for free, and how this program compares to other 3D software. In the last part of the chapter, you'll receive a quick tour of the SketchUp, which will help you prepare to create models with this exciting program.

1.1 SketchUp Basics

Before beginning a more detailed discussion of SketchUp, it's helpful to have some basic background information on the software, including the following:

▲ **You get SketchUp by downloading it from the Internet.** Just type http://sketchup.google.com into your web browser, and read through the first page of the Google SketchUp website. Click the links to download the application on to your computer, and then follow the installation instructions on the web.

▲ **SketchUp works with Windows and Mac OS X.** Google SketchUp is available for both operating systems, and it looks (and works) nearly the same way on both platforms.

▲ **A professional version is available.** Google offers a professional version of SketchUp (called Google SketchUp Pro) that can be purchased. It includes a few terrific features that certain users, like architects, production designers, and other design professionals need for exchanging files with other software. SketchUp Pro also includes a whole new sub-application for creating presentation documents that works natively with SketchUp models. It's called LayOut and is discussed later in this book. If you think you might need SketchUp Pro, you can download a free trial version from http://sketchup.google.com.

Many years ago, when photography was first invented, there was suddenly a new way to make pictures of things that didn't involve drawing, engraving, or painting. Nowadays, you can't throw a rock without hitting a photograph of something. *Everything* (it seems) can take pictures, including people's cellular phones. Thus, over a century after it was first created, photography remains the main way that visual information is communicated.

But what comes after photography? Google thinks it's 3D, and here's why: You live in 3D. The furniture you buy (or build) is 3D, and so is the route you take to work. Because so many of the decisions you need to make (e.g., buying a couch, or finding your way) involve 3D information, wouldn't it be nice to be able to experience that information in 3D?

Software like SketchUp lets you see 3D information on a 2D screen, which is good. However, affordable 3D printers and holography are just over the horizon. All that's left is to build a model of every single thing in the world—and guess who's going to do it? You are! By making SketchUp free for all users, Google is leading the 3D charge. Rather than relying on a small number of extensively trained users to get around to modeling everything in the universe, Google has made SketchUp available to anyone who wants to participate. After all, the idea behind Google is to organize the world's information, not to create it. By giving SketchUp away, the company has created an entirely new kind of information to organize. You'll learn more about Google's methods for storing and organizing this information later in the book, in the discussion of Google Earth and Google 3D Warehouse.

SELF-CHECK

1. SketchUp is:
   a. free.
   b. expensive.
   c. only for Macs.
   d. distributed by Yahoo.
2. You can download SketchUp from the Internet. True or false?
3. A professional version of SketchUp is available. True or false?
4. _____ has made SketchUp available to everyone.

1.2 Comparing SketchUp to Other 3D Modeling Programs

If you're reading this book, you're most likely interested in two things: building 3D models and using SketchUp to do so. The following sections tell you something about how SketchUp compares to other 3D modeling programs—specifically, how long it takes to learn to use the software, and what kind of models the software produces.

1.2.1 Traveling the SketchUp Learning Curve

When it comes to widely available 3D modeling software, it really doesn't get any easier than SketchUp. This software has been successful for one reason: Within several hours of launching the program for the first time, most people are able to learn SketchUp well enough to build a model. SketchUp doesn't require reading any thick manuals or understanding any special geometric concepts; instead, it's simply about grabbing your mouse and jumping in. Part of the reason for this is that the software is easy to use; another part is that SketchUp comes with a number of introductory tutorials that help users get up and running as quickly as possible.

So, how long should it take you to discover how SketchUp works? It depends on your background and experience, but in general, you can expect to be able to make a recognizable object in less than four hours. That's not to say you'll be an expert—it just means that SketchUp's learning curve is extremely shallow. You don't need to know much to get started, and you'll still be picking up new skills years from now.

But is SketchUp *easy*? Lots of people say so, but it's all relative. SketchUp is without a doubt easi*er* than most other modeling programs available today, but 3D modeling itself can be tricky. Some people catch on right away, and others take longer. But one thing is certain: If you want to build 3D models and you have an afternoon to spare, there's no better place to start than with SketchUp.

1.2.2 Understanding the Types of Models SketchUp Produces

Three-dimensional modeling software creates two basic types of models: **solid models** and **surface models.** Figure 1-1 illustrates the basic difference between the two.

Figure 1-1

Surface models are hollow   Solid models are solid

Surface models are hollow, whereas solid models are not.

Google SketchUp is a "surfaces" modeler. In other words, everything in SketchUp is basically made of the following elements:

▲ **Faces:** Thin (infinitely thin, actually) surfaces
▲ **Edges:** Straight lines

That's it. Even things that look thick, such as cinder-block walls, are in fact hollow shells. Making models in SketchUp is a lot like building things out of paper—albeit it *extremely* thin paper. Surface modelers like SketchUp are great for making models quickly, because all you really need to worry about is modeling what things *look* like. That's not to say that these modelers are less capable; it's just that they're primarily intended for visualization.

On the other hand, using a "solids" modeler is more like working with clay. When you cut a solid model in half, you create new surfaces where you cut; that's because objects are, of course, solid. Programs like SolidWorks, FormZ, and Inventor create solid models. People who make parts, like mechanical engineers and industrial designers, tend to work with solid models because they can use them to perform precise calculations. For example, being able to calculate the volume of an object means that you can figure out how much it will weigh. Also, special machines can produce real-life prototypes directly from solid-model files. This is helpful for seeing how lots of small components are going to fit together.

An important point to reinforce here is that there's no "best" type of modeling software. It all depends on three things: how you like to work, what you're modeling, and what you plan to do with your model when it's done.

FOR EXAMPLE

Polygonal vs. Curves-Based Modelers

While 3D modeling programs can be classified based upon whether they create solid or surface models, they can also be categorized based on the type of math they use to produce their models. More specifically, programs can be thought of as either **polygonal modelers** (of which SketchUp is an example) or **curves-based modelers.** Polygonal modelers use straight lines and flat surfaces to define everything; here, even things that *look* curvy aren't actually curvy. On the other hand, curves-based modelers use true curves to define lines and surfaces. This yields organic, flowing forms that are much more realistic than those produced by polygonal modelers, but curvy modelers put a lot more strain on the computers that have to run them (as well as the people who have to figure out how to use them). Ultimately, the choice between the two types of modelers involves a trade-off between simplicity and realism.

SELF-CHECK

1. _____ modelers use straight lines and flat surfaces to define everything.
2. A surface model is solid. True or false?
3. When you cut a solid model in half, you create new _____.
4. SketchUp is a solids modeler. True or false?

1.3 What You Should (and Shouldn't) Expect SketchUp to Do

It's wise to be skeptical of tools that claim to be able to do everything. Typically, it's better to rely on specialists, or tools that are designed to do one thing *really* well. SketchUp is an example of a specialist—one that was created to build 3D models. In fact, here's a list of the various tasks (all related to model building) that you can do with SketchUp:

▲ **Start a model in lots of different ways:** With SketchUp, you can begin a model in whatever way makes sense for what you're building:
  • *From scratch:* When you first launch SketchUp, you see nothing except a small person standing in the middle of your screen. If you want, you can even delete the person, leaving you with a completely blank slate on which to model anything you want.
  • *In Google Earth:* With this method, you can bring an aerial photograph of any place on Earth (including your home) into SketchUp and start modeling right on top of it.
  • *From a photograph:* You can also use SketchUp to build a model based on a photo of the thing you want to build. It's not really a beginner-level feature, but it's there.
  • *With another computer file:* SketchUp can also import images and CAD (computer-aided drawings produced with other software) files so that you can use them as a starting point for what you want to make.

▲ **Work "loose" or "tight":** One of the best things about SketchUp is that you can model without worrying about exactly *how big* something is. You can make models that are super-sketchy, but if you want, you can also make models that are absolutely precise. In this way, SketchUp is just like paper—the amount of detail you add is entirely up to you.

▲ **Build something real or make something up:** What you build with SketchUp really isn't the issue. You only work with lines and shapes, and how you arrange them is your call. SketchUp isn't intended for making buildings any more than it is for creating other things. It's just a tool for drawing in three dimensions.

▲ **Share your models:** After you've made something you want to show off, you can do a number of things:

- *Print:* Yes, you can print from SketchUp.
- *Export images:* If you want to generate an image file of a particular view, you can export one in any of several popular formats.
- *Export movies:* Animations are a great way to present three-dimensional information, and SketchUp can create them easily.
- *Upload to the 3D Warehouse:* This is a giant, online repository of SketchUp models that you can add to (and take from) all you want.

So, what *can't* SketchUp do? A few things, actually—but that's okay. SketchUp was designed from the outset to be the friendliest, fastest, and most useful modeler available. Fantastic programs are available that do the things in the following list, and SketchUp can exchange files with most of them:

▲ **Photorealistic rendering:** Most 3D modelers have their own built-in photo renderers, but creating model views that look like photographs is a rather specialized undertaking. SketchUp has always focused on something called **nonphotorealistic rendering (NPR)** instead. NPR is essentially technology that makes things look hand-drawn. If you want to make realistic views of your models, consider using one of the many third-party renderers that work well with SketchUp (discussed in Chapter 16).

▲ **Animation:** Although SketchUp can export animations, the movies you can make with this software only involve moving your "camera" around your model. True animation software also lets you move around the things *inside* your model. SketchUp doesn't do this; however, the professional version does allow you to export your models to a number of different programs that offer this more advanced type of animation.

▲ **Building Information Modeling (BIM):** BIM software lets you make models that automatically keep track of things like quantities, and it generates standard drawing views (plans and sections) from your model. SketchUp lets you draw edges and faces, but it has no earthly idea what you're drawing—that's just not how it works. You can use SketchUp with all the major BIM packages out there (via special importers and exporters), but it won't carry out BIM functions on its own.

FOR EXAMPLE

Edges and Faces

When you use SketchUp to draw a bunch of edges and faces in the shape of a staircase, all SketchUp knows is how many edges and faces it has to keep track of, and where they all go. There's no such thing as a *stair* in SketchUp—just edges and faces.

Coming to this realization has the tendency to worry some people. If you want a model of something, you have to make it out of edges and faces. SketchUp has some nice tools that let you create, delete, and otherwise arrange your geometry to make anything you want, but no Stair Tool is available to help you make stairs. Ditto for walls, windows, doors, or any of the other things that specialized architecture software programs offer. The thing to remember is that SketchUp was created to let you model *anything*, not just buildings, so its tools are designed to manipulate geometry. That's good news, believe or not, because it means that you're not restricted in any way—you can model anything you can imagine!

SELF-CHECK

1. SketchUp has always focused on photorealistic rendering. True or false?
2. With SketchUp you can:
   a. share your models.
   b. export movies.
   c. export images.
   d. all of the above.
3. SketchUp has BIM functions of its own. True or false?
4. You can make precise models with SketchUp. True or false?

1.4 Taking the Ten-Minute SketchUp Tour

Now, before learning how to use SketchUp, let's take a quick look at where you can find most of the important windows, menus, and related components within the program.

Figure 1-2

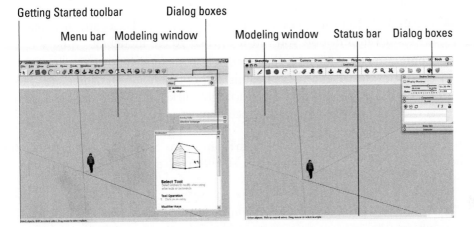

The main parts of SketchUp, in both the Windows (left) and Mac (right) versions.

As with most programs you already use, the SketchUp user interface has five main parts. Figure 1-2 shows all of them, in both the Windows and Mac versions of the program.

These five parts, plus an additional feature, can be described as follows:

▲ **Modeling window:** See that big area in the middle of the computer screen? That's the modeling window, and it's where you will spend 99 percent of your time in SketchUp. You build your model there; in fact, it's sort of a frame into a 3D world inside your computer. What you see in your modeling window is *always* a 3D view of your model, even if you happen to be looking at it from the top or side.

▲ **Menu bar:** For anyone who has used a computer in the last thirty years, the menu bar is nothing new. Each menu contains a long list of options, commands, tools, settings, and other features that pertain to just about everything you can do in SketchUp.

▲ **Toolbars:** These contain buttons that you can click to activate tools and commands; they are faster than using the menu bar. SketchUp has a few different toolbars, but only one is visible when you launch the program for the first time: the Getting Started toolbar. (Note that if your modeling window is too narrow to show all the tools on the Getting Started toolbar, you can click the arrow on the right to see the rest of them.)

▲ **Dialog boxes:** Some programs call these boxes "palettes," and some call them "inspectors." SketchUp doesn't call them anything. Its documentation (specifically, the SketchUp Help document you can access in the Help menu) refers to some of them as managers and some as dialog boxes, but for the sake of simplicity, this text will refer to them all as dialog boxes.

▲ **Status bar:** You can consider this your SketchUp dashboard. It contains contextual information you can use while you're modeling.

▲ **Context menus:** Right-clicking things in your modeling window usually cause a context menu of commands and options to open. These are always relevant to whatever you happen to right-click (and whatever you're doing at the time), so the contents of each context menu are different.

In addition, although the following aren't part of the SketchUp user interface (or the items described in the previous list), they're a critical part of modeling in SketchUp:

▲ **A mouse with a scroll wheel:** On most mice, you usually find a left button (the one you use the majority of the time), a right button (the one that opens the context menus), and a center scroll wheel that you can both roll back and forth and click down like a button. If your mouse doesn't have a scroll wheel, you should consider getting one that does—it will improve your SketchUp experience more than any single other thing you could buy.

▲ **A keyboard:** This sounds silly, but some people have tried to use SketchUp without a keyboard, although it's just not possible. So many of the things you need to do all the time (like make copies) involve your keyboard, so you'd better have one handy if you're planning to use SketchUp.

1.4.1 Using the Menu Bar

SketchUp's menus are generally straightforward; you won't find anything surprising in any of them. All the same, here's what they contain:

▲ **File:** This menu includes options for creating, opening, and saving SketchUp files. It's also where to go if you want to import or export a file, or make a printout of your model view.

▲ **Edit:** The Edit menu has all the commands that affect the bits of your model that are selected.

▲ **View:** This menu's a little tricky. You'd think it would contain all the options for flying around in 3D space, but it doesn't—those are found on the Camera menu. Instead, the View menu includes all the controls you use to affect the appearance of your model itself: what's visible, how faces look, and so on. The View menu also contains settings for turning on and off certain elements of SketchUp's user interface.

▲ **Camera:** This menu contains controls for viewing your model from different angles. In SketchUp, your "camera" is your point of view, literally.

▲ **Draw:** The Draw menu includes tools for drawing edges and faces in your modeling window.

▲ **Tools:** Most of SketchUp's tools are contained in this menu, except of course, the ones you use for drawing.

▲ **Window:** If you're ever wondering where to find a dialog box that you want to use, this is the place to look; they're all right here.

▲ **Plugins:** You can get extra tools for SketchUp—in other words, smaller programs that "plug in" to it and add functionality. Some of these programs show up on this menu after they're installed.

▲ **Help:** The Help menu contains some incredibly useful resources for understanding SketchUp as you go along. Pay particular attention to the video tutorials and the special SketchUp community link.

1.4.2 Using the Toolbars

The Getting Started toolbar contains a small subset of the tools that you can use in SketchUp. The idea behind this toolbar is that seeing all the tools right away tends to overwhelm new users, so having a limited selection is more helpful for most people.

To get access to more tools (through toolbars—you can always access everything through the menus), you can do the following, depending on which operating system you're using:

▲ **Windows:** Choose View⇨Toolbars to see a list of all the toolbars that are available. You may want to start with the Large Tool Set to begin, and then add toolbars as you need them (and as you figure out what they do).

▲ **Mac:** Choose View⇨Tool Palettes⇨Large Tool Set. To add even more tools, right-click the Getting Started toolbar (the one right above your modeling window) and choose Customize Toolbar. Now drag whatever tools you want onto your toolbar, and click the Done button.

1.4.3 Checking the Status Bar

Just below the modeling window lies an often overlooked feature of SketchUp: the status bar. This part of the screen contains helpful information including the following:

▲ **Context-specific instructions:** Most of the time, you can check the status bar to see what options might be available for whatever you're doing in SketchUp. Modifier keys (keyboard strokes that you use in combination with certain tools to perform additional functions), step-by-step instructions, and general information about what you're doing all appear in one place: right here.

▲ **The Value Control Box (VCB):** The VCB is where numbers show up (to put it as simply as possible). Chapter 2 goes into more detail about the VCB, but its basic purpose is to allow you to be precise while you're modeling.

1.4.4 Understanding the Dialog Boxes

Most graphics programs have multiple small controller boxes that float around your screen, and SketchUp is no exception. After the dialog boxes are open, you can "dock" them together by moving them close to each other (although many users end up with these boxes all over their screen). Dialog boxes in SketchUp contain controls for all kinds of things; here are a few that deserve special attention:

▲ **Preferences:** While the Model Info dialog box (see the next bullet point) contains settings for the SketchUp file you have open, the Preferences dialog box has controls for how SketchUp behaves *no matter what* file you have open. Pay particular attention to the Shortcuts panel, where you can set up keyboard shortcuts for any tool or command in the program. (Note that on a Mac, the Preferences dialog box is on the SketchUp menu, which doesn't exist in the Windows version of SketchUp.) Some Preference settings changes don't take effect until you open another SketchUp file, so don't worry if you can't see a difference right away.

▲ **Model Info:** This dialog box is the most important of all dialog boxes. It has controls for everything under the sun; you should definitely open it and take your time going through it. Chances are, the next time you can't find the setting you're looking for, it's in Model Info.

▲ **Entity Info:** This box is small, but it shows information about entities— edges, faces, groups, components, and lots of other things—in your model. Keeping it open is a good idea, because it helps you see what you have selected. This is especially useful when your model has many parts, some of which may be difficult to see!

▲ **Instructor:** The Instructor box only does one thing: It shows you (often with animations) how to use whatever tool happens to be activated. While you're discovering SketchUp, you should keep the Instructor dialog box open off to the side. It's a great way to learn about all the things the tool you're "holding" can do.

SELF-CHECK

1. What box shows you how to use an activated tool in SketchUp?
2. The _____ menu contains controls for viewing your model from different angles.
3. The SketchUp user interface has _____ main parts.
4. You can get extra plugins for SketchUp. True or false?

SUMMARY

As you have learned in this chapter, SketchUp has several great qualities. It's free, it's easy, and you don't have to be able to draw to create complex and precise models of 3D objects. In this chapter, you assessed the relationship between Google and SketchUp, you evaluated the capabilities and limitations of SketchUp, and you prepared to use SketchUp by learning about its different components and features. You are now well on your way to mastering the exciting world of SketchUp!

KEY TERMS

Building Information Modeling (BIM)	Software that enables users to make models that automatically keep track of things such as quantities, and that automatically generate standard drawing views (plans and sections) from the model.
Curves-based modelers	Modeling programs that use curves to define lines and surfaces.
Edges	In SketchUp, straight lines.
Faces	In SketchUp, infinitely thin surfaces.
Nonphotorealistic rendering (NPR)	Technology that makes objects look hand-drawn or otherwise not like a photograph. SketchUp is a nonphotorealistic rendering program.
Polygonal modelers	Modeling programs that use straight lines and flat surfaces to define everything; within these modelers, even things that look curvy aren't actually curvy.
Solid models	Models that are not hollow but are dense throughout.
Surface models	Models that are hollow.

ASSESS YOUR UNDERSTANDING

Go to www.wiley.com/college/chopra to evaluate your knowledge of SketchUp basics.
Measure your learning by comparing pre-test and post-test results.

Summary Questions

1. SketchUp is a _____ program.
2. SketchUp can produce images that look like they are hand-drawn. True or false?
3. SketchUp can produce solid and surface models. True or false?
4. SketchUp has animation capabilities, including moving the camera inside your model. True or false?
5. Modelers that use straight lines and flat surfaces to define everything are known as:
   (a) curves-based modelers.
   (b) polygonal modelers.
   (c) solid modelers.
   (d) surface modelers.
6. Straight lines are also known in SketchUp as:
   (a) surfaces.
   (b) faces.
   (c) edges.
   (d) solids.
7. The Value Control Box (VCB) is where _____ show up.
8. The SketchUp tools used for drawing are on the Tools menu. True or false?
9. Video tutorials are on the _____ menu in SketchUp.

Applying This Chapter

1. You want to build a deck on the back of your house, but you would like to draw a model of it first in SketchUp so you can experiment with different lengths and widths and determine what size would work best. How would you start your model?
2. Would you advise a mechanical engineering student who needs to make a model of a car part that shows the precise weight of the part to use SketchUp? Why or why not?

3. What are the five main parts of the SketchUp user interface and what is the purpose of each?
4. What are the main limitations and capabilities of SketchUp? In what situations would you use SketchUp, and in what situations would you recommend using a different modeling program?

Experimenting with SketchUp

Download SketchUp and spend an hour navigating through the software. Write down what you find easy to do and what you find difficult. Keep this list and write down directions for how to complete the difficult tasks as you work through this text.

Modifying SketchUp Models

Spend an hour searching through the SketchUp Component library (which you access in the Components dialog box, in the menu bar). Specifically, look for a model of a two-story house. Experiment and modify the model in two different ways. Write down the changes you made to the model and why.

2

ESTABLISHING THE MODELING MINDSET
Model Basics

Starting Point

Go to www.wiley.com/college/chopra to assess your knowledge of SketchUp models.
Determine where you need to concentrate your effort.

What You'll Learn in This Chapter

▲ How SketchUp represents three-dimensional space on a two-dimensional screen
▲ How to use the Orbit, Pan, and Zoom tools
▲ What inferences are and how to use them
▲ How to add color and texture to your work

After Studying This Chapter, You'll Be Able To

▲ Assess when and how to use edges and faces
▲ Evaluate how to represent three-dimensional objects
▲ Compare and contrast different SketchUp tools and when to use them
▲ Assess how to inject accuracy into your models

INTRODUCTION

SketchUp has so many great tools that it is tempting to start modeling right away. However, that is not the best approach. When you decided to learn how to drive a car, you probably didn't just get behind the wheel, step on the gas, and figure it out as you went along. You should approach SketchUp in much the same way you approached learning to drive; in other words, you should really know several things about the software before you get started. This chapter is dedicated to introducing those concepts, which can make your first few hours with SketchUp a lot more productive and fun.

After reading this chapter, you will be able to do the following:

▲ Assess when to use edges and faces—the basic components that SketchUp models are made of.

▲ Evaluate how SketchUp lets you work in 3D (three dimensions) on a 2D (flat) surface (namely, your computer screen). Understanding how SketchUp represents depth is everything when it comes to making models. If you've never used 3D modeling software before, pay close attention to the middle part of this chapter.

▲ Assess SketchUp tools and understand when to use them to accomplish different tasks—things like navigating around your model, drawing lines, selecting objects, and working with accurate measurements.

2.1 All About Edges and Faces

In SketchUp, everything is made up of one of two kinds of entities. edges and faces. They're the basic building blocks of every model you'll ever make.

Collectively, the edges and faces in your model are called **geometry**. Thus, when someone refers to geometry when discussing SketchUp, they're talking about edges and faces. Other modeling programs have other kinds of geometry, but SketchUp is pretty simple. That's a good thing—it means there's less to keep track of.

The drawing on the left in Figure 2-1 is a basic cube drawn in SketchUp. It's composed of 12 edges and 6 faces. The model on the right is a lot more complex, but the geometry's the same: It's all just edges and faces.

2.1.1 Understanding Edges

Edges are lines. You can use lots of different tools to draw them, erase them, move them, hide them, and even stretch them out. Here are some basic things you ought to know about SketchUp edges:

▲ **Edges are always straight.** Not only is everything in your SketchUp model made up of edges, but all of these edges are also perfectly straight. Even arcs and circles are made of small straight-line segments, as shown in Figure 2-2.

Figure 2-1

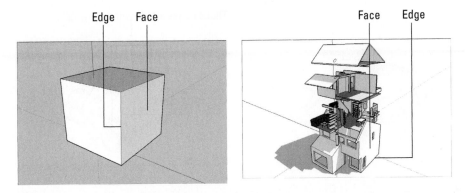

SketchUp models are made from edges and faces.

▲ **Edges don't have a thickness.** This idea can be a bit difficult to understand. In SketchUp, you never have to worry about how thick the edges in your model are, because that's just not how the software works. Depending on how you choose to *display* your model, your edges may look like they have different thicknesses. In reality, however, your edges themselves don't have a built-in thickness. You can read more about making your edges look thick in Chapter 8.

▲ **Just because you can't see the edges doesn't mean they're not there.** Edges can be hidden so that you can't see them; doing so is a popular way to make certain forms. Take a look at Figure 2-3. On the left is a model that looks rounded. On the right, the hidden edges are visible as dashed lines. See how even surfaces that look smoothly curved are made of straight edges?

Figure 2-2

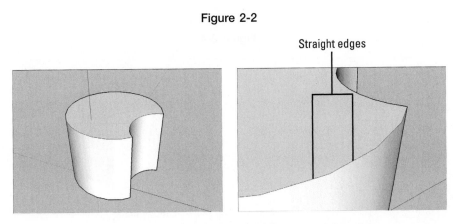

In SketchUp, even curved lines consist of straight edges.

Figure 2-3

These edges are smoothed, but still there

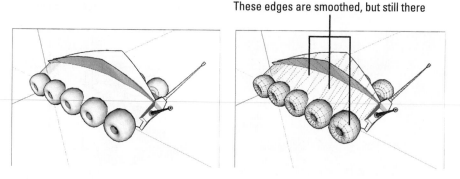

Even organic shapes and curvy forms are made of straight edges.

2.1.2 Understanding Faces

Faces are surfaces. If you think of SketchUp models as being made of toothpicks and paper, faces are basically the paper. Here's what you need to know about them:

▲ **You can't have faces without edges.** To have a face, you need to have at least three **coplanar** (on the same plane) edges that form a loop. In other words, a face is defined by the edges that surround it, and those edges all have to be on the same, flat plane. Because you need at least three straight lines to make a closed shape, faces must have at least three sides. There's no limit to the number of sides a SketchUp face can have, though, as long as they are coplanar. Figure 2-4 shows what happens when you get rid of an edge that defines one or more faces.

Figure 2-4

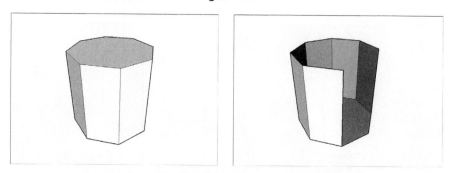

You need a closed loop of edges to make a face.

Figure 2-5

Each of these triangles is perfectly flat

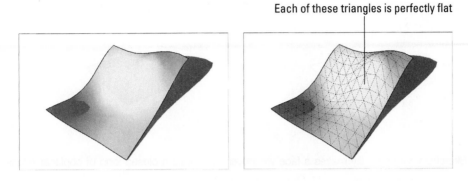

All faces are flat, even the ones that make up larger, curvy surfaces.

▲ **Faces are always flat.** In SketchUp, even surfaces that look curved are made up of multiple, flat faces. In the model shown in Figure 2-5, you can see that what looks like an organically shaped surface (on the left) is really made up of many smaller faces (on the right). To make multiple flat faces look like one big, curvy surface, the edges between them are smoothed; you can find out more about smoothing edges in Chapter 6.

▲ **Just like edges, faces don't have any thickness.** If faces are a lot like pieces of paper, they're *infinitely thin* pieces of paper—in other words, they don't have any thickness. To make a thick surface (for example, a 6-inch-thick wall), you need to use two faces side by side.

2.1.3 Understanding the Relationship Between Edges and Faces

Now that you know that models are made from edges and faces, you're most of the way to understanding how SketchUp works. Here's some additional information that should help fill in the gaps:

▲ **Every time SketchUp can make a face, it will.** There's no such thing as a "Face tool" in this software; SketchUp just automatically makes a face every time you finish drawing a closed shape out of three or more coplanar edges. Figure 2-6 shows this in action: As soon as the last edge that is drawn is connected to the first one to close the "loop," SketchUp creates a face.

▲ **You can't stop SketchUp from creating faces, but you can erase them if you want.** If a face you don't want ends up getting created, just right-click it and choose Erase from the context menu. That face will be deleted, but the edges that defined it will remain (see Figure 2-7).

Figure 2-6

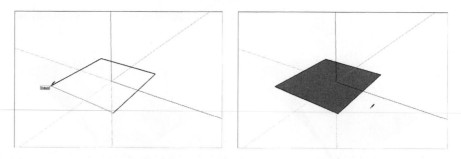

SketchUp automatically makes a face whenever you create a closed loop of coplanar edges.

Figure 2-7

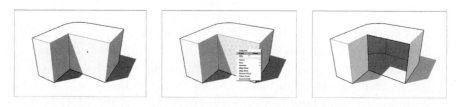

You can delete a face without deleting the edges that define it.

▲ **If you delete one of the edges that defines a face, that face will be deleted, too.** For example, when one of the edges in the cube is erased (with the Eraser tool, in this case), *both* of the faces that were defined by that edge disappear. This happens because it's impossible to have a face without also having all its edges.

▲ **Retracing an edge re-creates a missing face.** If you already have a closed loop of coplanar edges but no face (because you erased it, perhaps), you can redraw one of the edges to make a new face. Just use the Line tool to trace over one of the edge segments and a face will reappear (see Figure 2-8).

Figure 2-8

Drawing an edge from here...   ...to here...   ...causes this face to be created

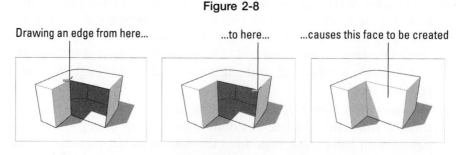

Just retrace any edge on a closed loop to tell SketchUp to create a new face.

Figure 2-9

Splitting a face with an edge, and then extruding one of the new faces.

▲ **Drawing an edge all the way across a face splits the face in two.**
When you draw an edge (such as by using the Line tool) from one side
of a face to another, you cut that face in two. The same thing happens
when you draw a closed loop of edges (like a rectangle) on a face—you
end up with two faces, one "inside" the other. In Figure 2-9, the face is
split in two with the Line tool, and then one of the faces is extruded a
bit with the Push/Pull tool.

▲ **Drawing an edge that crosses another edge *doesn't* automatically split
both edges.** In the left side of Figure 2-10, we've drawn an edge that
crosses one of the edges that defines a face. Doing this doesn't split any
of the edges, and more importantly, it *doesn't split the face*. Thus, if you
want to make the edge you just drew into two edges, you need to retrace
one of its segments with the Line tool (as shown in the middle image of
Figure 2-10). When you do this, you don't just end up with two edges
instead of one; you also end up splitting the face (as shown in the right
side of Figure 2-10).

Figure 2-10

Drawing an edge from here...   ...to here splits the face

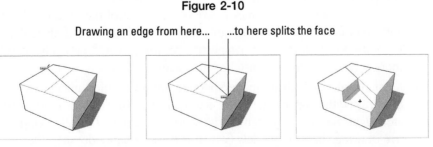

Crossing one edge with another doesn't cut either one of them. To split
an edge, you have to trace over part of it with the Line tool.

SELF-CHECK

1. _____ are always straight.
2. Coplanar means "on different planes." True or false?
3. Faces are always _____.
4. Faces are thick, whereas edges are thin. True or false?

2.2 Drawing in 3D on a 2D Screen

For computer programmers, letting you draw three-dimensional objects on your screen is a difficult problem. You wouldn't think it would be such a big deal; after all, people have been drawing in perspective for a very long time. If someone could figure it out 500 years ago, why should it give your computer any problems?

The thing is, human perception of depth on paper is a trick of the eye. And of course, your computer doesn't have eyes that enable it to interpret depth without thinking about it. You need to give your computer explicit instructions. In SketchUp, this means using drawing axes and inferences, as explained in the sections that follow.

FOR EXAMPLE

Drawing in Perspective?

Contrary to popular belief, modeling in SketchUp doesn't involve drawing in perspective and letting the software "figure out" what you mean. There are two reasons for this, which turns out to be a very good thing:

▲ **Computers aren't very good at figuring out what you're trying to do.** This has probably happened to you: You're working away at your computer, and the software you're using tries to "help" by guessing what you're doing. Sometimes it works, but most of the time it doesn't, and eventually, it can become quite annoying. Thus, even if SketchUp were *able* to interpret your perspective drawings, you'd probably spend more time correcting its mistakes than actually building something.

▲ **Most people can't draw in perspective anyway.** Unfortunately, creating drawings with proper perspective just isn't one of the things most of us are taught. So even if SketchUp did work by turning your 2D perspective drawings into 3D models (which it most certainly doesn't), the vast majority of those people who "can't draw" wouldn't be able to use it.

2.2.1 Giving Instructions with the Drawing Axes

Color Plate 1 is a shot of the SketchUp modeling window, right after you create a new file. (See insert for Color Plates.) See the three colored lines that cross in the lower-left corner of the screen? These are the **drawing axes,** and they're the key to understanding how SketchUp works. Simply put, you use SketchUp's drawing axes to figure out where you are (and where you want to go) in 3D space. When you're working with the colored axes, you need to keep two important things in mind:

▲ **When you draw, move, or copy something parallel to one of the colored axes, you're working in that "color's direction."** Take a look at Color Plate 2. In the first image, we're drawing a line parallel to the *red* axis, so we would say we're drawing "in the *red* direction." We know that the line we're drawing is parallel to the red axis because it turns red to let us know. In the second image, we're moving a box parallel to the *blue* axis, so we're "moving in the *blue* direction." We know we're parallel to the blue axis because a dotted, blue line appears to tell us so. (Note that the red and green axes define the ground plane in SketchUp, and the blue axis is vertical.)

▲ **The point of using the red, green, and blue axes is to let SketchUp know what you *mean*.** Remember that one problem with modeling in 3D on a computer is the fact that you're working on a 2D screen. Consider the example shown in Color Plate 3. If we click the cylinder with the Move tool and move the cursor *up,* how is SketchUp supposed to know whether we mean to move it *up* in space (above the ground) or *back* in space? That's where the colored axes come into play. If we want to move it *up,* we go in the *blue* direction. If we want to move it *back,* we follow the *green* direction (because the green axis happens to run from the front to the back of the screen).

When you're working in SketchUp, use the colored drawing axes *all the time*. They're not just handy; they're what make SketchUp work. Having colored axes (instead of axes labeled *x, y,* and *z*) lets you draw in 3D space without having to type commands to tell your computer where you want to draw. They make modeling in SketchUp quick, accurate, and relatively intuitive. All you have to do is make sure that you're working in your intended color direction as you model by lining up your objects with the axes and watching the screen tips that tell you what direction you're working in. After your first couple of hours with the software, paying attention to the colors becomes second nature.

2.2.2 Watching for Inferences

If you've spent any time experimenting with SketchUp, you've surely noticed all the colored squares, dotted lines, yellow tags, and other similar objects that appear as you move your cursor around your modeling window. All these elements are collectively referred to as SketchUp's **inference engine.** The sole purpose of this engine is to help you while you're building models. Without inferences, SketchUp wouldn't be very useful.

Point Inferences

Generally, SketchUp's inferences help you be more precise. **Point inferences** (see Color Plate 4) appear when you move your cursor over specific parts of your model. They look like small colored squares, and if you pause for a second, they're accompanied by a yellow tag that says what they are. For example, watching for the small green Endpoint inference (which appears whenever your cursor is over one of the ends of an edge) helps you accurately connect an edge you're drawing to the end of another edge in your model. Here's a list of SketchUp's various point inferences:

▲ Endpoint (green)
▲ Midpoint (cyan or light blue)
▲ Intersection (black)
▲ On Edge (red)
▲ Center (of a circle, green)
▲ On Face (dark blue)

Linear Inferences

As you've probably already noticed, color plays a big part in SketchUp's **user interface** (the way it looks). Perhaps the best example of this is in the software's **linear inferences,** or the "helper lines" that show up to help you work more precisely. Color Plate 5 is an illustration of all of the linear inferences in action, and here's a description of what they do:

▲ **On Axis:** When an edge that you're drawing is parallel to one of the colored drawing axes, the edge turns the same color as that axis.
▲ **From Point:** This inference is a little harder to describe. When you're moving your cursor, sometimes you'll see a colored, dotted line appear. This means that you're "lined up" with the point at the end of the dotted line. Naturally, the color of the From Point inference corresponds to whichever axis you're lined up "on." Sometimes, From Point inferences show up on their own, and sometimes you have to *encourage* them; see the "Encouraging Inferences" section later in this chapter for additional details.
▲ **Perpendicular:** When you're drawing an edge that's perpendicular to another edge, the edge that you're drawing turns magenta (reddish purple).

▲ **Parallel:** When it's parallel to another edge in your model, the edge that you're drawing turns magenta to let you know. You tell SketchUp which edge you're interested in "being parallel to" by encouraging an inference.

▲ **Tangent at Vertex:** This inference only applies when you're drawing an arc (using the Arc tool) that starts at the endpoint of another arc. When the arc you're drawing is tangent to the other one, the one that you're drawing turns cyan. Tangent, in this case, means that the transition between the two arcs is smooth.

In addition, one of the most important inferences in SketchUp is one that you probably didn't even realize was an inference. It's the fact that, unless you specifically start on an edge or a face in your model, you'll always be drawing on the ground plane by default. In other words, if you just start creating stuff in the middle of nowhere, SketchUp assumes that you want to be drawing on the ground.

2.2.3 Using Inferences to Help You Model

A big part of using SketchUp's inference engine involves locking and encouraging inferences—sometimes even simultaneously. At first, this will seem like a difficult skill, but with practice, it gets easier.

Locking Inferences

If you hold down Shift when you see any of the first four types of linear inferences described previously, that inference gets locked, and it stays locked until you release Shift. When you lock an inference, you constrain whatever tool you're using to only work in the direction of the inference you locked. Confused? Consider the following example for some clarity.

Color Plate 6 shows a situation in which it would be useful to lock a blue On Axis inference while using the Line tool. Here, we want to draw a vertical line that's exactly as tall as the peak of the house's roof, so here's what we do:

1. Click once to start drawing an edge.
2. Move the cursor up until we see the edge we're drawing turn blue. This is the blue On Axis inference that lets us know that we're exactly parallel to the blue drawing axis.
3. Hold down Shift to lock the inference. Here, our edge gets thicker to let us know it's locked, and now we can only draw in the blue direction (no matter where we move the cursor).
4. Click the peak of the roof to make our vertical edge end at exactly that height.
5. Release Shift to unlock the inference.

Encouraging Inferences

Sometimes, an inference you need doesn't show up on its own; when this happens, you have to encourage it. To encourage an inference, just hover your cursor over the part of your model you'd like to "infer" from, and then slowly go back to whatever you were doing when you decided you should use an inference. The following example demonstrates how to encourage an inference.

Color Plate 7 shows a model of a cylinder. We'd like to start drawing an edge that lines up perfectly with the center of the circle on top of the cylinder, but we don't want it to start at the center itself. Thus, we follow these steps:

1. Hover (don't click) over the edge of the circle for about two seconds.
2. Move slowly toward the middle of the circle until the Center Point inference appears.
3. Hover (still don't click) over the center point for a couple of seconds.
4. Move the cursor slowly in the direction of where we want to start drawing our edge. A dotted From Point inference should appear.
5. Click to start drawing the edge.

SELF-CHECK

1. What appears when you move your cursor over specific parts of your model?

   a. Linear inferences

   b. Point inferences

   c. Yellow tags

   d. All of the above

2. When you draw, move, or copy something parallel to one of the colored axes, you are working in that _____ direction.

3. To lock an inference, you hold down Shift. True or false?

4. The Endpoint inference is:

   a. green.

   b. blue.

   c. red.

   d. black.

2.3 Warming Up for SketchUp

There are seven activities you'll need to do every time you use SketchUp. You might think of these activities as "core competencies." Whatever you care to call them, these activities are all introduced in the following sections, so you can come back and get a quick refresher whenever you'd like.

2.3.1 Getting the Best View of What You're Doing

Using SketchUp without learning how to orbit, zoom, and pan is like trying to build a ship in a bottle . . . in the dark, with your hands tied behind your back, while using chopsticks. In other words, it's impossible!

Fully half of modeling in SketchUp involves using the aforementioned navigation tools, which allow you to change your view so you can see what you're doing. Most people who try to learn SketchUp on their own take too long to understand this. Thus, the following sections will help you avoid this problem.

The Orbit Tool

Hold a glass of water in your hand. Now twist and turn your wrist around in every direction so that the water's all over you and the rest of the room. Stop when the glass is completely empty. This is basically how the **Orbit** tool works!

Just as your wrist helps you twist and turn the glass to see it from every angle, think of using Orbit as a way to "fly around" your work. Figure 2-11 shows the Orbit tool at work.

Here are some things you should know about using Orbit:

▲ **The Orbit tool is on the Camera menu.** However, by far the least productive way to use Orbit is to choose it from the Camera menu.

▲ **Orbit is also on the toolbar.** The second-least productive way to activate Orbit is to click its button on the toolbar. This button looks like two red arrows trying to form a ball.

▲ **You can orbit using your mouse.** Here's how you should *always* orbit: Click the scroll wheel of your mouse and hold it down. Now move your mouse around. See your model swiveling around? Release the scroll wheel when you're done. Using your mouse to orbit means that you don't have to switch tools every time you want a better view, which saves you a significant amount of time.

The Zoom Tool

Hold your empty glass at arm's length. Close your eyes, and then bring the glass rushing toward you, stopping right before it hits you in the nose. Now throw the glass across the room, noticing how it shrinks as it gets farther away. That, in a nutshell, describes the **Zoom** tool.

Figure 2-11

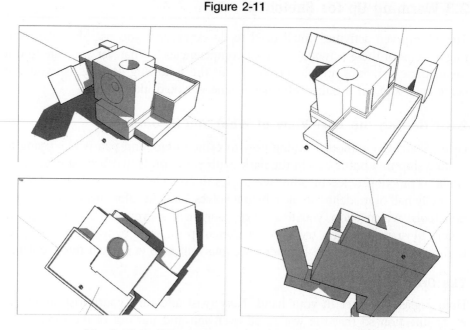

The Orbit tool lets you see your model from any angle.

You use Zoom to get closer to (and farther from) your model. If you're working on something small, you zoom in until it fills your modeling window. To see everything at once, zoom out. Figure 2-12 is a demonstration of the Zoom tool at work.

There are several things you need to know about Zoom:

▲ **Just like Orbit, you can activate the Zoom tool in several ways.** The worst way to activate Zoom is from the Camera menu; the second-worst way is to click the Zoom button in the toolbar. If you use Zoom either of these two ways, you actually zoom in and out by clicking and dragging

Figure 2-12

Zoomed in   Zoomed in even more

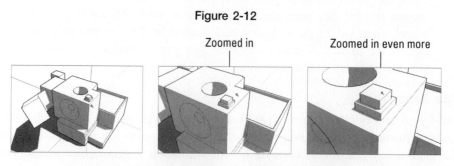

Use the Zoom tool to get closer to your model.

up and down on your screen. The best way to zoom is to roll your finger on the scroll wheel of your mouse to zoom in and out. Instead of clicking the scroll wheel to orbit, just roll your scroll wheel back and forth to zoom. Using your mouse to zoom means that you don't have to switch tools—as soon as you stop zooming, you revert to whatever tool you were using before.

▲ **Use Zoom Extents to see everything.** Technically, Zoom Extents is a separate tool, but it's related closely enough to be mentioned here. If you want your model to fill your modeling window (which is especially useful when you "get lost" with the navigation tools), just choose Camera⇨Zoom Extents.

When you use the Zoom tool, SketchUp zooms in on your cursor; just position it over whatever part of your model you want to zoom in on (or zoom out from). If your cursor isn't over any of your model's geometry (faces and edges), the Zoom tool won't work very well—you'll end up zooming either really slowly or really quickly.

The Pan Tool

Using the **Pan** tool is a lot like washing windows; in other words, you move the paper towel back and forth, but it stays flat and it never gets any closer or farther away from you. The Pan tool is basically for sliding your model view around in your modeling window. To see something that's to the right, you use Pan to slide your model to the left. It's as simple as that.

There are three basic things you should know about Pan:

▲ **Pan is on the Camera menu:** Once again, however, that's not where you should go to activate it.

▲ **Pan is also on the toolbar:** Again, you *could* access the Pan tool by clicking its button on the toolbar (it looks like a severed hand), but there's a better way . . .

▲ **Hold down your mouse's scroll wheel button and press Shift.** When you do both at the same time—basically, Orbit+Shift—your cursor temporarily turns into the Pan tool. When it does so, simply move your mouse to pan.

2.3.2 Drawing Edges with Ease

Being able to use the Line tool without having to think too much about it is *the* secret to being able to model anything you want in SketchUp. You use the Line tool to draw individual edges, and because SketchUp models are really just fancy collections of edges (albeit carefully arranged), anything you can make in SketchUp, you can make with the Line tool.

Figure 2-13

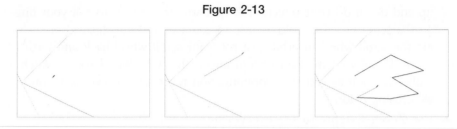

Use the Line tool to draw edges.

Drawing edges is just as simple. Just follow these steps:

1. Select the Line tool (some people call it the Pencil tool).
2. Click where you want your line to begin.
3. Move your cursor to the desired endpoint for your line, and click again to end. Figure 2-13 demonstrates the basic idea. When you draw a line segment with the Line tool, notice how SketchUp automatically tries to draw another line? This is called **rubber banding**—the Line tool lets you "continue" to draw edge segments, automatically starting each new one at the end of the previous one you drew.
4. When you want the Line tool to stop drawing lines, press Esc to "snip" the line at the last spot you clicked.

SketchUp lets you draw lines in two ways: You can either use the click-drag-release method or the click-move-click one. They both work, of course, you should train yourself to do the latter. You'll have more control with this method, and your hand won't get as tired. When you draw edges by clicking and *dragging* your mouse (click-drag-release), you're a lot more likely to "drop" your line accidentally. Because the Line tool only draws straight lines, think about using

FOR EXAMPLE

Turning Off "Rubber-Banding" Lines

Depending on what you're making and how you work, you might want to turn off the Line tool's rubber-banding behavior off. To do so, follow these steps:

1. Choose Window⇨Preferences (SketchUp⇨Preferences on a Mac).
2. Choose the Drawing panel from the list on the left in the Preferences dialog box.
3. Deselect the Continue Line Drawing check box.

it less like a pencil (even though it looks like one) and more like a spool of sticky thread.

Finally, note that the Eraser tool is specifically designed for erasing edges; use it by clicking the edges you don't like to delete them. You can also drag over edges with the Eraser, but that's a little harder to get used to.

2.3.3 Injecting Accuracy into Your Model

It's all well and fine to make a model, but most of the time, you need to make sure that your model is accurate. Without a certain level of accuracy, a model is not as useful for figuring things out. The key to accuracy in SketchUp is the small text box that lives in the lower-right corner of your SketchUp window (and is pointed out in Figure 2-14). This text box is called the Value Control Box, or VCB, and here are some of the things you can use it to do:

▲ Make a line a certain length.
▲ Draw a rectangle a certain size.

Figure 2-14

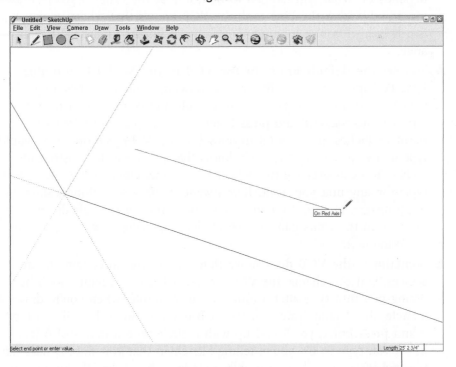

Value Control box

SketchUp's VCB (Value Control Box) is the key to working precisely.

▲ Push/pull a face a certain distance.

▲ Change the number of sides in a polygon.

▲ Move something a given distance.

▲ Rotate something by a certain number of degrees.

▲ Make a certain number of copies.

▲ Divide a line into a certain number of segments.

▲ Change your field of view (how much you can see).

Here are some things you should know about the VCB:

▲ **You don't have to click in the VCB to enter a number.** When they're first starting out with SketchUp, many people assume that they need to click in the VCB (to select it, presumably) before they can start typing. This isn't the case—just start typing, and whatever you type shows up in the VCB automatically. When it comes to being precise, SketchUp is always "listening" for you to type something in this box.

▲ **The VCB is context-sensitive.** This means that what it controls depends on what you happen to be doing at the time. If you're drawing an edge with the Line tool, the VCB knows that whatever you type is a length; if you're rotating something, it knows to "listen" for an angle.

▲ **You set the default units for the VCB in the Model Info dialog box.** Perhaps you want a line you're drawing to be 14 inches long. If you're set up to use inches as your default unit of measurement, just type **14** into the VCB and press Enter—SketchUp assumes that you mean 14 inches. If you want to draw something 14 *feet* long, you would type in **14'**, just to let SketchUp know that you mean feet instead of inches. You can override the default unit of measurement for the VCB by typing in any unit you want. If you want to move something a distance of 25 meters, type in **25m** and press Enter. You set the default units for the VCB in the Units panel of the Model Info dialog box (which is on the Window menu).

▲ **Sometimes, the VCB does more than one thing.** In certain circumstances, you can change the VCB's mode (what it's "listening for") by typing in a unit type after a number. For example, when you're drawing a circle, the default "value" in the VCB is the radius—thus, if you type 6 and press Enter, you'll end up with a circle with a radius of 6 inches. But if you type in **6s**, you're telling SketchUp that you want 6 *sides* (and not inches), so you'll end up with a circle with 6 sides. If you type in 6 and press Enter, and then type in **6s** and press Enter again, SketchUp will draw a hexagon (a 6-sided circle) with a radius of 6 inches.

▲ **The VCB lets you change your mind.** As long as you don't do any-thing after you press Enter, you can always type a new value into the VCB and press Enter again; there's no limit to the number of times you can change your mind.

▲ **You can use the VCB *during* an operation.** In most cases, you can use the VCB to be precise while you're using a tool. Here's how that works:

1. Click once to start your operation (such as drawing a line or using the Move tool).

2. Move your mouse so that you're going in the correct color direction. If you're using the Line tool and you want to draw parallel to the green axis, make sure that the edge you're drawing is green. Be sure not to click again.

3. Without clicking the VCB, just type in the dimension you want; you should see it appear in the VCB.

4. Press Enter to complete the operation.

▲ **You can also use the VCB *after* an operation.** Doing this revises what you've just done. These steps should give you an idea of what this means:

1. Complete your operation. This might be drawing a line, moving some-thing, rotating something, or any of the other things mentioned at the beginning of this section.

2. Before you do anything else, type in whatever dimension you intended, and then press Enter. Whatever you did should be redone according to what you typed in.

To give you a more concrete example of using the VCB after an operation, say you want to move a box (shown in Figure 2-15) a total of 10 meters in the red direction (parallel to the red axis). Here's what you should do:

1. Using the Move tool, click the box once to "pick it up."

2. Move your mouse until you see the linear inference that tells you that you're moving in the red direction.

3. Type in **10m**, and then press Enter. Your box will be positioned exactly 10 meters from where you picked it up.

4. Now, say you aren't happy with the 10 meters, so you decide to change it. Simply type in **15m**, and then press Enter again, and the box will move another 5 meters in the red direction. You can keep doing this until you're happy with the results.

Resizing with the Tape Measure Tool

Imagine that you've been working away in SketchUp, not paying particular atten-tion to how big anything in your model is, when you suddenly decide that you

Figure 2-15

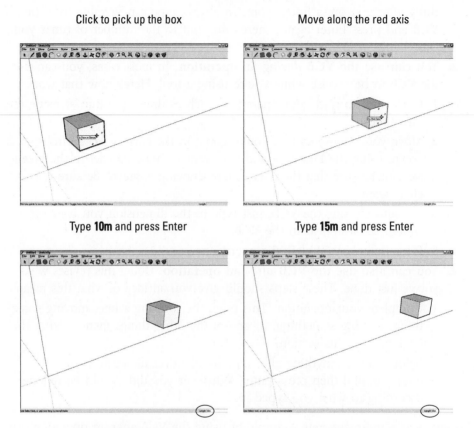

Click to pick up the box

Move along the red axis

Type **10m** and press Enter

Type **15m** and press Enter

Here, the box is first moved 10 meters, and then it's moved 15 meters.

need what you've made to be a specific size. SketchUp has a terrific trick for taking care of this exact situation: You can use the Tape Measure tool to resize your whole model based on a single measurement.

Here's how it works: Say, as depicted in Figure 2-16, you've started to model a simple staircase, and you now want to make sure that it's the right size. You know you want the riser height (the vertical distance between the steps) to be 7 inches, so this is what you do:

1. Select the Tape Measure tool (choose Tools⇨Tape Measure).
2. Make sure that the Tape Measure is in Measure mode by pressing Ctrl (Option on the Mac) until you don't see a plus sign (+) next to the Tape Measure cursor.
3. To measure the current distance (in this case, the riser height), click once to start measuring, and click again to stop.

Figure 2-16

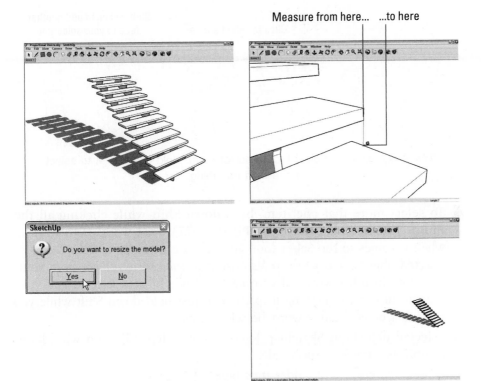

The Tape Measure tool allows you to resize your entire model at one time.

4. Type in the dimension you *want* what you just measured to be: 7 (for 7 inches).

5. In the dialog box that appears, which asks whether you want to resize the whole model, click the Yes button.

When you click the Yes button, the whole model is resized proportionately to the dimension you entered.

2.3.4 Selecting Parts of a Model

If you want to move something in your model, or rotate it, or copy it, or do any number of other things to it, you need to select it first. When you select an element, you're telling SketchUp that *this* is the part of the model you want to work with. To select things, use the Select tool, which looks exactly the same as the Select tool most other graphics programs—it's an arrow.

Here's everything you need to know about selecting things in SketchUp:

▲ **Simply click anything in your model to select it.** Do this while you're using the Select tool, of course.

Figure 2-17

Click to select a face

Shift + click to add another
face to your selection

Click things with the Select tool to select them. Hold down Shift to select
more than one thing.

▲ **To select more that one item, hold down Shift while clicking all the things you want to select (see Figure 2-17).** Shift works both ways when it comes to the Select tool. You can use it to *add* to your set of selected objects, and you can also use it to *subtract* an object from your selection. In other words, if you have multiple objects selected and you want to deselect something in particular, just hold down Shift while you click that object, and it won't be selected anymore.

▲ **Selected objects in SketchUp look different depending on what kind of objects they are.** Specifically:

- Selected edges and guides turn blue.
- Selected faces are covered in tiny blue dots.
- Selected groups and components are surrounded by a blue box.
- Selected section planes turn blue.

▲ **A much fancier way to select things in your model is to double- and triple-click them.** When you double-click a face, you select that face and all the edges that define it. Double-clicking an edge gives you that edge plus all the faces that are connected to it. When you *triple*-click an edge or a face, you select the whole object that it's a part of. Figure 2-18 illustrates this.

▲ **You can also select several things at once by dragging a box around them.** You have two kinds of selection boxes; which one you use depends on what you're trying to select (see Figure 2-19):

- *Window selection:* If you click and drag from *left to right* to make a selection box, you create a window selection. In this case, only things that are *entirely* inside your selection box are selected.
- *Crossing selection:* If you click and drag from *right to left* to make a selection box, you create a crossing selection. With one of these, anything your selection box touches (including what's inside) ends up getting selected.

Figure 2-18

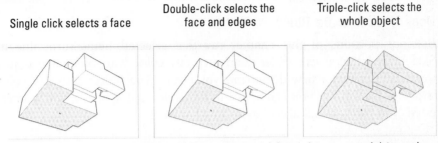

Single click selects a face

Double-click selects the
face and edges

Triple-click selects the
whole object

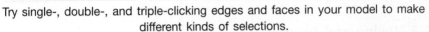

Try single-, double-, and triple-clicking edges and faces in your model to make
different kinds of selections.

Note that just because you can't see something doesn't mean it isn't selected.
Whenever you make a selection, it's a very good idea to orbit around to make
sure you've got only what you intended to select. Accidentally selecting too much
is an easy mistake to make.

Figure 2-19

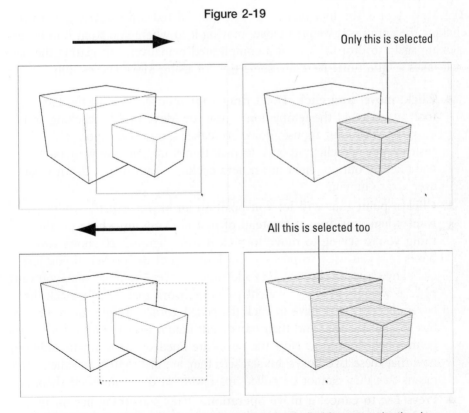

Only this is selected

All this is selected too

Dragging left to right selects everything completely inside your selection box.
Dragging right to left selects everything that your selection box touches.

FOR EXAMPLE

Does It Have to Be Blue?

Previous portions of this chapter say that selected items turn blue in SketchUp, but you can make them turn any color you want. Blue is just the default color for new documents you create. The "selected things" color is one of the settings you can adjust in the Styles dialog box. If you're interested, you can read all about styles in Chapter 8.

2.3.5 Moving and Copying

To move things in SketchUp, use the Move tool. To make a copy of something, use the Move tool in combination with a button on your keyboard: Ctrl in Windows, and Option on a Mac. It's really that simple.

Moving Things Around

The Move tool is the tool that looks like crossed red arrows. Using it involves clicking the entity you want to move, moving it to where you want it to be, and clicking again to drop it. It's not a complicated maneuver, but getting the hang of it takes a little time. Here are some tips for using Move successfully:

▲ **Click, move, and click. Don't drag your mouse.** As with the Line tool, try to avoid the temptation to use the Move tool by clicking and dragging with your mouse; doing so makes things a lot more difficult. Instead, practice clicking once to pick things up, moving your mouse without any buttons held down, and clicking again to put down whatever you're moving.

▲ **Click a point that will let you position an object *exactly* where you want when you drop it (instead of just clicking anywhere on the thing you're trying to move to pick it up).** Figure 2-20 shows two boxes that you want to precisely stack on top of each other. If you just click anywhere on the first box and move it over the other one, you can't place it where you want; SketchUp doesn't work that way. To stack the boxes precisely, you have to click the *bottom corner* of the soon-to-be top box to grab it there, and then move your cursor over the *top corner* of the bottom box to drop it. Now the boxes are lined up perfectly. In addition, now that these two boxes are stacked, they are also "glued together." This means that they cannot be pulled apart without distorting their shapes.

▲ **Press Esc to cancel a move operation.** Here's something beginners do all the time: They start to move something (or start moving something accidentally), and then they change their minds. Instead of pressing Esc,

Figure 2-20

Picking it up here...   ...doesn't let you stack properly

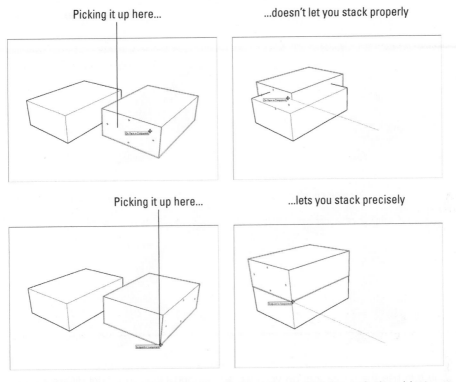

Picking it up here...   ...lets you stack precisely

To move objects precisely, choose precise points at which to grab the objects and put them down.

they try to use Move to put things back the way they were. Inevitably, this doesn't work. If you change your mind in the middle of moving something, just press Esc, and everything will go back to the way it was.

▲ **Don't forget about inferences.** To move something in one of the colored directions, just wait until you see the dotted On Axis linear inference appear, and then hold down Shift to lock yourself in that direction.

▲ **Don't forget about the VCB.** Always remember, you can move things precise distances using the Value Control Box.

Modeling with the Move Tool

In SketchUp, the Move tool is very important for modeling; it's not just for moving entire objects around. You can also use it to move just about anything, including **vertices** (edges' endpoints), edges, faces, and combinations of any of these. By only moving certain entities (all the things just mentioned), you can change the shape of your geometry pretty drastically. Figure 2-21 illustrates this.

Figure 2-21

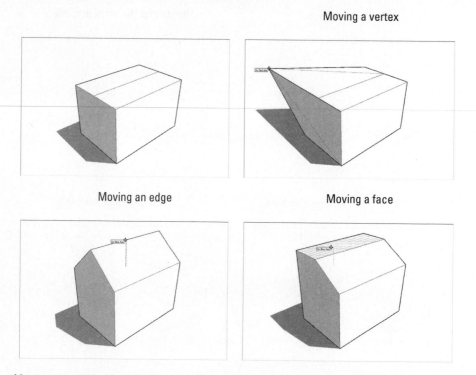

You can use the Move tool on vertices, edges, and faces to model different forms.

Using the Move tool to create forms (instead of just moving them around) is an incredibly powerful way to work, but isn't particularly intuitive. After all, nothing in the physical world behaves like the Move tool—you can't just grab the edge of a hardwood floor and move it up to turn it into a ramp in real life. In SketchUp, however, you can—and you should.

Using Auto-Fold

This will happen to you sooner or later when using SketchUp: You'll be trying to move a vertex, an edge, or a face, and you won't be able to go in the direction you want. SketchUp doesn't like to let you create **folds** (when extra faces and edges are created in place of a single face) with the Move tool, so it constrains your movement to directions that won't end up adding them. If SketchUp won't let you move whatever you're trying to move, *force it* to do so by doing one very important thing: Pressing and holding down Alt (Command on a Mac) while you're moving. When you do this, you're telling SketchUp that it's okay to proceed—in other words, to create folds if it has to. This is called Auto-Fold, and Figure 2-22 illustrates how it works.

Figure 2-22

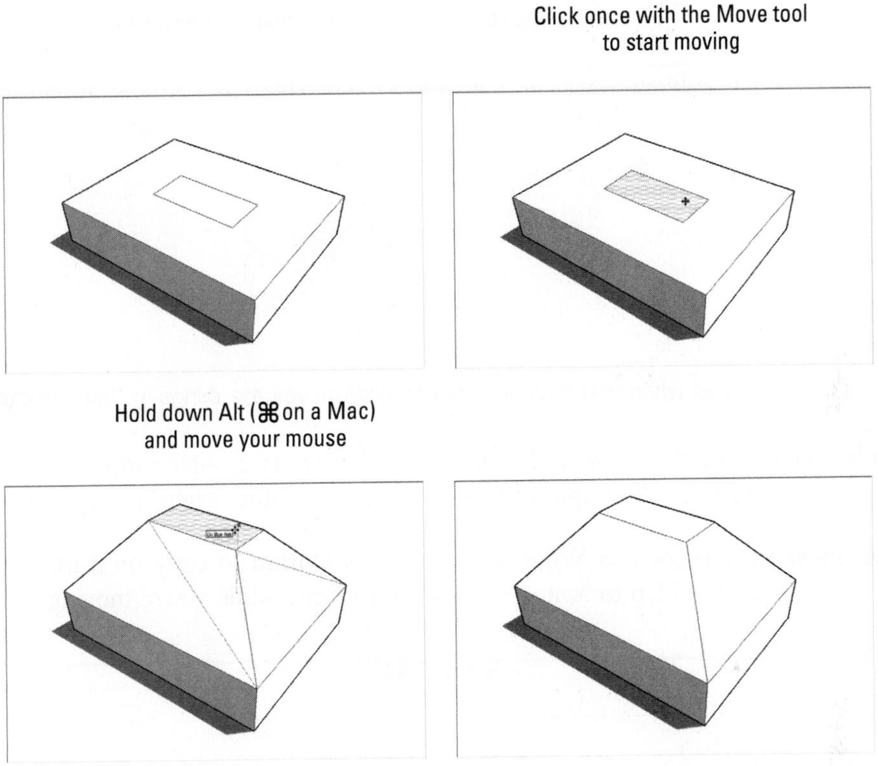

Click once with the Move tool
to start moving

Hold down Alt (⌘ on a Mac)
and move your mouse

Use Auto-Fold to force SketchUp to create folds in a model.

Deciding When to Preselect

The Move tool works in two different ways. Eventually, you'll need to use both of them, depending on what you're trying to move:

▲ **Moving a selection:** When you have a selection of one or more entities, the Move tool only moves the things you've selected. This comes in handy every time you need to move more than one object. Figure 2-23 shows a selection being moved with the Move tool.

▲ **Moving without a selection:** If you don't have anything selected, you can click anything in your model with the Move tool to move it around. Only the thing you click is moved. Figure 2-24 illustrates this.

Making Copies with the Move Tool

Lots of people spend time hunting around in SketchUp, trying to figure out how to make copies. This process is actually very simple: You just press a **modifier key** (a button on your keyboard that tells SketchUp to do something different)

Figure 2-23

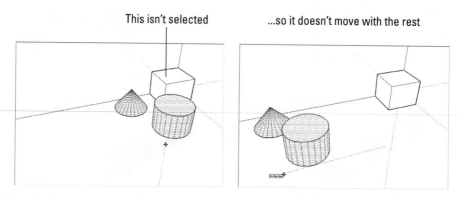

This isn't selected   ...so it doesn't move with the rest

Using the Move tool when you have a selection only moves the things in that selection.

while you're using the Move tool. Thus, instead of moving something, you move a copy of it. Here are a couple of things to keep in mind when doing this:

▲ **Press Ctrl to copy in Windows, and press Option to copy on a Mac.** This tells SketchUp to switch from Move to Copy while you're moving

Figure 2-24

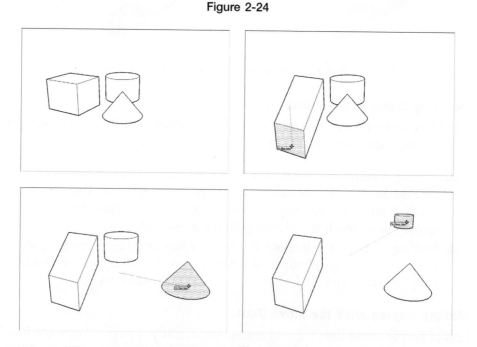

Without anything selected, you can click anything in your model with the Move tool to start moving it around.

Figure 2-25

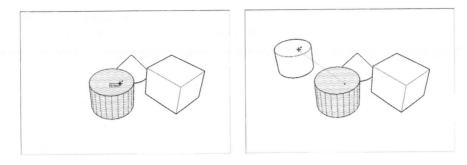

Press Ctrl (Option on a Mac) to tell SketchUp to make a copy
while you're moving something.

something with the Move tool. Your cursor will have a small "+" appear
next to it, and you'll see your copy moving when you move your mouse.
Figure 2-25 shows this in action. If you decide you don't want to make a
copy, just press Ctrl (Option) again to toggle back to Move; the "+" sign
will disappear.

▲ **Copying is just like moving, except you're moving a copy.** This means
that all the same rules that apply to using the Move tool apply to making copies, too.

▲ **You can make more than one copy at a time.** Perhaps you want to
make five equally spaced copies of a column, as shown in Figure 2-26.
All you have to do is move a copy to where you want the last column
to be, then type in **5/** and press Enter. This makes five copies of the
column and spaces them evenly between the first and last column in the
row. Alternatively, if you know how far apart you want your copies to

Figure 2-26

Move a copy

Typing **5/** yields 5 copies
between

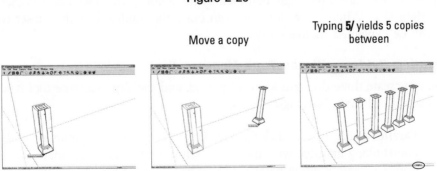

To make evenly spaced copies, type in the number of copies you want
followed by a slash (/), and then press Enter.

Figure 2-27

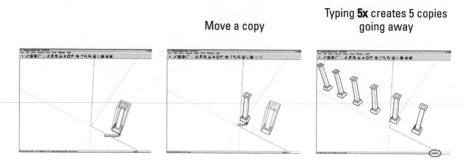

Move a copy

Typing **5x** creates 5 copies going away

To make multiple copies in a row, type in the number of copies you want, followed by an *x*, and press Enter.

be, you can move a copy that distance, type in **5x**, and press Enter. Your five copies will appear equally spaced in a row (see Figure 2-27).

2.3.6 Making and Using Guides

Sometimes you need to draw temporary lines while you're modeling. These temporary lines, called **guides**, are useful for lining things up, making things the right size, and generally adding precision and accuracy to what you're building.

In previous versions of SketchUp, guides were called construction geometry, because that's basically what they are: a special kind of entity that you create when and where you need them. They aren't part of your model, because they're not edges or faces. This means that you can choose to hide them or delete them, and they don't affect the rest of your geometry.

Figure 2-28 shows an example of guides in action. Here, we have positioned guides 12 inches from the wall and 36 inches apart to draw the sides of a doorway. We then use another guide 6 feet, 8 inches from the floor to indicate the top. Next, we draw a rectangle bounded by the guides, which we know is exactly the right size. When we're done, we can erase the guides with the Eraser tool, as will be explained momentarily.

Creating Guides with the Tape Measure Tool

You can create three different kinds of guides, and the Tape Measure tool is used to make all of them (see Figure 2-29).

▲ **Parallel guide lines:** Clicking anywhere (except the endpoints or midpoint) along an edge with the Tape Measure tells SketchUp that you want to create a guide parallel to that edge (see Figure 2-29). Just move your mouse and you'll see a parallel, dashed line; click again to place it wherever you want.

Figure 2-28

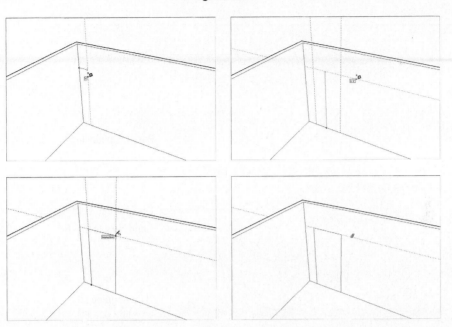

Use guides to measure things before you draw.

▲ **Linear guide lines:** To create a guide along an edge in your model, click one of the endpoints or the midpoint once, and then click again somewhere else along the edge.

▲ **Guide points:** You might want to place a point somewhere in space; you can do exactly that with guide points. With the Tape Measure tool, click an edge's midpoint or endpoint, and then click again somewhere else in space. A little *x* appears at the end of a dashed line—that's your new guide point.

Here's an important point about the Tape Measure tool: It has two modes, and it only creates guides in one of them. Pressing Ctrl (Option on a Mac) toggles between the modes. When you see a + next to your cursor, your Tape Measure can make guides; when there's no +, it can't.

Using Guides to Make Life Easier

As you're working along in SketchUp, you'll find yourself using guides all the time; they're an indispensable part of the way modeling in this software works. Here are some things you should know about using guides:

▲ **Position guides precisely using the VCB.** Check Section 2.3.3 ("Injecting Accuracy into Your Model") earlier in this chapter to find out how.

Figure 2-29

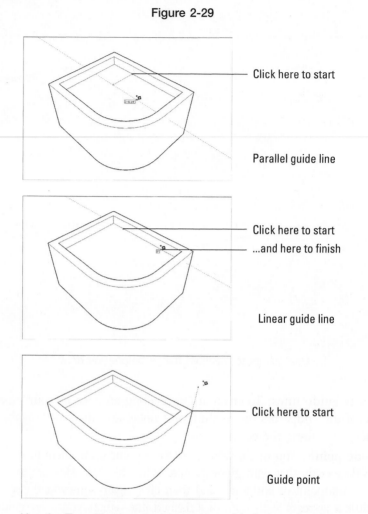

Click here to start

Parallel guide line

Click here to start
...and here to finish

Linear guide line

Click here to start

Guide point

Use the Tape Measure tool to create guide lines and points.

▲ **Erase guides one at a time.** Just click or drag over them with the Eraser tool to delete guides individually. You can also right-click them and choose Erase from the context menu.

▲ **Erase all your guides at once.** Choosing Edit⇨Delete Guides does just that.

▲ **Hide guides individually or all at once.** Right-click a single guide and choose Hide to hide it, or deselect View⇨Guides to hide all of them. It's a good idea to hide your guides instead of erasing them, especially while you're still modeling.

▲ **Select, move, copy, and rotate guides just like any other entity in your model.** Guides aren't edges, but much of the time, you can treat them as such.

2.3.7 Painting Faces with Color and Texture

When it comes to adding colors and textures—collectively referred to in SketchUp as **materials**—to your model, there's really only one place you need to look, and one tool you need to use: the Materials dialog box and the Paint Bucket tool, respectively.

The Materials Dialog Box

To open the Materials dialog box (or Colors dialog box on the Mac), choose Window⇨Materials. Figure 2-30 illustrates what you see when you do this. The Materials dialog box is radically different in the Windows and Mac versions of SketchUp, but that's okay, because they basically do the same thing.

In SketchUp, you can choose from two different kinds of materials to apply to the faces in your models:

▲ **Colors:** These are simple—colors are always solid colors. You can't have gradients (where one color fades into another), but you can make almost any color you want.

▲ **Textures:** Basically, a SketchUp texture is a tiny image (a photograph, really) that gets tiled over and over to cover the face you apply it to. If you paint a face with, say, a brick texture, what you're really

Figure 2-30

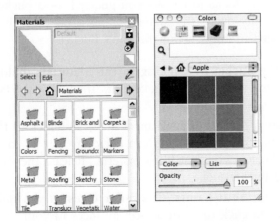

The Materials dialog box in Windows (left) and on the Mac (right).

doing is telling SketchUp to cover the surface with however many brick photo tiles it takes to do the job. The preview image you see in the Materials dialog box is actually a picture of a single texture image tile. (Note that on a Mac, you have to click the little brick icon in the Materials dialog box to see the textures libraries that ship with SketchUp; it's the drop-down list next to the little house icon.) SketchUp comes with many textures, but you can get even more from the Google SketchUp website (http://sketchup.google.com/bonus-packs.html). If that's still not enough, you can go online and choose from thousands more available that are for sale. And if that's *still* not enough, you can make your own, although the process of doing so is well beyond the scope of this book.

Here's some more interesting information about SketchUp materials:

▲ **Materials can be translucent.** Adjusting the Opacity slider makes the material you've selected more or less translucent, which makes seeing through windows in your model a lot easier.

▲ **Textures can have transparent areas.** If you take a look at the materials in the Fencing library, you'll notice that a lot of them look kind of strange; they have areas of black that don't seem right. These black areas are areas of transparency. When you paint a face with one of these textures, you'll be able to see through the areas that look black.

▲ **You can edit materials, and even make your own.** This can be considered a relatively advanced use of SketchUp, so it won't be covered in this book.

The Paint Bucket Tool

The Paint Bucket tool looks just like—you guessed it—a bucket of paint. Activating it automatically opens the Materials dialog box, which is handy. Here's everything you need to know about the Paint Bucket:

▲ **You "fill" the bucket by clicking in the Materials dialog box.** Just click a material to load your bucket, and then click the face you want to paint. It's as simple as that.

▲ **Holding down Alt (Command on a Mac) switches to the Sample tool.** With the Sample tool, you can click any face in your model to load your Paint Bucket with that face's material. Release the Alt key to revert to the Paint Bucket tool.

▲ **Holding down Shift paints all similar faces.** If you hold down Shift when you click to paint a face, all faces in your model that match the one you click will be painted, too. If things don't turn out the way you want, just choose Undo from the Edit menu to go back a step.

SELF-CHECK

1. Three SketchUp navigation tools are:

   a. Fly, Jump, and Pan.

   b. Orbit, Jump, and Pan.

   c. Fly, Zoom, and Pan.

   d. Orbit, Zoom, and Pan.

2. You should always use Orbit by using your _____.

3. The drawing mode in which SketchUp starts drawing a new edge at the end of the previous edge is called:

   a. zig-zagging.

   b. rubber banding.

   c. orbiting.

   d. snipping.

4. The VCB is _____-sensitive.

5. You can only make one copy at a time. True or false?

SUMMARY

The key to mastering SketchUp is the ability to select the correct tool for the task at hand. In this chapter, you surveyed many of the tools that are available to you. You compared these tools and how you can use them. You assessed when and how to use edges and faces and what role they have in representing three-dimensional objects. You also evaluated how to inject accuracy into your models.

KEY TERMS

Coplanar	On the same plane.
Drawing axes	Three colored lines visible in the SketchUp modeling window that enable users to work in three-dimensional space.
Folds	Edges and faces that are created in place of a single face.
Geometry	Edges and faces in SketchUp models.

Guides	Temporary lines that users can create to work more accurately in SketchUp.
Inference engine	Objects such as colored squares, dotted lines, yellow tags, and other similar objects that appear as the user moves his or her cursor around the SketchUp modeling window.
Linear inferences	Helper lines that allow a user to work more accurately.
Materials	The colors and textures in SketchUp models.
Modifier key	A button on the keyboard that users can push to take a different action than what they are currently doing.
Orbit	Ability to look at a SketchUp model from every angle; this is accomplished with the Orbit tool.
Pan	Sliding the model view around the modeling window; this is accomplished by using the Pan tool.
Point inferences	Small colored squares that appear when a SketchUp user moves the cursor over specific parts of their model.
Rubber banding	Drawing edge segments, automatically starting each new one at the end of the previous one.
User interface	The visual elements in a software program that the user uses to interact with the software, such as dialog boxes and buttons.
Vertices	The endpoints of edges.
Zoom	Getting closer or further away from the model; this is accomplished by using the Zoom tool.

ASSESS YOUR UNDERSTANDING

Go to www.wiley.com/college/chopra to evaluate your knowledge of SketchUp models.

Measure your learning by comparing pre-test and post-test results.

Summary Questions

1. The _____ tool is used to slide the model view around the modeling window.
2. There is only one way to activate the Zoom tool. True or false?
3. You can make copies by using a modifier key. True or false?
4. The key to accuracy in SketchUp is:
   (a) the Value Control Box.
   (b) the user interface.
   (c) the inference engine.
   (d) rubber banding.
5. SketchUp automatically makes a _____ every time you finish drawing a closed shape out of three or more coplanar edges.
6. If you want to get closer to your model, you can use:
   (a) the Pan tool.
   (b) the Orbit tool.
   (c) guides.
   (d) the Zoom tool.
7. You can use the _____ tool to create guides.
8. You can erase all of your guides at once or one at a time. True or false?
9. When selecting colors for your model, you have gradients to choose from. True or false?
10. If you want your model to automatically fill your modeling window, you would use:
    (a) Pan.
    (b) Orbit.
    (c) Zoom Extents.
    (d) Zoom.

Applying This Chapter

1. You are teaching your classmate how to use SketchUp to draw a model of a doghouse. What are the first three things you would teach him or her and why?

2. Name and describe four qualities of the Value Control Box.

3. You've started to model a staircase, and you want to make sure the riser height is 6 inches. How do you do this?

4. You are modeling a house with five equally-spaced columns. After you havedrawn the first column, what is the easiest way to add the other four columns?

Zoom, Pan, and Orbit

Open the Components dialog box (from the Window menu) and select a pre-created model. Zoom, pan, and orbit around this model using the appropriate tools.

Draw a Box

In SketchUp, draw a box. Use the Tape Measure tool to create linear and point guides. Save the box for future exercises.

3

BUILDING SIMPLE MODELS
Step-by-Step Instructions for Creating a Model of a Doghouse

Starting Point

Go to www.wiley.com/college/chopra to assess your knowledge of building simple models.
Determine where you need to concentrate your effort.

What You'll Learn in This Chapter

▲ How to set up SketchUp and change the default settings
▲ The first steps to take in building simple models
▲ The different ways you can change the appearance of a model
▲ How to add shadows to a model

After Studying This Chapter, You'll Be Able To

▲ Set up SketchUp to begin modeling
▲ Build a simple model
▲ Alter how your model looks by changing its color, texture, style, and shadows
▲ Share your model with others by exporting it as a JPEG

INTRODUCTION

If you can't wait to start using SketchUp, you've come to the right chapter! In this chapter, you'll learn how to make a simple model step by step, spin it around, paint it, and even apply styles and shadows. These pages are about *doing* and about the basics of putting together the various SketchUp features to produce a great model in no time.

More specifically, in this chapter, we'll walk through the steps necessary to create a model of a doghouse. The nice thing about doghouses is that they're a lot like human houses in several important ways: They have doors and roofs, and just about everybody has seen one.

In this chapter, you will build a doghouse. Don't get nervous! This chapter presents the steps in chronological order with very simple and easy-to-understand instructions, beginning with how to set up the program. In addition, you'll learn to alter how your model looks by changing its color, texture, and style and by adding shadows. Finally, you'll discover how to share your model with others.

3.1 Setting Up SketchUp

Because setup can be boring, this discussion is as brief as possible. To make sure that you're starting at the right place, simply follow these steps when setting up SketchUp on your computer:

1. **Launch Google SketchUp.** In other words, open the program on your computer.
2. **Choose your default settings.** If you've never launched SketchUp on your computer before, you'll see the Choose Default Settings dialog box upon startup (see Figure 3-1).

Here's what to do if the Choose Default Settings box appears on your screen:

▲ Choose Perspective View (on the left).
▲ Choose your preferred measurement system from the Units drop-down menu.
▲ Click the Continue button to close the dialog box.

If the Choose Default Settings dialog box doesn't appear, you (or someone else) have already chosen these settings. Don't worry—just follow these steps to set things straight:

▲ Choose Window➪Preferences (SketchUp➪Preferences on a Mac).
▲ On the left side of the System Preferences dialog box, choose Template to show the Template panel.

Figure 3-1

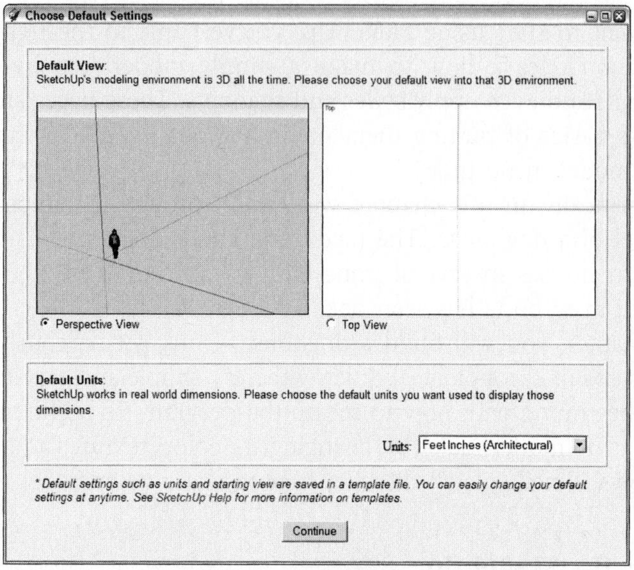

The Choose Default Settings dialog box appears
the first time you launch SketchUp.

▲ Choose one of the 3D templates from the drop-down list (see Figure 3-2).

▲ If you're on a Windows machine, close the System Preferences dialog box
by clicking OK. On a Mac, click the red button in the upper-left corner
of the dialog box.

▲ Finally, open a new file by choosing File⇨New.

Figure 3-2

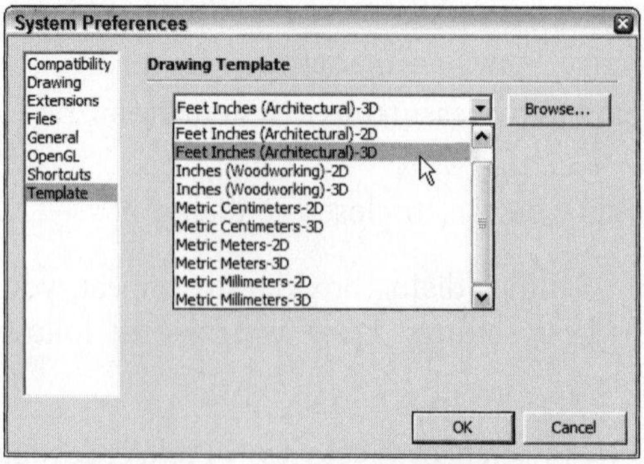

Choose one of the 3D templates from the list
in the System Preferences dialog box.

Figure 3-3

The Getting Started toolbar is located at the top of your modeling window.

3. **Close the Learning Center dialog box (which may have opened automatically when you launched SketchUp) for now. If the Learning Center isn't there in the first place, skip to step 4.** As long as the Show Tips at Startup check box has never been deselected (by you or someone else), the Learning Center dialog box will open every time you launch SketchUp. That's a good thing; don't deselect it just yet. Just close the Learning Center for now by clicking the small X in its upper-right corner. If you're on a Mac, click the red circle in the upper-left corner.

4. **Make sure that you can see the Getting Started toolbar.** Figure 3-3 shows the Getting Started toolbar. If it's not visible in your modeling window, choose View⟹Toolbars⟹Getting Started to make it show up. If you're on a Mac, choose View⟹Show Toolbar.

5. **Clear your modeling window.** If this isn't the first time SketchUp has been run on your computer, you might see dialog boxes all over your screen. If this is the case, open the Window menu and make sure that everything is deselected to get rid of these boxes.

SELF-CHECK

1. If the Choose Default Settings dialog box doesn't appear, then this is because someone else has already chosen the settings. True or false?

2. You can choose the units of _____ that you prefer to work with.

3. Sometimes the Learning Center dialog box opens automatically when you launch SketchUp. True or false?

3.2 Making a Quick Model

Figure 3-4 shows what your computer screen should look like at this point. You should see a row of tools across the top of your modeling window, a small figure of a man, and three colored drawing axes (red, green, and blue lines).

Figure 3-4

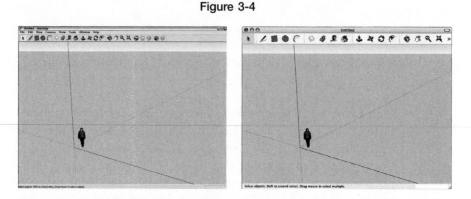

This is what your screen should look like in Windows (left) and on a Mac (right).

Now, you're ready to start creating your model of a doghouse! Simply follow these steps to build your model.

1. **Delete the little man on your screen.** Using the Select tool (the arrow on the far left of your toolbar), click on the man to select him (his name is Bryce, by the way), and then choose Edit⇨Delete.

2. **Choose Camera⇨Standard⇨Iso.** This switches you to an **isometric view** (3D view) of your model, which allows you to build an object without having to "move around."

3. **Draw a rectangle on the ground.** Use the Rectangle tool (between the pencil and the circle on your toolbar) to draw a rectangle by doing the following:

   • Click once to place one corner on the left side of your screen.

   • Click again to place the opposite corner on the right side of your screen.

   Remember that you're in a 3D, *perspective,* view of the world, so your rectangle will look more like a diamond—90-degree angles don't look like 90-degree angles in perspective. Figure 3-5 shows what you should be aiming for in this step.

   It's important to draw the right kind of rectangle for this example (or for any model you're trying to create in Perspective view), so try it a few times until it looks like the rectangle in Figure 3-5. To go back a step, choose Edit⇨Undo Rectangle, and the last thing you did will be undone. You can use Undo to go back as many steps as you like, so feel free to use it anytime.

4. **Use the Push/Pull tool to extrude your rectangle into a box.** Use this tool (it looks like a brown box with a red arrow coming of out the top) to "pull" your rectangle into a box by following these steps:

   • Click the rectangle once to start the push/pull operation.

   • Click again, somewhere above your rectangle, to stop pushing/pulling.

Figure 3-5

Click here to start drawing   Finish drawing here

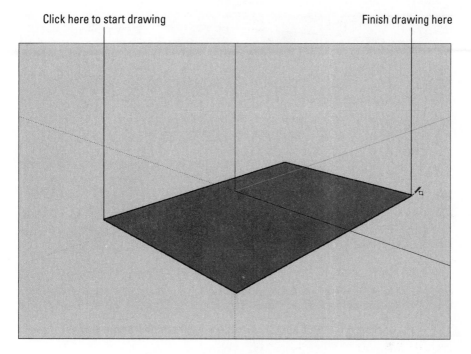

Draw a 3D rectangle on the ground.

At this point, you should have something that looks like Figure 3-6. If you don't, use Push/Pull again to make your box look about the right height.

Note that if you are pushing/pulling on your box and everything suddenly disappears, it's because you pushed/pulled the top of your box all the way to the ground. Just choose Edit⇨Undo and keep going.

5. **Draw diagonal lines for your roof.** Use the Line tool (it's shaped like a pencil) to draw two diagonal edges (lines) that will form your peaked roof, as shown in Figure 3-7. Follow these steps:

   • Click once at the midpoint of the top of your box's front face to start your line. You'll know you're at the midpoint when you see a small, light-blue square and the word *Midpoint* appears. Move slowly to make sure that you see this indicator.

   • Click again somewhere along one of the side edges of your box's front face to end your line. Wait until you see a red *On Edge* cue (just like the Midpoint indicator in the last step) before you click; if you don't, your new line won't end on the edge like it's supposed to.

   • Repeat the previous two steps to draw a similar (but opposite) line from the midpoint to the edge on the other side of the face. Don't

Figure 3-6

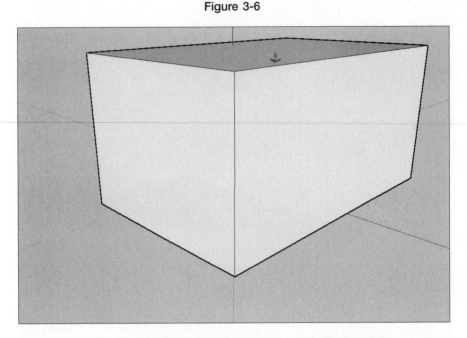

Use the Push/Pull tool to extrude your rectangle into a box.

worry about making your diagonal lines symmetrical; for the purposes of this exercise, it's not important that they are.

6. **Push/pull the triangles away to leave a sloped roof.** Use the Push/Pull tool (the same one you used in step 4) to get rid of the triangular parts of your box, leaving you with a sloped roof. Have a look at Figure 3-8 to see this in action, and follow these steps:

   • Select the Push/Pull tool, and then click the right triangular face once to start the push/pull operation.

Figure 3-7

Click here to start drawing   Click here to finish your first edge

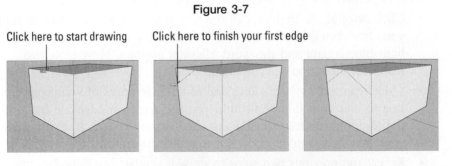

Draw two diagonal lines that will become your peaked roof.

Figure 3-8

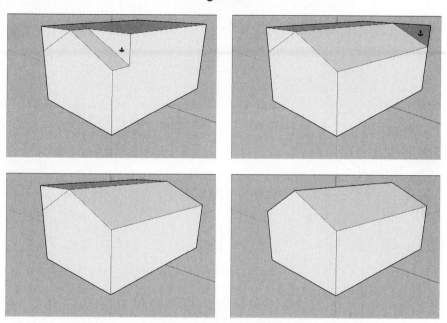

Use the Push/Pull tool to form a peaked roof on your box.

- Move your cursor to the right to "push" the triangle as far as it will go (even with the end of your box).
- Click again (on the triangle) to end the push/pull operation and to make the triangular face disappear.
- Still using the Push/Pull tool, double-click the left triangular face to repeat the previous push/pull operation, making that face disappear as well.

7. **Draw a rectangle on your front face.** Switch back to the Rectangle tool (which you used in step 3) and draw a rectangle on the front face of your pointy box. Make sure that the bottom of your rectangle is flush with the bottom of your box by watching for the red On Edge cue to appear before you click. Check out Figure 3-9 to see what it should look like when you're done.

   Remember, using the rectangle tool is a two-step process: You click once to place one corner and again to place the opposite corner. Try not to draw lines and shapes in SketchUp by dragging your cursor; doing so makes matters more difficult. Practice clicking once to start an operation (like drawing a rectangle) and clicking again to stop.

Figure 3-9

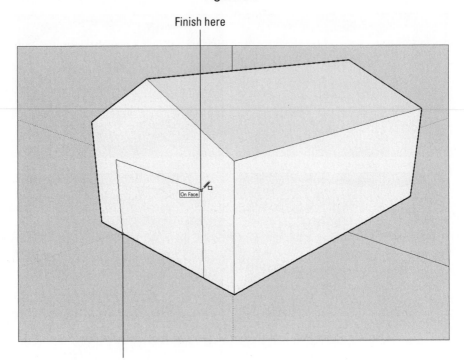

Finish here

Click here to start drawing

A rectangle drawn on the front of your pointy box.

8. **Draw an arc on top of the rectangle you just drew.** Use the Arc tool (to the right of the Circle tool) to draw an arc on top of your rectangle (see Figure 3-10). Follow these steps to draw an arc:
   - Click the upper-left corner of the rectangle to place one endpoint of your arc. Make sure that you see the green Endpoint hint before you click.
   - Click the upper-*right* corner of the rectangle to place the other endpoint of your arc.
   - Move your cursor up to "bow out" the line you're drawing into an arc, and click when you're happy with how it looks.

9. **Select the Eraser tool and then click the horizontal line between the rectangle and the arc to erase that line.** This creates the arched doorway to your doghouse.

10. **Push/pull the doorway inward.** Use the Push/Pull tool to push the "doorway" face you created in steps 7 through 9 in just a bit. Remember, you use Push/Pull by clicking a face once to start, moving your cursor to "push/pull" it in or out, and then clicking again to stop.

Figure 3-10

Click here to start   Click here second

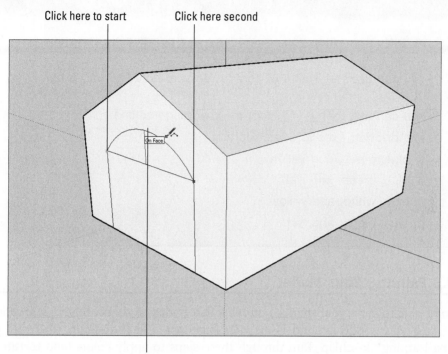

Click up here third

Draw an arc on top of your rectangle.

11. **Erase the horizontal line at the bottom of the doorway by clicking it with the Eraser tool.** This makes the line (and the whole face above it) disappear. Figure 3-11 illustrates what your finished doghouse should look like.

Figure 3-11

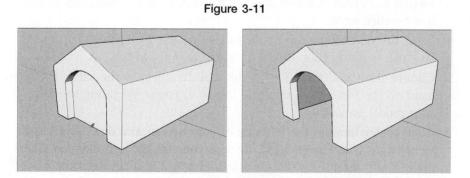

Create the door opening by erasing its bottom edge.

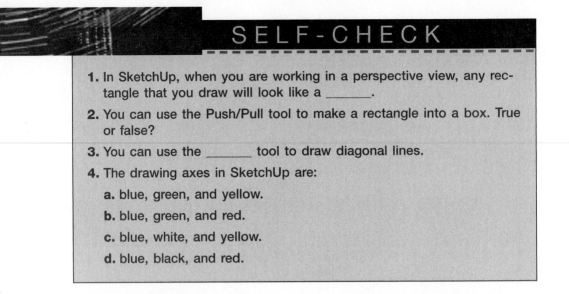

1. In SketchUp, when you are working in a perspective view, any rectangle that you draw will look like a _____.
2. You can use the Push/Pull tool to make a rectangle into a box. True or false?
3. You can use the _____ tool to draw diagonal lines.
4. The drawing axes in SketchUp are:

   a. blue, green, and yellow.

   b. blue, green, and red.

   c. blue, white, and yellow.

   d. blue, black, and red.

3.3 Painting Your Model

To be able to paint your model, you must first understand how to spin it around. Moving your model around is *the most important* skill to develop when you're first learning SketchUp. Run through these steps to apply colors (and textures) to the faces in your model—and to learn more about moving your model while you're doing it:

1. **Choose Window⇨Materials to open the Materials dialog box.** See Figure 3-12 for a picture of this dialog box. Click a color or texture that you like. When you do, you automatically "pick up" the Paint Bucket tool and fill it with your chosen material.
2. **Paint some of the faces in your model.** Do this by clicking any face you want to paint with the Paint Bucket tool.
3. **Switch materials.** Choose another material from the Materials dialog box by clicking it.
4. **Paint the rest of the faces you can see.** Refer to Figure 3-13 to see how this is done. Loop through steps 2 to 4 for as long as you like.
5. **Choose the Orbit tool.** This is the tool that's just to the left of the white hand on the toolbar. By selecting this tool, you're preparing to move your model around.
6. **Click somewhere on the left side of your screen and *drag* your cursor to the right (see Figure 3-14). Release your mouse button when you're done.** Your model spins! This is called orbiting. Orbit around some more, just to get the hang of it. If you're orbiting, and you've dragged your cursor over as far as it will go but you haven't orbited as much as you want to,

Figure 3-12

The Materials dialog box in Windows (left) and on a Mac (right).

Figure 3-13

Use the Paint Bucket tool to paint everything you can see.

Figure 3-14

Choose the Orbit tool and drag your cursor to spin your model around.

don't fret. Just release the mouse button, move your cursor to where it was when you started orbiting, and orbit some more by clicking and dragging. You usually can't see what you want to see with a single orbit; typically, you'll need a bunch of separate "drags" to get things looking the way you want.

7. **Zoom in and out if you need to by selecting the Zoom tool and dragging your cursor up and down in your modeling window.** The Zoom tool looks like a magnifying glass, and it's on the other side of the white hand icon. Dragging up zooms in, while dragging down zooms out.

8. **If needed, move around in two dimensions with the Pan tool by selecting it and then clicking and dragging the Pan cursor inside your modeling window.** The Pan tool is the white hand found between Orbit and Zoom. You use Pan to "slide" your model inside your modeling window without spinning it or making it look bigger or smaller. You can pan in any direction.

9. **Use the Orbit, Zoom, Pan, and Paint Bucket tools to finish painting your doghouse.** Now that you know how to move around your model, paint it as follows (Color Plate 8 shows what it should look like):

   • Paint the exterior walls reddish brown.

   • Paint the roof light blue.

   • Paint the interior yellow-orange.

When you're just starting out in SketchUp, it's easy to get a little lost with the navigation tools (Orbit, Zoom, and Pan); it happens to everybody. If you find yourself having difficulties, just choose Camera⇨Zoom Extents. When you do this, SketchUp automatically places your model directly in front of you; check out Figure 3-15 to see Zoom Extents in action. Zoom Extents is also a button on the toolbar; it's located next to the Zoom tool.

Figure 3-15

Click Zoom Extents

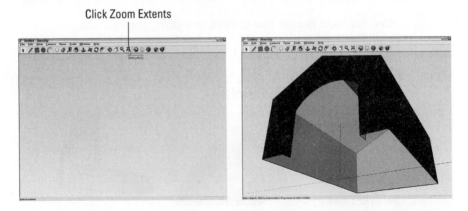

Use Zoom Extents anytime you can't determine where your model went.

SELF-CHECK

1. To paint your model, you would use the color tool. True or false?
2. The Materials dialog box includes colors and _____.
3. Orbit, Zoom, and Pan are navigation tools. True or false?
4. Which tool would you use to move your model around?
   a. Orbit tool
   b. Zoom tool
   c. Pan tool
   d. Zoom Extents

3.4 Giving Your Model Some Style

SketchUp Styles allow you to change your model's appearance—basically, the way it's drawn—with just a few clicks of your mouse. You can create your own styles, of course, but SketchUp also comes with a library of premade ones that you can use without knowing anything about how they work.

Follow these steps to try several different styles on your doghouse:

1. **Choose Window⇨Styles.** This opens the Styles dialog box.
2. **Click the Select tab.** This lets you see the Select pane.
3. **In the Libraries drop-down menu, choose the Assorted Styles library.** This is shown in Figure 3-16.

Figure 3-16

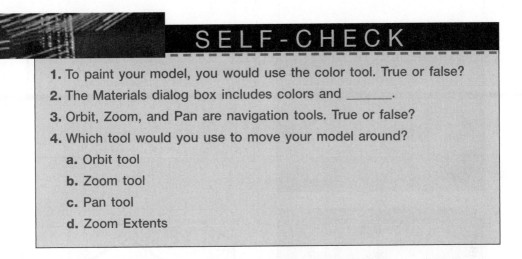

The Assorted Styles library is a sampler
of ready-mixed SketchUp styles.

Figure 3-17

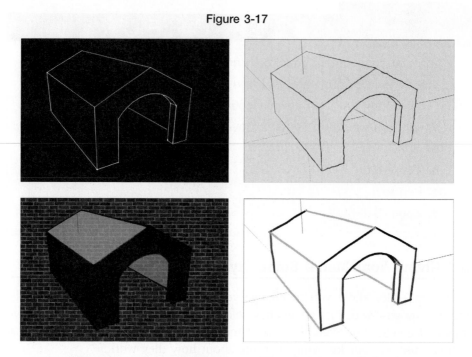

The same doghouse with four very different styles applied to it.

4. **Click through the different styles to see what they're about.** When you click a style in the Styles dialog box, that style is applied to your model. Figure 3-17 shows a model of a doghouse with a few different styles applied. Can you figure out which styles have been used?
5. **Go back to the default style.** This is the first style in the Default Styles library.

SELF-CHECK

1. How do you open the Styles dialog box?
2. SketchUp comes with a library of premade styles. True or false?

3.5 Adding Shadows

You're about to use what some people consider to be the one of SketchUp's best features: shadows. When you turn on shadows, you're activating SketchUp's built-in sun. The shadows you see in your modeling window are *accurate* for

Figure 3-18

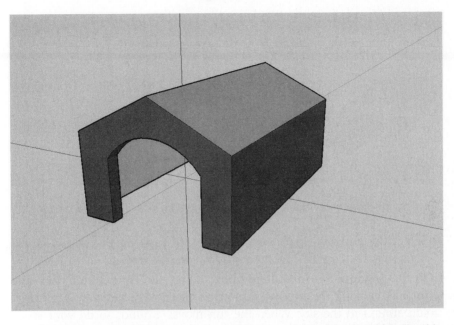

Use Orbit, Zoom, and Pan to navigate until your model looks something like this.

whatever time and location you set. For the purposes of this tutorial, though, don't worry about accuracy. Go through these steps to let the light shine in:

1. **Use Orbit, Zoom, and Pan to get an aerial, three-quarter view of your doghouse.** Your view should look much like the one shown in Figure 3-18.

2. **Choose Window⇨Shadows.** This opens the Shadow Settings dialog box, as shown in Figure 3-19.

Figure 3-19

Slide back and forth

The Shadow Settings dialog box controls
the position of SketchUp's built-in sun.

Figure 3-20

7:31 a.m.   3:16 p.m.

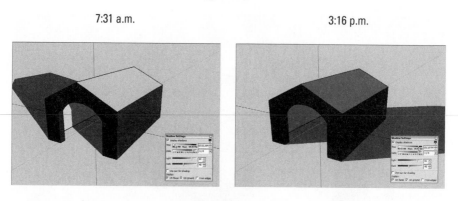

Moving the Time slider back and forth changes the position of your shadows.

3. **Select the Display Shadows check box to turn on the sun.** Your dog-house should now be casting a shadow on the ground.

4. **In the Shadow Settings dialog box, move the Time slider back and forth.** Changing the time of day means that you're moving SketchUp's sun around in the sky. When the sun moves around, so do your shadows. Take a look at Figure 3-20 to see how this works.

For more about fine-tuning light and shadows, refer to Chapter 9.

SELF-CHECK

1. When you turn on shadows, you're activating SketchUp's built-in _____.

2. The shadows in SketchUp are accurate for the time and location you set. True or false?

3. How do you open the Shadow Settings dialog box?

3.6 Sharing Your Model

Now that your model looks the way you want it to, you probably want to show it to someone. The easiest way to do this is by exporting your model to a **JPEG** image that you can attach to an email. Follow these steps, and you'll be on your way:

1. Navigate around (using Orbit, Zoom, and Pan) until you like the view of your model that you see in your modeling window.

2. Choose File⇨Export⇨2D Graphic.

> **FOR EXAMPLE**
>
> **What Is a JPEG?**
>
> JPEG stands for Joint Photographic Experts Group and is a compression technique for digital images. JPEG compression reduces file sizes to a small percentage of their normal size. Users can often choose the degree of compression they desire when saving files as JPEGs. The more compressed a file is, the lower the quality of the image.

3. In the Export dialog box that opens, choose JPEG from the Export Type drop-down menu.
4. Pick a location on your computer system, and give your exported image a name.
5. Click the Export button to create a JPEG image of what's visible in your modeling window.

Exporting a JPEG file is just one way to share models. You can share your model on Google Earth, as a printout, as an image or animation, or as a slick presentation that will (hopefully) impress all your friends.

SELF-CHECK

1. What is a JPEG?
2. Name two ways you can share your models.

SUMMARY

Congratulations! You have completed your first SketchUp model. In this chapter, you set up SketchUp and created a simple model of a doghouse. After some experimentation, you altered how your model appeared by adding color, texture, style, and shadows. You also shared your model with others by exporting it as a JPEG. These skills are the foundation for creating more intricate and complex models, as you will do in later chapters.

KEY TERMS

Isometric view	A kind of three-dimensional view of a model.
JPEG	A compressed file type for digital images.

ASSESS YOUR UNDERSTANDING

Go to www.wiley.com/college/chopra to evaluate your knowledge of building simple models.

Measure your learning by comparing pre-test and post-test results.

Summary Questions

1. A(n) _____ view is a three-dimensional view of your model.
2. What might a rectangle look like in 3D?
   (a) A rectangle
   (b) A diamond
   (c) A box
   (d) A circle
3. If you are turning a rectangle into a box using the Push/Pull tool and everything disappears, it is because you have pushed/pulled the top of your box to the ground. True or false?
4. The Line tool is shaped like a diagonal line. True or false?
5. The On Edge cue is:
   (a) blue.
   (b) yellow.
   (c) green.
   (d) red.
6. If you make a mistake, you can always go back one or more steps by choosing _____ from the Edit menu.
7. Styles allow you to change your model's appearance. True or false?
8. Exporting a _____ is one way to share your model.
9. You can share your model on Google Earth. True or false?
10. The Push/Pull tool looks like:
    (a) a pencil.
    (b) a rope.
    (c) a small man.
    (d) a brown box with a red arrow coming out of it.
11. You can use Undo for only the last two steps you completed. True or false?
12. You can find textures in the _____ dialog box.

Applying This Chapter

1. SketchUp gives you the ability to add shadows to your models. Why would you want to add shadows?

2. You make a model of your ideal house and want to share it with your friends. Name three ways you can share the model.

3. You are working on a model of your ideal house. How would you add color and textures to the model? Which color and textures would you choose?

4. How do you navigate around your model and why is the ability to do this important?

YOU TRY IT

Sharing Your Model

Follow the directions in this chapter and build a doghouse. After you are done, share your model by doing the following:

a. Exporting it as a JPEG file
b. Emailing it to a friend

Altering Your Model

Follow the directions in this chapter and build a doghouse. Once you are done, alter your model by:

a. Changing the color
b. Adding shadows
c. Changing the style
d. Adding a window

4

MODELING BUILDINGS
From Drafting a Floor Plan to Adding a Roof

Starting Point

Go to www.wiley.com/college/chopra to assess your knowledge of modeling buildings.
Determine where you need to concentrate your effort.

What You'll Learn in This Chapter

▲ Components of a floor plan
▲ The different drafting tools that SketchUp offers
▲ How to model interior and exterior walls
▲ Three different methods for creating stairs
▲ The different types of roofs

After Studying This Chapter, You'll Be Able To

▲ Draft a simple floor plan
▲ Convert a 2D plan to a 3D model
▲ Model stairs
▲ Create and insert doors and windows
▲ Create and add a roof to your model

INTRODUCTION

Even though SketchUp lets you make just about anything you can think of, certain forms are easier to make than others. Fortunately, these kinds of shapes are exactly the ones that people want to make with SketchUp most of the time. That's no accident! SketchUp was designed with architecture in mind, so the whole paradigm—the fact that SketchUp models are made of faces and edges, as well as the fact that the software offers certain tools—is perfect for making things like buildings.

But what about curvy, swoopy buildings? You can use SketchUp to make those, too, but they're a little harder, so they're not really a good place to start. Because most of us live in boxy places with right-angled rooms and flat ceilings, that kind of architecture is relatively easy to understand, and it is also easier to model with SketchUp.

In this chapter, you'll learn some of the fundamentals of SketchUp modeling in terms of making simple, rectilinear buildings. You will draft a simple floor plan. You will convert a 2D plan to a 3D model, and you will add stairs, doors, windows, and a roof to your model. By reading about how to build certain kinds of things, instead of just reading about what the individual tools do, you should find it easier to get started. Even if you're not planning to use SketchUp to model any of the things described in this chapter, you should still be able to apply these concepts to your own creations.

4.1 Drawing Floors and Walls

Most floors and walls are flat surfaces, so it's easy to model them with straight edges and flat faces in SketchUp. In fact, chances are good that the first thing you ever modeled in SketchUp looked a lot like the floor and walls of a building.

There are two different kinds of architectural models that most people want to create in SketchUp. Exactly how you approach modeling floors and walls depends entirely on the type of model you're making:

▲ **Exterior models:** An **exterior model** of a building is basically just an empty shell; you don't have interior walls, rooms, or furniture to worry about. This makes for a slightly simpler proposition for users who are just starting out.

▲ **Interior models:** An **interior model** of a building is significantly more complicated than an exterior-only one; dealing with interior wall thicknesses, floor heights, ceilings, and furnishings involves a lot more modeling prowess.

Figure 4-1

Single-face walls   Double-face walls

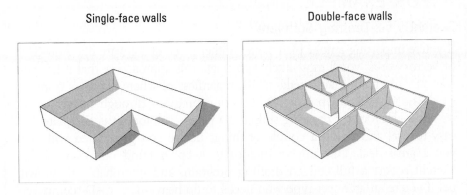

Use single faces for exterior models and double faces for interior ones.

Here's the thing: Because everything in SketchUp is made up of super-flat faces (they have no thickness), the only way to model a wall that's, say, 8 inches thick is to use two faces side by side and 8 inches apart. For models where you need to show wall thicknesses—namely, interior models—this is what you'll have to do. Exterior models are easier to make because you can use single faces to represent walls. Figure 4-1 shows the difference between single- and double-face walls.

One of the biggest mistakes new SketchUp users make is to attempt an "inside-outside" model right away. Making a model that shows both the interior and the exterior of a building at the same time is, to be honest, extremely difficult when you're just getting started. Instead, at this point, you should build two separate models if you need both interior and exterior views. If you require a combination model later on, you'll be able to build it in a quarter of the time it took you to build either of the first two!

4.1.1 Beginning in 2D

Of course, you can make a 3D model of a building's interior in many ways, but we're going to begin with a process that involves drawing a two-dimensional floor plan that includes all your interior and exterior walls, and then extruding it upward to be the right height. In this method, don't worry about doors, windows, or stairs until after your model is extruded. You will put these elements in afterward.

Switching to 2D View

If you're going to use SketchUp to draw a 2D plan, the first thing you need to do is orient your point of view. It's easiest to draw in 2D when you're directly above your work, looking down at the ground plane. You also want to make sure that you're not seeing things in perspective, which distorts your view of what you have.

FOR EXAMPLE

SketchUp vs. Drafting Software

If you're importing a floor plan from another piece of software like AutoCAD or VectorWorks, you'll most likely appreciate this approach in that it lets you take 2D information and make it 3D, regardless of where it comes from.

Although SketchUp is a 3D modeling program through and through, it's not a bad tool for drawing simple 2D plans. The toolset is adequate and easy to use, and doing a couple of things before you get started will help you a great deal. One important idea to keep in mind, however, is that SketchUp isn't a full-fledged drafting program, and it probably never will be. If you're an architect-type who needs to do heavy-duty CAD (computer-aided drawing) work, you should probably draft in another piece of software and import your work into SketchUp whenever you need 3D models. If you're just drawing your house or the place where you work, look no further—SketchUp should meet your needs.

Follow these simple steps to switch to a 2D view:

1. **Create a new SketchUp file.**
2. **Choose Camera⇨Standard⇨Top.** This changes your viewpoint so that you're looking directly down at the ground.
3. **Choose Camera⇨Parallel Projection.** Switching from Perspective to Parallel Projection makes it easier to draw plans in 2D. At this point, your modeling window should look like the one shown in Figure 4-2.

As always, feel free to delete Bryce (the human figure that appears on your screen when you create a new SketchUp file) at this point. When working in 2D, Bryce appears as a small diagonal line that's visible in your modeling window when you're in Top view. To get rid of Bryce, just right-click him and choose Erase from the context menu.

SketchUp's Drafting Tools

Here's some good news: You don't need many tools to draft a 2D plan in SketchUp. Figure 4-3 shows the basic toolbar; everything you need is located right there.

Let's take a closer look at the options on this toolbar:

▲ **Line tool:** You use the Line tool (which looks like a pencil) to draw edges, which are one of the two basic building blocks of SketchUp models. Fundamentally, you click to start drawing an edge and click again to finish it. (You can find more information about drawing lines in Chapter 2.)

Figure 4-2

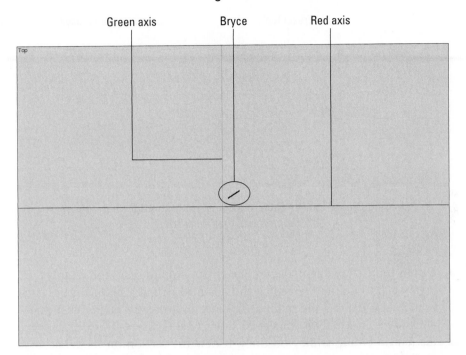

This is what your modeling window should look like before you start drawing in 2D.

▲ **Eraser tool:** You use the Eraser to erase edges (see Figure 4-4). Keep in mind that you can't use the Eraser to delete faces, though erasing one of the edges that defines a face automatically erases that face, too. Take a look at the section about edges and faces at the beginning of Chapter 2 for more detail on this. You can use the Eraser tool in two different ways:

- **Clicking:** Click on edges to erase them one at a time.
- **Dragging:** Drag over edges to erase them; this is faster if you have lots of edges you want to erase.

Figure 4-3

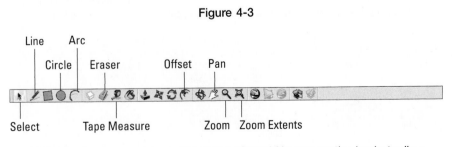

All the tools you need to draft in 2D in SketchUp are on the basic toolbar.

Figure 4-4

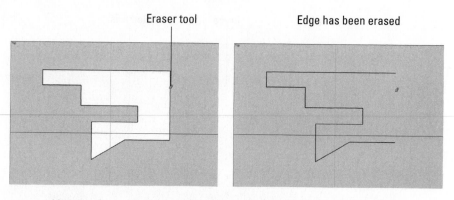

Use the Eraser tool to erase edges. Erasing an edge that defines
a face erases that face, too.

▲ **Circle tool:** Drawing circles in SketchUp is quite easy. You simply click once to define the center and again to define a point on the circle (which also defines the radius). To enter in a precise radius, just draw a circle, type in a radius, and press Enter (see Figure 4-5). For more information on typing while you draw, review the section on model accuracy in Chapter 2.

▲ **Arc tool:** To draw an arc, click once to define one end of the arc, again to define the other end, and a third time to define the bulge (how much the arc sticks out). If you'd like, you can type in a radius after you draw your arc by entering the radius, the units, and the letter *r*. If you want an arc with a radius of 4 feet, for instance, you first would draw your arc however big, then type in **4'r**, and then press Enter. This is shown in Figure 4-6.

Figure 4-5

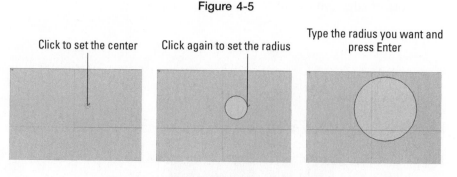

Drawing circles is easy with the Circle tool.

Figure 4-6

2. then click here...

1. Click here to start... | 3. then click here.

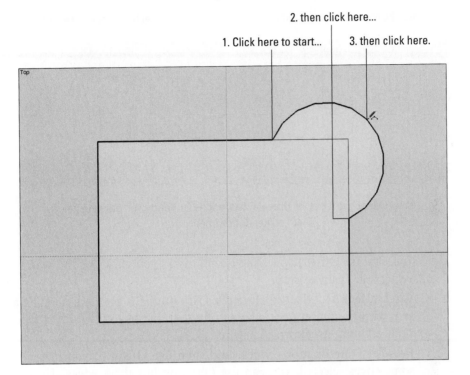

Using the Arc tool is a three-step operation.

▲ **Offset tool:** The Offset tool helps you draw edges that are a constant distance apart from edges that already exist in your model. Take a look at Figure 4-7. Using Offset on the shape in this figure lets us create another shape that's exactly 6 inches bigger all the way around (middle image) or exactly 6 inches smaller all the way around (right image). Offsetting edges is a useful way to create things like doorways and window trim.

Figure 4-7

Click to start drawing; then move your cursor

6 inch *outside* offset

6 inch *inside* offset

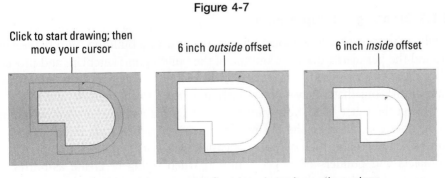

The Offset tool lets you create edges based on other edges.

Figure 4-8

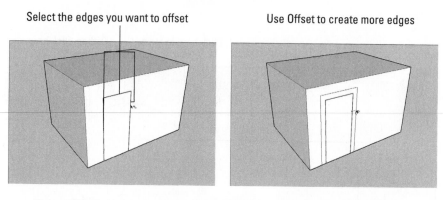

Using Offset on a set of preselected edges is handy for drawing things like doorframes.

You can use Offset in two ways; with both, you click once to start offsetting and again to stop:

- **Click a face to offset all its edges.** If nothing is selected, clicking a face with the Offset tool lets you offset all that face's edges by a constant amount, as shown in Figure 4-7.
- **Preselect one or more edges, and then use Offset.** If you have some edges selected, you can use Offset on just those edges. This comes in handy for drawing things like doorframes and balconies, as shown in Figure 4-8.

▲ **Tape Measure tool:** The Tape Measure is one of those tools that does many different things. To use it for measuring distances, click any two points in your model to measure the distance between them. The distance "readout" is in the VCB in the lower-right corner of your modeling window. You can also use this tool for resizing a model and for creating guides, as explained in Chapter 2.

4.1.2 Creating a Simple Plan

If all you're trying to do is model an exterior view of a building, simply measure around the perimeter, draw the outline of the building in SketchUp, and proceed from there (see Figure 4-9). Your walls will be only a single face thick (meaning paper-thin), but that's okay—you're only interested in the outside, anyway.

If, on the other hand, you want to create an *interior* view, matters are somewhat more complicated. The business of measuring an existing building so that you can model it on the computer is easier said than done—even experienced architects and builders often get confused when trying to create **as-builts**, as drawings of existing buildings are called. Closets, ventilation spaces, interior

Figure 4-9

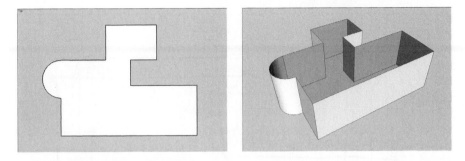

To make an exterior model, just measure the outside of your building
to draw an outline in SketchUp.

walls, and all kinds of other obstructions inevitably get in the way of obtaining good measurements. Thus, most of the time, you just have to give it your best shot and then tweak things a bit to make them right.

Drawing an Interior Outline

Because the main goal of creating an interior model of a building is to end up with accurate interior spaces, you will need to work from the inside out. If your tape measure is long enough, try to figure out a way to get the major dimensions first—this means the total interior width and length of the inside of your building. You might not be able to, but do your best. After that, it's really just a matter of working your way around, using basic arithmetic and logic to figure things out.

Often, it is extremely helpful to make a paper drawing before you start creating an interior outline with SketchUp. Figure 4-10 shows an example of a paper sketch that was used to model an existing house.

From this paper drawing, here's how you would draw a basic interior outline of the house:

1. **First, switch into 2D, overhead view.** The section "Switching to 2D View," found earlier in this chapter, explains how to do this.

2. **Using the Line tool, draw an edge 17 feet long (see the top two images in Figure 4-11), representing the western wall of the house.** To draw this, click once to start the edge, move your cursor up until you see the green linear inference (indicating that you're drawing parallel to the green axis), and click again to end your line. To make the edge 17 feet long, type in **17'** and then press Enter—the line will automatically resize itself to be exactly 17 feet in length. If you'd like, you can use the Tape Measure to double-check what you've done.

3. **Draw an edge 11 feet 10 inches long, starting at the end of the first edge, heading to the right in the red direction.** (See the bottom two

Figure 4-10

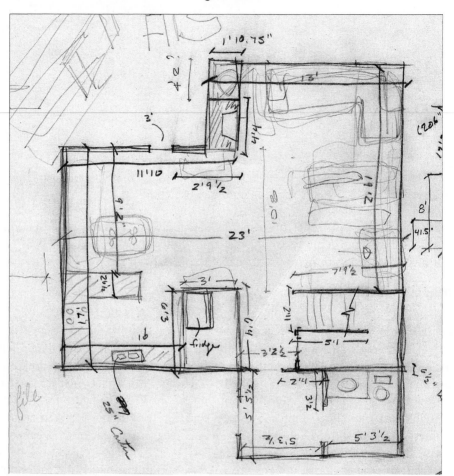

This paper sketch was used to model a house in SketchUp.

images in Figure 4-11.) To do this, do exactly what you did to draw the first edge, except move parallel to the red axis this time, type in **11'10**, and then press Enter.

4. **Keep going all the way around the house, until you get back to where you started (see Figure 4-12).** If you make a mistake, either use the Eraser to get rid of edges you're unhappy with or choose Edit⇨Undo to go back a step or two.

5. **If all your measurements don't add up, adjust things so that they do, and complete the outline.** When you complete your outline (forming a closed loop of edges that are all on the same plane), a face automatically appears. In this example, we have a total of 11 edges and 1 face.

Figure 4-11

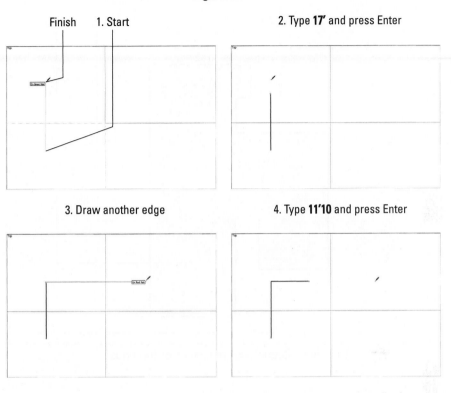

Finish   1. Start   2. Type **17′** and press Enter

3. Draw another edge   4. Type **11′10** and press Enter

Start by drawing an edge 17 feet long, and then draw a perpendicular
edge 11 feet 10 inches long.

When you're drafting in 2D, whatever you do, *do not* use the Orbit tool. Because you're working in 2D, you only need to use Zoom and Pan to navigate around your drawing (see Chapter 2 for more information on this). If you accidentally end up orbiting your model into a 3D view, follow the steps in the section "Switching to 2D View," found earlier in this chapter, to get things back in order. Finally, remember, if you ever get lost and no amount of zooming and panning gets you back to a view of your floor plan, choose Camera⇨Zoom Extents. Think of this as an emergency lever you can pull to fill your modeling window with your geometry.

Offsetting an Exterior Wall

Now that you've gotten this far, you can offset an exterior wall thickness, just to make it easier to visualize your spaces. Here's how to do this:

1. **Using the Offset tool, offset your closed shape by 8 inches to the outside (see Figure 4-13, left panel).** An offset of 8 inches is a pretty

Figure 4-12

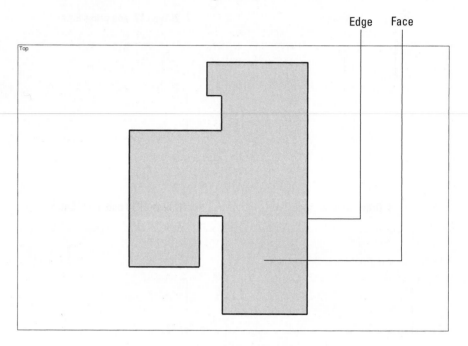

The completed interior perimeter of the house.

standard thickness for an exterior wall, especially for houses. This is how you can use the Offset tool to create 8-inch thick walls:

- Make sure that nothing in your drawing is selected by choosing Edit⇨Select None.
- Click once inside your shape.

Figure 4-13

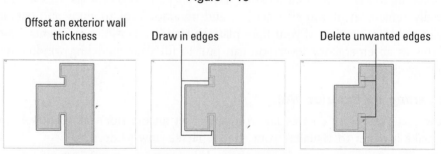

Use Offset to create an exterior wall thickness, and then clean up the image using the Line and Eraser tools.

- Click again outside the shape to make a second, bigger shape.
- Type in **8**, and then press Enter.

2. **Because you know there are no alcoves on the outside of the house (as shown in the sketch), use the Line tool to draw across them.** See the middle panel of Figure 4-13 for an illustration of how this is done.

3. **Use the Eraser tool to get rid of the extra edges (see Figure 4-13, right).** By deleting the extra edges, you go back to having only two faces: one representing the floor, and one representing the exterior wall thickness. It doesn't matter that the wall is thicker in several places than in others; you can always go back and remedy this later on.

Putting in Interior Walls

For this part of the process, it is extremely helpful to use guides. If you haven't done so already, read the last part Chapter 2, where you'll find a full description of guides and how to use them.

When drafting a floor plan in SketchUp, it often helps to ignore things like doors and windows. For now, wherever a doorway should be in a wall, just draw a solid wall instead. You can add in doors and windows after you've extruded your floor plan into a three-dimensional figure.

Here's how you can put in a few interior walls on the first floor of your house:

1. **With the Tape Measure tool, drag a parallel guide 5 feet, 3½ inches from the inside of the entryway (see Figure 4-14, left panel).** To do this, just click the edge from which you want to draw the guide, move your cursor to the right (to tell SketchUp which way to go), type in **5'3.5**, and press Enter.

2. **Draw a few more guides in the same way you drew the first one.** Working from the pencil drawing, figure out the location of each interior wall, and create guides to measure off the space (see Figure 4-14).

Figure 4-14

Create a parallel guide   Create more guides   Draw edges using your guides

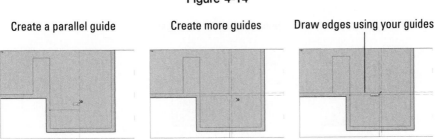

Draw a guide to help locate your first interior wall, create additional guides, and then draw edges using these guides.

Figure 4-15

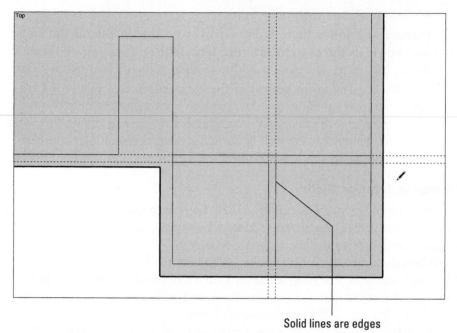

Solid lines are edges

Use the Line tool to create edges where your guides come together.

3. **Switching to the Line tool, draw in edges to represent the interior walls.** By using the guides, it's easy to draw your edges correctly. Figure 4-15 shows a close-up view (thanks to the Zoom tool) of what you should have so far.

4. **Use the Eraser to delete your guides.**

5. **Use the Eraser to get rid of all extra edge segments (see Figure 4-16).** By doing this, you go back to having only two faces in your

Figure 4-16

Erase your guides   Erase tiny unwanted edges

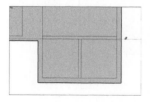
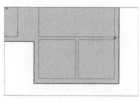
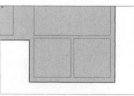

Using the Eraser, delete your guides and all the small edge segments left over from drawing the interior walls.

model (one for the floor and one for the walls). When it's time to extrude your plan into walls, removing these segments will make things much easier.

4.1.3 Going from 2D to 3D

Once you have a 2D plan in hand, the next step is to extrude it into a 3D model. This is basically a one-step process, and it involves one important tool: Push/Pull. In the following sections, you'll take the simple floor plan you drew earlier in the chapter and turn it into three-dimensional walls.

Changing Your Point of View

Before you pop up your plan into the third dimension, you need to change your point of view to get a better view of what you're doing. (See Figure 4-17.)

Figure 4-17

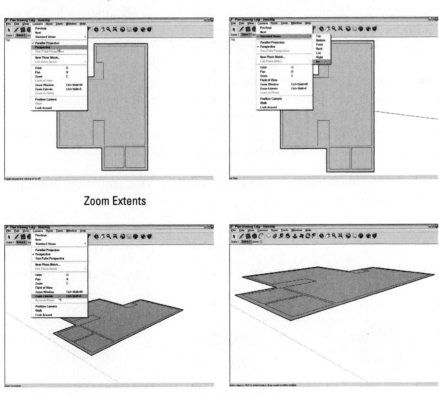

Switch to Perspective view   Switch to Iso view

Zoom Extents

Before starting to work in 3D, switch over to a 3D view.

To change your point of view, try following these steps:

1. **Choose Camera⇨Perspective.** This "turns on" SketchUp's perspective engine, meaning that you now can see things more realistically—the way people really see things in 3D.

2. **Choose Camera⇨Standard⇨Iso.** This switches you from a top view to an isometric (three-quarter) view. You could also do this with the Orbit tool. (Remember, there is always more than one way to do everything in SketchUp.)

3. **Choose Camera⇨Zoom Extents.** Zoom Extents also has its own button on the basic toolbar.

4. **Change the field of view from 35 to 45 degrees by choosing Camera⇨ Field of View, typing in 45, and pressing Enter.** By default, SketchUp's field of view is set to 35 degrees. (For more information on what this means, check out Chapter 10.)

Pushing and Pulling

The Push/Pull tool is a simple device; you use it to extrude flat faces into 3D shapes. It works (like everything else in SketchUp) by clicking—you click a face once to start pushing/pulling it, move your cursor until you like what you see, and then click again to stop push/pulling. That's it. (For more detail on Push/ Pull, see the nearby sidebar, "More Fun with Push/Pull.")

Note that Push/Pull only works on flat faces; if you need to do something to a curved face, you'll have to use another tool (such as the Intersect with Model feature, which is discussed later in this chapter).

To use Push/Pull to extrude your house's first-floor plan into a 3D model (as shown in Figure 4-18), this is what you should do:

1. **Select the Push/Pull tool from the toolbar.** This tool looks like a little box with a red arrow coming out of the top.

Figure 4-18

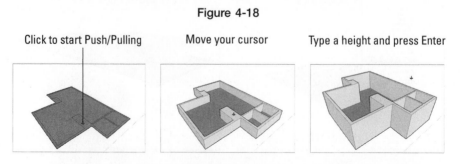

Click to start Push/Pulling   Move your cursor   Type a height and press Enter

Use Push/Pull to extrude one of your faces into all the walls in your house.

2. **Click the "wall's" face once to start extruding it.** If you click the "floor" face, you would end up extruding that instead. If you choose the wrong face by accident, press Esc to cancel the operation, and try again.

3. **Move your cursor up to pull up the walls, and click to stop extruding.** It doesn't matter how much you extrude your face, because you're going to add precision in the next step.

4. **Type in** 8' **and press Enter.** When you do this, your push/pull distance is revised to exactly 8 feet.

If you had forgotten to erase any small edge segments before you used Push/Pull, all of your walls might not have been "pulled up" at once. In this case, you could have used Push/Pull again on any faces that needed it.

MORE FUN WITH PUSH/PULL

Because Push/Pull is the tool that most people think of when they think of SketchUp, it might be helpful to know more about what it can do. The people who invented SketchUp actually *started* with the idea for Push/Pull—that's how closely SketchUp and Push/Pull are linked! Here are four things about Push/Pull that aren't immediately obvious when you first start using it:

▲ **Double-click with the Push/Pull tool to extrude a face by the last distance you pushed/pulled.** When you double-click a face, it automatically gets pushed/pulled by the same amount as the last face you used Push/Pull on.

▲ **Press Ctrl (Option on a Mac) to push/pull a *copy* of your face.** The first graphic in the following figure shows what this means. Here, instead of using Push/Pull the regular way, you can use a modifier key to extrude a copy of the face you're pushing/pulling. This comes in handy for quickly modeling things like multi-story buildings.

▲ **While pushing/pulling, hover over other parts of your geometry to tell SketchUp how far to extrude.** Take a look at the second graphic. Perhaps you want to use Push/Pull to extrude a cylinder that is exactly the same height as a box. Before you click the second time to stop pushing/pulling, hover over a point on the top of the box; now the cylinder is exactly that tall. To complete the operation, click while you're still hovering over the box. It's pretty simple, and it'll save you hours of time after you're used to doing it.

▲ **Pushing/pulling a face into another, coplanar face automatically cuts a hole.** In fact, this is how you make openings (like doors and windows) in double-face walls. The last graphic shows this in action.

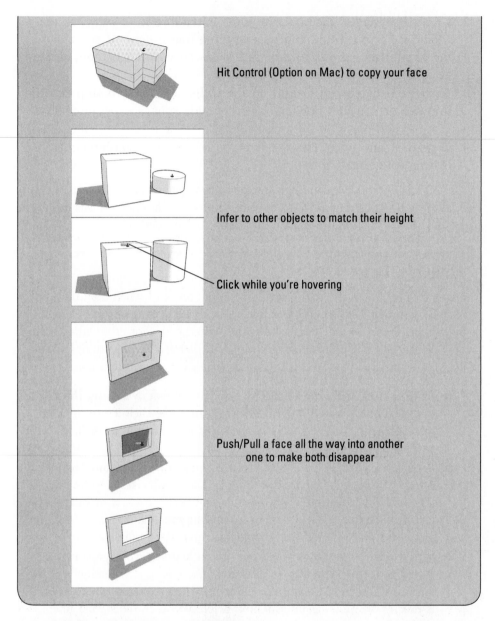

Hit Control (Option on Mac) to copy your face

Infer to other objects to match their height

Click while you're hovering

Push/Pull a face all the way into another one to make both disappear

4.1.4 Adding Doors and Windows

You can make openings in your walls in a couple of different ways. What you choose to do depends on what kind of building you're modeling, whether you're using single-face or double-face walls, and how much detail you plan to include in your model. You have two options:

▲ **Use SketchUp components that cut openings themselves.** SketchUp comes with numerous doors and windows that you can drag and drop into your model. One great thing about these is that they cut their own openings when you place them. Here's the catch, though: Sketch-Up's "Cut Opening" components only work on single-face walls, which means that they're really only useful for exterior building models. If you're building an interior model, you'll have to cut your own openings.

▲ **Cut openings yourself.** For double-face walls, this is your only option; luckily, it's easy to do. Basically, you draw an outline for the opening you want to create, and then you use Push/Pull to create the opening—it works the same way for both doors and windows.

Using SketchUp's Components

As mentioned earlier, as long as you're making an exterior model, you can use the doors and windows that come with SketchUp. These are components of the program, and you can read more about them in Chapter 5. Without going into too much detail at this point, however, here are a few basics related to components:

▲ **They're in the Components dialog box.** Choose Window⇨Components to open the dialog box, and then look in the Architecture library for the doors and windows.

▲ **You can find hundreds more online.** If you're connected to the Internet, choose File⇨3D Warehouse⇨Get Models. This brings up the 3D Warehouse, where you can freely download just about anything you're looking for. Chapter 11 goes into more detail about the 3D Warehouse, if you're interested.

▲ **They are editable.** There's much more detail about this in Chapter 5, but for now, here's the gist: If you don't like something about one of SketchUp's built-in doors or windows, you can change it.

▲ **They cut their own openings, but the openings aren't permanent.** When you move or delete a door or window component you've placed, its opening is deleted with it.

Adding a hole-cutting component to your model is easy, as you can see from Figure 4-19.

Follow these steps to do it yourself:

1. In the Components dialog box, click the component that you want to place in your model.
2. Place the component where you want it to be.
3. If you don't like where it is, use the Move tool (explained in Chapter 2) to reposition your component.

Figure 4-19

Click a component   Place it in your model

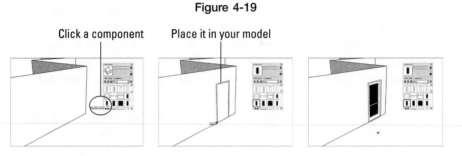

Placing window and door components in a model is simple.

Figure 4-20 shows a simple building to which a door and a couple of window components have been added. Notice how guides have been used to line things up—doing this is the best way to make sure everything's in the right spot.

Making Your Own Openings

Most of the time, you won't be able to get away with using SketchUp's built-in door and window components—the fact that they can't cut through two-faced walls means that they're limited to external use only. That's okay though, because

Figure 4-20

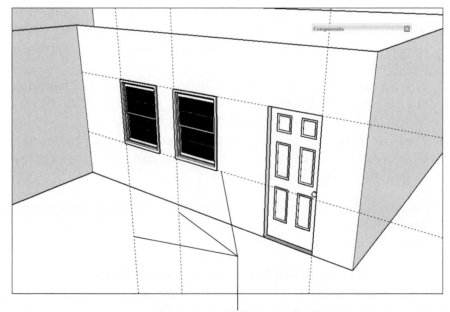

Guides

Use guides to help line up the components you add to your model.

Figure 4-21

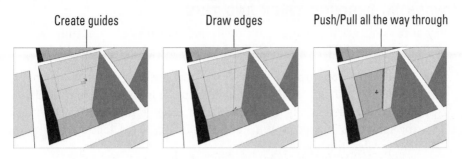

Create guides   Draw edges   Push/Pull all the way through

Use guides to plan where you want an opening, and then push/pull all
the way through both faces.

cutting your own holes in walls is quick and easy, and you'll always end up with
exactly what you want.

Figure 4-21 illustrates the basic steps in cutting a precise opening in a double-
face wall.

Here's a more detailed discussion of how to carry out these steps:

1. **Mark where you want your opening to be with guides.** For a refresher
   on using guides, refer to Chapter 2.

2. **Draw the outline of the opening you want to create, making sure
   to create a new face in the process.** You can use any of the drawing tools to do this, though it's usually best to stick with the Line tool
   when you're starting out. You'll know you've made a new face if the
   edges in your outline look thin. If they don't, check out the nearby
   sidebar, "Working Through Thick and Thin," for more information.

3. **Use Push/Pull to extrude your new face back into the thickness of
   the wall until it touches the face behind it.** If everything goes well,
   your face should disappear, taking with it the corresponding area of
   the face behind it. Now you have an opening in your wall. If your face
   doesn't disappear and no opening is created, it's probably for one of the
   following reasons:

   • **Your faces aren't parallel to each other.** This technique only works
     if both faces are parallel. Keep in mind that just because two faces
     look parallel doesn't mean that they are.

   • **You hit an edge.** If you push/pull your face into a face with an
     edge crossing it, SketchUp gets confused and doesn't cut an open-
     ing. Use Undo, get rid of the pesky edge (if you can), and try again.

Throughout this process, don't forget to orbit! If you can't quite push/pull what
you mean to push/pull, orbit around until you can see what you're doing.

WORKING THROUGH THICK AND THIN

Pay attention to which edges look thick and which ones look thin. When you're drawing in 2D, you can tell a lot from an edge's appearance:

▲ **Thin edges cut** *through* **faces.** Edges that are thin are ones that have "sunk in"; you can think of them like cuts from a razor-sharp knife. When you successfully split a face with an edge that you draw with the Line tool, it appears thin. The first image in the following figure shows what this looks like.

▲ **Thick edges sit** *on top* **of faces.** If the edge you just drew looks thicker than some of the other edges in your model, it isn't actually cutting through the face it's on—it's only sitting on top. An edge can sit on top of a face for a couple of reasons:

- *It has one end free.* So-called "free" edges are ones that aren't connected to other edges at both ends (as in the second image).

- *It crosses another edge.* Because edges don't automatically cut other edges where they cross, you have to manually split them. To make a thick edge thin (in other words, to make it "sink in"), use the Line tool to trace over each segment, as shown in the third image.

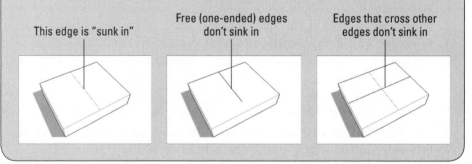

This edge is "sunk in"   Free (one-ended) edges don't sink in   Edges that cross other edges don't sink in

SELF-CHECK

1. A(n) _____ model of a building is basically an empty shell.

2. For models where you want to show wall thickness, what must you do?

3. _____ is the most important tool used to extrude a two-dimensional plan into a three-dimensional model.

4. Door and window components can cut through two-faced walls and are therefore ideal for interior models. True or false?

4.2 Creating Stairs

There are probably a million different ways to make stairs in SketchUp, but everyone has their own preferred method. In the following sections, you'll find three different methods that work equally well. Take a look at all of them, and then decide which works best for your situation.

Before we explore these methods, here's some simple stairway vocabulary, just in case you need it. Each of these elements is also shown in Figure 4-22.

▲ **Rise and run:** The **rise** is the total distance your staircase needs to climb. If the vertical distance from your first floor to your second flood (i.e., your floor-to-floor distance) is ten feet, that's your rise. The **run** is the total horizontal distance your staircase takes up. Thus, a set of stairs with a big rise and a small run would be very steep.

▲ **Tread:** A **tread** is an individual step—in other words, it's the part of the staircase you step on. When people refer to the size of a tread,

Figure 4-22

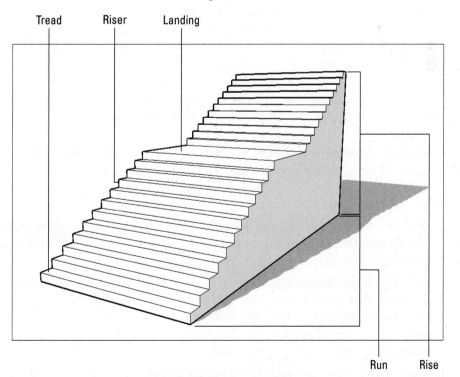

The anatomy of a staircase.

they're talking about the tread's depth, or the distance from the front to the back of the tread. Typically, this is anywhere from 9 to 24 inches, but treads of 10 to 12 inches are most comfortable to walk on.

▲ **Riser:** The **riser** is the part of the step that connects each tread in the vertical direction. Risers are usually about 5 to 7 inches high, but that depends on the building. Not all staircases have actual risers (think of steps with gaps between treads), but they all have a riser height.

▲ **Landing:** A **landing** is a platform somewhere around the middle of a set of stairs. Landings are necessary in real life, but modeling them can be a pain; figuring out staircases with landings is definitely more complicated. It's sometime easier if you think of your landings as really big steps.

4.2.1 The Subdivided Rectangles Method

This is the method most people use to draw their first set of stairs. It's intuitive and simple, but it's also a bit more time-consuming than the other methods described in this chapter.

The key to the subdivided rectangles method is to use a special trick you can do with edges: Called *Divide,* it lets you pick any edge and divide it into as many segments as you want. If you know how many steps you need to draw, but not how deep each individual tread needs to be, this comes in handy.

Figure 4-23 illustrates the subdivided rectangles method at work.

Here's a detailed look at how to use this method of creating stairs:

1. **Start by drawing a rectangle the size of the staircase you want to build.** It almost always works best to model steps as a group, separate from the rest of your building, and then move them into position when they're done. (You can read all about groups in Chapter 5.)

2. **With the Select tool, right-click one of the long edges of your rectangle and choose Divide from the context menu.** If your staircase is wider than it is long, right-click one of the short edges instead.

3. **Before you do anything else, type in the number of treads you want to create and press Enter.** This command automatically divides your edge into many more edges, eliminating the need to calculate how deep each of your treads needs to be. Essentially, each of your new edges will become the side of one of your treads.

4. **Draw a line from the endpoint of each of your new edges, dividing your original rectangle into many smaller rectangles.** You can use the

Figure 4-23

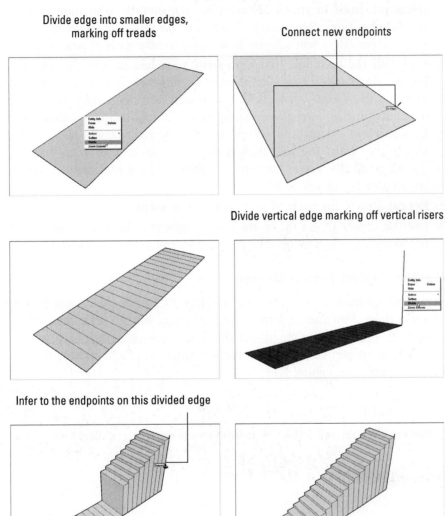

Divide edge into smaller edges, marking off treads

Connect new endpoints

Divide vertical edge marking off vertical risers

Infer to the endpoints on this divided edge

The subdivided rectangles method of building stairs.

Line or the Rectangle tool to do this; pick whichever one you're most comfortable with.

5. **From one of the corners of your original rectangle, draw a vertical edge.** This edge should be the height of your staircase's total rise.

6. **Use the Divide command to split your new edge into however many risers you need in your staircase (this is generally your number of treads, plus one).** Repeat steps 2 and 3 to do this. The endpoints of your new, smaller edges will tell you how high to make each of your steps.

7. **Push/Pull the rectangle that represents your last step to the correct height.** Here's where you need to use the "hover-click" technique described earlier in this chapter. Just click once to start pushing/pulling, hover over the endpoint that corresponds to the height of that tread, and click again. Your step will automatically be extruded to the right height. It's a good idea to start extruding your highest step first, but keep in mind that it doesn't go all the way to the top; you always have a riser between your last step and your upper floor.

8. **Repeat step 7 for each of your remaining steps.**

9. **Use the Eraser to get rid of any extra edges you don't need.** Be careful not to accidentally erase geometry on the part of your staircase you can't see.

4.2.2 The Copied Profile Method

This method for modeling a staircase relies, like the last one, on using Push/Pull to create a three-dimensional form from a 2D face, but it's a lot more elegant. In a nutshell, you draw the *profile*—or the side view—of a single step, and then you copy as many steps as you need, create a single face, and extrude the whole thing into shape (see Figure 4-24).

Figure 4-24

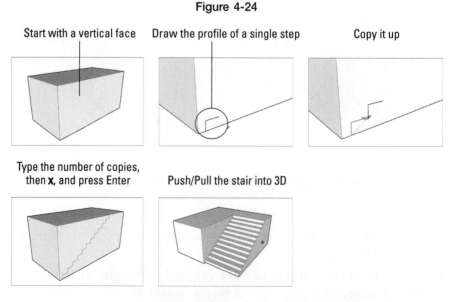

The copied profile method of drawing a staircase.

Here's a more detailed explanation of how to use the copied profile method:

1. **Start with a large, vertical face, making sure that it's big enough for the flight of stairs you want to build.** You're going to end up pushing/pulling the whole staircase out of the side of this face.

2. **In the bottom corner of the face, draw the profile (side outline) of a single step.** You can use the Line tool to do this, although you might want to use an arc or two, depending on the level of detail you need. (For a refresher on drawing lines accurately, refer to Chapter 2.)

3. **Select all the edges that make up your step profile.** Remember that you can hold down Shift while clicking with the Select tool to add multiple objects to your selection.

4. **Make a copy of your step profile and place it above your first profile.** If you're unfamiliar with how to make copies using the Move tool, refer to the section on moving and copying found near the end of Chapter 2.

5. **Type in the number of steps you'd like to make, type the letter *x*, and then press Enter.** For example, if you wanted ten steps, you would type in *10x*. This technique repeats the copy operation you just did by however many times you tell it to; adding an *x* at the end of the number tells SketchUp you want to make copies.

6. **Draw an edge to make sure that all your step profiles are part of a single face.** You don't have to do this step if your stair profiles already fit perfectly on your vertical face. If you measured carefully, they just might.

7. **Push/Pull the staircase face out to be the width you need it to be.** This is the part that seems like magic to most people!

This method of stairway building also works great in combination with the Follow Me tool, which is described in Chapter 6. For now, Figure 4-25 provides a brief preview of using Follow Me when creating stairs.

4.2.3 The "Treads Are Components" Method

Nothing beats this technique for modeling stairs, but it isn't really beginner-level stuff. It's only included here because it's something you should eventually know how to do, so don't worry if it seems a little over your head as you get started with SketchUp. Simply remember that this method is here if you need it.

The "treads are components" method involves, as you may have guessed, making each tread in your staircase into an instance of the same component. Basically, you build one simple tread that's the right depth, make it into a com-

Figure 4-25

Profile   Extrusion path for Follow Me

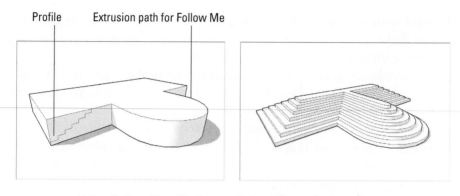

Using Follow Me with the copied profile method produces
some impressive geometry.

ponent, and copy multiple instances into a full flight of stairs. Because every step is "linked," anything you do to one automatically happens to all of them. If you don't know the first thing about components, now would be a terrific time to start from the beginning of Chapter 5—it'll fill you in.

Go through the following steps to build a staircase using the "treads are components" method:

1. **Model a single step, including the tread and the riser.** You can make this very simple at this stage, if you'd like; all that matters is that the tread depth and the riser height are correct. You can adjust everything else later. Figure 4-26 shows a simple example of this.

2. **Make a component out of the step you just built.** Chapter 5 goes into great detail about making and using components, but here's the short version (see Figure 4-27):
   • Select all the edges and faces that make up your step.
   • Choose Edit⇨Make Component.

Figure 4-26

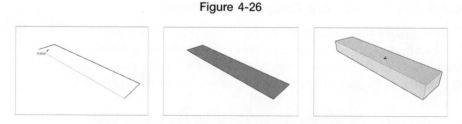

Model a single step, making sure that the tread depth and
riser height are accurate.

Figure 4-27

Create a component

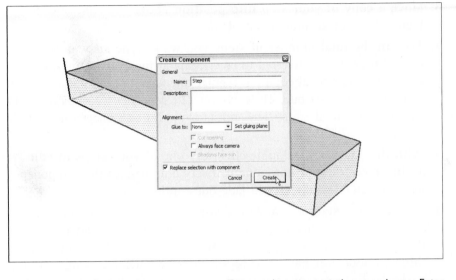

Move a copy up

Type number you want, then **x**, and press Enter

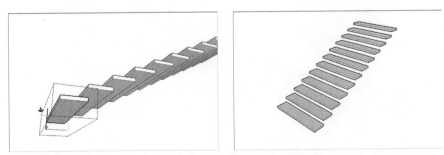

Edit one instance...

...and they all change

Make your step into a component instance, move a copy into position above
the original, and then create an array.

- In the dialog box that opens, name your component "Step," and then click the Create button. Your step is now a component instance.

3. **Move a copy of your step into position above the first one.** See Figure 4-27 for an illustration of this.

4. **Type in the total number of steps you want, type an *x*, and then press Enter.** This is referred to as creating a **linear array,** meaning that you're making several copies at regular intervals, in the same direction you moved the first one. Thus, typing **12x** generates 12 steps the same distance apart as the first step and its copy. The last image on the right in Figure 4-27 illustrates this.

5. **With the Select tool, double-click any one of your steps to edit all instances of your component.** Everything besides the component instance you're editing should fade out a little.

6. **Change your staircase however you'd like.** This is the fun part. Having your staircase made up of multiple component instances means that you have all the flexibility to make drastic changes to the whole thing without ever having to repeat yourself. Add a **nosing** (a bump at the leading edge of each tread), a **stringer** (a diagonal piece of structure that supports all your steps), or even a handrail by getting creative with how you modify a single component instance. Figure 4-28 shows some of what you can do. The color insert in this book also shows the "treads are components" method applied to building a circular stair.

Figure 4-28

Series of component instances

A single component instance

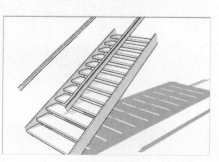
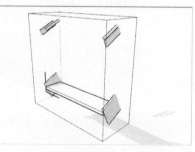

On the left, a flight of stairs with side stringers and a handrail. On the right, a single component instance from this staircase.

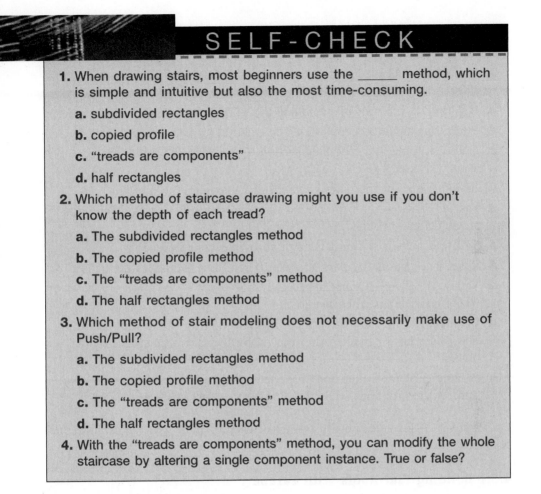

1. When drawing stairs, most beginners use the _____ method, which is simple and intuitive but also the most time-consuming.

   a. subdivided rectangles

   b. copied profile

   c. "treads are components"

   d. half rectangles

2. Which method of staircase drawing might you use if you don't know the depth of each tread?

   a. The subdivided rectangles method

   b. The copied profile method

   c. The "treads are components" method

   d. The half rectangles method

3. Which method of stair modeling does not necessarily make use of Push/Pull?

   a. The subdivided rectangles method

   b. The copied profile method

   c. The "treads are components" method

   d. The half rectangles method

4. With the "treads are components" method, you can modify the whole staircase by altering a single component instance. True or false?

4.3 Creating a Roof

If you're lucky, the roof you want to model is fairly simple. Unfortunately, home builders sometimes get creative, constructing roofs with dozens of different features that make modeling them difficult. For this reason, we're going to keep things fairly simple: The following sections are dedicated to showing you how to identify and model some of the basic roof forms. After that, you'll learn about a great tool you can use to assemble complicated roofs from less-complicated pieces.

Before learning how to create roofs, let's review some general terminology related to roof types and components:

▲ **Flat roof:** Flat roofs are just that, except they aren't—if a roof were really completely flat, it would collect water and leak. That's why even roofs that look flat are sloped very slightly.

▲ **Pitched roof:** Any roof that isn't flat is technically a pitched roof.

▲ **Shed roof:** A shed roof is one that slopes from one side to the other.

▲ **Gabled roof:** Gabled roofs have two planes that slope away from a central ridge.

▲ **Hip roof:** A hip roof is one where the sides and ends all slope together.

▲ **Pitch:** The angle of a roof surface is referred to as its pitch.

▲ **Gable:** A gable is the pointed section of wall that sits under the peak of a pitched roof.

▲ **Eaves:** Eaves are the parts of a roof that overhang the building.

▲ **Fascia:** Fascia is the trim around the edge of a roof's eaves where gutters are sometimes attached.

▲ **Soffit:** A soffit is the underside of an overhanging eave.

▲ **Rake:** The rake is the part of a gabled roof that overhangs the gable.

▲ **Valley:** A valley is formed when two roof slopes come together; this is where water flows when it rains.

▲ **Dormer:** Dormers are the little things that pop up above roof surfaces. They often have windows, and they serve to make attic spaces more usable.

▲ **Parapet:** Flat roofs that don't have eaves have parapets. These are extensions of the building's walls that go up a few feet past the roof itself.

Figure 4-29 provides an illustration of each of these roof types and components.

4.3.1 Building Flat Roofs with Parapets

SketchUp is ideal for modeling flat roofs that feature parapets. In fact, by using a combination of the Offset tool and Push/Pull, you should be able to make a parapet in under a minute. Figure 4-30 provides a quick visual representation of this process.

Here are the steps involved in modeling this type of roof:

1. **With the Offset tool, click the top face of your building.**
2. **Click again somewhere inside the same face to create another face.**
3. **Type in the thickness of your parapet, and then press Enter.** This redraws your offset edges to be a precise distance from the edges of your original face. How thick should your parapet be? It all depends on your building, but most parapets are between 6 and 12 inches thick.
4. **Push/pull your outside face (the one around the perimeter of your roof) into a parapet.**
5. **Type in the height of your parapet, and then press Enter.**

Figure 4-29

Gabled roof   Dormer   Valley   Hip roof   Flat roof   Parapet   Shed roof

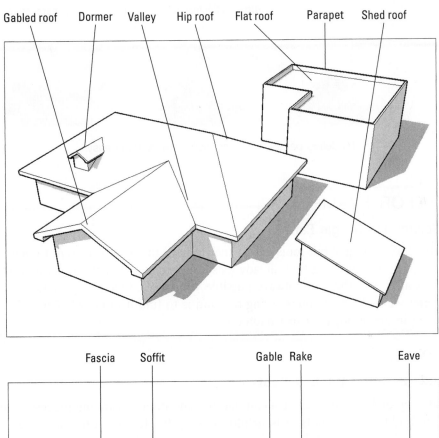

Fascia   Soffit   Gable Rake   Eave

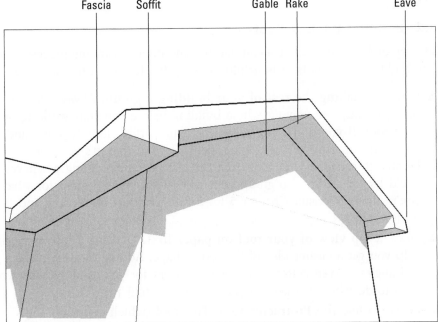

Some different kinds of roofs and their various parts.

Figure 4-30

Offset to the inside   Push/Pull your parapet up

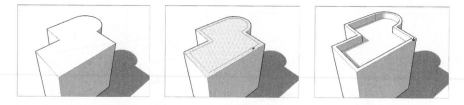

Modeling parapets on flat-roofed buildings is easy.

FOR EXAMPLE

Roofing via Google Earth

One tricky thing about roofs is that they're hard to see. If you want to make
a model of something that already exists, it helps to be able to get a good
look at it, and that's not always possible with roofs. One neat way to get a
better view of a roof you're trying to build is to find it in Google Earth. For
more information, refer to Chapter 11.

4.3.2 Building Pitched Roofs

Modeling pitched roofs can be a complicated and often frustrating process. Thus,
before building such roofs, it is helpful to keep the following tips in mind:

▲ **Start by making the rest of your building a group.** Always, *always*
make a group out of your whole building before you start working on
your roof. If you don't, your geometry will start sticking together and
you'll end up erasing walls by accident. Beyond that, it's very handy to
be able to separate your roof from the rest of your building whenever
you'd like. You can also group your roof, if that makes sense for what
you're doing. Consult Chapter 5 for a full rundown on making and
using groups.

▲ **Draw a top view of your roof on paper first.** Drawing a top view can
help you get a clearer idea of the roof's shape. Adding measurements
and angles is even better, as it makes it easier for you to know what you
need to do when you get around to using SketchUp.

▲ **Learn to use the Protractor tool.** This tool (which is on the Tools
menu) is for measuring angles and, more importantly, creating angled
guides. Because sloped roofs are all about angles, you will probably

need to use the Protractor sooner or later. The best way to find out how it works is to open the Instructor dialog box by choosing Window⇨ Instructor and then activating the Protractor tool.

Creating Eaves for Buildings with Pitched Roofs

One good way to create eaves (overhangs) on pitched roofs is to use the Offset tool, as shown in Figure 4-31.

Figure 4-31

Make a group   Retrace (or Copy and Paste) the roof line

Offset an overhang   Delete the inside face

Push/Pull a fascia thickness

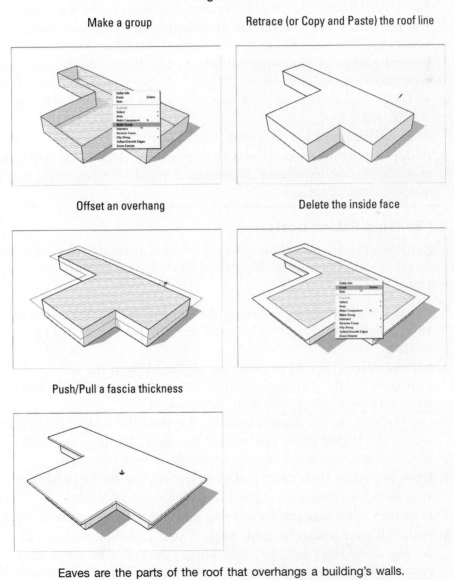

Eaves are the parts of the roof that overhangs a building's walls.

Follow these steps to get the general idea:

1. **Make a group out of your whole building before you start modeling the roof.** This makes it easier to keep your roof separate, which in turn makes your model easier to work with.

2. **Use the Line tool to create an outline of the parts of your roof that will have eaves of the same height.** The goal here is to end up with a single face to offset. A lot of buildings have complex roofs with eaves of all different heights. For the sake of this step, just create a face which, when offset, will create roof overhangs in the right places.

3. **Use the Offset tool to create an overhanging face.** For instructions on how to use Offset, see the section earlier in this chapter.

4. **Erase the edges of your original face.** A quick way to do this (with the Select tool) is as follows:
   • Double-click inside your first face. This selects both it and the edges that define it.
   • Press Delete to erase everything that's selected.

5. **Push/Pull your overhanging roof face to create a thick fascia.** Different roofs have fasciae of different thicknesses. If you don't know yours, just take your best guess.

4.3.3 Building Gabled Roofs

You can approach the construction of a gabled roof in many different ways, but the method described below and depicted in Figure 4-32 works well on a consistent basis.

1. **Create a roof overhang, following the steps in the previous section.** Most gabled roofs have eaves, so you'll probably need to do this for your building.

2. **Use the Protractor tool to create an angled guide at the corner of your roof.** See the previous section of this chapter for more information about drawing angled guides with the Protractor.

3. **Use the Line tool to draw a vertical edge from the midpoint of your roof to the angled guide you created in step 1.** The point at which your edge and your guide meet is the height of your roof ridge.

4. **Draw two edges from the top of your vertical line to the corners of your roof.** This should cause two triangular faces to be created.

5. **Erase the vertical edge you drew in step 3 and the guide you drew in step 1.**

6. **Push/Pull your triangular gable back.** If your gabled roof extends all the way to the other end of your building, push/pull it back that far. If your roof runs into another section of roof (as in Figure 4-33), extrude

Figure 4-32

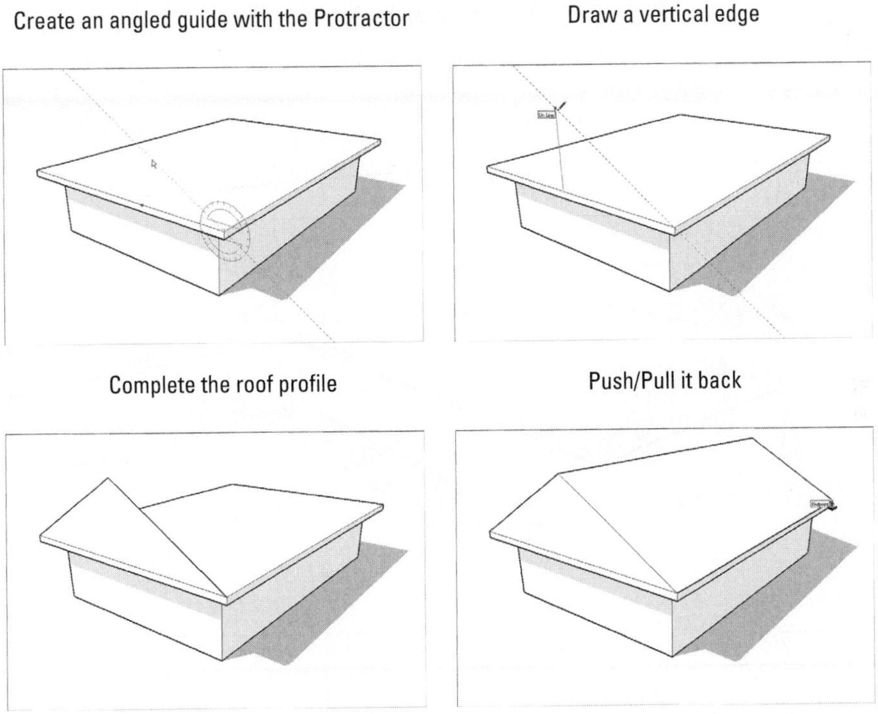

Create an angled guide with the Protractor

Draw a vertical edge

Complete the roof profile

Push/Pull it back

Gabled roofs are relatively easy to make in SketchUp.

it back until it's completely "buried." The section "Putting Your Roof Together," found later in this chapter, has more information on what to do when you're making a complex roof.

7. **Finish your eaves, fascia, soffit, and rake(s) however you want.** There are many different kinds of gabled roof details, so we can't cover them all here. However, Figure 4-34 shows a few common features of gabled roofs.

FOR EXAMPLE

Rise Over Run Ratios

Architects and builders often express angles as *rise over run ratios*. For example, a 4:12 (pronounced "four in twelve") roof slope rises 4 feet for every 12 feet it runs. Accordingly, a 1:12 slope is very shallow, while a 12:12 slope is very steep. When using the Protractor tool, SketchUp's VCB understands angles expressed as ratios, as well as those expressed in degrees. Thus, typing **6:12** yields a slope of 6 in 12.

Figure 4-33

Push/Pull it all the way into the other roof pitch

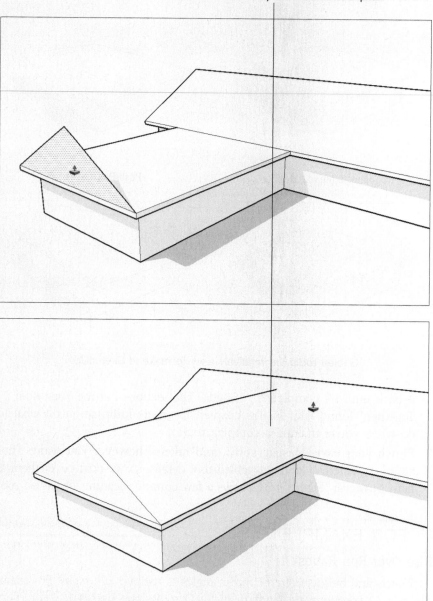

If your gabled roof is part of a larger roof structure, it might run into another roof pitch.

Figure 4-34

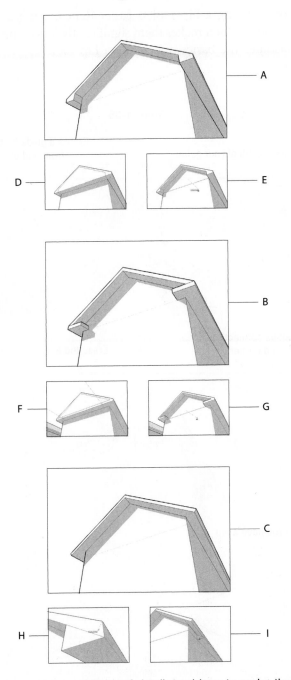

Some common gabled roof details and how to make them.

4.3.4 Building Hip Roofs

Believe it or not, building a hip roof is easier than making a gabled one! Hip roofs don't have rakes, which makes them significantly less complicated to model. Figure 4-35 illustrates the basics of creating a hip roof.

Figure 4-35

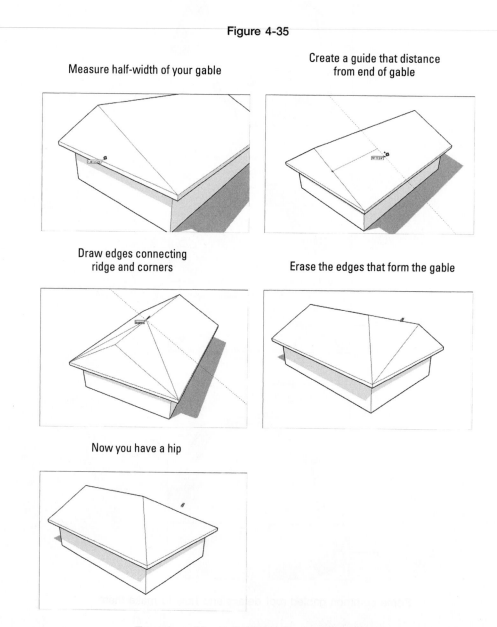

Measure half-width of your gable

Create a guide that distance from end of gable

Draw edges connecting ridge and corners

Erase the edges that form the gable

Now you have a hip

To make a hip roof, start with a gabled one.

Here are the steps associated with drawing a hip roof in more detail:

1. **Follow steps 1 through 5 in the section "Building Gabled Roofs" to begin making a hip roof.**

2. **Measure the distance from the midpoint of the gable to the corner of the roof.** Because hip roofs have pitches that are the same on all sides, you can use a simple trick to figure out where to locate the hip in your roof. It's a lot easier than using the Protractor.

3. **With the Tape Measure, create a guide (the distance you just measured) from the end of the gable.**

4. **Draw edges from the point on the ridge you just located to the corners of your roof.** This does two things: It splits the sides of your roof into two faces each and creates a new face (which you can't see yet) under the gabled end of your roof.

5. **Erase the three edges that form the gabled end of your roof, revealing the "hipped" pitch underneath.** Now all three faces of your roof are the same pitch—just the way they should be.

6. **If appropriate, repeat the process on the other end of your roof.**

COMPLEX HIP ROOFS AND THE FOLLOW ME TOOL

SketchUp also has a tool called Follow Me (described in detail in Chapter 6), which you can use to create complex hip roofs in about one-fifth the time it would normally take to make them. At its core, Follow Me works a bit like Push/Pull, except it lets you extrude faces along predetermined paths. You can use this tool to create very complicated geometry.

When it comes to hip roofs, the Follow Me technique only works if your roof meets the following conditions:

▲ The pitch needs to be the same on all roof surfaces.
▲ The roof needs to be "hipped" all the way around.

Follow these steps to use Follow Me to create a complex hip roof (as shown in the accompanying images):

1. Over the widest part of your building, draw a triangle that represents the slope of your roof. It should only be a half-gable, as shown in the images.

2. Select the top surface of your building.

3. With the Follow Me tool (available on the Tools menu), click the half-roof profile you drew in step 1 once.

4. Select your whole roof by triple-clicking it with the Select tool. (You may want to hide the rest of my building at this point, too.)

5. Right-click anywhere on the roof and choose Intersect⇨Intersect with Model from the context menu.

6. Use the Eraser to clean up your roof by erasing any geometry that isn't supposed to be part of it (you'll find plenty). You'll probably also have to draw in edges every now and then. If you make a mistake, just use Undo and try again.

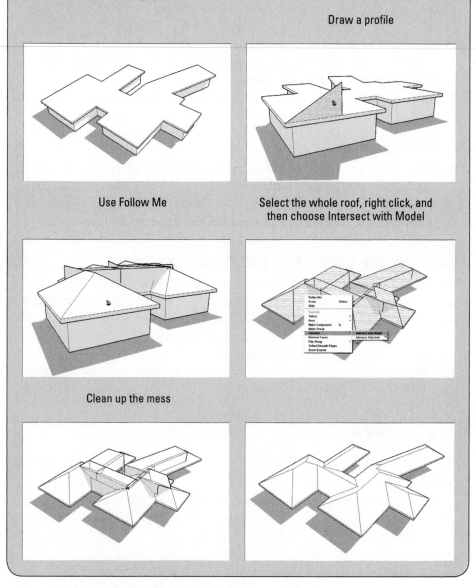

Draw a profile

Use Follow Me

Select the whole roof, right click, and then choose Intersect with Model

Clean up the mess

4.3.5 Putting Your Roof Together

In general, the newer and more expensive a house is, the more roof slopes it has. This can make modeling difficult! Thankfully, SketchUp includes a relatively little-known feature that often helps when it comes to making roofs with numerous pitches: Intersect with Model.

Getting to Know Intersect with Model

Here are the basic things you need to know about the Intersect with Model tool:

▲ **Intersect with Model makes new geometry from existing geometry.**
   That's how it works: It takes faces you've selected and creates edges
   wherever they intersect. You use Intersect with Model in cases where
   you need to create forms that are the *union* (both put together), *difference*
   (one minus the other), or *intersection* (the part they have in common)
   of other forms. Figure 4-36 illustrates this. Perhaps you want to make a
   model that's a cube with a cylinder-shaped chunk taken out of it. To do
   this, you would model the cube and the cylinder. After positioning them
   carefully, you could then use Intersect with Model to create edges where
   the two shapes' faces come together. After that, you can use the Eraser to
   get rid of the edges you don't want (the rest of the cylinder, in this case).

▲ **Intersect with Model and the Eraser tool go hand in hand.** Anytime you
   use Intersect with Model, you need to follow up by spending some time
   deleting the geometry you don't want. This isn't a bad thing, but it does
   mean that you need to be good at orbiting, zooming, and panning around
   your model. It also means that you need to be handy with the Eraser.

▲ **Most of the time, choose to Intersect with Model.** This tool has three different
   modes (just introduced in SketchUp 6), but most of the time, you'll end
   up using just the basic one. In any case, here's what all three of the tools do:

   • **Intersect with Model:** This creates edges everywhere your selected
     faces intersect with other faces in your model—whether the other
     faces are selected or not.

Figure 4-36

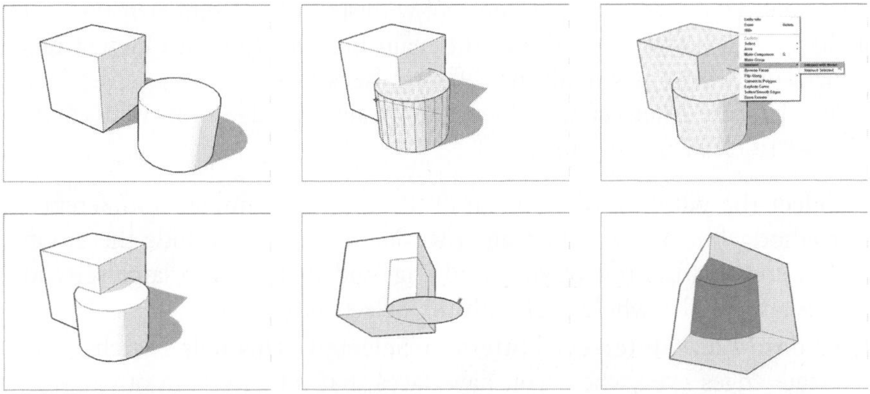

Using Intersect with Model to cut a partial cylinder out of a cube.

FOR EXAMPLE

SketchUp and Boolean Operations

Most 3D modeling programs let you carry out Boolean operations, meaning that you're encouraged to make models by adding, subtracting, and intersecting different shapes to make new ones. For *solids* modelers (like Solid-Works, Inventor, and FormZ), this makes sense, because this paradigm is a lot like sculpting with clay. But because SketchUp is more paper-like than clay-like, Boolean operations are not technically possible. Intersect with Model is about as close as SketchUp comes to letting you work this way.

- **Intersect Selected:** This option only creates edges where *selected* faces intersect with other *selected* faces. This is handy if you're trying to be a bit more precise.
- **Intersect with Context:** This one's a little trickier: Choosing this option creates edges where faces *within the same group or component* intersect. For this reason, it's only available when you're editing a group or component.

▲ **Intersect with Model doesn't have a button.** To use it, you have to do either of the following:
- Right-click and choose it from the context menu.
- Choose Edit⇨Intersect.

Using Intersect with Model to Make Roofs

When it comes to creating roofs, you can use Intersect with Model to combine numerous gables, hips, dormers, sheds, and so on into a single roof. It's not easy, and it requires a fair amount of planning, but it works great when nothing else will.

Figure 4-37 shows a complicated roof with several different elements. Gabled roofs have been pushed/pulled into the main hip roof form at different heights, but edges don't exist where all the different faces meet.

Now, let's use Intersect with Model to create the edges you want, and then the Eraser to clean up the mess:

1. **Select the whole roof.** You can do this using a number of different methods, but one way that often works best is to first hide the group that contains the rest of your building, and then draw a large selection box around the whole roof with the Select tool.
2. **Choose Edit⇨Intersect⇨Intersect Selected.** This tells SketchUp to create edges everywhere you have faces that intersect—in other words, everywhere they "pass through" each other without an edge.

Figure 4-37

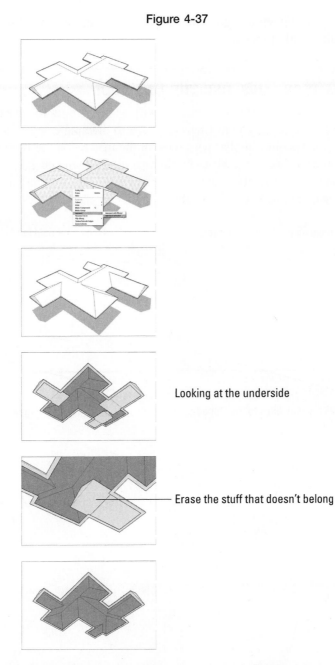

Looking at the underside

Erase the stuff that doesn't belong

Here's a typically complex roof that could be unified using Intersect with Model.

3. **Get out your Eraser and *carefully* delete all the extra geometry on the inside of your roof.** This can be a lot of work, but it's much easier than using the Line tool and SketchUp's inference engine to determine

where everything should go. The last image in Figure 4-37 shows the end result of this process.

WHEN ALL ELSE FAILS, USE THE LINE TOOL

Fancy tools like Follow Me and Intersect with Model are useful most of the time, but for some roofs, you just have to resort to drawing edges. If that's the case, you'd best become familiar with most of the material at the beginning of Chapter 2, because you're going to be doing a lot of inferencing.

For example, consider the following figure. In it, the Line tool and SketchUp's inference engine are used to add a gabled dormer to a sloped roof surface.

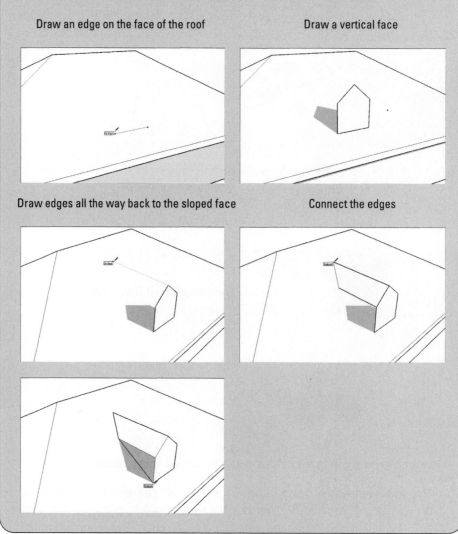

Draw an edge on the face of the roof

Draw a vertical face

Draw edges all the way back to the sloped face

Connect the edges

SELF-CHECK

1. SketchUp is ideal for making what kind of roof quickly?
2. The _____ tool is useful in creating eaves.
3. Building a hip roof is easier than making a gabled roof because a hip roof does not have:
   a. a pitch.
   b. eaves.
   c. rakes.
   d. parapets.
4. The Intersect with Model tool can be used to combine numerous gables, hips, dormers, and sheds into a single roof. True or false?

SUMMARY

Congratulations! You've modeled your first house with SketchUp. SketchUp was designed with architecture in mind. Because of this, you can model simple buildings such as doghouses to more intricate buildings such as airports and museums. In this chapter, however, we focused on modeling simple house forms. You drafted a simple floor plan and converted your two-dimensional plan to a three-dimensional model. You created doors and windows for your house, and added stairs. You also chose and created the type of roof you want your house to have.

KEY TERMS

As-built	A drawing of an existing building.
Dormer	A structure above a roof surface that serves to make attic space more usable.
Eave	A part of a roof that overhangs the building.
Exterior model	A model of the outside of a building, which does not include interior walls, rooms, or furniture.
Fascia	The trim around the edge of a roof's eaves where gutters are sometimes attached.
Flat roof	A roof that appears flat but is sloped very slightly.

Gable	The pointed section of wall that sits under the peak of a pitched roof.
Gabled roof	A roof with two planes that slope away from a central ridge.
Hip roof	A roof where the sides and ends all slope together.
Interior model	A model of the inside of a building, which must take into account interior wall thicknesses, floor heights, ceilings, and furnishings.
Landing	A platform somewhere around the middle of a set of stairs.
Linear array	Several copies at regular intervals and in the same direction.
Nosing	A bump at the leading edge of a tread on a stair.
Parapet	The extension of a building's walls that go up a few feet past the roof.
Pitch	The angle of a roof surface.
Pitched roof	A roof that isn't flat.
Rake	The part of a gabled roof that overhangs the gable.
Rise	The total vertical distance a staircase climbs.
Riser	The part of a step that connects each tread in the vertical direction.
Run	The total horizontal distance a staircase takes up.
Shed roof	A roof that slopes from one side to the other.
Soffit	The underside of an overhanging eave.
Stringer	A diagonal piece of structure that supports all the steps in a staircase.
Tread	An individual step, or the part of a staircase that you step on.
Valley	The place where the bottoms of two roof slopes come together.

ASSESS YOUR UNDERSTANDING

Go to www.wiley.com/college/chopra to evaluate your knowledge of modeling buildings.

Measure your learning by comparing pre-test and post-test results.

Summary Questions

1. It is easier to build two separate models, one showing the interior and one showing the exterior, than to create one model that shows both the interior and the exterior of a building at once. True or false?

2. When creating three-dimensional models, at what point should you add windows and doors?

    (a) After drawing an interior outline

    (b) After offsetting exterior walls

    (c) After putting in interior walls

    (d) After extruding the floor plan into a three-dimensional figure

3. To make an interior model, it is best to measure the exterior of the building and work from the outside in. True or false?

4. Which tool should you never use when drafting in 2D?

    (a) Line tool

    (b) Orbit tool

    (c) Offset tool

    (d) Arc tool

5. It is helpful to use guides when putting in interior walls. True or false?

6. A _____ is an individual step.

    (a) tread

    (b) rise

    (c) run

    (d) landing

7. It can be helpful to think of a landing as a really big:

    (a) riser.

    (b) step.

    (c) tread.

    (d) edge.

8. The copied profile method for modeling staircases, combined with the Follow Me tool, can produce some elaborate geometry. True or false?

9. The "treads are components" method for modeling staircases is the best technique for beginners. True or false?

10. A _____ is any kind of roof that is not flat.
    (a) pitched roof
    (b) shed roof
    (c) gabled roof
    (d) hip roof
11. You should wait to group your whole building until your roof is completed. True or false?
12. The process for building hip roofs starts out the same as that for building gabled ones. True or false?

Applying This Chapter

1. What tools would you use for the following tasks?
    (a) Drawing edges
    (b) Erasing edges
    (c) Drawing circles
    (d) Drawing arcs
    (e) Drawing edges that are a constant distance apart from edges that already exist
    (f) Measuring distances
2. Why can it be difficult to measure an existing building?
3. What are components and in what circumstances would you use them?
4. List three circumstances in which you would want to use the Push/Pull tool.
5. List and describe four different types of roofs.
6. How can you add doors and windows to a model?

First Steps

You want to create a model of your favorite museum. What are the first three steps you take in creating this model and why?

Creating Staircases

You are creating a set of steps for a model of your house. Which method (subdivided rectangles method, copied profile method, "treads are components" method) do you use and why? Write two to three paragraphs explaining the method you chose and why.

Creating Roofs

You are creating a house with a roof with four slopes. What would you use to help you accomplish this and why? Open SketchUp and create this roof.

5

KEEPING YOUR MODEL ORGANIZED
Using Groups, Components, the Outliner, and Layers

Starting Point

Go to www.wiley.com/college/chopra to assess your knowledge of keeping your model organized.
Determine where you need to concentrate your effort.

What You'll Learn in This Chapter

▲ The definitions of groups, components, Outliner, and layers
▲ Different ways groups can be used
▲ What makes groups different from components
▲ Items stored in the Outliner dialog box
▲ How layers in SketchUp differ from layers in other software programs

After Studying This Chapter, You'll Be Able To

▲ Compare and contrast groups, components, the Outliner, and layers
▲ Assess ways to group objects together
▲ Evaluate ways components can make it easier to keep a model organized
▲ Evaluate ways to use the Outliner to keep track of groups and components
▲ Assess how to add layers and how to move entities to different layers

INTRODUCTION

As everybody knows, living life can be a messy ordeal, and modeling in SketchUp is no exception. As you crank away at whatever it is you're building, you will reach a time when you stop, orbit around, and wonder how your model got to be such a mess. It's inevitable.

Luckily, SketchUp includes a number of different ways to keep your geometry (edges and faces) from getting out of control. Because big, unwieldy, disorganized models are a pain to work with—they can slow your computer, or even cause SketchUp to crash—you should definitely get in the habit of "working clean."

In this chapter, you will compare and contrast four main tools that SketchUp provides for organizing your model: groups, components, the Outliner, and layers. You will evaluate how to use groups and components to keep your model organized. You will explore the Outliner dialog box and all it has to offer. You will also assess how to add layers and how to move objects to different layers. Finally, the chapter ends with a detailed example of how all four methods can be used together to make your life easier.

5.1 Taking Stock of Your Organization Options

When it comes to sorting out the thousands of edges and faces in your model, it's all about lumping things together into useful sets. After you've separated things out, you can name them, hide them, and even lock them so that you (or somebody else) can't mess them up. This whole chapter is dedicated to the different tools SketchUp provides to help keep your model straight, but here's a brief rundown of each of these tools, just to put things in perspective:

▲ **Groups:** Making a **group** is like gluing together some of the geometry in your model. Edges and faces that are grouped together act like mini-models inside your main model. You use groups to make it easier to select, move, hide, and otherwise work with parts of your model that need to be kept separate.

▲ **Components:** SketchUp **components** are a lot like groups, but they have several extra handy properties. You use components when your model includes multiple copies of the same thing, like windows, furniture, and trees. After you're up and running with SketchUp, you'll end up using components often.

▲ **Outliner:** The **Outliner** dialog box is basically a fancy list of all the groups and components in your SketchUp model. It shows you which groups and components are nested inside other ones, lets you assign names for them, and gives you an easy way to hide parts of your model

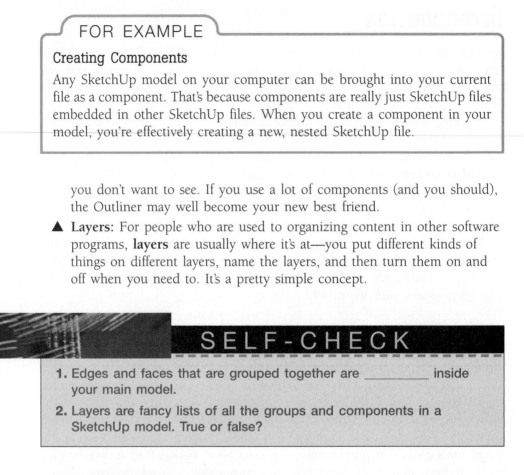

FOR EXAMPLE

Creating Components

Any SketchUp model on your computer can be brought into your current file as a component. That's because components are really just SketchUp files embedded in other SketchUp files. When you create a component in your model, you're effectively creating a new, nested SketchUp file.

you don't want to see. If you use a lot of components (and you should), the Outliner may well become your new best friend.

▲ **Layers:** For people who are used to organizing content in other software programs, **layers** are usually where it's at—you put different kinds of things on different layers, name the layers, and then turn them on and off when you need to. It's a pretty simple concept.

SELF-CHECK

1. Edges and faces that are grouped together are _____ inside your main model.
2. Layers are fancy lists of all the groups and components in a SketchUp model. True or false?

5.2 Grouping Things Together

Anyone who's worked with SketchUp for even a short time has probably noticed something: SketchUp geometry (the edges and faces that make up a model) is *sticky.* That is to say, stuff in a model wants to stick to other stuff. The people who invented SketchUp built it this way on purpose; however, the reasons why they did so take a while to explain. In any case, making and using groups is the key to keeping elements in your model from sticking together.

There are many reasons why you may need to make groups when using SketchUp; the following are a few of those reasons:

▲ **Grouped geometry doesn't stick to anything.** Perhaps you've modeled a building, and you want to add a roof. You want to be able to remove the roof by moving it out of the way with the Move tool, but every time you try to do this, you end up pulling the whole top part of the house along with the roof (like the middle image in Figure 5-1). Making the

Figure 5-1

The house is being stretched

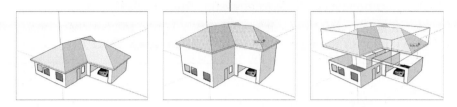

Making the roof into a group means that it won't stick to the rest of your building.

roof a separate group allows you to let it sit on top of your house without sticking there, making it easier to deal with, as shown in the right image in Figure 5-1.

▲ **Using groups makes it easier to work with your model.** For example, you can select all the geometry in a group by clicking it once with the Select tool. You can move groups around and make copies with the Move tool. To edit a group, you double-click it with the Select tool. To stop editing it, you simply click outside it, somewhere else in your modeling window.

▲ **You can name groups.** If you turn a selection of geometry in your model into a group, you can give it a name. In the Outliner (which is described later in this chapter) you can see a list of the groups (and components) in your model, and if you've given them names, you can see what you have.

Follow these steps to create a group:

1. **Select the geometry (edges and faces) you'd like to turn into a group.** The simplest way to select multiple entities (edges and faces) is to click them one at a time with the Select tool while holding down Shift. You can also use the Select tool to drag a box around the entities you want to select, but this can be tough, depending on where the entities are.

2. **Choose Edit⇨Make Group.** You can also right-click and choose Make Group from the context menu that pops up.

If you want to "ungroup" the geometry in a group, you need to explode it. To do this, right-click the group and choose Explode from the context menu. The edges and faces that were once grouped together won't be grouped anymore.

5.3 Working with Components

Even though components are incredibly important, there's nothing too magical about them—they're just groupings of geometry that make working in SketchUp faster, easier, and more fun. In a lot of ways, components are really just fancy groups—they do a lot of the same things. In the following sections, you'll learn about what makes components special and see some examples of what you can do with them. Next, you'll have a quick tour of the Components dialog box, in which you'll discover where components live and how you can organize them. The last part of this section is devoted to making your own components. It's not hard, and once you're able to make components, you're well on your way to SketchUp success.

The following are a few of the reasons why components are important:

▲ **Everything that's true about groups is true about components.** That's right: Components are just like groups, only better (in some ways, at least). Components don't stick to the rest of your model, you can give them meaningful names, and you can select them, move them, copy them, and edit them easily—just like you can with groups.

▲ **Components update automatically.** When you use multiple copies (these are called *instances*) of the same component in your model, they're all linked. Changing one makes all of them change, which saves loads of time. Consider a window component that you created and made two copies of, as shown in Figure 5-2. When you add something (in this case, some shutters) to one instance of that component, *all* the instances are updated. Now you have three windows, and they all have shutters.

▲ **Using components can help you keep track of quantities.** You can use the Components dialog box to count, select, substitute, and otherwise manage all the component instances in your model. Figure 5-3 shows a big (and ugly) building designed to go with the window component from the previous figure. Because the windows are component instances, you have a lot more control over them here than you would if they weren't components.

Figure 5-2

These windows are instances
of the same component

Changing one instance of a component changes all the other instances, too.

▲ **You can make a component cut an opening automatically.** Perhaps you've made a window, and you'd like that window to poke a hole through whatever surface you stick it to. SketchUp components can be set up to cut their own openings in faces. These openings are temporary; thus, when you delete the component, the hole disappears. Check out Figure 5-4 to see this in action. Note, however, that components that are set up to automatically cut openings can only do so through a single face. As a result, if your wall is two faces thick, your components will cut through only one of the faces.

▲ **You can use your components in other models.** It's a simple operation to make any component you build available for use whenever you're working in SketchUp, no matter what model you're working on. If you have a group of parts or other things you always use, making your own component library can save you a lot of time and effort. There's more information about creating your own component libraries later in this section.

Figure 5-3

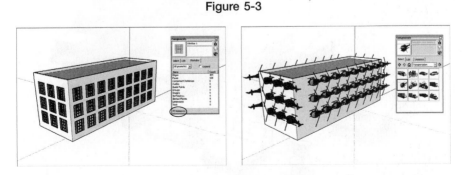

Quickly count all the Window 1 instances in your model (left), or even swap
them out for another component.

Figure 5-4

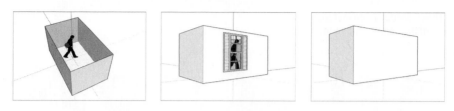

Components can cut their own holes in surfaces, which is handy
for windows and doors.

▲ **Components are great for making symmetrical models.** Because you can flip a component instance and keep working on it, and because component instances automatically update when you change one of them, using components is a great way to model anything that's symmetrical. And if you look around, you'll notice that most of the things we use are symmetrical. Chapter 6 dives headlong into modeling symmetrical things like couches and hatchbacks; Figure 5-5 shows some examples of symmetrical objects from SketchUp's default component library.

5.3.1 Exploring the Components Dialog Box

It's all fine and well that SketchUp lets you turn bits of your models into components, but wouldn't it be nice if you had someplace to *keep* them? And wouldn't

Figure 5-5

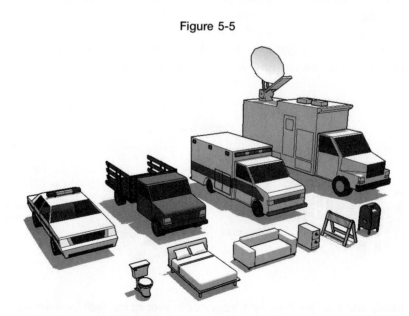

What do all these things have in common? They're symmetrical!

it be great if you could use components made by other people to spiff up your model, instead of having to build everything yourself? As you've probably already guessed, both of these things are possible in SketchUp, and both involve the Components dialog box, which you can find on the Window menu.

The Components dialog box is made up of four major areas, which are described in the following sections.

Information and Buttons

This part of the dialog box doesn't have an "official" name, so let's simply refer to it as the Information and Buttons area. Figure 5-6 points out the elements in this area.

Here's what everything in the Information and Buttons area does:

▲ **Name:** This is where the name of the component you select appears. If it's a component in your model, it's editable. If it's in one of the default libraries, it's not. A component is considered to be in your model if it appears in your In Model library, which you can read about later in this chapter.

▲ **Description:** Some, but not all, components have descriptions associated with them. You can write one when you're creating a new component, or you can add one to an existing component in your model. As with component names, you can only edit descriptions for models if the models are in your In Model library.

Figure 5-6

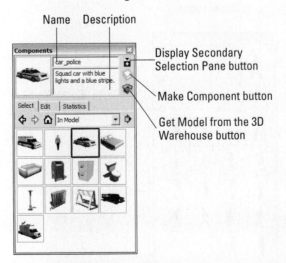

The Information and Buttons area of the Components dialog box.

▲ **Display Secondary Selection Pane button:** Clicking this button opens a second view of your libraries at the bottom of the Components dialog box. You can use this to manage the components on your computer system.

▲ **Make Component button:** Clicking this button creates a component from whatever geometry you have selected in your modeling window. There are also other ways to create new components, which are explained in the next section.

▲ **Get Model from the 3D Warehouse button:** The 3D Warehouse is an online repository of thousands—maybe hundreds of thousands—of SketchUp components that you can use in your model.

The Select Pane

This is where your components "live" (if they can be said to live anywhere). You use the Select pane to view, organize, and choose components. Figure 5-7 shows the Select pane in all its glory.

The functions of the various parts of the Select pane are as follows:

▲ **Back and Forward buttons:** Use these to toggle between component libraries that you've recently viewed.

Figure 5-7

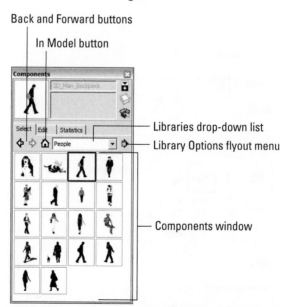

Back and Forward buttons

In Model button

Libraries drop-down list

Library Options flyout menu

Components window

The Select pane in the Components dialog box.

▲ **In Model Library button:** SketchUp automatically keeps track of the components you've used in your model and puts a copy of each of them in your In Model library. Each SketchUp file you create has its own In Model library, which contains the components that exist in that model. Clicking the In Model Library button displays the components in your In Model library, if you have any.

▲ **Libraries drop-down list:** Clicking this shows a list of the component libraries you have on your computer system. SketchUp comes prein-stalled with a few default libraries, but you can create your own if you want to. Libraries are essentially folders on your computer that contain SketchUp files. When you tell SketchUp that a particular folder is a component library, it displays each SketchUp model in that folder as a component that you can use in whatever model you're working on at the moment. For more information on creating your own libraries of compo-nents, keep reading.

▲ **Components window:** This window displays the components in the currently selected component library. Click a component to use it in your model.

▲ **Library Options flyout menu:** Here's where you manage the component libraries on your computer system. Several options exist on this menu; they are as follows:

   • **Open an Existing Library:** This lets you choose a folder on your computer system to use as a component library. Any SketchUp models in that folder can be used as components in your current model.

   • **Create a New Library:** This allows you to create a folder some-where on your computer system that you can use as a component library. This is handy if you have a number of components that you use all the time; putting them all in one place makes them easier to find.

   • **Save Library As:** When you choose this option, SketchUp lets you save your In Model library (consisting of all the components in your current model) as a library all by itself. As you can imagine, this option is only available when you're viewing your In Model library.

   • **Add Library to Favorites:** If you have a library that you use a lot, choose this option to add it to the Favorites section of the Libraries drop-down list. That way, it'll be easier to access quickly.

▲ **Expand:** Because components can be made up of other nested compo-nents, a component you use in your model might really consist of *lots* of components. Choosing Expand displays all the components in your model, whether or not they're nested inside other components. Most of the time, you'll probably want to leave Expand deselected.

▲ **Purge Unused:** Choose this to get rid of any components in your In Model library that aren't in your model anymore. Be sure to use this before you send your SketchUp file to someone else; it'll seriously reduce your file size and make things a whole lot neater.

On top of the all the buttons, menus, and windows you can immediately see in the Select pane of the Components dialog box, some hidden options exist that most people don't find until they go looking for them; they're on the context menu that pops up when you right-click a component in your In Model library, and they are as follows:

▲ **Select Instances:** Perhaps you have 15 instances (copies) of the same component in your model, and you want to select them all. Just make sure that you're viewing your In Model library, and then right-click the component (in the Components dialog box) whose instances you want to select all of. Choose Select Instances, and your work's done. This can save you tons of time, particularly if you have component instances all over the place.

▲ **Replace Selected:** Say you want to swap in a different component for one that's currently in your model. Simply select the component instances (in your modeling window) that you want to replace, and then right-click the component (in the Components dialog box) that you want to use instead. Choose Replace Selected from the context menu to perform the swap.

Ready for an even better tip? Use Select Instances and Replace Selected together to help you work more efficiently. For example, instead of placing 20 big, heavy tree components in your model (which can seriously slow things down), use a smaller, simpler component instead (like a stick). When you're finished modeling, use Select Instances to select all the stand-in components at once, and then use Replace Selected to swap in the real component.

The Edit Pane

Because the options in this part of the Components dialog box are similar to the ones you get when you make a new component, you should check out the section "Creating Your Own Components," later in this chapter, for the whole scoop. You can only use the options in the Edit pane on components in your In Model library—everything will be grayed out for components that "live" any other place.

The Statistics Pane

The Statistics pane is a useful place to spend some time. You use it to keep track of all the details related to whatever component you have selected in the Components dialog box. See Figure 5-8 for an example.

This pane is especially useful for doing the following things:

▲ **Checking the size of your components:** The information in the Edges and Faces areas of this pane lets you know how much geometry is in a component. If you're worried about file size or your computer's performance, try to use small components—ones with low numbers of faces and edges.

▲ **Seeing what components are inside your components:** The Component Instances line lists how many component instances are in your selected component. If you switch from All Geometry to Components in the drop-down list at the top of the pane, you can see a list of all the constituent components: subcomponents within your main component.

Figure 5-8

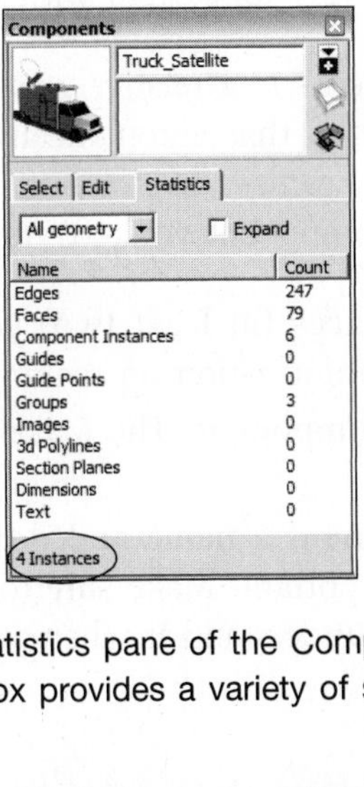

The Statistics pane of the Components
dialog box provides a variety of statistics.

The Statistics pane *doesn't* show details for components you have selected in your actual model; it only shows information about the component that's selected in the Select pane of the Components dialog box. To see information about whatever component (or other kind of object) you have selected in your modeling window, use the Entity Info dialog box (located in the Window menu).

5.3.2 Creating Your Own Components

Now you've learned about the benefits of using components in your models, you're probably ready to start making your own. Thankfully, creating and using components is probably the single best SketchUp habit you can develop. Here's why:

▲ **Components keep file sizes down.** When you use several instances of a single component, SketchUp only has to remember the information for one of them. This means that your files are smaller, which in turn means that you'll have an easier time emailing, uploading, and opening them on your computer.

▲ **Components show up in the Outliner.** If you're a person who's at all interested in not wasting time hunting for things you've misplaced, you should create lots of components. Doing so means that you'll be able to see, hide, unhide, and rearrange them in the Outliner, which is described later in this chapter.

▲ **Components can save your sanity.** Hooray! You've finished a model of the new airport—and it only took three weeks! Too bad the planning commission wants you to add a sunshade detail to every one of the 1,300 windows in the project. If you made that window a component, you're golden. If, on the other hand, that window *isn't* a component, you're going to be spending a very long night with your computer.

Creating simple components is a relatively easy process, but making more complicated ones—components that automatically cut openings, stick to surfaces, and always face the viewer—can be a little trickier. Follow these steps, regardless of what kind of component you're trying to make:

1. **Select the edges and faces (at least two) you'd like to turn into a component.** For more information on making selections, see Chapter 2.
2. **Choose Edit⇨Make Component.** The Make Component dialog box opens (see Figure 5-9).
3. **Give your new component a name and description.** Of these two, the name is by far more important. Make sure to choose one that's descriptive enough that you'll understand it when you open your model a year from now.

Figure 5-9

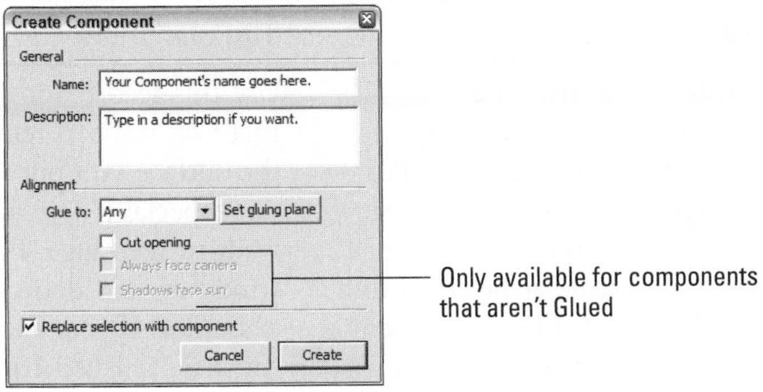

The Make Component dialog box.

4. **Set the alignment options for your new component.** Wondering what all this stuff means? For a quick introduction to each option and tips for using it, see Table 5-1.

5. **Select the Replace Selection with Component check box, if it isn't already selected.** This drops your new component into your model right where your selected geometry was, saving you from having to insert it yourself from the Components dialog box.

6. **Click the Create button to create your new component.**

Components can only cut through one face at a time. If your model's walls are two faces thick, you'll have to cut your window and door openings manually.

5.3.3 Editing, Exploding, and Locking Component Instances

Right-clicking a component instance in your modeling window opens a context menu that offers lots of useful choices. Here's what some of those choices let you do:

▲ **Edit Component:** To edit all instances of a component at once, right-click any instance and choose Edit Component from the context menu. The rest of your model will fade back, and you'll see a dashed bounding box around your component. When you're done, click somewhere outside the bounding box to finish editing; your changes have been made in every instance of that component in your model.

▲ **Make Unique:** Sometimes you want to make changes to only one or a few of the instances of a component in your model. In this case, select the instance(s) you want to edit, right-click one of them, and choose Make Unique from the context menu. This turns the instances you

Table 5-1: Component Alignment Options

Option	What It Does	Tips and Tricks
Glue To	This option makes a component automatically stick to a specific plane. For example, a chair will almost always be sitting on a floor. It will almost *never* be stuck to a wall, turned sideways. When a component is glued to a surface, using the Move tool only moves it around on that surface—never perpendicular to it (up and down, if the surface is a floor).	Use this feature for objects that you want to remain on the surface you put them on, especially objects you'll want to rearrange. Furniture, windows, and doors are prime examples. If you want to "unstick" a glued component from a particular surface, right-click it and choose Unglue from the context menu.
Set Gluing Pane	This sets a component's gluing pane, which is an invisible rectangle that tells SketchUp what part of that component should stick to things after you select Glue To. For simple things like chairs, the gluing pane is under the chair legs. For flat-screen TVs, it's behind the back surface.	Click the Set Gluing Pane Button to choose where you want your component's gluing pane to be (it looks like a gray, translucent rectangle. Click once to center your axes, again to establish the red direction, and a third time to establish the green and blue directions. Practice a few times to get it right—it's not the easiest thing to do.
Cut Opening	For components "on" a surface, select this check box to automatically cut an opening in surfaces you stick the component to.	As with pre-made components, this opening is temporary. If you delete the component instance, the opening will disappear. If you move the component instance, the opening will move, too.
Always Face Camera	This option makes a component *always* face you, no matter how you orbit around. To make your 2D Face-Me components (as they're called)	Using flat, "lightweight" components instead of 3D "heavy" ones is a great way to have lots of people and trees in your model

work, rotate your component to-be so that it's perpendicular to your model's green axis before you choose Make Component.

without bogging down your computer.

Shadows Face Sun	This option is only available when the Always Face Camera check box is selected, and it is selected by default.	You should leave this check box selected unless your Face-Me component meets the ground in two or more separate places, as shown in Figure 5-10.

Figure 5-10

Incorrect shadow

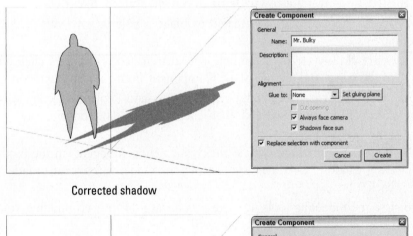

Corrected shadow

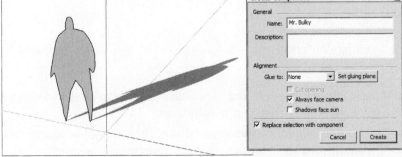

Deselect the Shadows Face Sun check box if your component touches the ground in more than one place.

selected into a separate component. Now edit any of them; only those instances you "made unique" will reflect your changes.

▲ **Explode:** When you explode a component instance, you're effectively turning it back into regular geometry. Explode is a lot like Ungroup in other software programs (in SketchUp, you use Explode to "disassemble" both components and groups).

▲ **Lock:** Locking a group or a component instance means that nobody— including you—can mess with it until it's unlocked. You should use this on parts of your model you don't want to change accidentally. To unlock something, right-click on it and choose Unlock.

MAKING YOUR OWN DOORS AND WINDOWS

If you really enjoy modeling, nothing beats making your own window and door components. Here's what you need to know (check out the illustration for visual instructions):

1. Start by drawing a rectangle on a vertical surface, like a wall.
2. Delete the face you just created to make a hole in your vertical surface.
3. Select all four edges of the hole you just created. Then right-click one of the edges and choose Make Component from the context menu.
4. Make sure that Glue to Any, Cut Opening, and Replace Selection with Component are all selected, then click the Create button to create your new component.
5. With the Select tool, double-click your new component (in the modeling window) to edit it; the rest of your model will appear to fade back a bit.
6. Use the modeling tools just like you always do to keep building your door or window any way you want.
7. When you're done, click outside your component to stop editing it.

If the opening you create ever closes up, one of two things probably happened:

▲ **A new surface was created.** Try deleting the offending surface to see whether that fixes things; it usually does.

▲ **The cutting boundary was messed up.** The cutting boundary consists of the edges that define the hole your component is cutting. If you take away those edges, SketchUp doesn't know where to cut the hole anymore. Drawing them back in usually sets things straight.

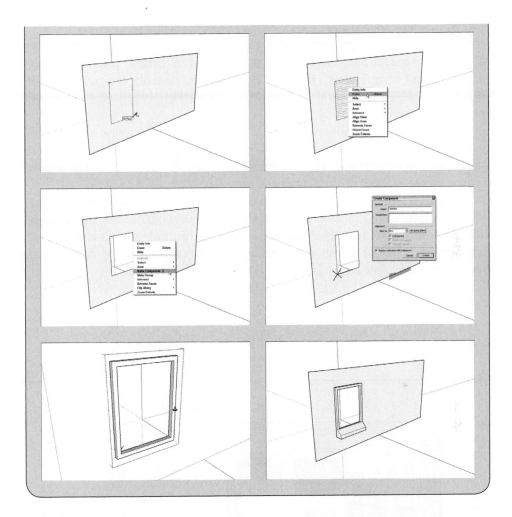

1. Using components has little effect on file size. True or false?
2. Explode is similar to _____ in other software programs.
3. The gluing pane is a rectangle that is:
    a. red.
    b. blue.
    c. invisible.
    d. black.

5.4 Using the Outliner

Most halfway-complicated SketchUp models consist of dozens, if not hundreds, of groups and components. These groups and components are nested inside each other and a lot of them are heavy, computer-killing behemoths like three-dimensional trees and shrubs.

Without a list, how are you going to manage all your groups and components? How are you going to keep track of what you have, hide what you don't want to see, and (more importantly) *unhide* what you *do* want to see? The answer to these questions lies in the Outliner dialog box.

You can open the Outliner dialog box by choosing Window⇨Outliner. Figure 5-11 shows what this box looks like when a model consists of a simple room with some furniture in it. The individual items of furniture are all components that were found in the Components dialog box (after downloading the Architecture Bonus Pack, that is).

Figure 5-11

This symbol means this is a component instance

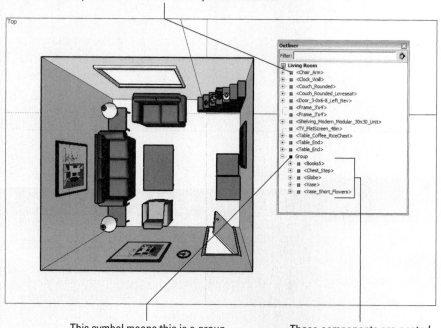

This symbol means this is a group

These components are nested inside a group

The Outliner, when there are a few components within a model.

The Outliner dialog box has the following features:

▲ **Search filter box:** If you type a word or phrase into this box, the Outliner will only show the items in your model that include that word or phrase in their name. For example, if you were to type in *coffee*, only the coffee table component would be visible.

▲ **Outliner Options flyout menu:** This handy little menu contains three options:

• **Expand All:** Choose this option to have the Outliner show *all* the nested groups and components in your model (provided they're on visible layers).

• **Collapse All:** This option collapses your Outliner view so that you only see *top-level* groups and components—ones that aren't nested inside other groups and components.

• **Sort by Name:** Select this option to make the Outliner list the groups and components in your model alphabetically.

▲ **Outliner List window:** This is where all the groups and components in your model are listed. Groups and components that have nested groups and components inside them have an Expand/Collapse toggle arrow next to their names. When they're expanded, their constituent groups and components appear as an indented list below them.

It's important to note that the Outliner only shows groups and components that exist on layers that are visible in your model. In other words, anything on a hidden layer won't appear in the Outliner, so you should be extra careful if you're using both the Outliner and layers to organize your model.

If you're going to use lots of groups and components (and you should), having the Outliner open on your screen is one of the best things you can do to model efficiently. Here's why:

▲ **Use the Outliner to control visibility.** Instead of right-clicking groups and components in your model to hide them, use the Outliner instead. Just right-click the name of any element in the Outliner and choose Hide. When you do, the element is hidden in your modeling window, and its name is grayed out and italicized in the Outliner. To unhide it, just right-click its name in the Outliner and choose Unhide.

▲ **Drag and drop elements in the Outliner to change their nesting order.** Don't like having the component you just created nested inside another component? Simply drag its name in the Outliner to the top of the list. This moves it to the top level, meaning that it's not embedded in anything. You can also use the Outliner to drag groups and components "into" other ones, too.

▲ **Find and select things using the Outliner.** When you select something in the Outliner, its name gets highlighted, and it gets selected in your modeling window. This is a much easier way to select nested groups and components, especially if you're working with a complex model.

SELF-CHECK

1. The nesting order of elements cannot be changed within the Outliner. True or false?
2. The Outliner presents information in collapsible rows. True or false?
3. If you wanted to find the trees in your model, you could type "trees" into the _____ filter box.
4. Which of the following are listed in the Outliner List window?
   a. Groups
   b. Components
   c. Layers
   d. Groups and components

5.5 Discovering the Ins and Outs of Layers

In a 2D program like Photoshop or Illustrator, the concept of layers makes a lot of sense: You can have content on any number of layers, sort of like a stack of transparencies. You find a distinct order to your layers, so anything that's on the top layer is visually "in front of" everything on all the other layers. Figure 5-12 shows what this means.

Figure 5-12

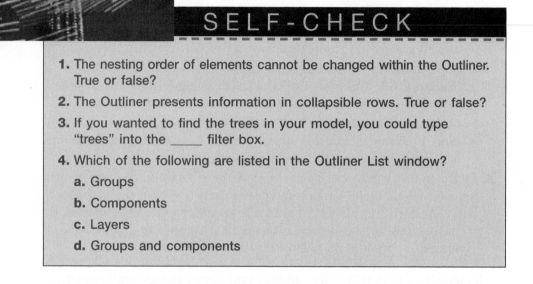

In 2D software, layers are pretty straightforward.

But hold on a second—SketchUp isn't a 2D program; it's a 3D program. So how can it have layers? How can objects in three-dimensional space be "layered" on top of each other so that things on higher layers appear "in front of" things on lower ones? In short, they can't—it's impossible. This means that layers in SketchUp are different from layers in most other graphics programs, and that's confusing to lots of people.

SketchUp has a layers system because some of the very first SketchUp users were architects, and many, *many* architects use drawing software called AutoCAD. Because AutoCAD uses layers extensively, layers were incorporated into SketchUp to maximize compatibility between the two products. When you import a layered AutoCAD file into SketchUp, its layers show up as SketchUp layers, which is rather convenient.

So what are SketchUp layers for? Layers are for controlling visibility. You use them to gather particular kinds of geometry so that you can easily turn that geometry on (make it visible) and turn it off (make it invisible) when you need to. That said, layers *don't* work the same way as groups and components; your edges and faces aren't isolated from other parts of your model, which can cause major confusion if you're not careful.

5.5.1 Using Layers in SketchUp

You can find the Layers dialog box on the Window menu. It's a pretty simple piece of machinery, as you can see in Figure 5-13.

Here's what everything does:

▲ **Add Layer:** Clicking this button adds a new layer to your SketchUp file.
▲ **Delete Layer:** Click this button to delete the currently selected layer. If anything is on the layer you're trying to delete, SketchUp will

Figure 5-13

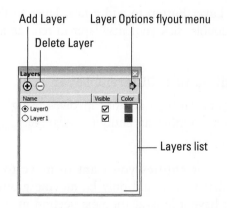

The Layers dialog box.

ask you what you want to do with it; choose an option and select Delete.

▲ **Layer Options flyout menu:** This contains the following useful options:

- **Purge:** When you choose Purge, SketchUp deletes all the layers that don't contain geometry. This is a handy way to keep your file neat and tidy.

- **Color by Layer:** Notice how each layer in the list has a little color swatch next to it? Choosing Color by Layer temporarily changes all the colors in your SketchUp model to match the colors assigned to each layer. To see what's on each layer, this is the way to go.

▲ **Layers list:** This is a list of all the layers in your SketchUp file. You need to know the following about the three columns in this list:

- **Name:** Double-click a layer's name to edit it. Giving your layers meaningful names is a good way to quickly find what you're looking for.

- **Visible:** This check box is the heart and soul of the Layers dialog box. When it's selected, the geometry on that layer is visible; when it's not, it's not.

- **Color:** You can choose to view your model using Color by Layer, which is described in the previous list. You can choose which color to assign to each layer by clicking the Color swatch.

5.5.2 Adding a New Layer

Follow these steps to add a layer to your SketchUp file:

1. **Choose Window⇨Layers.** This opens the Layers dialog box.
2. **Click the Add Layer button to add a new layer to the Layers list.** If you want, you can double-click your new layer to rename it.

5.5.3 Moving Entities to a Different Layer

Moving things from one layer to another involves using the Entity Info dialog box. Follow these steps to move an entity (an edge, face, group, or component) to a different layer:

1. **Select the entity or entities you want to move to another layer.**
   Keep in mind that you should only be moving groups and components to other layers; have a look at the next section in this chapter to find out why.

2. **Choose Window⇨Entity Info.** This opens the Entity Info dialog box. You can also open it by right-clicking your selected entities and choosing Entity Info from the context menu.

3. **In the Entity Info dialog box, choose a layer from the Layer drop-down list.** Your selected entities are now on the layer you chose from the list.

Layers can be really helpful, but you need to know how to use them; if you don't, bad things can happen. Here's some more detail:

▲ **Do all your modeling on Layer0.** Always make sure that Layer0 is your current layer when you're working. (The current layer is the one whose radio button is selected.) Keeping all your "loose" geometry (that's not part of a group or component) together in one place is the *only* way to make sure that you don't end up with edges and faces all over the place. SketchUp, unfortunately, lets you put geometry on whatever layer you want, which means that you can end up with a face on one layer, and one or more of the edges that define it on another. When that happens, it's next to impossible to work out where everything belongs; you'll spend literally hours trying to straighten things out. This property of SketchUp's layers system is a major stumbling point for new SketchUp users; knowing to keep everything on Layer0 can save you a lot of anguish.

▲ **Don't move anything but groups and components to other layers.** If you're going to use layers, follow this rule: *Never* put anything on a layer other than Layer0 unless it's a group or a component. Doing so ensures that you don't end up with stray edges and faces on separate layers.

▲ **Use layers to organize big groups of similar things.** More complicated SketchUp models often include things like trees, furniture, cars, and people. These kinds of things are almost always already components, so they're perfect candidates for being kept on separate layers. For instance, you might make a layer called Trees and put all your tree components on it. This makes it easy to hide and show all your trees all at once. This will also speed your workflow by improving your computer's performance (trees are usually big, complicated components with lots of faces).

▲ **Don't use layers to organize interconnected geometry; use the Outliner instead.** "Interconnected geometry" means things like building floor levels and staircases. These are parts of your model that aren't meant to be physically separate from other parts (like vehicles and people are). When you put Level 1 on one layer and Level 2 on another, more often than not, you'll get confused about what belongs where: Is the staircase part of Level 1 or Level 2? Instead, make a group for Level 1, a group for Level 2, and a group for the staircase.

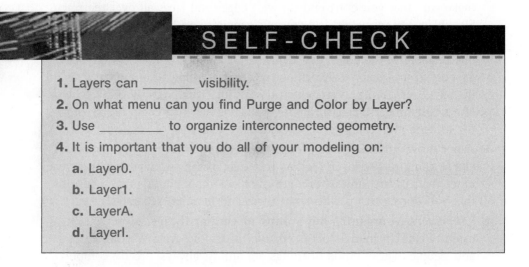

FOR EXAMPLE

Iterations

Feel free to use layers to iterate. **Iteration** is the process of doing multiple versions of the same thing. Lots of designers work this way to figure out problems and present different options to their clients. Using layers is a great way to iterate: You can move each version of the thing you're working on to a different layer, and then turn the layers on and off to show each version in turn. Just remember to follow the rule about only using groups and components on separate layers (mentioned previously), and you'll be fine.

SELF-CHECK

1. Layers can _____ visibility.
2. On what menu can you find Purge and Color by Layer?
3. Use _____ to organize interconnected geometry.
4. It is important that you do all of your modeling on:
   a. Layer0.
   b. Layer1.
   c. LayerA.
   d. LayerI.

5.6 Putting It All Together

Say that Figure 5-14 shows a model of a small house that we're building in SketchUp (which can be found on the fourth and fifth page of this book's color insert). Here, we're using all of SketchUp's organizational tools to help manage our model's complexity while we're working:

▲ **Each floor level is a group.** By working with each floor level as a separate group, we're able to use the Outliner to hide whichever one we're not working on. This makes it easier to see what we're doing. We're including the house's only staircase in the first floor group, because that turns out to be the easiest thing to do. We've also decided to include the interior walls on each level of the house in that level's group. Because we don't think we'll ever have to hide them, it wasn't worth making them a

Figure 5-14

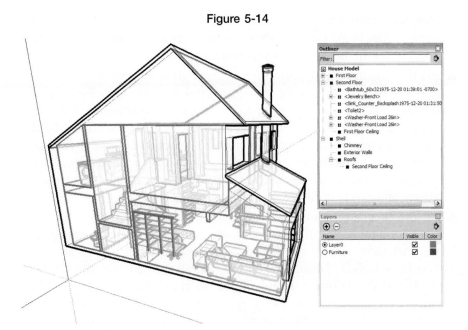

We're using all of SketchUp's organizational tools to build this model.

separate group. For what it's worth, the same thing probably applies to most buildings, unless you plan to study different floor plans with different interior wall arrangements.

▲ **The roof and exterior walls are groups inside of another group.** We want to be able to "remove" the roof and the exterior walls separately, so we've made each of them a group. We also want to be able to hide and unhide them both at the same time, so we made a group called "Shell" that includes both of them. Using the Outliner, we can selectively show or hide just the geometry we want (see Figure 5-15). The floor levels,

Figure 5-15

All groups are visible   Shell group is hidden   Only First Floor group is visible

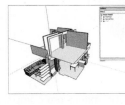
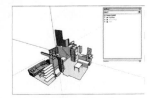

Each floor of the house, as well as the roof and the exterior walls, is a group.

roof, and exterior walls of the house are groups instead of components because they're *unique*—in other words, because we only have one first floor, it doesn't need to be a component.

▲ **All the furniture and plumbing fixtures are components.** All the components used to furnish the house are ones we built ourselves, took from the Components dialog box, or found in the 3D Warehouse. But we only have one couch: Why make it a component instead of a group? By making every piece of furniture in the model a component, we're able to see a list of our furniture in the In Model library of the Components dialog box (see Figure 5-16). We can also save that as a separate component library and use it in future models.

▲ **All the furniture is on a separate layer.** Because furniture components can be a little heavy (they're taxing on a computer system), and because we want to be able to see the house without furniture, we created a new layer (called "Furniture") and moved all the furniture onto it. Using the Layers dialog box, we can control the visibility of that layer with a single click of the mouse. But why not just create a group from all the furniture components and use the Outliner to hide and unhide them all, instead of bothering with layers? Good question. The answer is because it's easier to change a component's layer than it is to add it to an existing

Figure 5-16

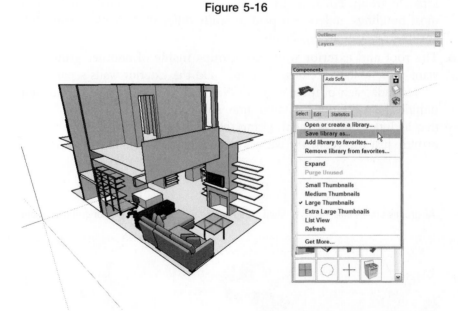

Because all of the pieces of furniture are components, we can use the Components dialog box to make our own custom component library.

group. To add something to a group, we would need to use the Outliner to drag and drop it in the proper place; with complex models, this can be a hassle. Changing a component's layer is just a matter of using the Entity Info dialog box to choose from a list.

SELF-CHECK

1. It's usually best to make the floor levels, roof, and exterior walls of a house groups instead of components because they are _____.
2. It is easier to change a component's layer than it is to add it to an existing group. True or false?

SUMMARY

Congratulations! You can now organize your model. This will save you time and will make modeling easier and much more enjoyable in the future. Keeping your model organized will also help you avoid slowing down your computer or crashing SketchUp.

In this chapter, we focused on the tools you need to keep your model organized: groups, components, layers, and components. You compared groups and components and when to use each. You used the Outliner dialog box to improve the organization of your model. You also assessed how to use layers, add layers, and move entities to different layers.

KEY TERMS

Components	Edges and faces grouped together into objects that display certain useful properties.
Group	Collection of edges and faces that are grouped together and act like a mini-model within the main model.
Iteration	The process of doing multiple versions of the same thing.
Layers	A collection of geometry (including groups and components) that can be made visible or invisible all at once.
Outliner	A dialog box that lists all of the groups and components in a model.

ASSESS YOUR UNDERSTANDING

Go to www.wiley.com/college/chopra to evaluate your knowledge of keeping your model organized.

Measure your learning by comparing pre-test and post-test results.

Summary Questions

1. Components are used when a model includes several copies of the same thing. True or false?

2. Which of the following is a characteristic of groups?

    (a) Grouped geometry sticks to everything.

    (b) Groups have no names.

    (c) Groups cannot be moved.

    (d) Ungrouping geometry requires that it be exploded.

3. When you use multiple instances (copies) of the same component, updates to all the instances occur _____.

4. Using components is a great way to model anything that is _____.

5. Libraries are folders on your computer that contain SketchUp files. True or false?

6. The Statistics pane shows details for components you have selected in your actual model. True or false?

7. Which of the following is true with regard to components?

    (a) They keep file sizes down.

    (b) They don't appear in the Outliner.

    (c) Component instances must be updated manually.

    (d) They cannot cut openings.

8. One benefit of using layers is that they can be used to organize large groups of similar items. True or false?

9. Using components can help you keep track of _____ of items.

10. Which of the following options in the Outliner displays a list of all the groups and components in your model?

    (a) Display

    (b) List

    (c) Expand

    (d) Library List

11. Which option should you use to make changes only to a few of the instances of a component in your model?

    (a) Alter Selectively

    (b) Make Unique

    (c) Edit Component

    (d) Select One

12. _____ All changes your Outliner view so that you only see top-level groups and components.

13. Sort by Name lists the groups and components in your model alphabetically.

14. The _____ enables you to check the size of your components.

Applying This Chapter

1. Name and describe three reasons why you would need to make groups.

2. List and describe the four major areas of the Components dialog box.

3. How do you move entities to a different layer?

4. Name two reasons you should use components and why you would want to create your own components.

5. What are libraries, and why would you use them?

6. What is Layer0 and when would you use it?

Doors and Windows

Within the model of the house that you've been working on, make your own doors and windows. What happens if the cutting boundary is messed up?

Organize Your Model

Create a model of a simple doghouse surrounded by trees, with one dog outside the doghouse. Using groups, components, the Outliner, and layers, organize the model so that you can easily show or hide certain subsets of objects.

6

CREATING EVERYDAY OBJECTS
Tools, Techniques, and Tips

Starting Point

Go to www.wiley.com/college/chopra to assess your knowledge of creating everyday objects.
Determine where you need to concentrate your effort.

What You'll Learn in This Chapter

▲ How things are put together
▲ How to use components to make symmetrical models
▲ How to extrude around circles and along paths with Follow Me
▲ How to round off corners

After Studying This Chapter, You'll Be Able To

▲ Create bilaterally symmetrical forms by building half of the form, creating a component, and copying and flipping the component
▲ Build radially symmetrical forms by modeling one portion of the form, making it into a component, and rotating copies of the component around a center point
▲ Design lathed forms using the SketchUp's Follow Me tool
▲ Construct pipes, gutters, and moldings by extruding a 2D face along a 3D path
▲ Create rounded edges using fillets and the Follow Me tool

INTRODUCTION

There's more to life than modeling buildings. Even though SketchUp is excellent at letting you make models of built structures, you can use it to build just about anything you can think of—all it takes is time, ingenuity, and the ability to take a step back and break things down into their basic parts. SketchUp provides some fantastic tools for creating forms that aren't in the least bit boxy, but these tools are not as obvious as Push/Pull and Rectangle, so most people never find them. This chapter is devoted to helping you discover SketchUp's "rounder" side.

In this chapter, you'll learn about tools, techniques, and other tips for creating forms that are distinctly unbuilding-like. Ideally, you will use these tools to push the limits of what you think SketchUp can do.

6.1 Modeling Symmetrically

First, take a hard look at the shape of the things you might want to model. Everything in the world (as you've probably realized) can be categorized as either of the following formal types:

▲ **Symmetrical:** Objects that exhibit **bilateral symmetry** are made of mirrored halves. You are (more or less) bilaterally symmetrical, and so is your car. Another kind of symmetry is **radial symmetry;** objects that are radially symmetric have similar parts regularly arranged around a central point. Starfish are good examples of this, as are umbrellas and apple pies. If you were going to build a model of something that exhibits some form of symmetry, building one part and making copies would be a smart way to do it.

▲ **Asymmetrical:** Some things—for example, puddles, oak trees, and many houses—aren't symmetrical. There's no real trick to making these things; you just have to settle in and get to work.

The fact is, a vast number of objects exhibit some kind of symmetry. This makes modeling a great deal easier, because it means you don't often have to model things in their entirety. With SketchUp's Components feature (described at length in Chapter 5), you can make a *piece* of something, copy it, flip it over (if necessary), and put it in position. Better yet, any changes you make to one part are automatically reflected in the others—because that's what components do.

You can take advantage of both bilateral and radial symmetry with SketchUp components. To do so, you just assemble those components as follows, depending on what type of symmetry your object has:

▲ **Bilateral symmetry:** To make a model of something that's bilaterally symmetrical, you just build half, make it into a component, and flip over a copy.

▲ **Radial symmetry:** Radially symmetrical objects can be (conceptually, anyway) cut into identical "wedges" that all radiate from a central axis. You can use components to model things like car wheels and turrets by building a single wedge and rotating copies of the wedge around a central point.

For examples of these processes, see Figure 6-1.

The following is a list of reasons why you should work with components whenever you're building a symmetrical object:

▲ **It's faster.** This one's obvious. Not having to model the same objects twice provides you with more time for doing other things.

▲ **It's smarter.** Everybody knows that things change, and when they do, it's nice not to have to make the same changes more than once. Using component instances means never having to make the same change more than one time.

Figure 6-1

Axis of symmetry

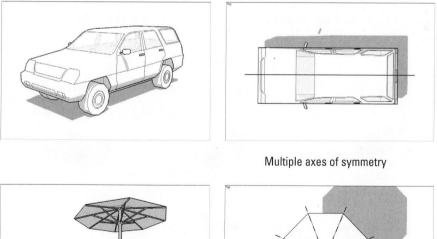

Multiple axes of symmetry

Bilateral symmetry (top) and radial symmetry (bottom) make it much easier to use SketchUp.

▲ **It's fun.** Modeling something and then watching it repeat in numerous other places is fun, and the overall effect impresses others. Somehow, people think you're smarter if they see things appearing "out of nowhere."

6.1.1 Building Bilaterally Symmetrical Forms

Bilaterally symmetrical forms are everywhere. Most animals you can name, the majority of the furniture in your house, your vehicle—they can all be modeled by building half, creating a component, and flipping over a copy.

Follow these steps to get the general idea of how to start building a bilaterally symmetrical model in SketchUp (see Figure 6-2):

1. **Make a simple box.** You can do this however you want, but perhaps the easiest way is to draw a rectangle and push/pull it into 3D.
2. **Draw a diagonal edge on the corner of your box.** The point of this step is to mark one side of your box so that when you flip it over, you aren't confused about which side is which.
3. **Turn your box into a component.** Chapter 5 has detailed information on how to do this, but here's the condensed version:
   - Select everything you want to make into a component.
   - Choose Edit⇨Make Component.
   - Name your component if you'd like, and then click the Create button.

Figure 6-2

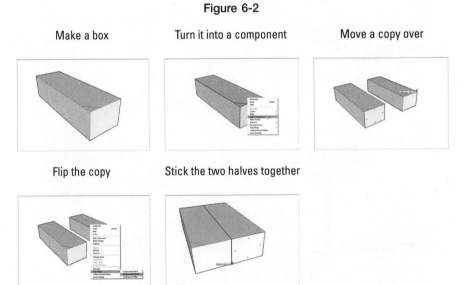

Make a box   Turn it into a component   Move a copy over

Flip the copy   Stick the two halves together

Creating a bilaterally symmetrical model.

4. **Make a copy of your new component instance.** The last part of Chapter 2 has information about moving and copying objects in SketchUp, but here's a simple version:

   - Choose the Move tool.
   - Press Ctrl (Option on a Mac) to toggle from Move to Copy mode. You should see a little plus sign (+) next to your cursor.
   - Click your component instance.
   - Move your copy beside the original, and click again to drop it. Make sure that you move in either the red or the green direction; doing so makes things easier in the next step.

5. **Flip the copy over.** To do this, right-click the copy and choose Flip Along from the context menu. If you moved your copy in the red direction in the previous step, choose Flip Along⇨Component's Red. Choose Flip Along⇨Component's Green if you moved in the green direction.

6. **Put the two halves together.** Using the Move tool (this time without Copy toggled on), pick up your copy *from the corner* and move it over, dropping it *on the corresponding corner* of the original. Take a look at the last image in Figure 6-2 to see what this looks like. Doing this precisely is important if you want your model to look right.

Now you're set up to start building objects with bilateral symmetry! If you'd like, you can carry out a quick test to make sure things went smoothly (see Figure 6-3). To do so, follow these steps:

1. With the Select tool, double-click one of the halves of your model to edit it.
2. Draw a circle on the top surface and push/pull it into a cylinder.

If the same thing happens on the other side, you're good to go. If the same thing *doesn't* happen on the other side, it's possible that one of the following situations holds true:

▲ **You're not really editing one of your component instances.** If you aren't, you're drawing *on top of* your component instead of *in* it. You'll know you're in Component Edit mode if the rest of your model looks grayed out.

▲ **You never made a component in the first place.** If your halves don't have blue boxes around them when you select them, they're not component instances. Start a new file and try again, paying particular attention to step 3 in the preceding list.

Figure 6-3

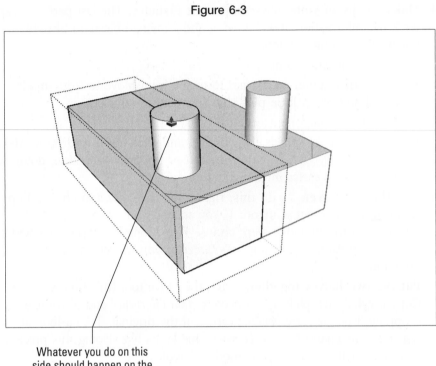

Whatever you do on this
side should happen on the
other side, too

Test your setup to make sure that everything works.

MAKING TWO HALVES LOOK LIKE ONE WHOLE

Look carefully at the little boat in the figure that follows. Notice how the edges in the middle clearly show that it's made out of two halves? If you were to erase those edges, your whole model would disappear, because those edges are defining faces, and without edges, faces can't exist.

Instead of erasing those unwanted edges, you can hide them by using the Eraser while pressing Shift. See the second and third images of the boat? When you hold down Shift as you drag over the edges you want to hide with the Eraser, they disappear.

There are two important things you need to know about hidden edges:

▲ **Hidden edges aren't gone forever.** Actually, this applies to any hidden geometry in your model. To see what's hidden, choose View↪Hidden Geometry. To hide it again, just choose the same thing.

▲ **To edit hidden edges, you have to make them visible.** If you need to make changes to your model that involve edges you've already hidden, you can either view your hidden geometry (see the previous point) or unhide them altogether. Just show your hidden geometry, select the edges you want to unhide, and choose Edit⇨Unhide⇨Selected.

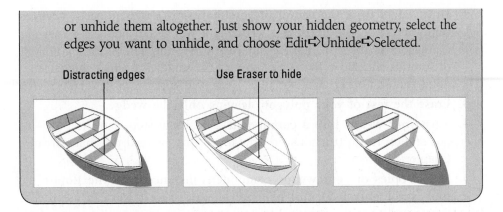

6.1.2 Building Radially-Symmetrical Forms

It's just as easy to model objects that exhibit radial symmetry as it is to model those with bilateral symmetry; all you need to do is start out slightly differently. The only thing you must decide before you start is how many "wedges"—or how many identical parts—your object is made of.

To set yourself up to model something with radial symmetry, you start by modeling one wedge, then you make it into a component, and then you rotate copies around the center. Follow these steps to get the hang of it:

1. **Draw a polygon with as many sides as the number of segments you need for the object you're modeling.** Here's the easiest way to draw a polygon in SketchUp, as shown in Figure 6-4:
   - Choose Tools⇨Polygon to select the Polygon tool.
   - Click once to establish the center (consider doing this on the axis origin), move your cursor, and then click again to establish the radius. Don't worry about being accurate right now.
   - Before you do anything else, type in the number of sides you'd like your polygon to have and press Enter.

Figure 6-4

Make a polygon   Define a wedge   Erase the rest

Draw a polygon to start, draw two edges to create a wedge, and erase the
rest of your polygon.

2. **Draw edges from the center of your polygon to two adjacent vertices (endpoints) on the perimeter, creating a wedge.** To find the center of a polygon (or a circle), hover your cursor over the outline for a couple of seconds and move the cursor toward the middle; a center inference point should appear.

3. **Erase the rest of your polygon, leaving only the wedge.**

4. **Turn your wedge into a component.** Check out step 3 in the previous section for instructions on how to do this, or read the first part of Chapter 5.

5. **Make copies of your wedge component instance with the Rotate tool (see Figure 6-5).** Just like with the Move tool, you can use the Rotate tool to make copies. You can even make an **array** (a series of copies that are equally spaced apart) than one copy at a time). Here's how to do it:

   • Select the edges and face of your wedge.

   • Choose Tools⇨Rotate to select the Rotate tool.

Figure 6-5

Click to define center of rotation

Click to start rotating

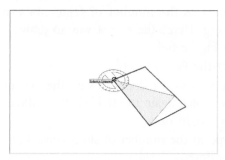 

Press Ctrl (Option on Mac) to rotate copy

Make more copies

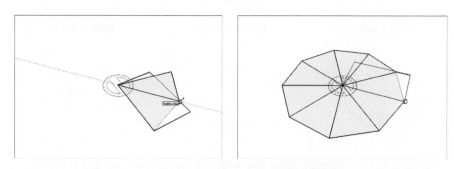

Use the Rotate tool to make copies of your wedge component instance.

- Press Ctrl (Option on a Mac) to tell SketchUp that you want to make a copy; a + should appear next to your cursor.
- Click the pointed end of your wedge to set your center of rotation.
- Click one of the opposite corners of your wedge to set your rotation start point.
- Click the other corner to make a rotated copy of your wedge.
- Before you do anything else, type in the number of additional wedges you want, followed by the letter *x,* and then press Enter.

6. **Test your setup, if you'd like.** Follow the steps at the end of the previous section in this chapter to test your setup.

Remember, you might want to consider hiding the edges in your component instances. Doing so can make your finished model look much better.

MODELING WITH THE SCALE TOOL

In this book, not much time is spent on the Scale tool because it's not difficult to figure out. However, it is important to point out something many new SketchUp users don't realize: Using the Scale tool to alter the *shape* of your model (instead of just the size) is an incredibly powerful way to work. The following figure shows what this means. The basic idea is to reshape your geometry by only selecting certain faces and edges, and then scaling those. You can see a good example of how this works in the Color Insert of this book, where it shows how to create the tapered bottom of a rowboat by scaling its bottom surface.

Here are some additional things you should know about the Scale tool:

▲ Press Ctrl (Option on a Mac) to scale about the center.
▲ Use the corner grips (the little green cubes) to scale proportionally.
▲ Use the side grips to squeeze or stretch your selection.

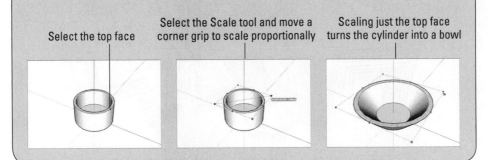

Select the top face | Select the Scale tool and move a corner grip to scale proportionally | Scaling just the top face turns the cylinder into a bowl

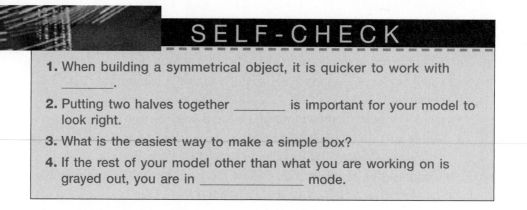

S E L F - C H E C K

1. When building a symmetrical object, it is quicker to work with _____.

2. Putting two halves together _____ is important for your model to look right.

3. What is the easiest way to make a simple box?

4. If the rest of your model other than what you are working on is grayed out, you are in _____ mode.

6.2 Extruding Shapes with Follow Me

Follow Me is an excellent example of a powerful SketchUp tool with an underwhelming name. The problem that faced the software designers when they were trying to determine what to call this feature was this: It does what other 3D modeling programs dedicate two or three other tools to doing. Thus, the designers chose an unconventional name because Follow Me is a wholly unconventional tool.

In the following sections, you'll learn how to use Follow Me to create a number of different types of shapes. Examples of these shapes are shown in Figure 6-6 and are as follows:

▲ **Bottles, spindles, and spheres:** These are all examples of **lathed forms,** or 3D forms created by spinning a 2D shape around a central axis. These can be created by spinning a 2D profile (shape) around a central axis to create a 3D model.

Figure 6-6

Follow Me lets you create all kinds of different shapes.

▲ **Pipes, gutters, and moldings:** If you look closely, all three of these things are basically created by extruding a 2D face along a 3D path; the result is a complex 3D form.

▲ **Fillets and other cut-away profiles**: A **fillet** is a thin strip of material. In SketchUp, you can cut fillets and other shapes away from the edges of forms to create rounded edges. This can also be accomplished using Follow Me.

6.2.1 Using Follow Me

At its core, Follow Me lets you create forms that are extrusions. It's a bit like Push/Pull, except that it doesn't just work in one direction. You tell Follow Me to follow a path, and it extrudes a face all along that path. This means that you need three things to use Follow Me:

▲ **A path:** In SketchUp, you can use any edge, or series of edges, as a path. All you have to do is make sure that they're drawn before you use Follow Me.

▲ **A face:** Just like with Push/Pull, Follow Me needs a face to extrude. You can use any face in your model, but it needs to be created before you start using Follow Me.

▲ **Undo:** Imagining what a 2D face will look like as a 3D shape isn't easy—it usually takes several tries to get a Follow Me operation right. That's what Undo is for, after all.

Follow these steps to use Follow Me; refer to Figure 6-7 to see how the steps work:

1. **Draw a face to use as an extrusion profile.** In this example, we're creating a pipe, so our extrusion profile is a circular face.

Figure 6-7

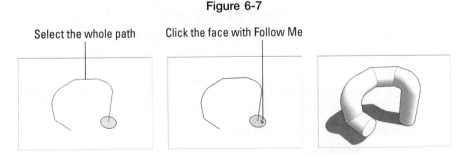

Using Follow Me to create a simple extruded shape.

2. **Draw an edge (or edges) to use as an extrusion path.** Although the edge (or edges) is touching the face in this case, it doesn't have to for Follow Me to work.

3. **Select the complete extrusion path you want to use.** Refer to the section on making selections in Chapter 2 for pointers on using the Select tool effectively.

4. **Activate the Follow Me tool.** To do this, choose Tools⇨Follow Me.

5. **Click the face you want to extrude once.** Magic! Your face (extrusion profile) is extruded along the path you chose in step 3, creating a 3D form (in this case, a section of pipe).

If you want to use Follow Me all the way around the perimeter of a face, you don't need to spend time selecting all the individual edges. Just select the face and then use Follow Me; the tool automatically runs all the way around any face you have selected.

You can use Follow Me another way, too: Instead of preselecting a path (as in step 3 of the preceding list), you can click any face with Follow Me and attempt to drag it along edges in your model. While this works on simple things, preselecting a path works a lot better—it's really the only option for using Follow Me in a predictable way.

6.2.2 Making Lathed Forms Like Spheres and Bottles

A surprising number of things can be modeled by using Follow Me to perform a *lathe* operation. A lathe is a tool that carpenters and machinists use to spin a block of raw material while they carve into it—this is how baseball bats are made, for instance.

A simple example of a lathed object is a sphere. Here's how you might make one with Follow Me:

1. **Draw a circle on the ground.**

2. **Rotate a copy of your circle up by 90 degrees, as shown in Figure 6-8.** If you're wondering how to do this, follow these steps:
   - Select the face of your circle with the Select tool.
   - Choose Tools⇨Rotate to activate the Rotate tool.
   - Press Ctrl (Option on a Mac) to tell SketchUp you want to make a copy.
   - Click a green endpoint inference along the edge of your circle *and hold down* your mouse button to drag. Don't let go just yet.
   - Still dragging, move your cursor over to the endpoint on the *exact opposite* side of your circle; then release your mouse button.

Figure 6-8

Click and hold down
mouse button

Drag here

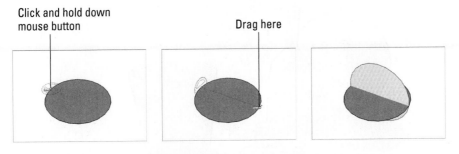

Using the Rotate tool to make a rotated copy of a circle.

Now your *axis of rotation* is a line right through the center of your circle.

- Click anywhere on the edge of your circle, and then move your mouse over a little bit.
- Type in **90** and press Enter.

3. **Make sure that one of your circles is selected.**

4. **With the Follow Me tool, click the circle that's not selected once (see Figure 6-9).** Now you have a sphere. The Follow Me tool "lathed" your circular face around the path you selected—the other circle.

Note, however, that if you really need a sphere, the easiest way to get one is in the Components dialog box. The Shapes library that comes installed with SketchUp has a selection of spheres (and cones and other things) you can choose from.

Under normal circumstances, you only have to model half a profile to use Follow Me to make it three-dimensional. Figure 6-10 shows a few different examples of 3D objects.

Figure 6-9

Select one circle   Click the other with Follow Me

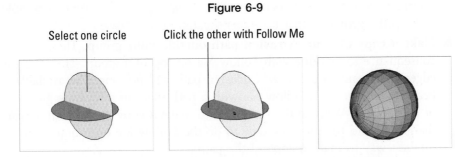

Clicking one circle with Follow Me while the other one is selected produces a sphere.

Figure 6-10

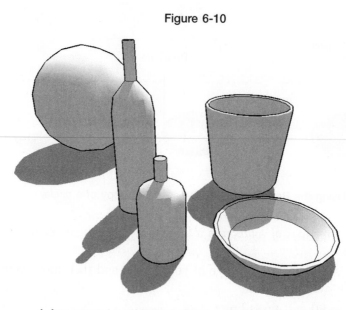

A few examples of lathed objects created with Follow Me.

6.2.3 Creating Extruded Shapes Like Gutters and Handrails

Much of the time, you'll want to use Follow Me to create geometry (edges and faces) that's attached to another part of your model. An example of this might be modeling a gutter that runs all the way around the roof of a house. In this case, you're likely to already have the path along which you want to extrude a profile (the edge of the roof).

When you're using Follow Me to extrude a face along a path that consists of edges that already exist as part of your model, there are two things you should *always* do:

▲ **Before using Follow Me, make the rest of your model a separate group.** Follow Me can sometimes mess things up, so you want to be able to keep the geometry that it creates separate, just in case.

▲ **Make a copy of your extrusion path outside your group.** There's a consequence to working with Follow Me on top of a group: The edge (or edges) you want to use as an extrusion path will no longer be available, because you can't use Follow Me with a path that's in a separate group or component. What to do? You need to make a copy of the path *outside* the group, and then use the *copy* to do the Follow Me operation. Here's the best way to make a copy of the path:

• With the Select tool, double-click your group to edit it.

• Select the path you want to use for Follow Me.

- Choose Edit⇨Copy.
- Exit (stop editing) your group by clicking somewhere else in your modeling window.
- Choose Edit⇨Paste in Place. Now you have a copy of the path you want to use, and it's outside your group.

When you're using an existing edge (or series of edges) as an extrusion path, the hard part is getting your profile in the right place. You have a choice of two ways to proceed; which one you use depends on what you need to model:

▲ **Draw the profile in place.** Do this only if the extrusion path is parallel to one of the colored drawing axes.

▲ **Draw the profile on the ground and then move it into position.** If your extrusion path doesn't start out parallel to a colored drawing axis, you should probably draw your profile somewhere else and move it into place later.

WHY YOUR COMPUTER IS SO SLOW

When you use Follow Me with an extrusion profile that's a circle or an arc, you're creating a piece of 3D geometry that's very big. In other words, this geometry has lots of faces, and faces are what make your computer slow down. Without going into detail about how SketchUp works, keep this in mind: The more faces you have in your model, the worse your computer's performance will be. At a certain point, you'll stop being able to orbit, your scenes (which are explained in Chapter 10) will stutter, and you'll be frustrated.

The first pipe in the figure that follows has been extruded using Follow Me. It was made with a 24-sided circle as an extrusion profile, and it has 338 faces. Hidden Geometry is turned on (in the View menu) so that you can see how many faces the pipe has.

The second pipe uses a 10-sided circle as an extrusion profile. As a result, it only has 116 faces. What an improvement!

The third pipe also uses a 10-sided circle as an extrusion profile, but the arc in its extrusion path is made up of only 4 segments, instead of the usual 12. It has a total of 52 faces. Even better!

The second image in the figure shows all three pipes with Hidden Geometry turned off. Is the difference in detail worth the exponential increase in the number of faces? Most of the time, the answer is no.

To change the number of sides in a circle or an arc, just before or just after you create it, follow these steps:

1. Type in the number of sides you'd like to have.
2. Type an s to tell SketchUp that you mean "sides."
3. Press Enter.

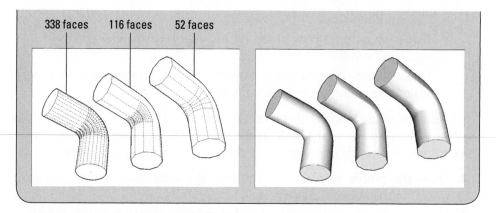

Drawing Your Profile in Place

Consider that you have a model of a house. You want to use Follow Me to add a gutter that goes all the way around the perimeter of the roof. You decide to draw the profile in place (right on the roof itself), because the edges of the roof are drawn parallel to the colored drawing axes. This means that you'll have an easier time using the Line tool to draw "in midair."

The trick to drawing an extrusion profile that isn't on the ground is to start by drawing a rectangular face. You then draw the profile on the face and erase the rest of the rectangle. Figure 6-11 shows how you would draw the profile of a gutter directly on the corner of a roof; the steps that follow explain the same things in words:

1. **Zoom in on what you're doing.** Get close, and fill your modeling window with the subject at hand.
2. **Using the Line tool, draw a rectangle whose face is perpendicular to the edge you want to use for Follow Me.** This involves paying careful attention to SketchUp's inference engine; watch the colors to make sure that you're drawing in the right direction.
3. **Use the Line tool (and SketchUp's other drawing tools) to draw your profile directly on the rectangle you just created.** The important thing here is to make sure that your extrusion profile is a single face; if it's not, Follow Me won't work the way you want it to.
4. **Erase the rest of your rectangle, leaving only the profile.**

Drawing Your Profile Somewhere Else

The awful thing about handrails is that they're almost always at funny angles, and thus not parallel to a colored axis. In such cases, it's not convenient to draw your extrusion profile in place. Here, it's best to draw the profile on the ground and move it into position afterwards.

Here's the trick: Draw a "tail"—a short edge—perpendicular to your extrusion profile. You can use this tail to help you line up your profile with the edge you

Figure 6-11

This part of roof   Watch the color inferences

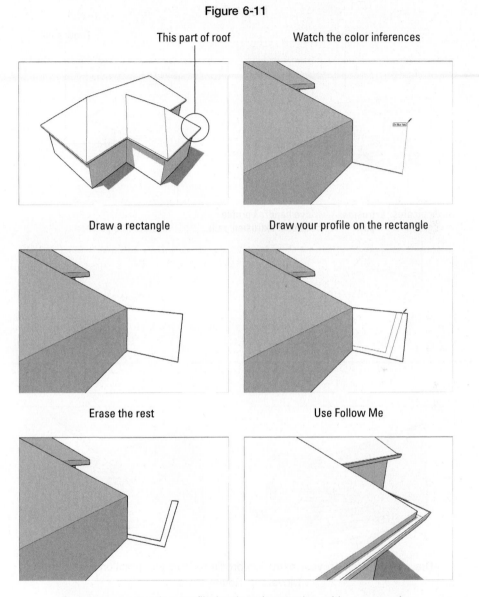

Draw a rectangle   Draw your profile on the rectangle

Erase the rest   Use Follow Me

Drawing an extrusion profile in place by starting with a rectangle.

want to use as an extrusion path for Follow Me. The following steps, and Figure 6-12, describe how you would draw and position a profile for a handrail:

1. **Draw your extrusion profile flat on the ground.**
2. **Draw a short edge perpendicular to the face you just drew.** This "tail" should come from the point where you want your profile to attach to the extrusion path.

Figure 6-12

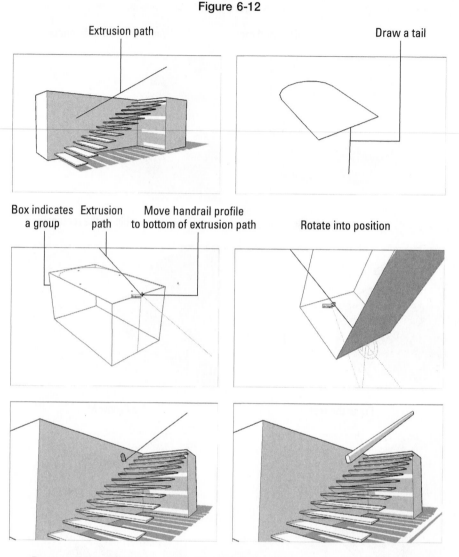

Draw a short tail on your extrusion profile to help you position it with the
Move and Rotate tools.

3. **Make your profile and its tail into a group.** This makes it easier to
   move and rotate around all at once. See Chapter 5 for information on
   creating and using groups, if you need it.

4. **Using the Move tool, place your profile at the end of the extrusion
   path.** To make sure that you position it accurately, pick it up by clicking
   the point where the tail meets the face, and drop it by clicking the end
   of the extrusion path.

5. **With the Rotate tool, rotate your profile into position.** Here's where you need to use a bit of skill. See the nearby sidebar, "Wrapping Your Head Around the Rotate Tool," for guidance. The Rotate tool is easy to use when you get the hang of it.

6. **Explode the group you created in step 3, and delete your tail.** To explode a group, right-click it and choose Explode from the context menu.

WRAPPING YOUR HEAD AROUND THE ROTATE TOOL

In the last version of SketchUp, the software's designers introduced a feature that allows you to establish your axis of rotation (the invisible line around which you're rotating) *while you're using the Rotate tool.* This makes it many times easier to rotate things.

By default, the Rotate tool "sticks" itself to whatever plane you happen to be hovering over—that's why it changes color as you move its big, round cursor all over your screen. When it's blue, its axis of rotation is the blue axis; the same goes for red and green. When it's black, its axis of rotation doesn't line up with any of the colored drawing axes.

If you want to show SketchUp the axis of rotation you want to use *while* you're using the Rotate tool, you can. In this case, using Rotate goes from being a three-step operation to a five-step one (refer to the following figure for a visual explanation):

1. Click once to establish your center of rotation, but *don't let go*—keep your finger on your mouse button.

2. Drag your cursor around (still holding the mouse button down) until your axis of rotation is where you want it. As you drag, you'll notice your Rotate cursor changing orientation; the line from the center of the cursor to your mouse is the axis of rotation.

3. Release your mouse button to set your axis of rotation.

4. Click (but don't drag) the point at which you want to "pick up" whatever you're rotating.

5. Click again to drop the thing you're rotating where you want it.

Whew! It takes practice, but it's worth it. The efficiency you gain by being able to rotate things in free space is huge. Here are two more things you should also know about Rotate, while we're on the subject:

▲ **Type in a rotate angle during or after you rotate something.** Check out the section about modeling with accuracy in Chapter 2 for more information on using the Value Control Box (VCB) to be precise while you're modeling.

▲ **Press Ctrl (Option on a Mac) to make a copy.** This works just like it does in the Move tool, which you can also read about in Chapter 2.

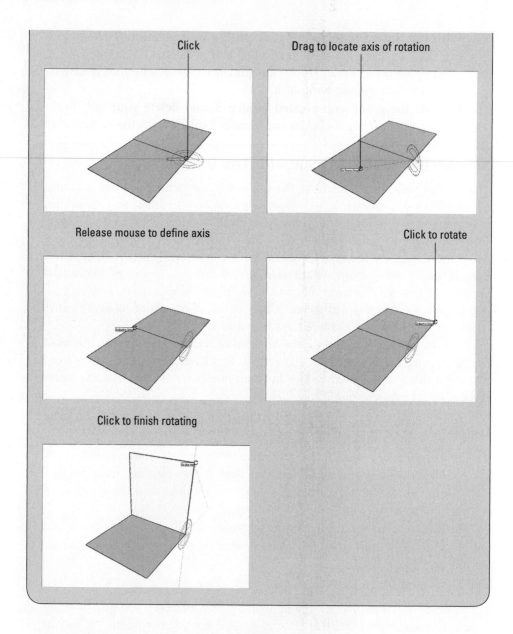

Click

Drag to locate axis of rotation

Release mouse to define axis

Click to rotate

Click to finish rotating

6.2.4 Subtracting From a Model with Follow Me

What if you want to model a bar of soap? Or a sofa cushion? Or any object that doesn't have a sharp edge? The best way to round off edges in SketchUp is to use Follow Me. In addition to using this tool to *add* to your model, you can also use it to *subtract* from your model.

Here's how it works: If you draw an extrusion profile on the end face of a longish form, you can use Follow Me to "remove" a strip of material along

Figure 6-13

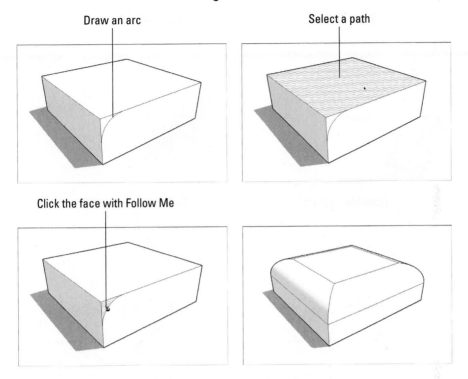

Creating a filleted edge with Follow Me.

whatever path you specify. Figure 6-13 demonstrates this concept on the top of a box.

If the extrusion path you want to use for a Follow Me operation consists of the entire perimeter of a face (as is the case in Figure 6-13), you can save time by just selecting the face instead of all the edges that define it.

But what if you want to create a corner that's rounded in *both* directions, as so many corners are? That one's a little trickier to do in SketchUp, but because it's such a common problem, let's take a closer look at how to do it. The basic technique involves using Follow Me on a corner you've already rounded with the Push/Pull tool. After you have a corner that's filleted with an arc of the correct radius, you can use copies (or component instances, if you're clever) of that corner several times, wherever you need them. It's not an elegant solution, but it's possible, and it works when you need it to.

Figure 6-14 gives a step-by-step, visual account of this process, while the following list explains it in words:

1. **Draw a box.** It doesn't really matter how big the box is, as long as it's big enough for the fillet you want to apply.

Figure 6-14

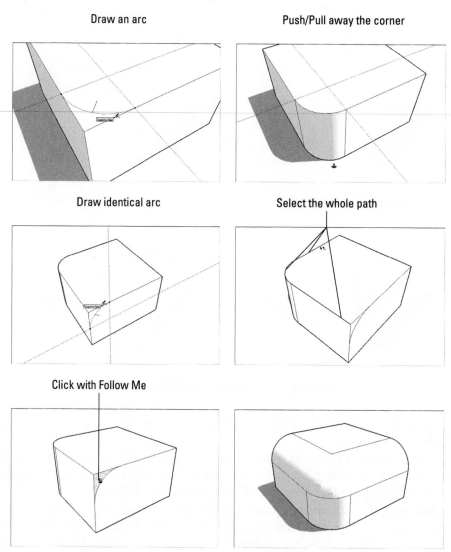

Draw an arc   Push/Pull away the corner

Draw identical arc   Select the whole path

Click with Follow Me

Making a corner that's filleted in both directions.

2. **With the Arc tool, draw an arc on the corner of the box.** When you're drawing an arc on a corner, keep an eye out for the inferences that help you draw properly:

   • After clicking to place one endpoint of your arc, as you cut across the corner, the point at which your line turns magenta is where your endpoints are *equidistant* (the same distance) from the corner across which you're cutting.

- After clicking to place your second endpoint, you will see a point at which the arc you're drawing turns magenta—this means your arc is *tangent to* (continuous with) both edges it's connected to. You want this to be the case, so you should click when you see magenta.

3. **Push/Pull the new face down to round off the corner.**

4. **Draw another, *identical* arc on one of the corners directly adjacent to the corner you just rounded.** This is where you'll have to refer to Figure 6-14. Pictures are better than words when it comes to explaining things such as which corners are adjacent to which.

5. **Select the edges shown in Figure 6-14.**

6. **Activate the Follow Me tool.**

7. **Click the arc corner face to extrude it along the path you selected in step 4.**

8. **Hide or smooth out any edges that need hiding or smoothing.** For information about hiding edges, see the sidebar "Making Two Halves Look Like One Whole," earlier in this chapter. Also check out the nearby sidebar "Smoothing Out Those Unsightly Edges," for the whole scoop on how to smooth edges.

After you have a fully rounded corner, you can use a number of them to make anything you want; it just takes a little planning. Figure 6-15 shows a simple bar of soap that was created out of eight rounded corners that were copied and flipped accordingly. The text (in case you're wondering) was created with SketchUp's 3D Text tool, which you can find on the Tools menu.

Figure 6-15

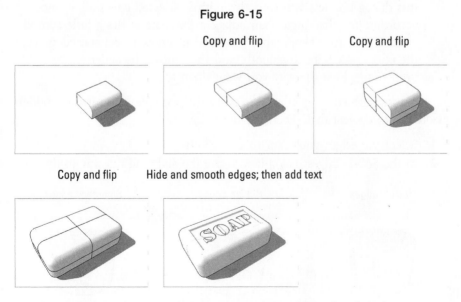

Copy and flip

Copy and flip

Copy and flip   Hide and smooth edges; then add text

Assembling multiple rounded corners to make objects is relatively easy.

SMOOTHING OUT THOSE UNSIGHTLY EDGES

If you're wondering how to get rid of all the ugly lines you end up with when you use Follow Me, the answer is simple: You can *smooth* edges, just like you can hide them. The difference between hiding and smoothing is illustrated by the images of the cylinders in the figure that follows:

▲ When you *hide* an edge between two faces, SketchUp still treats those faces as though your edge is still there—it just doesn't show the edge. Materials you've applied to each face stay separate, and each face is "lit" separately by SketchUp's sun. The latter fact is the reason why simply hiding the edges between faces that are supposed to represent a smooth curve doesn't make things look smooth; you still end up with a faceted look.

▲ When you *smooth* an edge between two faces, you're telling SketchUp to treat them as a single face, with a single material and smooth-looking shading. The difference is significant, as you can see in the second cylinder.

You can smooth edges in two different ways:

▲ **Use the Eraser.** To smooth edges with the Eraser tool, hold down Ctrl (Option on the Mac) while you click or drag over the edges you want to smooth.

▲ **Use the Soften Edges dialog box.** Located on the Window menu, this dialog box lets you smooth multiple selected edges all at once, according to what angle their adjacent faces are at. It's a little complicated at first, but here's what you need to know to get started: Select the edges you want to smooth, and then move the slider to the right until things look the way you want them to.

To unsmooth edges, you need to make them visible first; turn on Hidden Geometry to do just that. Then, do the following:

1. Select the edges you want to unsmooth.
2. In the Soften Edges dialog box, move the slider all the way to the left.

| Visible edges | Hidden edges | Smoothed edges |

SELF-CHECK

1. A simple example of a lathed object is a sphere. True or false?
2. You can use _____ to create a number of different types of shapes.
3. If you want to draw an extrusion profile that isn't on the ground, you should start by drawing a _____ face.
4. To view hidden edges, select View⤳_____.

SUMMARY

In this chapter, you learned how to create everyday objects such as wastebaskets, bottles, and soap. In doing so, you learned even more about SketchUp than if we had concentrated on buildings for the entire book. More specifically, in this chapter, you assessed symmetry and bilaterally symmetrical forms by building half of the form, creating a component, and copying and flipping the component. You built radially symmetrical forms by modeling one portion of the form, making it into a component, and rotating copies of the component around a center point. You then created lathed forms. Finally, you also evaluated the all-purpose Follow Me tool and used it to construct pipes, gutters, and moldings. These skills will serve you well in your models and designs.

KEY TERMS

Array	A series of copies that are equally spaced apart.
Bilateral symmetry	Mirrored halves.
Fillet	A thin narrow strip of material.
Lathed form	3D form created by spinning a 2D shape around a central axis.
Radial symmetry	Having similar parts arranged around a central point.

ASSESS YOUR UNDERSTANDING

Go to www.wiley.com/college/chopra to evaluate your knowledge of creating everyday objects.

Measure your learning by comparing pre-test and post-test results.

Summary Questions

1. Radially symmetrical forms have similar parts regularly arranged around a center point. True or false?

2. When you hide edges in a model, these edges are permanently deleted. True or false?

3. When creating a radially symmetrical form, you should draw a polygon with:

   (a) one more side than the number of segments you need for the object you're modeling.

   (b) one less side than the number of segments you need for the object you're modeling.

   (c) as many sides as the number of segments you need for the object you're modeling.

   (d) three hundred sixty sides (one for each of the degrees in a circle).

4. In SketchUp, you can cut away a thin strip of material called a _____ from the edge of a form to create a rounded edge.

5. At its core, Follow Me lets you create forms that are:

   (a) lathes.

   (b) extrusions.

   (c) paths.

   (d) faces.

6. When using Follow Me along a path that consists of edges that are already part of your model, you should always:

   (a) make sure the rest of your model is not a separate group.

   (b) delete these edges first.

   (c) rotate the edges around a central axis.

   (d) make a copy of your extrusion path outside your group.

7. In the current version of SketchUp, you can establish your axis of rotation while you're using the Rotate tool. True or false?

8. You can smooth edges by using the _____ tool or the Soften Edges dialog box.

Applying This Chapter

1. Name and describe the three things that you need to use Follow Me.
2. You've been asked to create a model of a wine bottle. How would you do this?
3. You've made a model of a vase, but you have many visible edges in your model. How would you smooth these edges out to make them invisible?
4. Give an example of when you would draw a profile in place and why.

Balcony Railing

Take your model of a house and create a balcony that consists of a flat platform and a handrail. Write down the list of steps you take to accomplish this as you are completing this task.

Add to Your House

Within the model of your house, add four wine bottles, three trash baskets, and one bar of soap. Write down the steps you take to create each one of these objects.

7

MODELING WITH PHOTOGRAPHS
Using Photo Match to Build Models

Starting Point

Go to www.wiley.com/college/chopra to assess your knowledge of modeling with photographs.
Determine where you need to concentrate your effort.

What You'll Learn in This Chapter

▲ Ways you can use photographs in your models
▲ How to use Texture Tweaker
▲ How to begin your model with Photo Match
▲ How to use Photo Match to match your model to a photograph

After Studying This Chapter, You'll Be Able To

▲ Paint faces in your model with photographs
▲ Tweak your textured faces with the Texture Tweaker
▲ Model on top of photo-textured faces
▲ Build a model from scratch with Photo Match

INTRODUCTION

It's almost impossible to find someone who doesn't take pictures. Aside from the millions of digital cameras out there, lots of mobile phones have cameras in them, too. In addition, more and more people are scanning existing photographs and saving them in digital form. In SketchUp, you can use photos from all of these sources in a couple of different ways:

▲ If you have a model you'd like to "paint" with photographs, you can do that in SketchUp. You can apply photos to faces and then use the information in the pictures to help you model.

▲ If you want to use a photo to help you model something from scratch, you can do that in SketchUp as well. New in version 6, a feature called Photo Match makes it (relatively) simple to bring in a picture, set things up so that your modeling window view matches the perspective in the photo, and then build what you see by "tracing" with SketchUp's modeling tools.

Neither of these techniques is especially easy, and they both require some familiarity with SketchUp's basic modeling techniques. Thus, if you haven't at least skimmed through Chapter 4, you might consider doing so before attempting the steps described in this chapter.

In this chapter, you will paint faces in your model with photographs; you will use Texture Tweaker; you will model on top of photo-textured faces; and you will build a model from scratch with Photo Match.

7.1 Painting Faces with Photos

Here's an interesting fact regarding the SketchUp feature you're about to learn about: Nobody really seems to know what it's called. During its development, the SketchUp team referred to it as the Texture Tweaker, mostly because both words start with the same letter, and they thought that was catchy. For some reason, however, this feature is called the Position Texture tool in SketchUp's Help documentation, even though it's not really a tool, at least not in the traditional sense. There's no button for the Texture Tweaker/Position Texture tool; you can only get to it by choosing a command from a menu. All the same, it's one of SketchUp's most useful "hidden" features.

Here are some of the things you can do with the Texture Tweaker:

▲ Stick artwork to 3D prototypes or packaging designs.
▲ Create photo-realistic buildings that you can *upload* (send) to Google Earth (see Chapter 11 for more detail on this).
▲ Figure out where things like windows, doors, signs, and ornamentation belong on your building models.

7.1.1 Adding Photos to Faces

Technically, painting surfaces with pictures using 3D software is referred to as **mapping**. Different software programs have different methods for mapping pictures to faces, and luckily, SketchUp's is very straightforward. Mapping photos of building facades to your building models with the Texture Tweaker/Position Texture tool has a number of benefits:

▲ Using photographs can make your models look more realistic.

▲ Taking advantage of details that are visible in a photograph (instead of modeling them) results in a smaller, easier-to-manage model.

▲ You can use a photograph to help you locate building elements, like doors, windows, and signs, if you plan to model them.

▲ Models to which you apply photo textures can be submitted to the 3D Warehouse, where they might be used on Google Earth's default Buildings layer. (Chapter 11 has all the details on this.)

SketchUp uses many different terms to refer to the elements that you can paint faces with, but generically, they're all called materials. Materials can be colors or textures; textures are image-based, and colors are a single, solid hue. When you import an image to map it to a face, it becomes a texture—just like any of the other textures in your Materials dialog box.

Follow these steps to map an image to a face. However, before you begin, note that you need to have at least one face in your model. If you don't, you won't have anything to map your texture to:

1. **Choose File⇨Import.** The Open dialog box opens.

2. **Select the image file you want to use as a texture.** You can use JPEGs, TIFFs, PNGs, and PDFs as textures in SketchUp. All of these are common image-file formats.

3. **Select the "Use as texture" option (see Figure 7-1).**

4. **Click the Open button.** This closes the Open dialog box, switches your active tool to Paint Bucket, and "loads" your cursor with the image you chose to import.

5. **Click once in the lower-left corner of the face you want to "paint" (see Figure 7-2).** Where you click tells SketchUp where to position the lower-left corner of the image you're using as a texture. You can click anywhere on the face you're trying to paint, but using the lower-left corner keeps things simple.

6. **Click somewhere else on the face you're painting to locate the upper-right corner of the image texture (see Figure 7-2).** Image textures in SketchUp are made up of *tiles*. To make a large area of

Figure 7-1

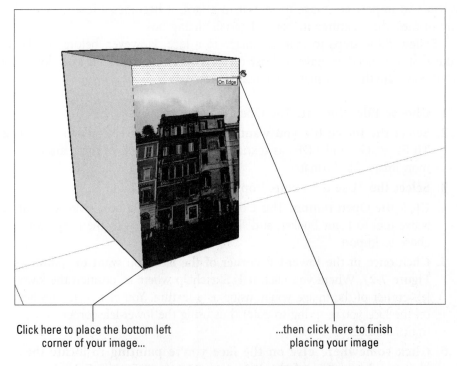

Use as texture

Make sure to pick "Use as texture."

Figure 7-2

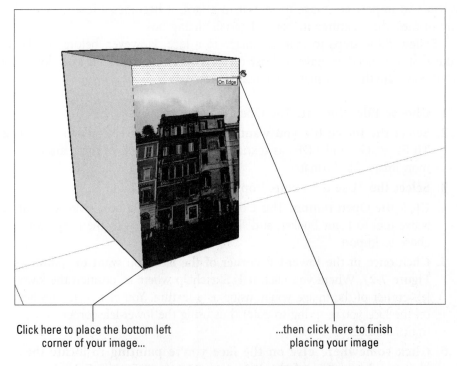

Click here to place the bottom left
corner of your image...

...then click here to finish
placing your image

Click once to locate the lower-left corner of the image you're using as a texture,
and then again to locate the upper-right corner.

texture (like a brick wall), SketchUp uses multiple tiles right next to each other. In the case of a brick wall, it may look like there are thousands of bricks, but it's really just the same tile of about 50 bricks repeated over and over again. Because SketchUp treats imported image textures just like any other texture, what you're really doing when you click to locate the upper-right corner of your image is this: You're telling SketchUp how big to make the tile for your new photo texture. Don't worry too much about getting it right the first time, though—you can always tweak things later on (hence the name Texture Tweaker).

Unless the proportions of your image perfectly match the face onto which it was mapped, you should see your image repeating. Don't worry—that's normal. SketchUp automatically tiles your image to fill the whole face. If you want to edit your new texture so that it doesn't look tiled (and you probably do), keep reading. You can scale, rotate, skew, or even stretch your texture to make it look however you want.

7.1.2 Editing Your Textures

After you've successfully mapped an image to a face, you're probably going to want to change it somehow: make it bigger, flip it over, rotate it around, and so on. This is where the Texture Tweaker/Position Texture tool comes in.

The Position Texture tool is actually more of a mode; thus, let's refer to it as Texture Edit mode. Within this mode, you can be in either of two submodes. The names of these submodes are less important than what they do, so here's a description of how they work:

▲ **Move/Scale/Rotate/Shear/Distort Texture mode:** As you'd expect, you use this mode to move, scale, rotate, shear, or distort your texture. Its technical name is *Fixed Pin mode*; you'll learn why a little later in the chapter.

▲ **Stretch Texture mode:** Stretch Texture mode lets you edit your texture by stretching it to fit the face it's painted on. If you want to map a photograph of a building façade to your model, this is the mode you want to use. In SketchUp's Help documentation, Stretch Texture mode is called *Free Pin mode*.

Note that you can only edit textures on flat faces; the Texture Tweaker doesn't work on curved faces. To find out more about working with textures and curved faces, see the section "Mapping Photo Textures to Curved Surfaces," found later in this chapter.

Moving, Scaling, Rotating, Shearing, and Distorting Your Texture

Moving, scaling, rotating, shearing, and/or distorting your texture involves use of the Texture Tweaker, as described in the following steps:

1. **With the Select tool, click the face with the texture you want to edit.**

2. **Choose Edit⇨Face⇨Texture⇨Position.** This enables Move/Scale/Rotate/Shear/Distort Texture mode. You should be able to see a transparent version of your image, along with four pins, each a different color. Have a look at Color Plate 9 to see what this looks like. Also note that if all your pins are yellow, you're in Stretch Texture mode. Right-click your textured face and make sure there's a check mark next to Fixed Pins to switch into the correct mode. (A quicker way to get to Edit mode is to right-click the textured face and then choose Texture⇨Position from the context menu.)

3. **Edit your texture.** At this point, the things you can do to edit your texture are located in two different places. Right-clicking your texture opens a context menu with the following options:

   • **Done:** Tells SketchUp you're finished editing your texture.

   • **Reset:** Undoes all the changes you've made to your texture, and makes things look like they did before you started altering them.

   • **Flip:** Flips your texture left to right or up and down, depending on which suboption you choose.

   • **Rotate:** Rotates your texture 90, 180, or 270 degrees, depending on which suboption you choose.

   • **Fixed Pins:** When this option is selected, you're in **Move/Scale/Rotate/Shear/Distort Texture mode** (Fixed Pin mode). Deselecting it switches you over to Stretch Texture mode, which is described later in this chapter.

   • **Undo/Redo:** Goes back or forward a step in your working process.

   Dragging each of the colored pins has a different effect (see Figure 7-3):

   • **Scale/Shear (Blue) pin:** This pin scales and shears your texture while you drag it. **Shearing** keeps the top and bottom edges parallel while making the image "lean" to the left or right.

   • **Distort (Yellow) pin:** This pin distorts your texture while you drag it; in this case, the distortion looks like kind of a perspective effect.

   • **Scale/Rotate (Green) pin:** This pin scales and rotates your texture while you drag it.

   • **Move (Red) pin:** This pin moves your texture around while you drag it. Of all four colored pins, this one may be most useful. You can use it to precisely reposition brick, shingle, and other building material textures in your models.

Figure 7-3

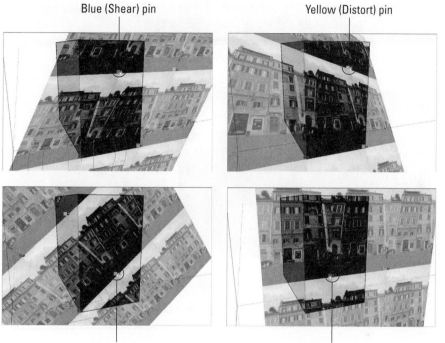

Blue (Shear) pin   Yellow (Distort) pin

Green (Rotate) pin   Red (Move) pin

Dragging each of the colored pins does something different.

Instead of just dragging around the colored pins, try single-clicking one of them to pick it up; this lets you place it wherever you want (just click again to drop it). This comes in especially handy when you're using the Move and Rotate pins.

4. **Click anywhere outside your texture in your modeling window to exit Edit mode.** You can also right-click and choose Done from the context menu, or press Enter.

Stretching a Photo Over a Face

To better understand how this feature works, think about having a photograph printed on a piece of stretchy fabric. Now, imagine that you stretch the fabric until the photo looks the way you want. Finally, you hold the fabric in place with pins.

In SketchUp, follow these steps to stretch your texture using the Texture Tweaker's Stretch Texture mode:

1. **With the Select tool, click the face with the texture you want to edit.**

Figure 7-4

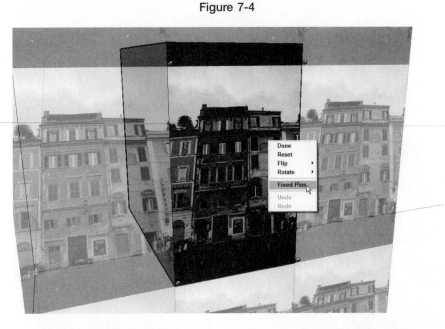

You know you're in Stretch Texture mode when all the pins are yellow.

2. **Choose Edit⇨Face⇨Texture⇨Position.** A quicker way to get to Edit mode is to right-click the textured face and choose Texture⇨Position from the context menu.

3. **Right-click your texture and *deselect* the Fixed Pins option (make sure that no check mark is next to it).** Deselecting Fixed Pins switches you to Stretch Texture mode (or Free Pin mode, if you're reading Sketch-Up's online Help). Instead of four different-colored pins with little symbols next to them, you should see four identical yellow pins. Figure 7-4 shows you what to expect.

4. **Click a pin to pick it up.** Your cursor should clench up into a fist, and the pin should follow it as you move your mouse around. Remember, you can press Esc to drop the pin you're carrying without moving it; pressing Esc cancels any operation in SketchUp.

5. **Place the pin at the corner of the building in your photograph by clicking once.** If the pin you're "carrying" is the upper-left one, drop it on the upper-left corner of the building in your photograph, as shown in Figure 7-5.

6. **Click and drag the pin you just moved to the corresponding corner of the face you're working on.** If the pin you just moved is the upper-left one, drag it over to the upper-left corner of the face whose texture you're "tweaking." Check out Figure 7-6 to see this in action.

Figure 7-5

Place the pin here

Place the pin at the corresponding corner (upper-left to upper-left, for instance)
of the building in your photo.

Figure 7-6

Move pin here

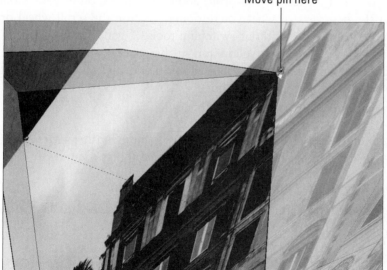

Drag the pin you just placed to the corresponding corner
of the face you're working on.

Figure 7-7

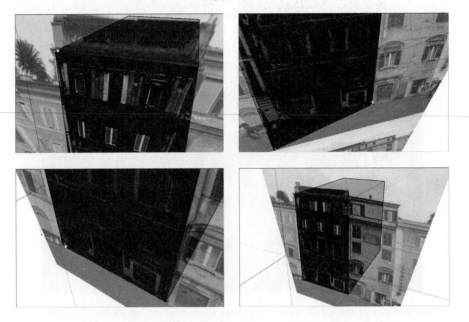

Repeat steps 4–6 for each of the other three yellow pins.

7. **Repeat steps 4–6 for each of the three remaining pins (see Figure 7-7).**
   If you need to, feel free to orbit, zoom, and pan around your model to get the best view of what you're doing; just use the scroll wheel on your mouse to navigate without switching tools. A good way to work is to pick up and drop each yellow pin in the general vicinity of the precise spot you want to place it. Then zoom in and use your better point of view to do a more accurate job.

8. **Press Enter to exit Texture Edit mode.**

If you don't like what you see, just go back and edit the texture again; there's no limit to the number of times you can change things around.

Scaling Your Model Until the Photo Looks Right

When you're happy with the way your texture is stretched to fit the face, one of two things will be true:

▲ **The proportions are correct.** If the proportions are correct, the photo won't look stretched or squashed. This will only be the case if the face to which you applied the photo texture was already exactly the right size.

Figure 7-8

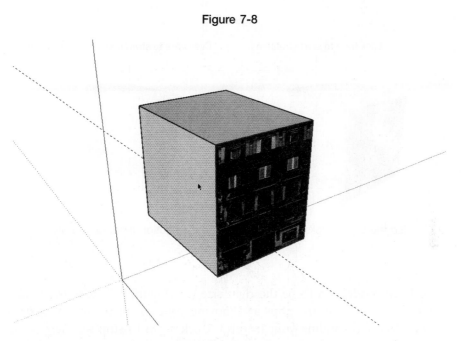

Select everything you want to stretch.

▲ **The proportions aren't correct.** If the photo texture you just "tweaked" looks stretched or squashed, the face it's on is the wrong size. No worries—you just need to stretch the whole face until the texture looks right. Better yet, if you know how big the face is *supposed* to be (in real life), you can stretch it until it's correct.

Follow these steps to stretch a face until the texture looks right:

1. **Use the Tape Measure tool to create guides that you can use to accurately stretch your face.** In this case, say you know that the building you're modeling is supposed to be 50 feet wide. (Using the Tape Measure tool and guides is described in Chapter 2, just in case you need a refresher.)

2. **Select the face you want to stretch.** If your model is at a fairly early stage, just select the whole thing. Triple-click the face with the Select tool to select it and everything attached to it. Figure 7-8 shows the whole model selected.

3. **Choose Tools⇨Scale to activate the Scale tool.** When the Scale tool is active, everything that's selected in your model should be surrounded by SketchUp's Scale Box. Its 27 little green cubes (they're called grips) and thick, yellow lines are hard to miss.

Figure 7-9

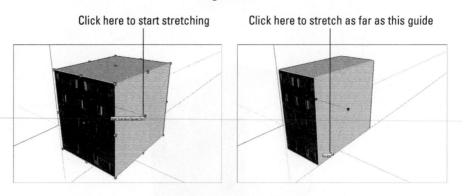

Click here to start stretching   Click here to stretch as far as this guide

Use the Scale tool's grips to stretch your selection (texture and all).

4. Scale your selection to be the right size (see Figure 7-9). Use the Scale tool by clicking on the grips and moving your cursor to stretch whatever's selected (including your texture). Click again to stop scaling.

To scale something precisely using a guide, click a scale grip to grab it and then hover over the relevant guide to tell SketchUp that's where you want to scale *to*. Click again to finish the scale operation.

7.1.3 Modeling on Top of Photo Textures

After you place a photo texture on the right face and in the correct place on that face, you may want to use the information in your photograph to help you add geometry to your model. It's a great way to be more or less accurate without having to measure much, and the combination of photo textures and a few simple push/pull operations can be very convincing.

One Thing You Must Know

Modeling with photo-textured faces isn't hard, but you *must* know one critical step before you can do it: You have to make sure that your texture is *projected*.

Figure 7-10 shows what happens when you try to push/pull an opening in a photo-textured face: On the left, when the texture *isn't* projected, the inside faces are painted with random parts of the texture. On the right, when it *is* projected, note how the "inside" faces that are produced by the push/pull operation appear striped. This is known as painting with "stretched" pixels, and the result is typically more appropriate for what you're doing.

Figure 7-10

Textures not projected

Wallpaper effect

Textures are projected

Stretched Pixels effect

No Textures

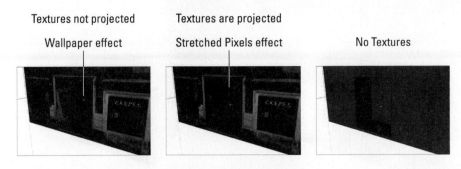

Pushing/pulling an opening in a textured face when the texture *isn't* projected (left),
and when it *is* projected (middle).

Thus, it's a good idea to make sure that your face's texture is projected *before* you start drawing on top of it. Happily, telling SketchUp to make a photo texture projected is just a matter of flipping a switch. Simply right-click the face with the photo texture and choose Texture➪Projected from the context menu. If you see a check mark next to Projected, your texture is already projected; don't choose anything.

Modeling with Projected Textures: A Basic Workflow

Follow these steps to get the hang of working with projected textures (see Figure 7-11):

1. **Make a basic rectangular box.**
2. **Apply a photo texture to one of the side faces.** Check out the section "Adding Photos to Faces," earlier in this chapter.
3. **Right-click the textured face and choose Texture➪Projected from the context menu.** Make sure that Projected has a check mark next to it.
4. **Draw a rectangle on the textured face and push/pull it inward.** Notice the "stretched pixels" effect?
5. **Add other angles or features to your model, if you like.** Figure 7-11 illustrates an angled face.
6. **Switch to the Paint Bucket tool.**
7. **Hold down Alt (⌘ on a Mac) and click somewhere on the textured face to sample the texture. (Your cursor should look like an eyedropper when you do this.)** This "loads" your Paint Bucket with the projected texture.
8. **Release the Alt (⌘ on a Mac) key to switch back to the Paint Bucket cursor, and click the angled face once to paint it with the projected texture.** You should see the "stretched pixels" effect here, too.

Figure 7-11

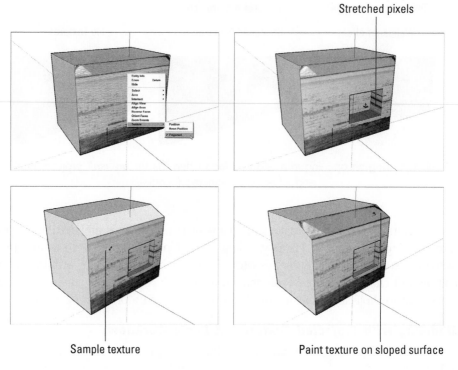

Working with projected textures.

Mapping Photo Textures to Curved Surfaces

Mapping projected textures to curved surfaces is complicated. Nevertheless, you *can* do it with a little effort. The key is to line up a flat surface with the curved surface to which you want to apply the photo texture. You then "paint" the flat surface with the texture, make it projected, sample it, and finally, paint the curved surface with the projected, sampled texture.

Follow these steps to get the basic idea (see Figure 7-12):

1. **Create a curved surface.** In this case, let's draw a couple of arcs on the top face of a rectangular block and then use Push/Pull to create a curved surface by "pushing" one of the top faces down to make it disappear.

2. **Create a flat surface that lines up with your curved surface.** Use the Line tool and SketchUp's inferencing system to draw a flat face that lines up with (and is the same size as) the curved surface.

Figure 7-12

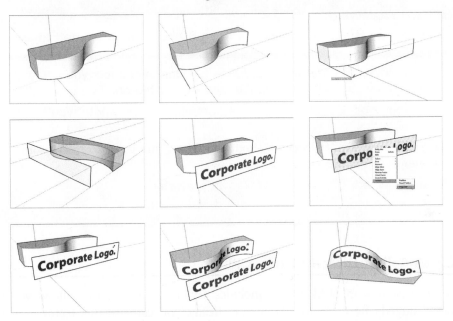

Mapping projected textures to curved surfaces is possible, but it isn't easy.

3. **Apply a photo texture to your flat surface and make sure that it's positioned correctly.** You can refer to the earlier parts of this chapter for detailed instructions on how to do this.

4. **Right-click the textured face and choose Texture⇨Projected.** This ensures that the texture is projected, which is the key to this entire operation.

5. **Use the Paint Bucket tool with the Alt key (⌘ on a Mac) held down to sample the projected texture.** This "loads" your Paint Bucket tool with the projected texture.

6. **Use the Paint Bucket tool *without* pressing anything on your keyboard to paint the curved surface with the projected texture.** If everything goes as it's supposed to, the photo texture should be painted on your curved surface; the pixels in the image should look stretched in some places.

7. **Delete the flat surface that you originally mapped the image to; you don't need it anymore.**

If you're trying to do this on your own curved surface and things don't seem to be working, your curved surface is probably part of a group or component. Either explode or double-click to edit the group or component before carrying out step 6, and see if that helps.

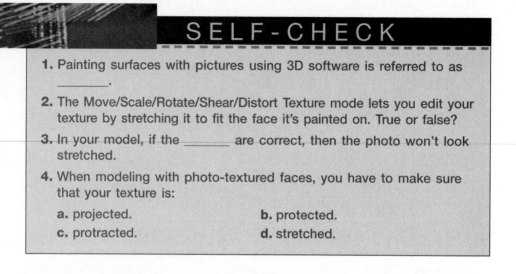

SELF-CHECK

1. Painting surfaces with pictures using 3D software is referred to as _____.

2. The Move/Scale/Rotate/Shear/Distort Texture mode lets you edit your texture by stretching it to fit the face it's painted on. True or false?

3. In your model, if the _____ are correct, then the photo won't look stretched.

4. When modeling with photo-textured faces, you have to make sure that your texture is:

   a. projected. **b.** protected.

   c. protracted. **d.** stretched.

7.2 Modeling Directly from a Photo

The newest version of SketchUp includes a fantastic feature that allows you to model directly from photos. More specifically, you can use this feature, called Photo Match, to do the following:

▲ **Build a model based on a photograph:** If you have a good photograph (or multiple photographs) of the thing you want to model in SketchUp, Photo Match can help you set things up so that building your model is much easier.

▲ **Match your model view to a photograph:** Perhaps you have a model of a building and a photograph of the spot where the building will be constructed. You can use Photo Match to position your "camera" in SketchUp to be exactly where the real-life camera was when the photograph was taken. Then, you can create a composite image that shows what your building will look like in context.

Photo Match only works on photographs of objects with at least one pair of surfaces that are at right angles to each other. Luckily, this includes millions of things you might want to build. Still, if the thing you want to Photo Match is entirely round, or wavy, or even triangular, Photo Match won't work.

7.2.1 Understanding Colors in Photo Match

Like some of SketchUp's other features, Photo Match is more of a *method* than a tool: You use it to set things up, you model a bit, you use the Photo Match dialog box a bit, and so on. If you don't know the basics of modeling in SketchUp yet, you won't have any luck with Photo Match—it's really more of an intermediate-level feature, if such a thing exists.

Color Plate 10 shows what your screen might look like when you're in the throes of Photo Match. It's a bit daunting, but after you've used it once or twice, it's not so bad. This image is included in the color section of this book because Photo Match (at least at the beginning of the process) uses color as a critical part of its user interface. Specifically, the following elements of Photo Match's interface will show up in your modeling window:

▲ **Photograph:** The photograph you pick to create a new Photo Match shows up as a kind of background in your modeling window; it stays there as long as you don't use Orbit to change your view. To bring it back, click the Scene tab (at the top of your modeling window) labeled with the photograph's name.

▲ **Perspective bars:** These come in two pairs: one green and one red. You use them when you're setting up a new Photo Match by dragging their ends (grips) to line them up with *perpendicular* pairs of *parallel* edges in your photograph. For a clearer explanation of how this works, see the next section in this chapter.

▲ **Horizon line:** This is a yellow, horizontal bar that, in most cases, you won't have to use. It represents the horizon line in your model view, and as long as you placed the perspective bars correctly, it takes care of itself.

▲ **Vanishing point grips:** These are found at both ends of the horizon line, and once again, as long as you did a good job of setting up the perspective bars, you shouldn't have to touch them.

▲ **Axis origin:** This is the spot where the red, green, and blue axes meet. You position it yourself to tell SketchUp where the ground surface is.

▲ **Scale line/vertical axis:** Clicking and dragging this blue line lets you roughly scale your photograph by using the colored Photo Match grid lines. After you're done, you can always scale your model more accurately using the Tape Measure tool (check out Chapter 2 for more information on how to do this).

You also need to work with a few things that appear outside your modeling window:

▲ **Photo Match scene tab:** When you create a new Photo Match, you create a new scene, too (you can read all about scenes in Chapter 10). Clicking a Photo Match scene tab returns your view to the one you set up when you created (or edited) that Photo Match. It also makes that Photo Match's photograph reappear, which is handy if you've orbited into another view.

▲ **Match Photo dialog box.** This is Photo Match "mission control." It's where you can find almost all the controls you need for creating, editing, and working with your Photo Match.

7.2.2 Creating a New Photo Match

Setting up a new Photo Match is generally a step-by-step procedure. Whether you're building a new model using Photo Match or lining up an existing model with a photograph, you start by getting your modeling window ready to create a new Photo Match. How you do this depends on what you're trying to do:

▲ **Using a photograph to build a model:** If this is what you want to do, open a new SketchUp file and you're ready to go.

▲ **Lining up a model you've built already with a photograph:** This case requires you to reorient your view and then reposition your drawing axes before you're ready to create a new Photo Match.

Follow these steps to do this:

1. Orbit around until your model view more or less matches the camera position in your photograph.
2. Choose Tools⇨Axes.
3. Click to place your Axis Origin (where your colored axes meet) somewhere on your model. Try to choose a spot that's also visible in your photograph, if there is one.
4. Click somewhere in the lower-left quadrant of your modeling window to make sure that the red axis runs from the upper-left to the lower-right corner of your screen.
5. Watch your linear inferences (described in Chapter 2) to be sure that your repositioned red axis is parallel to some of the edges in your model.
6. Click somewhere in the upper-right quadrant of your modeling window to make sure that the blue axis is pointing up.

After your modeling window is set up, follow these steps to create a new Photo Match in your SketchUp file:

1. **Choose Camera⇨Match New Photo.** This opens the New Photo Match dialog box.
2. **In the dialog box that opens, select the image on your computer that you want to use as the basis for your Photo Match and click the Open button.** The dialog box closes, and you see the image you chose in your modeling window. You also see a jumble of colorful lines all over the place. Don't worry—it's all part of the Photo Match interface. Figure 7-13 gives you an idea of what this will look like, and Color Plate 10 shows the same image in color. (Note that Photo Match requires that you use certain kinds of photographs in order for it to work properly. See the

Figure 7-13

Scale Line/Vertical Axis   Perspective Bars   Photograph   Match Photo dialog box

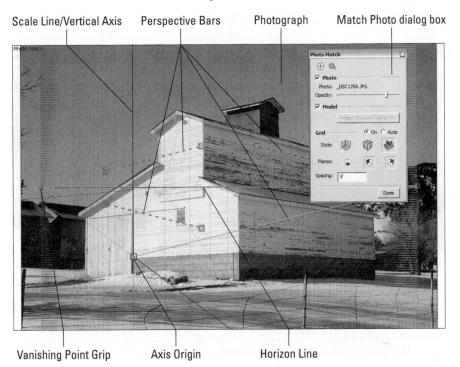

Vanishing Point Grip   Axis Origin   Horizon Line

The Photo Match interface includes your picture, plus lots of other things.

sidebar "Taking the Right Kind of Picture," later in this chapter, for pointers on what kinds of photos you can and can't use for Photo Match.)

3. **In the Match Photo dialog box (which should open automatically), choose the style that matches your photograph.** The style buttons in the Match Photo dialog box correspond to three different types of photographs you might be using. Choose Inside if your photo is an interior view, Above if it's an aerial shot, or Outside if your photo is an exterior view taken from a human vantage point. Figure 7-14 shows examples of each of these scenarios.

4. **Begin positioning the perspective bars, starting with the two green ones, by lining them up with any two parallel edges (the tops and bottoms of windows are good candidates, as are rooflines, tabletops, and ceiling tiles).** Take a deep breath—this is easier than it looks. You move each perspective bar one at a time, dragging each end into position separately. Color Plate 11 shows what this looks like in color. The following tips can help you get the bars positioned correctly:

   • Zoom in and out (using the scroll wheel on your mouse) to get a better view of your photograph while you're placing your perspective bars. The more accurate you can be, the better things will turn out.

Figure 7-14

Inside   Above   Outside

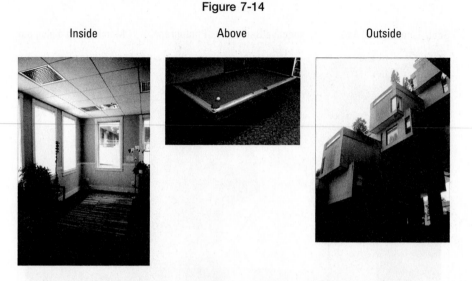

Choose the style that best describes your photograph's camera position.

- Pick nice, long edges in your photograph to match your bars to; you'll get better results that way.
- If you're working with an existing model, it might help to hide it while you place your perspective bars; sometimes it gets in the way. Just deselect the Model check box in the Match Photo dialog box to temporarily hide it.

5. **Line up the two red perspective bars with a different set of parallel edges—just be sure that these parallel edges are *perpendicular* (at right angles) to the first pair.** If they're not perpendicular, Photo Match doesn't work. Color Plate 12 shows what it looks like when all four perspective bars have been positioned properly.

6. **Drag the axis origin (the little square where the axes come together) to a place where your building touches the ground.** This is how you tell SketchUp where the ground plane is. Try to make sure your axis origin is right at the intersection of two perpendicular edges—this will make things easier later on. Color Plate 13 shows what this looks like. Note that if you're using Photo Match with an existing model, dragging the axis origin moves your model, too. Line up your model with the photograph so that the spot where you placed the axis origin is right on top of the corresponding spot in your photo. Don't worry about size right now; you'll deal with that in a moment.

7. **Roughly set the scale of your photograph by clicking and dragging anywhere on the blue scale/vertical axis line to zoom in or out until your**

photograph looks to be at about the right scale. You do this by first setting your grid spacing in the Match Photo dialog box and then using the grid lines in your modeling window to "eyeball" the size of your photo until it looks about right. Color Plate 14 shows an example where the grid spacing is set at 5 feet (the default setting). Because we know the barn in our photo is about 20 feet tall, we zoom in or out until it's about 4 grid lines high, because 4 times 5 feet is 20 feet. If you're trying to match an existing model to your photo, just zoom in or out until your model looks like it's the right size. You don't have to be very exact at this stage of the game. You can always scale your model later by using the Tape Measure tool.

8. **Click the Done button in the Match Photo dialog box.** When you click the Done button, you stop editing your Photo Match. All the colorful lines and grips disappear, and you're left with the photo you brought in and your model axes. It may have seemed complicated, but what you did was pretty simple: You used Photo Match to create a scene (scenes are described in Chapter 10) with a camera position and lens settings that match the ones used to take the picture that's on your screen. In effect, you're now "standing" exactly where the photographer was standing when the photograph was taken.

TAKING THE RIGHT KIND OF PICTURE

Your level of success with Photo Match depends to some extent on the photograph you start out with. Here are some tips for what kind of images are good candidates for Photo Match:

▲ **Cropped photos won't work.** Photo Match uses your photo's center point to help figure out its perspective; if you try to use a picture that's been *cropped* (in other words, some of the original shot has been cut away), the center point will be different, and things won't work properly.

▲ **Make sure that the edges of two perpendicular surfaces are visible in the shot.** You need to be able to see planes that are at right angles to each other to be able to use Photo Match.

▲ **Shoot at a 45-degree angle if you can.** Because of the way perspective works, you'll get a more accurate result if you use a photograph where you can see both perpendicular surfaces clearly. If one of them is sharply distorted, you'll have a harder time. The images in the following figure show what this means.

▲ **Watch out for lens distortion.** When you take a picture with a wide-angle lens, some of the straight lines in the image "bow" a little bit, depending on where they are in the frame. Try to use photos taken with a normal or telephoto lens: 50mm to 100mm is a good bet.

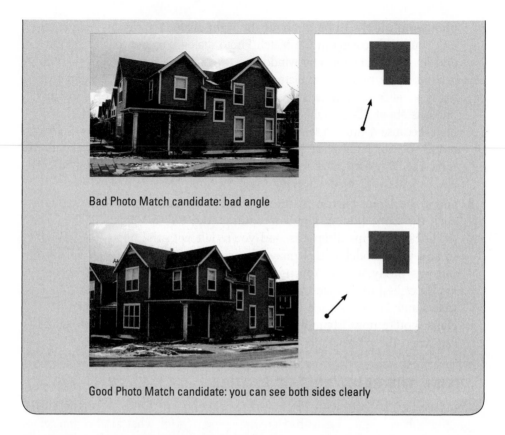

Bad Photo Match candidate: bad angle

Good Photo Match candidate: you can see both sides clearly

7.2.3 Modeling with Photo Match

Setting up a new Photo Match was just the first step. Now it's time to use SketchUp's modeling tools (with a little help from the Match Photo dialog box) to build a model based on the photograph you "matched." Here are a couple of the basic concepts to keep in mind when doing this:

▲ **It's not a linear process.** Building a model using a Photo Matched photo entails going between drawing edges, orbiting around, drawing some more edges, going back to your Photo Match scene, and drawing yet more edges. Every photo is different, so the ones you work with will present unique challenges that you'll (hopefully) have fun figuring out.

▲ **Don't forget the photo textures.** By far one of the best features of Photo Match is its ability to automatically photo-texture your model's faces using your photograph as "paint."

Follow these steps to start building a model with Photo Match:

1. **Click the Photo Match scene tab to make sure that you're lined up properly.** If you orbit away from the vantage point you set up with

Figure 7-15

Scene tab for this Photo Match

Clicking the scene tab for your Photo Match takes you back to that vantage point (and brings back your photograph).

Photo Match, you'll know it; your photograph will disappear. You can easily get back by clicking the scene tab for your Photo Match. It's labeled with the name of your photo, and it's at the top of your modeling window (see Figure 7-15).

2. **Trace one of the edges in your photograph with the Line tool.** Make sure that you're drawing in one of the three main directions: red, green, or blue. Color Plate 15 shows this in action. It's a good idea to start drawing at the axis origin; it'll help to keep you from getting confused.

3. **Keep tracing with the Line tool until you have a rectangular face.** The key here is to make sure that you keep watching the color of your edges as you draw. You always want to see your lines turn red, green, or blue when you're starting out. Have a look at Color Plate 16 to see what this looks like. Be careful not to orbit while you're drawing—if you do, repeat step 1 and keep going. You *can* zoom and pan all you want, though.

4. **Click the Project Textures from Photo button in the Match Photo dialog box.** Every time you do this, SketchUp paints the faces in your model with the photograph you used to create your Photo Match. The face you created in step 3 should now be photo-textured according to the image you used to model it. Orbit around and you'll see what this means (see Color Plate 17).

5. **Click the Photo Match scene tab to return to your Photo Match view.**

6. **Use SketchUp's modeling tools to continue to "trace" the photograph in three dimensions.** Here are some pointers for doing this successfully:

   • **Always start an edge at the end of an edge you've already drawn.** If you don't, your geometry won't make any sense, and you won't end up with what you expect.

   • **Never draw an edge in "midair."** This is basically the same as the previous point, but it bears repeating: If you don't draw edges based on other edges, you won't get good results.

   • **Orbit frequently to see what's going on.** You'll be surprised what you have sometimes—tracing a 2D image in 3D is tricky business. Get in the habit of orbiting around to check on things and draw certain edges. Click the Photo Match scene tab to return to the proper view.

   • **Use other tools (like Push/Pull and Offset) when appropriate.** Nothing prevents you from using the full complement of SketchUp's modeling tools when using Photo Match. However, using only Line and Eraser while drawing the basic skeleton of your model keeps things simple.

   • **Pay attention to the colors.** With a photograph as an underlay, it's a little harder to see what you're doing. But with Photo Match, watching to make sure that you're drawing the edge you intend to draw is critical.

   • **Draw angles by "connecting the dots."** If you need to trace an edge in your photo that doesn't line up with any of the colored axes (an angled roofline, for example), figure out where the endpoints are by drawing perpendicular edges and connecting them with an angled line. Color Plate 18 shows this in detail.

   • **If you want, keep pressing the Project Textures from Photo button to use the photograph to paint your model.** Of course, using Project Textures from Photo only works on faces that are visible in the photograph. For everything else, you need to use the Paint Bucket and the Texture Tweaker.

If you have more than one picture of the thing you want to model, you can use more than one Photo Match to help you build it. Just get as far as you can with the first Photo Match and then create a new one, using the geometry you created as an "existing building." Color Plate 19 shows the beginnings of a model of Habitat 67 in Montreal. Here, two pictures were used to create two Photo Matches in the same SketchUp file, which made it possible to build more of the model than could be seen in a single picture.

SELF-CHECK

1. With Photo Match, you can do the following:

   a. Build a model based on a photograph.

   b. Match your model view to a photograph.

   c. Position your camera in SketchUp to be exactly where the real-life camera was when the photo was taken.

   d. All of the above

2. The axis origin is:

   a. a yellow horizontal bar.

   b. where the red, green, and blue axes meet.

   c. a blue line.

   d. where the blue, yellow, and green axes meet.

3. When you click the _____ button, you stop editing your Photo Match.

4. You can use more than one Photo Match at a time. True or false?

SUMMARY

Using photos in your models expands your options and allows you to produce more accurate and realistic models. While it is not easy to paint with photographs or use Photo Match, the abilities these skills give you are well worth the effort of learning the techniques.

In this chapter, you painted faces in your model with photographs. You assessed the Texture Tweaker and applied it to your model. You modeled on top of photo-textured faces and also built a model from scratch with Photo Match. These skills will serve you well in your use of SketchUp.

KEY TERMS

Mapping	Painting surfaces with pictures using 3D software.
Move/Scale/Rotate/Shear/ Distort Texture mode	Mode to use when manipulating textures in SketchUp; also called Fixed Pin Mode.
Shearing	Action that keeps the top and bottom edges of an image parallel while making the image lean to the left or right.
Stretch Texture mode	Mode to use to edit a texture by stretching it to fit the face it is painted on. Also known as Free Pin Mode.

ASSESS YOUR UNDERSTANDING

Go to www.wiley.com/college/chopra to evaluate your knowledge of modeling with photographs.

Measure your learning by comparing pre-test and post-test results.

Summary Questions

1. With the _____, you can "paint" artwork on 3D prototypes or packaging designs.
2. Models to which you apply photo textures can be submitted to the 3D Warehouse. True or false?
3. Free Pin mode is also referred to as the _____ mode.
4. When you create a new Photo Match, you create a new _____.
5. The perspective bars come in two pairs: yellow and blue. True or false?
6. Modeling with Photo Match is a linear process. True or false?
7. The key to mapping photo textures to curved surfaces is to:
   (a) sample a flat surface.
   (b) line up a flat surface with the curved surface to which you want to apply the photo texture.
   (c) paint the curved surface with a texture.
   (d) paint the flat surface with a texture.

Applying This Chapter

1. What are three things you can do with the Texture Tweaker?
2. You have a photo that you want to add to your model of a house. List the steps you would take to add this photo to the faces of your model.
3. Why would you want to model on top of photo textures?
4. You want to create a new Photo Match in your SketchUp file. What steps do you take to do this and why?

Adding a Photo to a Model of a House

In SketchUp, create an exterior model of a real-life house in your neighborhood. Next, take a photo of the outside of that house, and use the Texture Tweaker to map this photo to the appropriate faces in your model.

Building a Model from Scratch

Take a photograph of a coffee table or other simple piece of furniture. Use Photo Match to build a model of the object in your photograph from scratch.

8

CHANGING YOUR MODEL'S APPEARANCE
Applying Styles

Starting Point

Go to www.wiley.com/college/chopra to assess your knowledge of using styles in SketchUp.
Determine where you need to concentrate your effort.

What You'll Learn in This Chapter

▲ When and where to use styles
▲ How to apply styles to your models
▲ Ways to make changes to existing styles
▲ How to create new styles
▲ Methods for saving the styles you create
▲ How to how make, use, and share entire styles libraries

After Studying This Chapter, You'll Be Able To

▲ Critique when you should and should not apply styles to a model
▲ Prepare a model that incorporates SketchUp's built-in styles
▲ Assess methods for making changes to pre-made styles
▲ Design new styles by mixing elements of one or more built-in styles
▲ Analyze different ways to save styles
▲ Construct styles libraries and share them with other SketchUp users

INTRODUCTION

This chapter provides a complete rundown of one of SketchUp's best features: styles. But what are styles? At the most basic level, **styles** are all about deciding how your geometry—all of your faces and edges—will actually look. For a better idea of what styles can do, refer to Color Plate 21.

Of course, with styles, as with many other parts of life, it is possible to get too much of a good thing. Thus, this chapter begins with a quick critique of when you should and should not apply styles to a model. Next, you'll learn how to prepare a model that incorporates SketchUp's built-in styles, as well as how to make changes to various elements of these pre-made styles. After that, you'll discover how to create your own styles by combining portions of styles that already exist. Finally, the chapter closes with an examination of how to save styles, construct entire styles libraries, and share your styles with other SketchUp users.

8.1 Choosing How and Where to Apply Styles

One important thing to remember about styles is that they're endless. With a million permutations of dozens of settings, you could quite literally spend all day altering the way your model looks. Thus, keeping one guiding question in mind—Does this setting help my model say what I want it to say?—will help you focus on what's important. There's no doubt styles are fun to use, but making them *useful* is the key to keeping them under control.

To make smart decisions about SketchUp styles, you should consider at least two factors when you're "styling" your model:

▲ **The subject of your model's "level of completeness":** For instance, you might consider reserving "sketchy" styles for models that are still evolving. The message this sends is "this isn't permanent/I'm open to suggestions/all of this can change if it has to." As your design gets closer to its final form, the appearance of your model should generally get less rough and more polished, and your styles should reflect this change. In this way, you can use styles to communicate how much input your audience can have and what decisions still need to be made.

▲ **How much your audience knows about design:** When it comes to how styles are perceived, there's a big difference between an architecture-school jury and a nondesigner client who's building a house for the first time. Design professionals are more experienced at understanding 3D objects from 2D representations, so they don't need as many visual "clues" to help them along. The essence of styles is really to provide these clues, so here's a rule of thumb: The more your audience knows about design, the simpler you should keep your styles.

Figure 8-1

Abusing styles is easy. Remember, a simpler model often has a greater effect.

Before you dive into styles, also remember that a little style goes a long way. No matter how tempting it is to go crazy with the styles settings, please resist the urge. Remember that the purpose of styles is to help your model communicate and *not* to make it look "pretty" or "cool." If the *style* of your work is getting noticed more than the content of your work, tone down your uses of styles. Figure 8-1 shows an example of going overboard with styles and then reining things in.

SELF-CHECK

1. Design professionals are experienced at understanding 3D objects from _____ representations.
2. A little style goes a long way. True or false?
3. Use of "sketchy" styles lets people know that your model is not open to suggestions and changes. True or false?

8.2 Applying Styles to Your Models

The easiest way to get started with styles is to apply the pre-made styles that come with SketchUp. You will find plenty of them, which is great, because seeing what's been done is the best way to see what's possible. In addition, as you read through this section of the chapter, you'll no doubt get ideas for your own styles, and that's where the fun begins.

Applying an existing SketchUp style to your model is a four-step process:

1. Choose Window⇨Styles to open the Styles dialog box.
2. Click the Select tab to make sure that you're looking at the Select pane.
3. Choose a styles library from the Styles Libraries drop-down list.
4. Click a style in the Styles window to apply it to your model.

This may come as a surprise, but it's not possible to view your model without any style at all. This is because styles are really just combinations of display settings. Some styles are fancier than others, but no matter what you do, you always have to have a style applied. If you want to get a relatively neutral view of your model, try choosing a style from among the selection provided in the Default Styles library.

One of the best things about SketchUp is that it offers so much pre-made content. Whether that content is styles, components, or materials, SketchUp comes with numerous examples to get you started. Figure 8-2 is a shot of the Styles Libraries drop-down list you'll see when SketchUp 6 is "new out of the box." As the figure shows, a variety of different styles are built right in to the software.

Here's what everything included in the Styles Libraries drop-down list does:

▲ **In Model:** The In Model library shows you all of the styles you've applied to your model. It keeps track of every style you've *ever* applied to the model, whether that style is still applied or not. Thus, to see a current list of styles in your SketchUp file, you must do the following:

1. Choose the In Model styles library to show a list of all styles you've applied to your model.

2. Click the Library Options flyout menu and choose Purge Unused to get rid of any styles that you aren't currently using.

▲ **Styles:** The name of this option is a little confusing, because it doesn't actually take you to a styles library. Instead, it provides a view of your Styles folder, which is the place on your computer that contains your styles libraries. If you look carefully, this list is the same one you see in the middle section of the Styles Libraries drop-down list. So why is it

Figure 8-2

The Styles Libraries drop-down list is where
you'll find all of your styles.

there? Having it readily accessible means that you can add libraries to your Styles folder from right inside SketchUp.

▲ **Assorted Styles:** Consider this library a sampler of effects that you can get with the styles settings. A couple of them are very useful, and some are just downright impressive. If you're ever trying to convince a friend to use SketchUp, head for this library of styles first.

▲ **Color Sets:** The styles in this library are different combinations of edge, face, and background colors. If you decide to depart from black and white, flip through this list to see whether you like any of these color combinations.

▲ **Default Styles:** With the exception of the first style in this library (which is the default style for all new SketchUp files you create), these styles are as minimal as it gets: white background, black edges, white-and-gray front-and-back faces, and no fancy edge effects. Consider using these styles to get back to a clean starting point for your models; it's usually easier to start simple and build from there.

▲ **Paper Watermarks:** Each of the styles in this library has a different **watermark,** or background. Using one of these makes it seem like your model is drawn on a particular kind of surface. Before using watermarks, however, it's usually best to think carefully about the message you're sending by presenting your digital model on a piece of "canvas."

▲ **Sketchy Edges:** The Sketchy Edges styles in SketchUp 6 are the result of more than a year's work on nonphotorealistic rendering. Basically, these styles involve using real hand-drawn lines instead of digital ones to render edges. The result is that you can make your models look more like manual sketches than ever before. As mentioned earlier in the chapter, you can use Sketchy Edges styles to convey any of the following ideas:

• That your design is in process

• That your model is a proposal and not a finished product

• That you welcome feedback in any and all forms

▲ **Straight Lines:** All the styles in the Straight Lines library are variations on a very simple theme: The edges in these styles are rendered with progressively thicker, perfectly straight lines with square corners. You won't get a technical pen effect with these styles, though; they still make for a relatively rough rendering of your model.

RUNNING FROM REALISM: NPR STYLES

In the world of 3D modeling software, the trend in recent years has been toward *photorealism.* Today, the standard of perfection is usually how close a model comes to looking like a photograph, and in many cases, that standard has been met.

But what about models of buildings or other things that aren't completely finished? Perhaps you're an architect who's designing a house for a client. If you aren't sure what kind of tile you'll end up using on your roof, how are you supposed to make a photorealistic rendering of it? You *could* just go ahead and throw any old tile up there as a placeholder, but that could backfire. Your client could hate the tile and decide not to hire you without ever telling you why, and all because of something you didn't even choose.

What you need is a way to show only the decisions you've made so far, and that is exactly why architects, interior designers and other such professionals make sketches and doodles instead of photorealistic renderings. When you're designing, decisions don't all happen at once, so you need to be able to add detail as your design evolves. Sketching allows you to do that because it offers a continuum from "cartoony" to photographic, with everything in between. The following figure is an illustration of this.

Programs like SketchUp offer what's called *NPR*, or *nonphotorealistic rendering*, as a way to solve this problem for people who design in 3D. Instead of dedicating processor power to making representations that look like photographs, the people who created SketchUp went in the opposite direction—they made a tool that lets you make drawings that are useful throughout the design process. And because SketchUp's NPR engine works in real time, you can make changes on the fly, in front of your audience.

1. The In Model library shows you the styles that you last used on your model. True or false?

2. The Sketchy Edges styles in SketchUp 6 are the result of _____ rendering.

3. A watermark is a background. True or false?

4. In which of the following libraries are the styles different combinations of edge, face, and background colors?

   a. Styles library   **b.** Colors library library

   c. Texture   **d.** Color Sets library

8.3 Making Changes to Styles

If you're handy in the kitchen, you've probably heard the saying that cooking is an art and baking is a science. Cooking allows you to experiment—adding a little of this and a dash of that won't destroy your final result. When it comes to baking, however, taking liberties with a recipe can be a train wreck. Luckily, in SketchUp, making your own styles has a lot more in common with cooking than it does with baking. Go ahead and experiment; you can't do any irreversible harm. Playing with styles doesn't affect the geometry in your model in any way, and because styles are just combinations of settings, you can always go back to the way things were before you started.

To experiment with styles, you need to understand the Edit and Mix panes of the Styles dialog box, along with their corresponding tabs. In the remainder of this chapter, you'll learn about the various settings in these two panes. Note, however, that of the panes in the Styles dialog box, Edit is definitely the most complex of the group. Because you'll find so many controls and settings here, SketchUp's designers broke the Edit pane up into five tabs. Here's a short description of each:

▲ **Edge:** The Edge tab contains all the controls that affect the appearance of edges in your model. This includes their visibility, their color, and other special effects that you can apply.

▲ **Face:** This tab controls the appearance of faces in your model, including their default colors, their visibility, and their transparency.

▲ **Background:** The Background tab has controls for setting the color and visibility of the background, the sky, and the ground plane in your model.

▲ **Watermark:** New for SketchUp 6, watermarks are images that you can use as backgrounds or as overlays. The Watermark tab gives you control over these.

▲ **Modeling:** The Modeling tab provides controls for setting the color and visibility of numerous elements in your model, including section planes and guides.

The following sections explain each tab in detail and provide suggestions for using some of the settings.

8.3.1 Tweaking Edge Settings

The Edge tab is tricky because it changes ever so slightly depending on what kind of style you currently have applied to your model. Specifically, NPR styles have different settings than regular, non-NPR styles. Remember, NPR stands for nonphotorealistic rendering, wherein SketchUp uses digitized, hand-drawn lines to render the edges in your model. All the styles in the Sketchy Edges library,

Figure 8-3

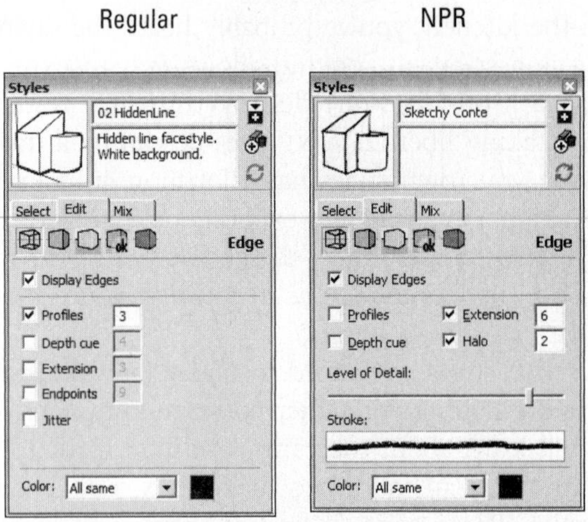

Regular   NPR

The appearance of the Edge tab is slightly different
when using regular styles as opposed to NPR styles.

as well as all but two—Google Earth and Standard CAD—in the Assorted Styles library, are NPR styles. Because you can create your own styles based on existing ones, all the styles you create using Edge settings from one of these NPR styles will be an NPR style, too.

Figure 8-3 shows both the regular and the NPR versions of the Edge tab, which you open by choosing Window⇨Styles, selecting the Edit tab, and then clicking the box icon on the far left.

Display Edges

Most of the time, you'll be viewing your model with Edges turned on. Because SketchUp is an edge-based modeler, it's hard to do any work with them turned off! However, Figure 8-4 shows what a model looks like when this option has been turned off (among other options, which are explained in the following sections). Some cases in which you might not want to display edges include the following:

▲ If you're trying to make your model look as photorealistic as possible.
▲ If you plan to export your model to a program that doesn't display
   edges, and you want to preview how it will look.

Profiles

Selecting the Profiles check box tells SketchUp to use a thicker line for edges that outline shapes in your model. If you're using a non-NPR style, you can type

Figure 8-4

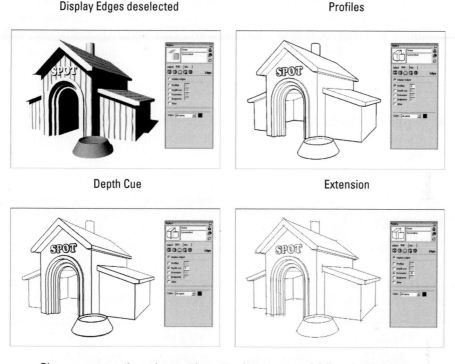

Choose among the edge settings to give your model the desired look,
from realistic to sketchy.

in the thickness of the profile lines you'd like to see. Like all the values in this tab, profile thickness is measured in pixels.

Using profile lines is a standard drawing convention that's been around for a long time. You use these lines primarily to add depth to views of your model by making things in the foreground seem to "pop out." Refer to Figure 8-4 to see what a difference profiles can make.

Depth Cue

Using different line thicknesses to convey depth is another popular drawing convention. With this method, objects closest to the viewer are drawn with the thickest lines, whereas the most distant things in the scene are drawn with the thinnest lines. The number of line thicknesses varies according to taste, but it's usually somewhere between 3 and 6.

Depth Cue is SketchUp's automatic way of letting you apply this effect to your models. When its check box is selected, Depth Cue dynamically assigns line thicknesses (draftspersons call them "line weights") according to how far away from you things are in your model. In non-NPR styles, you can tell SketchUp how many line weights you want. The number you type in is both your desired number of line weights *and* the thickness of the fattest line SketchUp will use. Consider using a maximum line weight of 5 or 6 pixels, and note that SketchUp will always make the thinnest lines 1 pixel thick because that's the finest line your computer monitor can display. Figure 8-4 shows a model with Depth Cue set to 5 pixels.

Here are some guidelines for using Depth Cue:

▲ **Depth Cue looks best on pure line drawings.** When you're using color and materials, there's usually plenty of other information in your view that can supply "depth."

IN A FOG?

If you're looking for something else to provide a sense of depth in your model views, look no further than the Fog feature. New for this version of SketchUp, Fog does exactly what it says—it makes your model look like it's enshrouded in fog (see figure below). Follow these three steps to let the fog roll into your model:

1. Choose Window➪Fog to open the Fog dialog box.
2. Select the Display Fog check box to turn on the fog effect.
3. Experiment with the controls until you like what you see.

Unfortunately, the process of controlling how Fog looks is not particularly scientific. You just play around with the sliders until you have the amount of fog you want. However, just in case you absolutely need to know, here's what the sliders do:

▲ **Top slider (0%):** This controls the point in space at which Fog begins to appear in your model. When it's all the way to the right (toward infinity), you can't see any fog.

▲ **Bottom slider (100%):** This controls the point in space at which the fog is completely opaque. As you move the slider from left to right, you're moving the "completely invisible" point farther away.

▲ **Use Depth Cue on large objects, like architecture or furniture.** In general, people who draw things like buildings, heavy machinery, or large industrial objects use the multiple-line-weights method, and people who draw smaller things like blenders and staplers use profile lines.

▲ **When using Depth Cue, consider turning off Profiles.** These two drawing conventions don't always work well together, so consider using only one or the other.

Extension

This tells SketchUp to extend the edges in your model by the number of pixels you type into the Extension text box (see Figure 8-4). You should note that Extension is measured in pixels, which means that your extensions will appear shorter when you're zoomed in close to your model, and longer when you're zoomed out.

Extending edges is a great way to make your model look sketchy, even if you're not using one of the NPR styles. You can use edge extensions to do the following:

▲ Indicate that your model is a quick sketch and not something you slaved over.

▲ Show that dimensions and proportions are still up for debate.

Endpoints

When drafting by hand, many people like to begin and end their lines by grinding their pencil into the paper, just to give their drawings a little flourish. Emphasizing endpoints with a darker, thicker line or dot is a way of making your drawings stand out more. For an example of this effect, see Figure 8-5.

SketchUp lets you achieve this effect with the Endpoints feature, which is available only in non-NPR styles. When using this feature, simply type in the

Figure 8-5

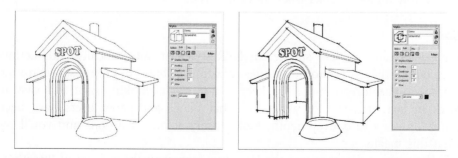

Endpoints give your model more visual impact. Used with Extension and Profiles or Depth Cue, they look even better.

Figure 8-6

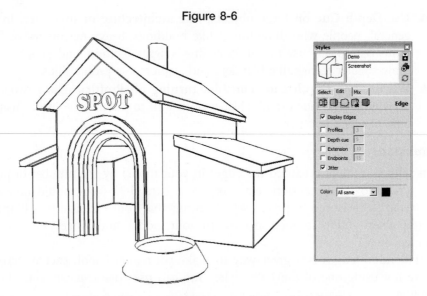

Turn on Jitter to randomize your lines automatically.

number of pixels you'd like SketchUp to emphasize at the end of each edge segment. As you can see in Figure 8-5, Endpoints can be especially effective when used in combination with Extension and Depth Cue.

Jitter

Most people either love Jitter or hate it. When it's on (it's only available for non-NPR styles), SketchUp "jitters" your edges, making it look like you rendered your model with a somewhat shaky hand. Before NPR styles came along, Jitter was the best way to make your model look hand-drawn. Use it if you want to, but be careful—not everyone will approve of your decision. You might consider using it in the same situations where you decide to use Extensions. Figure 8-6 shows how a model looks when Jitter is turned on.

Halo

What Halo does is very simple: In NPR styles, it automatically ends certain lines before they run into other ones, creating a "halo" of empty space around objects in the foreground. This keeps your model looking neat and easy to read. In fact, this is a drawing trick that pencil-and-paper users have been using for years to convey depth; look closely at most cartoons and you'll see what this means.

The number you type into the Halo box represents the amount of "breathing room" SketchUp gives your edges. The unit of measure is pixels, but there's no

Figure 8-7

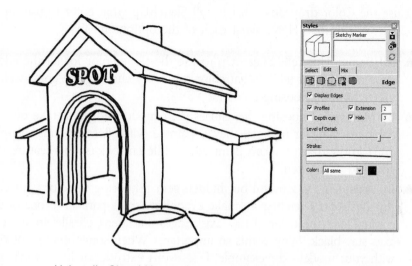

Halo tells SketchUp to give your edges their space.

real science to it; just play with the number until things look right to you. Take a look at Figure 8-7 to see Halo in full effect.

Level of Detail

When you slide the Level of Detail controller (which only appears when you've applied an NPR style) back and forth, you're effectively telling SketchUp how busy you want your model to look. The farther to the right you slide it, the more of your edges SketchUp displays. You should experiment with this setting to see what looks best for your model. Figure 8-8 shows what happens when you slide the Level of Detail controller from left to right.

Figure 8-8

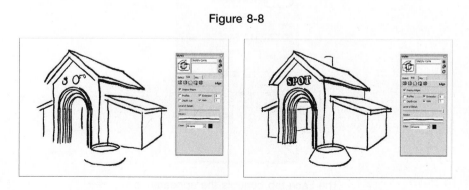

Level of Detail controls how many of your edges SketchUp draws.

Color

You use the Color drop-down list to tell SketchUp what color to use for all the edges in your model. Here's what each of the options means:

▲ **All Same:** This tells SketchUp to use the same color for all the edges in your model. You tell it what color to use by clicking the color well on the right and choosing a color.

▲ **By Material:** Choosing this causes your model's edges to take on the color of whatever material they're painted with. Because most people don't know that they can paint edges different colors, this feature doesn't get used very often.

▲ **By Axis:** This is a useful but hidden gem. Choosing to color your edges "by axis" tells SketchUp to make everything that's parallel to one of the colored axes the color of that axis. Edges that aren't parallel to any of the axes stay black. Why is this so important? When something is not right with your model—for example, faces won't extrude, or lines won't "sink in"—switching your edge colors to by axis is the first thing you should do. You'll be surprised to see how many of your edges aren't what they seem.

8.3.2 Changing the Way Faces Look

The Face tab of the Styles dialog box is very simple—at least compared to the Edge tab. This area of the SketchUp user interface controls the appearance of faces, or surfaces, in your model. From here, you can affect their color, visibility, and translucency. Figure 8-9 shows the Face tab, which you can open by choosing Window

Figure 8-9

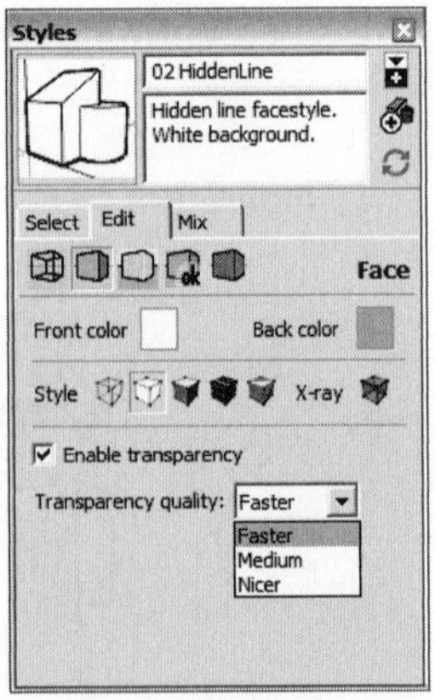

The Face tab controls the appearance
of your model's faces.

Drawing axes   Sky

Color Plate 1: The colored drawing axes are the key to how SketchUp works (Chapter 2).

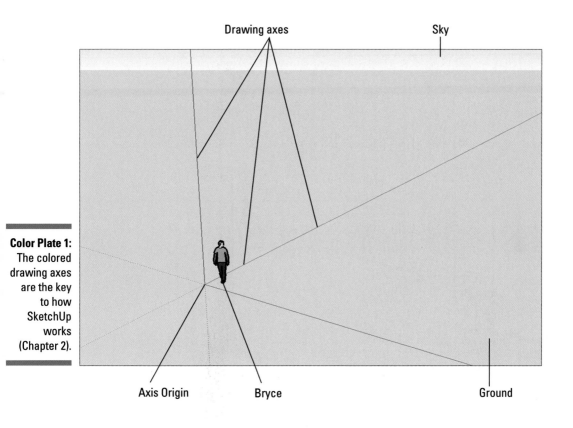

Axis Origin   Bryce   Ground

Drawing in the red direction   Moving in the blue direction

Color Plate 2: Going in the right color direction (Chapter 2).

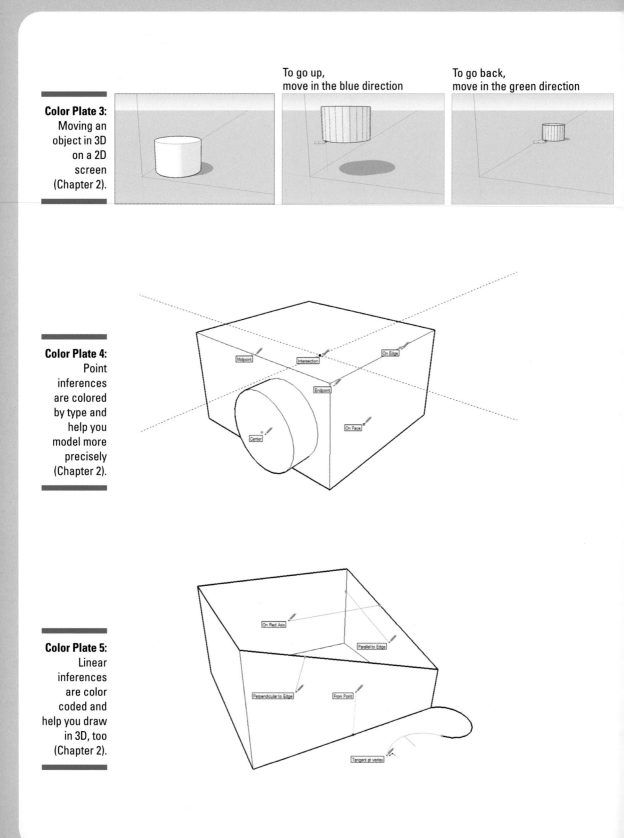

Color Plate 3:
Moving an object in 3D on a 2D screen (Chapter 2).

To go up, move in the blue direction

To go back, move in the green direction

Color Plate 4:
Point inferences are colored by type and help you model more precisely (Chapter 2).

Midpoint
Intersection
On Edge
Endpoint
On Face
Center

Color Plate 5:
Linear inferences are color coded and help you draw in 3D, too (Chapter 2).

On Red Axis
Parallel to Edge
Perpendicular to Edge
From Point
Tangent at vertex

Hold down Shift to lock
yourself in the blue direction

Hover over the point to which
you want to infer; then click to
end your edge

Color Plate 6:
Locking an
inference
helps you
draw in the
right direction
(Chapter 2).

Hover over the center point
inference

Move slowly away in the red
direction

Color Plate 7:
Encouraging
an inference
(Chapter 2).

Color Plate 8:
Orbit (spin)
your model to
paint all the
faces
(Chapter 3).

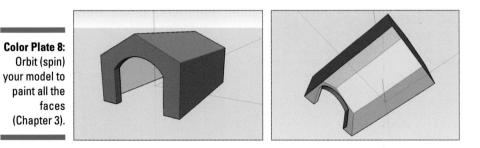

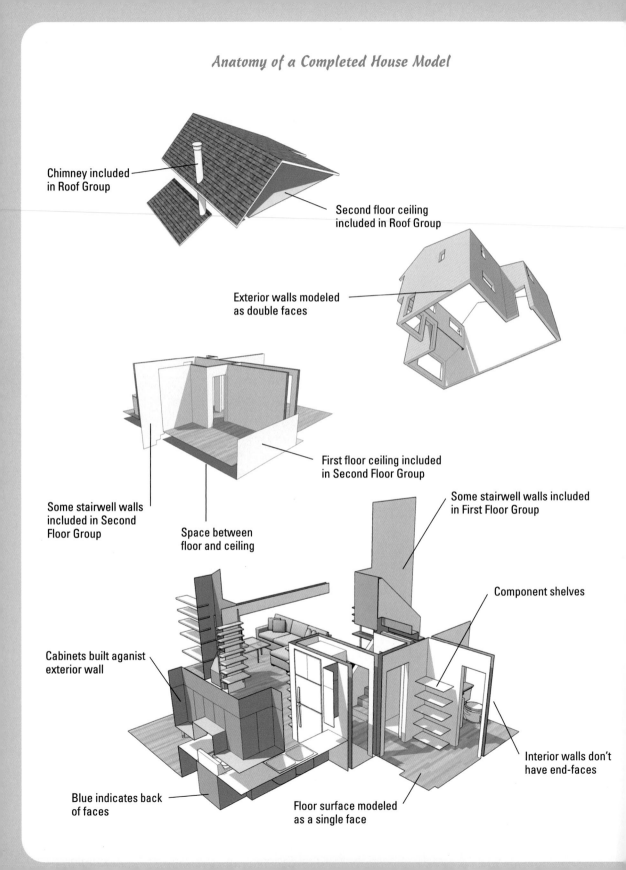

Anatomy of a Completed House Model

Chimney included in Roof Group

Second floor ceiling included in Roof Group

Exterior walls modeled as double faces

First floor ceiling included in Second Floor Group

Some stairwell walls included in First Floor Group

Some stairwell walls included in Second Floor Group

Space between floor and ceiling

Component shelves

Cabinets built aganist exterior wall

Interior walls don't have end-faces

Blue indicates back of faces

Floor surface modeled as a single face

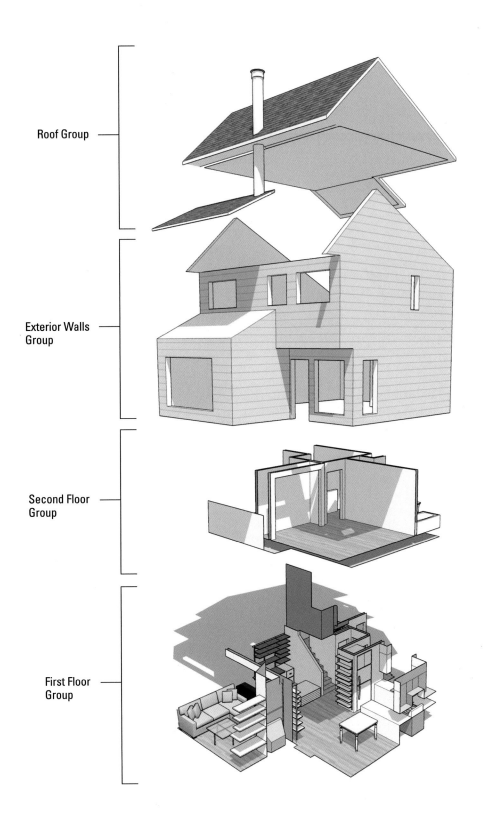

Roof Group

Exterior Walls
Group

Second Floor
Group

First Floor
Group

Building a Circular Stair with Components

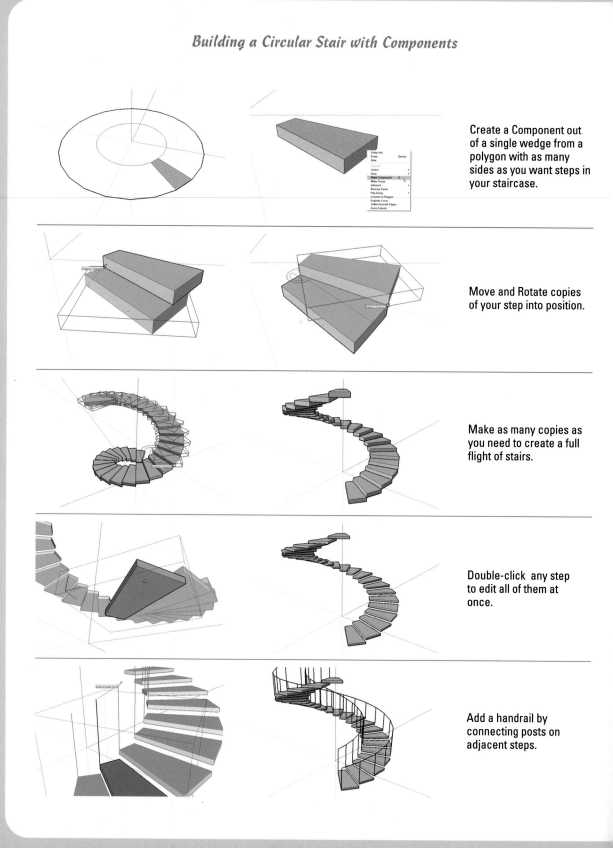

Create a Component out of a single wedge from a polygon with as many sides as you want steps in your staircase.

Move and Rotate copies of your step into position.

Make as many copies as you need to create a full flight of stairs.

Double-click any step to edit all of them at once.

Add a handrail by connecting posts on adjacent steps.

Building a Simple Boat with Mirrored Components and the Scale Tool

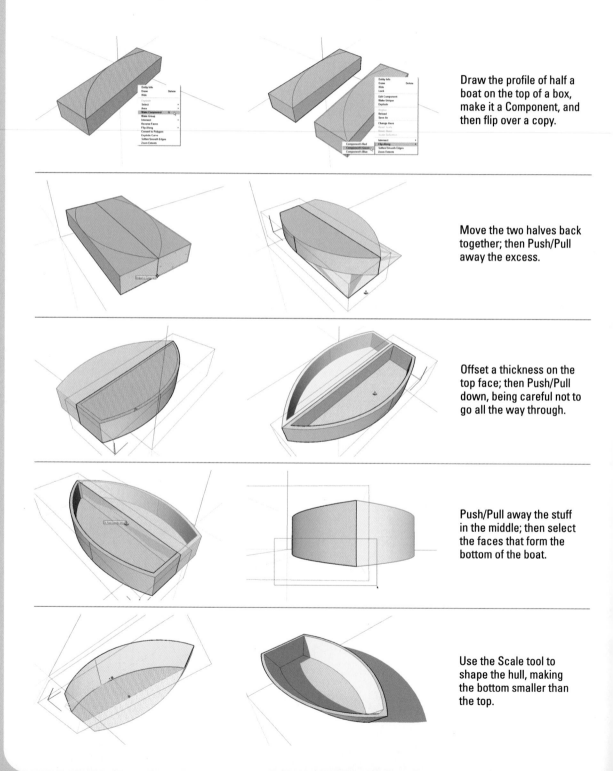

Draw the profile of half a boat on the top of a box, make it a Component, and then flip over a copy.

Move the two halves back together; then Push/Pull away the excess.

Offset a thickness on the top face; then Push/Pull down, being careful not to go all the way through.

Push/Pull away the stuff in the middle; then select the faces that form the bottom of the boat.

Use the Scale tool to shape the hull, making the bottom smaller than the top.

Color Plate 9: A transparent version of your image, along with four colored pins, appears when editing textures (Chapter 7).

Perspective Bars Photograph Photo Match dialog box

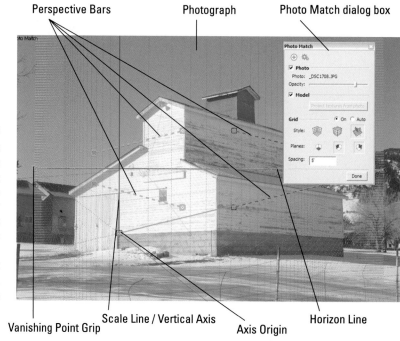

Color Plate 10: The Photo Match interface shows your picture, plus tools to create a model from it (Chapter 7).

Vanishing Point Grip Scale Line / Vertical Axis Axis Origin Horizon Line

Line up each Perspective bar with an edge in your photograph

Color Plate 11:
Lining up the
Perspective
bars
(Chapter 7).

Perspective bars lined up

Color Plate 12:
All four
Perspective
bars, properly
lined up with
edges in the
picture
(Chapter 7).

Move the Axis Origin to a logical place

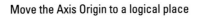

Color Plate 13:
Placing the
Axis Origin in
a good spot
(Chapter 7).

4 grid lines high (approx.)

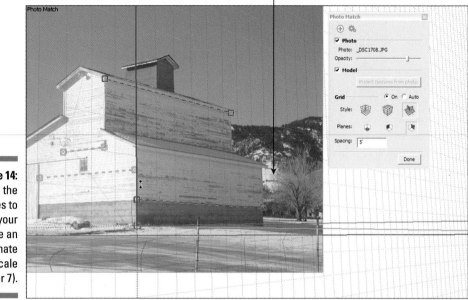

Color Plate 14:
Using the
grid lines to
give your
picture an
approximate
scale
(Chapter 7).

Draw an edge from here...   ...to here

Color Plate 15:
Tracing an
edge in one of
the three main
directions
(Chapter 7).

Color Plate 16: Creating a face to match a surface in the photograph (Chapter 7).

Color Plate 17: Projecting textures from a picture onto a face; then orbiting around to see the result (Chapter 7).

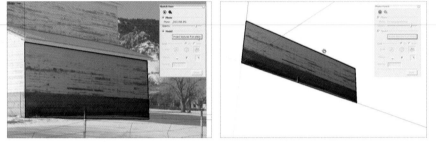

Draw this diagonal edge by connecting the dots

Edge

Color Plate 18: Using the endpoints of perpendicular edges to draw a diagonal (Chapter 7).

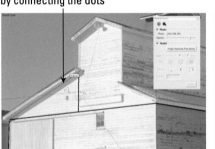 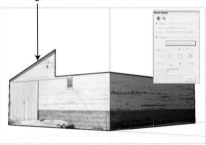

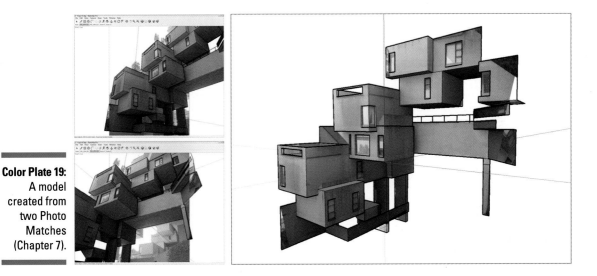

This edge should be blue

Their color tells me these edges aren't right

This edge should be green

Styles

04 Shaded with texture:

Default colors, shaded with textures facestyle. White

Select | Edit | Mix

Edge

☑ Display Edges

☑ Profiles   3
☐ Depth cue   4
☐ Extension   3
☐ Endpoints   9
☐ Jitter

Color: All same

All same
By material
By axis

Color Plate 21:
Use Styles to
make your
model look
any way
you want
(Chapter 9).

⇨Styles, selecting the Edit tab, and clicking the box icon that's second from the left. The following sections describe each of the elements of this tab in detail.

Choosing Default Colors for Front and Back Faces

In SketchUp, every face you create has a back and a front. You can choose what colors to use by default for all new faces you create by clicking the Front and Back color wells and picking a color. Try sticking with neutral tones for your defaults; you can always paint individual faces later on.

Sometimes when you're modeling in SketchUp, a face will be turned "inside out." This happens for lots of reasons (which all have to do with programming), but all you need to know is how to flip them back. Follow these steps to flip a face around so that the right side is showing:

1. Select the face you want to flip.
2. Right-click and choose Reverse Faces.

Knowing which face is the front and which is the back is especially important if you plan to export your model to another program. Some of these, like 3D Studio Max, use the distinction between front and back to make important distinctions about what to display. In these cases, showing the wrong side of a face can end up producing unexpected results.

Choosing a Face Style

Even though these are called Face styles, they have nothing to do with styles. Face styles might as well be called Face modes because that's what they are: different modes for viewing the faces in your model. You can flip between them as much as you like without affecting your geometry. All they do is change the way SketchUp draws your model on the screen. Each one has its purpose, and all are shown in Figure 8-10:

▲ **Wireframe:** In Wireframe mode, your faces are invisible. Because you can't see them, you can't affect them. Only your edges are visible, which makes this mode handy for doing two things:

- When you're selecting edges, switch to Wireframe mode to make sure that you've selected what you meant to select. Because no faces block your view, this is the best way to make sure that you're getting only what you want.

- After you've used Intersect with Model, you'll usually have stray edges in your model. Wireframe is the quickest way to erase them because you can see what you're doing. See Chapter 4 for details on Intersect with Model.

▲ **Hidden Line:** Hidden Line mode displays all your faces using whatever color you're using for the background; it's as simple as that. If you're

Figure 8-10

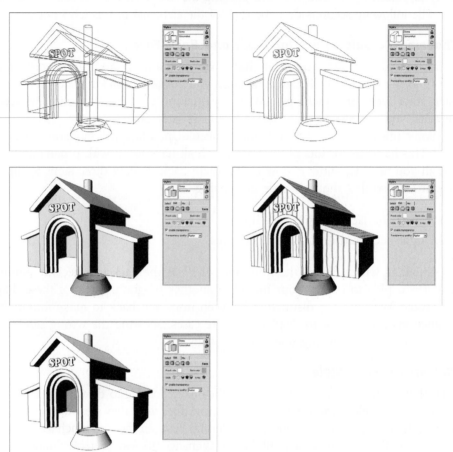

Use Face styles to change the way your faces appear.

trying to make a clean, black-and-white line drawing that looks like a technical illustration, make your background white. Consider using Hidden Line mode with Extensions and either Profiles or Depth Cue, depending on your subject matter. Shadows look great, too.

▲ **Shaded:** This Face style displays your faces with colors on them. Faces painted with a solid color appear that color. Faces to which you've added textures are shown with a color that best approximates their overall color. For example, if your texture has a lot of brown in it, SketchUp will pick a brown and use that. For models with a lot of textures, switching to Shaded mode can speed up orbiting, zooming, and otherwise navigating around. Thus, unless you absolutely need to see the textures you've applied to your faces, you might consider staying in Shaded mode as you're working on your model.

▲ **Shaded with Textures:** Use Shaded with Textures when you want to see your model with textures visible. Because this mode puts a lot of strain on your computer, it can also be the slowest mode to work in. Thus, you might think about turning it on only when you're working on a small model, or when you need to see the textures you've applied to your faces. Obviously, if you're going for a photorealistic effect, this is the mode to choose. It's also the mode that best approximates what your model will look like when (and if) you export it to Google Earth.

▲ **Display Shaded Using All Same:** When you want to quickly give your model a simplified color scheme, use this Face style; it uses your default front and back face colors to paint your model. Think of it as a compromise between the Hidden Line and Shaded modes—color, but not too much color.

Seeing Through Walls with X-Ray Mode

X-Ray mode is a simple on-off proposition; you use it when you want to be able to see through faces by making them translucent (see Figure 8-11). Unlike using translucent materials on some of your faces (like glass and water), flipping on X-Ray lets you see through *all* your faces. For instance, you might use it when you want to see through a wall or a floor to show what's behind it. If you're in a plan (overhead) view, it's also a great way to demonstrate how a floor level relates to the one below it.

Figure 8-11

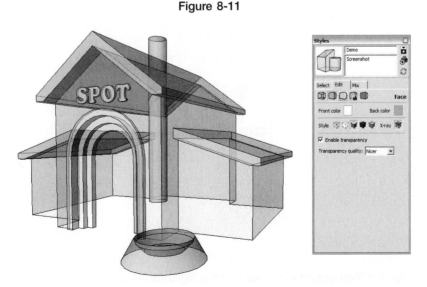

Turn on X-Ray to see through everything in your model.

Adjusting Transparency

Because how well SketchUp runs on your computer depends on what's in your model, and because displaying transparency (as in translucent materials) is an especially taxing operation for SketchUp and your computer to handle, you can decide how to display translucent materials:

▲ **Enable transparency:** Deselect this check box to display translucent materials as opaque. You should turn off transparency to speed Sketch-Up's performance if you find that it's slowed down.

▲ **Transparency quality:** If you decide to display transparency, you can further fine-tune your system's performance by telling SketchUp how to render that transparency.

Thus, you have the choice of better performance, nicer graphics, or an average of the two. Which one you choose depends on the size and complexity of your model, the speed of your computer, and the nature of your audience.

8.3.3 Setting Up the Background

In the Background tab of the Styles dialog box, you choose colors and decide whether you want to be able to see a sky and a ground plane. Check out Figure 8-12 to get a view of the Background tab, along with an idea of how this works. To open these options in your own copy of SketchUp, choose Window⇨Styles, select the Edit tab, and click the middle icon at the top of the tab.

Figure 8-12

Use the Background tab to turn on the sky and the ground and to choose colors for these elements.

You have the following options on the Background tab:

▲ **Background:** Click the color well to choose a color for the background of your model. If you're going for a blueprint or blackboard effect, pick a dark color and then change your edge color to white in the Edge tab.

▲ **Sky:** If you turn on the Sky feature, SketchUp paints everything above the horizon with any color you want; click the color well to choose one. The sky is rendered as a **gradient** that gets lighter as it gets closer to the horizon. This makes things slightly more realistic, but the real purpose of the Sky tool is to provide a point of reference for your model. In 3D views of big things like architecture, it's nice to be able to see the horizon. Another reason for turning on the sky is to "set the mood"—keep in mind that the sky isn't always blue. Play around and see what you like.

▲ **Ground:** Just like the Sky tool, you can choose to display a ground plane in your model. You can pick the color by clicking the color well, and you can even choose to have the ground be translucent. Before turning on this feature, note that it can be very hard to find a ground color that looks good, no matter what you're building. Also note that you can't dig into the earth to make sunken spaces (like courtyards) with the ground turned on. Instead of turning on this feature, consider making your own ground planes with faces and edges. It's more flexible, and it often looks better. If you find that you need to see the ground, or that you want to, you can choose to *not* be able to see it when you're below it, which is a useful option. Just deselect the Show Ground from Below check box to make this happen.

8.3.4 Working with Watermarks

Watermarks, which are brand-new for SketchUp 6, are much easier to understand if you don't think about them as actual watermarks. They're not anything like watermarks, in fact—they're much more useful. Think of them this way: Watermarks are graphics that you can apply either *behind* or *in front of* your model to produce certain effects. Here are a few of the things you can do with SketchUp watermarks:

▲ Simulate a paper texture, just like the styles in the Paper Watermarks library.

▲ Apply a permanent logo or other graphic to your model view.

▲ Layer a translucent or cutout image in the foreground to simulate looking through a frosted window or binoculars.

▲ Add a photographic background to create a unique model setting.

Understanding the Watermark Controls

Figure 8-13 shows the Watermark tab of the Styles dialog box. Here's a brief introduction to what the controls do:

▲ **Display Watermarks:** Displaying watermarks is an all-or-nothing proposition; if you have more than one, you can turn them all on or all off.

▲ **Add Watermark:** Click this button to add a new watermark to your model view. You're asked to select an image file on your computer, and you're then taken through the Choose Watermark procedure to set things up.

▲ **Remove Watermark:** Select the watermark you want to delete and then click this button to remove it.

▲ **Edit Watermark:** Selecting a watermark and then clicking this button opens the Edit Watermark dialog box, where you can change your watermark's properties. Editing a watermark is similar to creating a new one, which is described in the next section.

▲ **Watermark List:** This list shows all your watermarks in relation to something called Model Space, which is the space occupied by your model. All watermarks are either in front of or behind your model, making them overlays or underlays, respectively.

▲ **Move Up or Down:** Use these buttons to change the "stacking" order of the watermarks in your model view. Select the watermark you want to move in the list and then click one of these buttons to move it up or down in the order.

Figure 8-13

The Watermark tab, new for SketchUp 6.

Adding a Watermark

Watermarks are by no means simple, but working with them is. Follow these steps to add a watermark to your model view:

1. **Click the Add Watermark button to begin the process of adding a watermark.** The Open dialog box appears.

2. **Find the image you want to use as a watermark and then click the Open button to open the first Choose Watermark dialog box (see Figure 8-14).** You can use any of these graphics file formats: TIFF, JPEG, PNG, and GIF.

3. **Type in a name for your watermark in the Name box.**

4. **Choose whether you want your new watermark to be in the background or in the foreground as an overlay, and then click the Next button.**

5. **Decide whether to use brightness for transparency.** Selecting this check box tells SketchUp to make your watermark transparent, which kind of simulates a real watermark. *How* transparent each part becomes is based on how bright it is. White is the brightest color, so anything white in your watermark becomes completely transparent. Things that are black turn your background color, and everything in between turns a shade of your background color.

6. **Adjust the amount that your watermark blends with what's behind it, and click the Next button.** In this case, Blend is really just a synonym for Transparency. By sliding the Blend slider back and forth, you can adjust the transparency of your watermark. Blend comes in handy for making paper textures because that process involves using the same watermark twice: once as an overlay and once as an underlay. The overlay version gets "blended" in so that your model appears to be drawn on top of it. To see how this works, apply one of the Paper Texture styles to your model, and then edit each of the watermarks to check out its settings.

7. **Decide how you want your watermark to be displayed and then click the Finish button.** You have three choices for how SketchUp can display

Figure 8-14

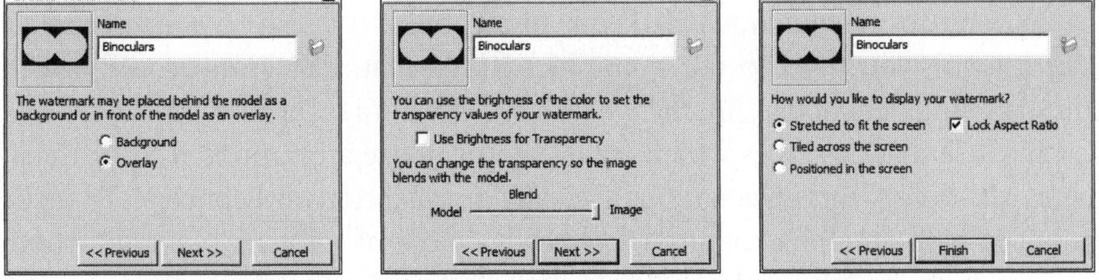

The Choose Watermark series of dialog boxes.

Figure 8-15

Stretched to fit

Tiled

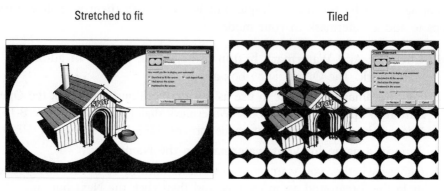

Positioned in lower right

You can display watermarks stretched, tiled, or positioned in your modeling window.

your watermark: stretched to fit the entire window, tiled across the window, and positioned in the window. Each is illustrated in Figure 8-15. If you select Stretched to Fit the Entire Window, be sure to select the Locked Aspect Ratio check box if your watermark is a logo that you don't want to appear distorted.

FOR EXAMPLE

Watermarks and Alpha Channels

If you want to make a watermark out of an image that isn't a solid rectangle (like a logo), you need to use a graphics file format, like PNG or GIF, which supports alpha channels. An *alpha channel* is an extra layer of information in a graphics file that describes which areas of your image are supposed to be transparent. It sounds complicated, but it's really a straightforward concept. To make an image with an alpha channel, you need a piece of software like Photoshop. Try searching for "alpha channels" on Google for more information.

Editing a Watermark

You can edit any watermark in your SketchUp file at any time. Follow these simple steps to edit a watermark:

1. **Select the watermark you want to edit in the Watermark list.** You can find the Watermark list on the Watermark tab, in the Edit pane of the Styles dialog box.

2. **Click the Edit Watermark button to open the Edit Watermark dialog box.** The Edit Watermark button looks like a couple of small gears; it's right next to the Add and Delete Watermark buttons above the Watermark list.

3. **Use the controls in the Edit Watermark dialog box and click the OK button when you're done.** For a complete description of the controls in this dialog box, see the previous section in this chapter.

8.3.5 Tweaking Modeling Settings

All you need to know about the controls in the Modeling tab (see Figure 8-16) of the Styles dialog box is that there's not much to know. You use these controls to adjust the color and visibility of all the elements of your model that aren't geometry. To open these options, choose Window⇨Styles, select the Edit tab, and click the box icon on the far right, at the top of the tab.

The controls found on the Modeling tab work as follows:

▲ **Controls followed by color wells:** Click the wells to change the color of that type of element.

Figure 8-16

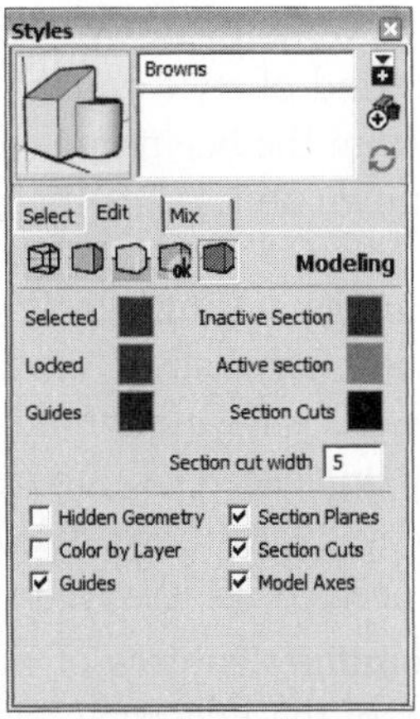

The controls on the Modeling tab are every bit as simple as they look.

▲ **Section cut width:** This refers to the thickness of the lines, in pixels, that make up the section cut when you're using a section plane. For more about this, have a look at the information on cutting sections in Chapter 10.

▲ **Controls preceded by check boxes:** Use these to control the visibility of that type of element in your model. Three of these controls bear special mention because they can be a bit confusing:

- **Color by Layer:** This tells SketchUp to color your geometry according to the colors you've set up in the Layers dialog box.

- **Section Planes:** This refers to the section plane objects that you use to cut sections. They're gray with four arrows on their corners.

- **Section Cuts:** Unlike section planes, this setting controls the visibility of the section cut effect itself. With this deselected, your section planes won't appear to be cutting anything.

SELF-CHECK

1. In Wireframe mode, your faces are _____.
2. Flipping on X-Ray lets you see through all your faces. True or false?
3. When does the Level of Detail controller appear?
4. In SketchUp, the ground is rendered as a gradient that gets lighter as it gets closer to the horizon. True or false?

8.4 Mixing Styles to Create New Ones

In SketchUp, you can make new styles in two very different ways; which way you choose depends on what kind of style you're trying to make. If you've been reading through this chapter from the beginning, you're already familiar with the first method of creating your own styles, but the second will be new to you:

▲ **Use the Edit pane to change settings until you like what you see.** This method is handy and quick, especially if you already know what all the controls do. You can *almost always* use the Edit pane to make your style adjustments. There's only one exception: It's impossible to switch from a regular to an NPR (Sketchy Edges) Edge style (or vice versa) using only the Edit pane; for that, you need to use the next method of creating new styles.

▲ **Use the Mix pane to combine features of multiple styles.** Instead of working through the tabs of the Edit pane, flipping controls on and off, sliding sliders, and picking colors, the Mix pane lets you build new styles by dropping existing ones onto special "category" wells. This is the only way you can switch a style's edge settings between NPR and non-NPR lines.

NPR refers to the styles in the Assorted Styles and Sketchy Edges Styles libraries. These nonphotorealistic rendering styles use scanned, hand-drawn lines to draw the edges in your model. You *can't* make your own NPR styles from lines you draw and scan in yourself, but you can adapt the existing ones by editing them and saving the changed versions as new styles.

The basic principle of the Mix pane is that you use the *secondary selection pane* (which appears automatically when you choose the Mix pane) to choose styles from which you want to sample certain settings. The secondary selection pane is the lower part of the Styles dialog box, from the word "Select" down, as you can see in Figure 8-17. You drag (on a Mac) or sample (in Windows) these styles onto one or more of the *category wells* to apply the settings you want to your current style. The category wells are the five long "Settings" rectangles in the middle of the Styles dialog box, as shown in Figure 8-17.

Follow these steps to change a style using the Mix pane:

1. **Choose Window⇨Styles and click the Mix tab in the Styles dialog box to open the Mix pane.** As part of the Mix pane, the secondary

Figure 8-17

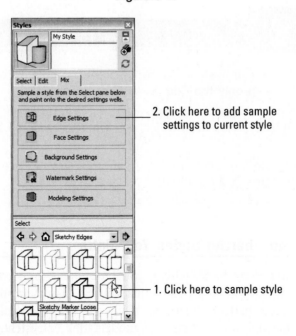

Drag and drop styles to update the style you're working on.

selection pane opens at the bottom of the dialog box. This provides you with a way to view your styles without having to switch from the Mix pane to the Select one.

2. **Find the style you want to sample from in the secondary selection pane. You can call this your source style.** Say that you're working on a new style, and you want your edges to look just like those in the Sketchy Marker Loose style that came with SketchUp. In this example, choose the Sketchy Edges library from the Styles Libraries drop-down list, where you'll find the Sketchy Marker Loose style.

3. **If you're using Windows, click the source style from the Styles list in the secondary selection pane to sample it and then click the category well that corresponds to the style setting you want to apply. If you're using a Mac, drag your source style from the Styles list in the secondary selection pane to the category well that corresponds to the style setting you want to apply.** In this case, sample the Sketchy Marker Loose style from the secondary selection pane and drop it on the Edge Settings Category well because you want the edge settings from that style to be applied to the style you're working on.

4. **To save your style after you're done adding all the various elements, see the following section.**

SELF-CHECK

1. In SketchUp, it's impossible to switch from a regular to an NPR Edge style using only the Edit pane. True or false?

2. The basic principle of the Mix pane is that you use the _____ pane to choose styles from which you want to sample certain settings.

3. When using the Mix pane, the _____ are the five long "Settings" rectangles in the middle of the Styles dialog box.

8.5 Saving and Sharing Styles You Make

As you're working along in SketchUp, you'll want to create your own styles. You'll also want to save those styles so that you can use them in other models. In addition, if you're part of a team, it's likely that everyone will want to have access to the same styles so that all your models look consistent. The following sections describe how to do all of these things, and more.

8.5.1 Saving the Styles You've Made

When it comes to creating your own styles, you can approach things in two different ways. Each of these ways gets its own button (see Figure 8-18):

▲ **Create new style:** Clicking this button creates a new style with the settings you currently have active. When you create a new style, it shows up in your In Model library of styles and is saved with your model. The Create button can be found in the upper-right corner of the dialog box, and looks like a couple of objects with a "+" sign on it.

▲ **Update style with changes:** This button updates the current style with any settings changes you've made in the Edit or Mix panes. If you want to modify an existing style without creating a new one, this is the way to go. You can find the Update button right below the Create button in the upper-right corner of the dialog box; it looks like two arrows chasing each other in a circle.

Updating an Existing Style

To make adjustments to a style in your model, you need to update it. Follow these steps to update a style:

1. **Apply the style you want to update to your model.** If you need help with this, follow the steps in the section, "Applying Styles to Your Models," earlier in this chapter.

Figure 8-18

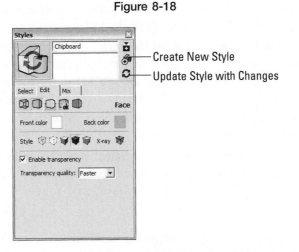

The Update and Create buttons in the Styles dialog box allow you to create new styles in different ways.

2. **Use the controls in the Edit pane to make changes to the style.** For a complete description of how to modify a style, check out the section "Making Changes to Styles," earlier in this chapter.

3. **Click the Update Style with Changes button in the Styles dialog box to update the style with your changes.**

You use the Update Style with Changes button to rename existing styles, too. Just type the new name into the Name box (at the top of the Styles dialog box), press Enter, and then click the Update button.

When you update a style, only the copy of the style that's saved with your model is updated. You aren't altering the copy of the style that shows up in every new SketchUp file you create.

Creating a New Style

Creating a new style adds it to your In Model library of styles, which means that you can come back and apply it to your model anytime you like. Follow these steps to create a new style:

1. **Click the Create New Style button in the Styles dialog box.** This duplicates the style that was applied to your model before you clicked the Create New Style button. Your new style appears in your In Model library as [*name of the original style*]1.

2. **Use the controls in the Edit pane to set up your style the way you want.** Have a look at the section "Making Changes to Styles," earlier in this chapter, for a rundown on using the controls in the Edit pane of the Styles dialog box. Frequently, you'll want to make a new style *after* you've already made changes to an existing one. If you want to create a new style that reflects modifications you've already made, just switch steps 1 and 2 around.

3. **Use the Name box (at the top of the Styles dialog box) to give your new style a name and press Enter.** If you want, you can also give your new style a description in the Description box, though you might want to wait until later. After all, it's hard to describe something you haven't made yet.

4. **Click the Update button.** This updates your new style with all the changes you made in steps 2 and 3.

5. **Check the In Model library in the Select pane to make sure that your new style is there.** Click the In Model button (which looks like a little house) to see your In Model Styles library. Your new style should appear alphabetically in the list.

If a bunch of styles exist in your In Model library that you aren't using anymore and you want to clean things up, right-click the Library Options flyout menu and choose Purge Unused. This gets rid of any styles that aren't currently applied to any scenes in your model. Have a look at Chapter 10 to find out more about scenes.

Remember, creating a new style *doesn't* automatically make it available for use in other SketchUp files. To find out how to do this, have a look the section "Sharing Styles with Other Models," later in this chapter.

SELF-CHECK

1. Clicking the Create button creates a new style with the settings you currently have active. True or false?

2. When you update a style, only the copy of the style that's saved with your model is updated. True or false?

3. Creating a new style adds it to your _____ library of styles, which means that you can come back and apply it to your model anytime you like.

4. To get rid of styles that aren't currently applied to any scenes in your model, right-click the Library Options flyout menu and choose _____.

8.6 Working with Style Library Options

After you've updated or created a style, you'll probably want to make that style available for use in other SketchUp models. To make this happen, you need to understand styles libraries: how to make them, how to use them, and how to share them with other people. This section explores your many library options; the next section explains how to save and share a library for yourself or on a network.

To see how you can use libraries to manage your styles, take a closer look at the Library Options flyout menu in the Select pane of the Styles dialog box (click the arrow icon to the right of the Libraries drop-down list). On that menu, you see the following options:

▲ **Open or Create a Library (Windows users):** Lets you either choose a library that already exists or make a new one. Whichever you do, the library you end up with is added to your Libraries drop-down list.

▲ **Open an Existing Library (Mac users):** Lets you choose an existing styles library from anywhere on your computer or network. A styles library isn't a special kind of file; it's any folder that contains one or more styles. You can keep your styles libraries anywhere you want on your computer or network.

▲ **Create a New Library (Mac users):** Lets you create a new styles library anywhere on your computer or network. Because libraries are really just folders, this is a nifty shortcut for creating a new folder without having to leave SketchUp. After you've created a new library, you can put styles in it. Select the Add to Favorites check box in the Add New Library dialog box to automatically add your new library to the Libraries drop-down list.

▲ **Save Library As:** Allows you to save copies of the styles in your In Model library to a location on your computer or network. If you don't see this option, make sure that your In Model library is selected in the Libraries drop-down list.

▲ **Add Library to Favorites:** Adds the currently selected library to the Favorites section of the Libraries drop-down list. Your Favorite Styles libraries are available in every SketchUp model you're working on, which makes this a great way to gather together libraries that might exist any-where on your computer or network.

▲ **Remove Library from Favorites:** Pops open a dialog box that lets you choose which libraries to remove from the Favorites section of your Libraries drop-down list.

▲ **Thumbnails and List View:** Allows you to view your styles in a number of different ways. List view is particularly important if you have styles with subtle differences that don't show up in the Preview Thumbnail view.

▲ **Get More:** Opens a web browser window and takes you to a place on the Internet where you can download more styles. You need to be online for this option to work.

8.6.1 Creating and Sharing a Library for the Styles You Make

Follow these steps to create a library to contain your styles:

1. **Choose Window➪Styles to open the Styles dialog box.**
2. **Click the Select tab to make sure that you're looking at the Select pane.**
3. **Click the Library Options flyout menu and choose Create a New Library.** This opens the Add New Library dialog box.
4. **Navigate to the folder on your computer or network where you would like to create your library.** You can locate your new library anywhere you like, but it's usually best to put it in the same folder as the other styles libraries on your computer:
   • **Windows:** C:/Program Files/Google/Google SketchUp 6/Styles
   • **Mac:** Hard Drive/Library/Application Support/Google SketchUp 6/SketchUp/ Styles
5. **Click Make New Folder if you're on a Windows computer, or New Folder if you're on a Mac.** The new folder you create will become your new library.

6. **Type in a name for your new library.**
7. **If you're on a Mac, make sure that the Add to Favorites check box is checked.**
8. **Click the Save button.** The Add New Library dialog box closes, and your library is added to the Favorites section of the Libraries drop-down list. It will be there in every SketchUp model you open on this computer.

8.6.2 Sharing Styles with Other Models

Follow these steps to make a style available for use in other SketchUp files:

1. **Choose Window⇨Styles, and in the Style dialog box that appears, click the Select tab.**
2. **Click the In Model button to display your In Model library.** The In Model button looks like a small house. The In Model library contains all the styles you've used in your model, including the ones you've created.
3. **Click the Show Secondary Selection Pane button.** When you click this button, which looks like a black-and-white rectangle and is in the upper-right corner of the Styles dialog box, a second copy of the Select pane pops out of the bottom of the Styles dialog box (see Figure 8-19). You

Figure 8-19

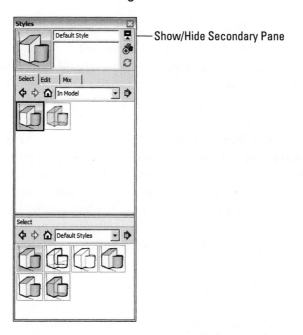

Use the secondary selection pane to manage your styles without leaving SketchUp.

Figure 8-20

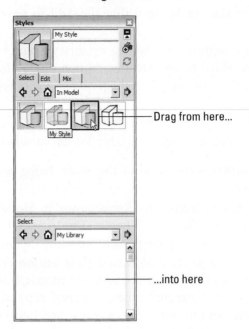

Drag from here...

...into here

Drag your style from the top Styles list to the bottom one.

use this pane to drag and drop styles between folders on your computer, which makes it easier to keep them organized.

4. **In the secondary selection pane, choose the library to which you want to add your style.** If you've created a library specifically for the styles you make, choose that one, or you can pick any of the libraries in the Libraries drop-down list.

5. **Drag your style from the In Model styles list to the Styles list in the secondary selection pane (see Figure 8-20).** By dragging and dropping your style from the upper list to the lower one, you're making it available to anyone who has access to that library. This means that you can use it in other SketchUp models you build on your computer. To share it with other members of your team, copy your style to a library somewhere where other people can get to it, such as on a network.

1. The Get More button on the Library Options menu allows you to view your styles in a number of different ways. True or false?

2. It's usually best to put a new styles library in the same folder as the other styles libraries on your computer. True or false?

3. To share it with other members of your team, copy your style to a _____ somewhere where other people can get to it.

4. The _____ button looks like a black-and-white rectangle and is in the upper-right corner of the Styles dialog box.

SUMMARY

Within SketchUp, styles determine how the geometry of your models—both their edges and their faces—appears. This chapter explored various instances in which you should and should not apply styles to a model. It showed you how to prepare a model that uses SketchUp's built-in styles, and it explained how to make changes to these existing styles. Next, the chapter demonstrated how to create your own styles by combining portions of styles that already exist, and it closed with a look at how to save styles and create and share style libraries. Understanding the various methods described in this chapter will not only help you use SketchUp more efficiently, but it will also allow you to create models that have even greater visual appeal.

KEY TERMS

Gradient	A gradual change in color over a given distance. For instance, in SketchUp, the sky is rendered as a gradient that gets lighter as it gets closer to the horizon.
Style	A collection of settings that determines how the geometry appears in a given SketchUp model.
Watermark	A graphic element that can be applied either behind or in front of a model to produce certain effects.

ASSESS YOUR UNDERSTANDING

Go to www.wiley.com/college/chopra to evaluate your knowledge of using styles in SketchUp.

Measure your learning by comparing pre-test and post-test results.

Summary Questions

1. Design professionals are more experienced at understanding 3D objects from 2D representations, so they expect additional visual "clues" in a model. True or false?

2. It's not possible to view a model without any style at all. True or false?

3. Typically, you should reserve "sketchy" styles for models that are:

   (a) closed to audience input.

   (b) still evolving.

   (c) in their final form.

   (d) required to be highly accurate.

4. Consider the _____ library a sampler of the effects that you can get with the styles settings.

5. Which of the following is **not** one of the tabs on the Edit pane?

   (a) Watermark

   (b) Face

   (c) Background

   (d) Foreground

6. The _____ tab on the Edit pane is tricky because it changes slightly depending on whether you're using NPR or non-NPR styles.

7. In SketchUp, use _____ to layer a translucent or cutout image in the foreground to simulate looking through a frosted window or binoculars.

8. The controls on which of the following tabs of the Styles dialog box allow you to adjust the color and visibility of all the elements of your model that aren't geometry?

   (a) Modeling

   (b) Edges

   (c) Watermark

   (d) Background

9. The _____ pane allows you to build new styles by dropping existing ones onto special category wells.

   (a) Edge

   (b) Mix

(c) Edit

(d) NPR

10. When you create a new style, it shows up in your In Model library of styles and is saved with your model. True or false?

11. Creating a new style automatically makes it available for use in other SketchUp files. True or false?

12. Your Favorite Styles libraries are available:

(a) only in models that you designate as "favorites."

(b) only in models that you create from scratch.

(c) in every SketchUp model you're working on.

(d) to all users on your network.

13. In the Library Options flyout menu, _____ view is particularly important if you have styles with subtle differences that don't show up in the Preview Thumbnail view.

(a) Existing Library

(b) Favorites

(c) Get More

(d) List

Applying This Chapter

1. In general, when should you consider toning down your use of elaborate styles within a model?

2. What are some reasons you might opt to use nonphotorealistic rendering when creating a model?

3. Describe a few situations in which you might not want to display edges in a model.

4. What are some of the Styles settings you can select (or deselect) to make SketchUp run more efficiently on your computer?

5. In what two ways can you make new styles using SketchUp? Describe each method.

6. How can you get rid of styles that aren't currently applied to any of the scenes in your model?

7. What are the basic steps for making a style available for use in other SketchUp files?

YOU TRY IT

Experiment with Your Model

Using the model of a house that you have already created, add the following effects and save each as a new model:

- Jitter
- Halo
- Transparency
- Change face styles

If you do not already have a model of a house, create a model of a simple doghouse and experiment with the effects listed above. Save each version of the doghouse as a different model.

Create a New Style

Experiment with combining elements of existing styles. Create a new style that you like and that looks good when applied to your model. Give your new style a name and save it for use with other models you create.

9

WORKING WITH LIGHT AND SHADOW
Adding Realism to Models

Starting Point

Go to www.wiley.com/college/chopra to assess your knowledge of working with light and shadow.
Determine where you need to concentrate your effort.

What You'll Learn in This Chapter

▲ What the Shadows dialog box is
▲ Why shadows are important to models
▲ What information is needed to create accurate shadows
▲ What a simple shadow animation looks like

After Studying This Chapter, You'll Be Able To

▲ Assess how to use the Shadows dialog box
▲ Evaluate how shadows make models look more realistic
▲ Create and display accurate shadows in your model
▲ Create a simple shadow animation

INTRODUCTION

The ability to cast shadows is one of the most impressive features in SketchUp. Displaying shadows is an easy operation—it's a matter of clicking a single button—and the Shadows feature offers lots of ways to make your models look more realistic, more accurate, and more readable.

Typically, you add shadows to a SketchUp drawing for two key reasons:

▲ **To display or print a model in a more realistic way:** Turning on shadows adds depth and realism and gives your model an added level of complexity that makes it look like you worked harder than you really did.

▲ **To study the effect of the sun on what you've built (or plan to build) in a specific geographic location:** Shadow studies are an integral part of the design of any built object. If you're making a sunroom, you need to know that the sun is actually going to hit it, no? You can use SketchUp to show exactly how the sun will affect your creation, at every time of day, on every day of the year.

This chapter starts with a brief description of how all the controls work, without going into much detail about choosing one setting over another. You will assess how to use the Shadows dialog box. You will also evaluate how shadows make models look more realistic. The middle portions are devoted to running through each of the above scenarios and using the controls to make SketchUp do exactly what you want it to. In the last part of the chapter, you'll dive into some more advanced material—how to animate your shadows to see how they change over time. By the end of this chapter, you will be able to create and display accurate shadows in your model and create a simple shadow animation.

9.1 Discovering SketchUp's Shadow Settings

The basic thing to understand about shadows in SketchUp is that, just like in real life, they're controlled by changing the position of the sun. If SketchUp were another kind of program, you might have to type in information about azimuths and angles, but luckily, it's not. Because the sun moves in exactly the same way every year, you just pick a date and time, and SketchUp automatically displays the correct shadows by figuring out where the sun should be.

Using shadows in SketchUp is something you can figure out without fear of altering your model. Turning on shadows and adjusting them can never do anything to your model except change the way it's displayed. Nothing you've built can be affected in any way, so feel free to experiment with shadow settings.

You do all these simple maneuvers in the Shadow Settings dialog box, shown in Figure 9-1. The sections that follow introduce how the controls work so that you can apply them to your model.

Figure 9-1

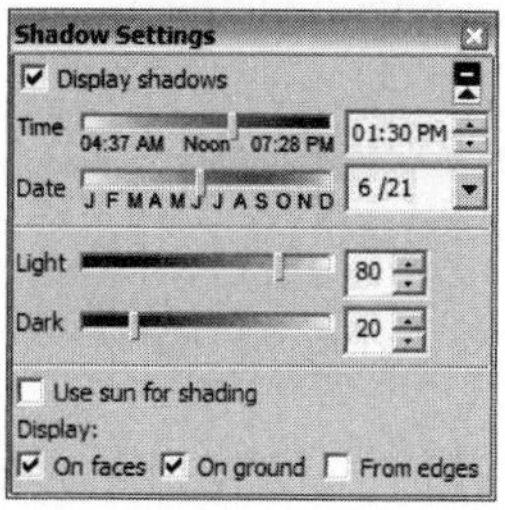

The Shadow Settings dialog box.

9.1.1 Turning On the Sun

Shadows aren't on by default, so the first thing you need to know about applying shadows is how to turn them on. Follow these simple steps:

1. **Choose Window⇨Shadows to display the Shadow Settings dialog box.**
2. **At the top of the dialog box, select the Display Shadows check box.** Clicking it "turns on" the sun in SketchUp, casting shadows throughout your model.

9.1.2 Setting a Shadow's Time and Date

The Shadow Settings dialog box has time and date controls, which you use to change the position of the SketchUp "sun." The time and date you choose, in turn, controls the appearance of shadows in your model:

▲ **Setting the time:** Move the Time slider back and forth, or type a time into the box on the right. Use a colon (:) to separate the hours from the minutes, and type in **AM** or **PM** if you're using 12-hour time. Notice the little times at each end of the slider? These represent sunrise and sunset for the day of the year you've set in the Date control, described in the next point.

▲ **Setting the date:** Just like the time of day, you set the day of the year by moving the Date slider back and forth, or by typing in a date in the box on the right. Use a forward slash (/) to separate the month from the day, entering the month first. If you slide the Date control back and forth, notice that the sunrise and sunset times change in the Time control.

To toggle the extra shadow controls open or closed, click the triangular Expand button in the upper-right corner of the Shadow Settings dialog box.

9.1.3 Choosing Where Shadows Are Displayed

The Display check boxes in the Shadow Settings dialog box enable you to control *where* shadows are cast. Depending on your model, you may want to toggle these on or off. Figure 9-2 shows shadows only on faces (top), only on the ground (middle), and from the edges of the model (bottom):

▲ **On Faces:** Deselecting the On Faces check box means that shadows will not be cast on faces in your model. This is on by default, and should

Figure 9-2

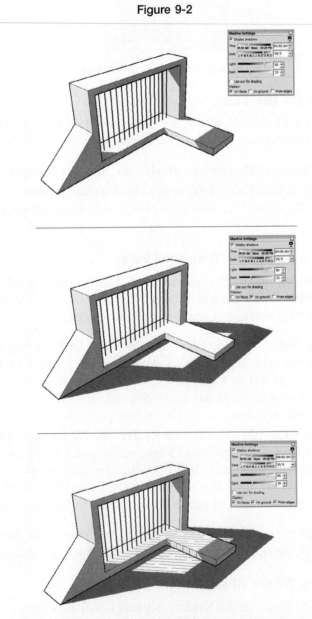

Shadows on faces, on the ground, and from edges.

probably be left on, unless you only want to cast shadows on the ground.

▲ **On Ground:** Deselecting the On Ground check box causes shadows not to be cast on the ground plane. Again, this is on by default, but sometimes you'll want to turn it off. A prime example of this is when something you're building extends underground.

▲ **From Edges:** Selecting the From Edges check box tells SketchUp to allow edges to cast shadows. This applies to single edges that are not associated with faces—things like ropes, poles, and sticks are often modeled with edges like these.

FOR EXAMPLE

Controlling Contrast

You can use the Shadow Settings dialog box to control the overall contrast in your model view, as shown in Figure 9-3 in the next section. The Light and Dark sliders seem simple, but it's not immediately obvious to most people how they work. Most of the time, you'll want to leave these settings the way they are, but here's what they do, just in case you want to work with them:

▲ **The Light slider controls the lightness of surfaces that are not in shadow.** Sliding it all the way to the left is like a solar eclipse—everything looks like it's in the shade. The default setting for Light is 80.

▲ **The Dark slider controls the darkness of shadows cast both on surfaces and on the ground.** Sliding it all the way to the right is like having no shadows. The default setting for Darkness is 20.

The Use Sun for Shading check box is confusing because it doesn't actually control shadows, even though it's in the Shadow Settings dialog box. It does affect the appearance of your model, however:

▲ **When it's selected, you see more contrast in your model view.** That's because SketchUp is lighting surfaces as if shadows are turned on, regardless of whether they are.

▲ **When it's deselected, things look flatter.** You should deselect this check box when you're working with photos mapped onto faces; doing so makes it easier to see what you're doing. Select the Use Sun for Shading check box again when you're ready to present your work.

SELF-CHECK

1. Adding shadows enables you to display or print a model in a more _____ way.
2. SketchUp shadows are controlled by the changing position of the sun. True or false?
3. You can change the position of the SketchUp sun with the _____ _____.
4. Selecting the On Ground check box causes shadows not to be cast on the ground plane. True or false?

9.2 Using Shadows to Add Depth and Realism

Shadows in SketchUp are easy to apply and to adjust. The previous sections dealt with the basic controls in the Shadow Settings dialog box. The following sections show how to use those controls to add depth, realism, and nuance to your models.

There are several situations when you'll need to use shadows to make your drawings read better; most of them fit into one of the following categories:

▲ **Indoor scenes:** The sun is the only source of lighting that SketchUp has, so any shadows you use in interior views have to come from it.

▲ **Objects that aren't in any particular location:** For things like cars and furniture, it doesn't matter that the shadows are geographically accurate; all that matters it that they help make your model look good.

▲ **2D views:** Without shadows, it's next to impossible to read depth in 2D views of 3D space.

9.2.1 Lighting Indoor Spaces

Adding shadows to interior views presents an interesting problem: There are no lights besides the sun in SketchUp, so how can you make anything look realistic? With a ceiling in your room, everything's dark. If you leave off the ceiling, however, your model doesn't look right. A few techniques can solve this problem:

▲ **Decrease the darkness of the shadows.** Sliding the Dark slider to the right brightens your view considerably. You'll still be able to see the

Figure 9-3

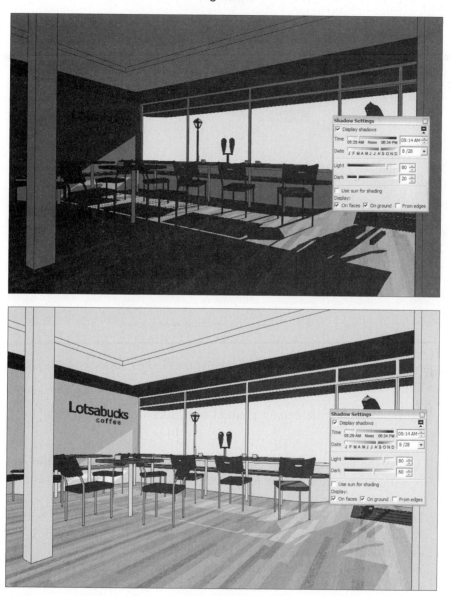

Brighten the room by decreasing the Dark setting.

shadows cast by the sun coming through windows and other openings. Figure 9-3 illustrates this.

▲ **Make an impossible ceiling.** As long as you haven't modeled anything on top of the interior you're planning to show, you can tell the ceiling

Figure 9-4

Tell the ceiling not to cast a shadow.

not to cast a shadow. That way, sunlight will shine directly onto your furniture, casting complex shadows.

Figure 9-4 shows the ceiling method in action; follow these steps to do it yourself:

1. **Adjust the settings in the Shadow Settings dialog box until the sun is shining through one or more windows in your view.** This ensures that shadows cast by objects in your room look like they're caused by light from the windows. To make it seem like overhead lighting is in your space, set the time of day to about noon. The shadows cast by furniture and similar objects will be directly below the objects themselves. One more thing: If you have lighting fixtures on the ceiling, remember to set them not to cast shadows in the Entity Info dialog box (described below).

2. **Choose Window⇨Entity Info.** This opens the Entity Info dialog box.

3. **Select any faces that make up the ceiling.** Hold down Shift to select more than one thing at a time.

4. **In the Entity Info dialog box, deselect the Cast Shadows check box.** The ceiling now no longer casts a shadow, brightening your space considerably.

5. **Repeat steps 3 and 4 for the following faces and objects:**
   - The wall with the windows in it.
   - The windows themselves.
   - Any walls in your view that are casting shadows on the floor of your space.
6. **Move the Dark slider over to about 50.** This brightens things even more and makes your shadows more believable.

If you try the first two methods and shadows don't seem to be working, *don't bother turning on shadows.* Instead, try this:

1. **In the Shadow Settings dialog box, deselect the Display Shadows check box to turn off shadows.**
2. **Select the Use Sun for Shading check box to add some contrast.**
3. **Slide the Dark slider all the way to the left and the Light slider all the way to the right to add even more contrast.**
4. **Move the Time slider around until things look good.** Try to make walls with windows in them darker than walls that might be "lit" by those windows. Figure 9-5 demonstrates this technique.

Figure 9-5

Increase the contrast in your view without using shadows.

9.2.2 Making 3D Objects "Pop"

Adding shadows to freestanding things like tables and lamps is a mostly aesthetic undertaking; just adjust the controls until things look good. Here are some things to keep in mind (which are illustrated in Figure 9-6):

▲ **Take it easy on the contrast.** This is especially true when it comes to very complex shapes or faces with photos mapped to them. When your model has too much contrast, it can be hard to read. To decrease the contrast, do the following:

1. Move the Dark slider over to about 40.

2. Move the Light slider down to 60 or 70.

▲ **Shorten your shadows.** It's strange to see objects lit as though the light source is very far away; overhead lighting looks more natural. To make your shadows look better, follow these steps:

1. Set the Date slider to a day in the early autumn.

2. Set the Time slider to a time between 10 a.m. and 2 p.m.

▲ **Rotate your model around.** Remember that you can't get every possible shadow position by using only the controls in the Shadow Settings dialog box. To get the effect you want, you might have to rotate your model by selecting it and using the Rotate tool.

▲ **Select the From Edges check box.** Lots of times, modelers use free edges to add fine detail to models (think of a harp or a loom). Selecting

Figure 9-6

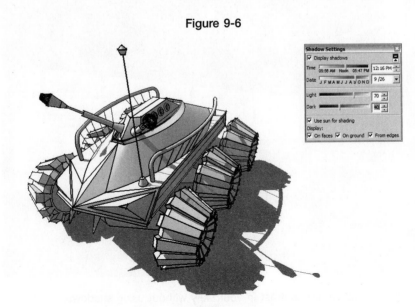

Tips for making objects stand out with shadows.

the From Edges check box tells SketchUp to allow those edges to cast shadows.

▲ **Pay attention to the transparency of faces.** When you have a face painted with a transparent material, you can decide whether that face should cast a shadow—chances are that it shouldn't. In SketchUp, the rule is that materials that are more than 50 percent transparent cast shadows. So, if you don't want one of your transparent-looking faces to cast a shadow, do one of the following:

• Select the face, and then deselect the Cast Shadows check box in the Entity Info dialog box.

• Adjust the opacity of the face's material to be less than 50 percent in the Materials dialog box.

9.2.3 Conveying Depth in 2D Views

Have you ever looked at a roof plan or building **elevation** (a straight-on, 2D view of the exterior) or a floor plan of an interior design project and had difficulty reading it? One of the main reasons that 2D drawings are so hard to read is that they usually don't convey *depth*. Without knowing how close or far away things are, everything turns into a flat jumble of lines. Of course, experienced draftspersons can use line weight (thickness) and tone to convey depth. SketchUp's style settings, which you can read about it Chapter 8, provide some help, but your best bet is to use shadows.

Take a look at Figure 9-7 to see what a difference the addition of shadows can make to a 2D overhead view of a row of buildings. In Parallel Projection mode, which is how 99 percent of 2D drawings are made, there's no way to know how high any of the buildings are. Turning on shadows reveals a whole new layer of information.

When adding shadows to 2D views of your model, here are some things to keep in mind:

▲ **The convention in architecture is to cast shadows at a 45-degree angle.** If you want your views to look somewhat official, play with the

Figure 9-7

Adding shadows to a 2D view provides important extra information.

Time and Date sliders until your shadows are cast at about 45 degrees from your model.

▲ **Lighten your shadows.** Because the purpose of this exercise is to increase the legibility of your 2D views, you don't need to be dramatic. To be able to see what's happening in your shadows, move the Dark slider in the Shadow Settings dialog box up to about 50.

▲ **The same is true for elevations.** An elevation is a 2D view of the side of a building or a sectional view of an interior, with furniture. Feel free to use shadows to make these drawings clearer, too. Architects do it all the time, and it makes a difference.

SELF-CHECK

1. Shadows are on by default. True or false?
2. SketchUp uses the following sources of light:
   a. Sun and artificial lights added in by the user
   b. Artificial lights only
   c. Sun only
   d. The user can choose between using only the sun or using only artificial lights
3. Without _____, it's almost impossible to read depth in 2D views of 3D space.
4. If you have a transparent-looking face and you don't want it to cast a shadow, you can select the face, and then deselect the _____ check box in the Entity Info dialog box.

9.3 Creating Accurate Shadow Studies

One of the most useful features in SketchUp is the ability to display accurate shadows. To do this, three pieces of information are necessary:

▲ The time of day.
▲ The day of the year.
▲ The latitude of the building site.

The sun's position (and thus the position of shadows) depends on geographic location—that is to say, **latitude**. The shadow cast by a building at 3:00 on March 5 in Minsk is very different from that cast by a similar building, at the same time of day, on the same date in Nairobi.

If you're displaying shadows on a model of a piece of furniture, geographic location probably isn't important; the shadows are for effect only. But if you're trying to see how much time your pool deck will spend in the sun during the summer months, you need to give SketchUp your geographic location.

9.3.1 Telling SketchUp Your Geographic Location

Few people know the precise latitude of where they live. SketchUp makes it easy to **geolocate** your model—tell it where it is supposed to be. How you do so depends on which version of SketchUp you're using:

▲ Google SketchUp 6 (free): If you're using the free version of SketchUp, you can geolocate your model by importing a Google Earth snapshot. See Chapter 11 to learn how to do this.

▲ Google SketchUp Pro 6: Users of the Pro version of SketchUp have access to some nifty additional functionality. If you're using Pro, you have a choice of methods for geolocating your model:

• You can import a Google Earth snapshot (which is explained in Chapter 11) or

• You can use the Location panel in the Model Info dialog box, as shown in Figure 9-8. Read the next part of this chapter to find out how it works.

Figure 9-8

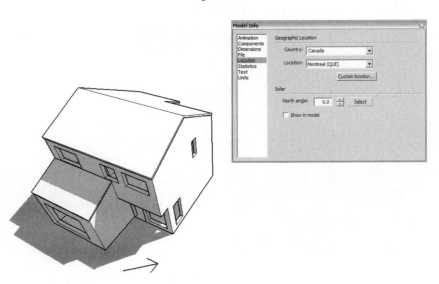

Giving your model a geographic location with SketchUp Pro.

To give your model a geographic location using the Location panel in SketchUp Pro, follow these steps:

1. **Somewhere on the ground in your model, draw a short line to indicate the direction of north.** If you're working with imported geometry (from AutoCAD, for instance), you might already have a north indicator.

2. **Choose Window⊏⊐Model Info to open the Model Info dialog box.**

3. **On the left side of the Model Info dialog box, choose Location.** If the Country drop-down list says Custom or N/A, stop here. Your model has already been geographically located by importing a Google Earth snapshot, and you don't need to go through any of the following steps (see Chapter 11 for more imformation). Shadows will be accurate for wherever you were in Google Earth when you imported your snapshot. Close the Model Info dialog box and skip the next seven steps.

4. **Choose a country from the Country drop-down list.**

5. **Choose a location from the Location drop-down list.** If the location you want isn't listed, choose the closest one, or click the Custom Location button to enter a set of coordinates. To find coordinates for almost anywhere in the world, try searching for "city, country coordinates" on Google.

6. **Instead of typing in a north angle (which may be overly complicated), click the Select button to the right of the North angle box.** Back in your model window, your cursor will have become a large circle with four lines radiating out from the center, as shown in Figure 9-9.

7. **Click the southern end of the line you drew in step 1.**

Figure 9-9

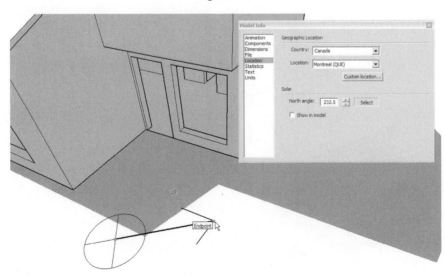

Telling SketchUp where north is.

8. Click the northern end of the same line, finishing the operation.

9. If you want, select the **Show in Model** check box to display the direction of north as a yellow line.

10. **Close the Model Info dialog box.** The shadows in SketchUp are now specific to the geographic location you've just set up. If you like, you can erase the line you drew in step 1.

9.3.2 Displaying Accurate Shadows for a Given Time and Place

Now that you've told SketchUp where your model is, it's a fairly simple process to study how the sun will affect your project, as shown in Figure 9-10.

To study how the sun will affect your project, follow these steps:

1. Orbit, zoom, and pan around until you have a good view of the part of your project you want to study.

2. Choose Window⇨Shadows to open the Shadow Settings dialog box.

3. Select the Display Shadows check box to turn on SketchUp's sun.

4. Type a month and day into the box to the right of the Date slider, and press Enter.

5. Move the Time slider back and forth to see how the shadows will move over the course of that day.

6. Pick a time of day using the Time controls.

Figure 9-10

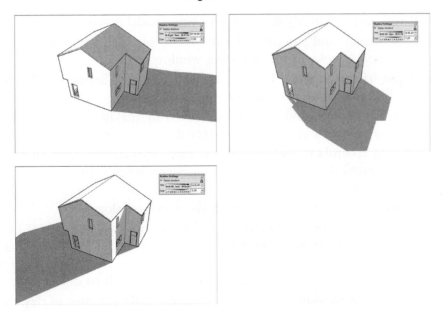

Studying the effect of the sun on your model.

FOR EXAMPLE

Uses for Shadows

Even if you're not an architect, you might want to study shadows accurately for these reasons:

▲ To figure out where to locate the plants in your garden that need the most light (or the most shade).

▲ To see when sunlight will be coming straight through the skylight you're thinking of installing.

▲ To make sure that the overhang behind your house will provide enough shade at lunchtime in the summer.

7. Move the Date slider back and forth to see how the sun will affect your project at that time of day over the course of the year.

9.3.3 Animating a Shadow Study

It's a relatively easy next step to create a simple animation that shows shadows moving over time. To do this, you'll use scenes, a feature also discussed in Chapter 10, where you'll find more detailed coverage of scenes in general.

To create a simple animation showing the movement of shadows in your model over time, follow these steps:

1. **If you haven't already done so, give your model a geographic location.**
2. **Orbit, zoom, and pan around until you're satisfied with the way your model looks in the modeling window.**
3. **If you haven't already done so, open the Shadow Settings dialog box by choosing Window⇨Shadows.**
4. **Turn on the sun (and thus the shadows) by making sure that the Display Shadows check box is selected.**
5. **Use the controls to pick a time and date.** Try picking a time early in the morning—it'll make for a better animation when you're done (see Figure 9-11).
6. **Choose Window⇨Scenes to open the Scenes dialog box.**
7. **Click the Add button (which looks like a plus sign in a circle) in the Scenes dialog box.** This adds a scene to the list in the Scenes dialog box and a tab at the top of your modeling window (see Figure 9-12). If it's the first scene you've created in this model, it will be called Scene 1.
8. **Back in the Shadows dialog box, choose a different time of day.** A time late in the afternoon works well.

Figure 9-11

Pick a time in the morning.

9. **Back in the Scenes dialog box, click the Add button again.** This adds Scene 2 to the list in the dialog box and another tab at the top of your modeling window.

10. **Click the tab you created in step 7.** See the shadows moving? Clicking back and forth between the tabs causes the shadows to animate between the times of day you set up in the Shadow Settings dialog box. You can keep changing the date and time, adding more scenes if you like.

11. **When you're ready to animate all the scenes you've created, flip to Chapter 13 to find how to export the animation you just created as a movie file.**

To do a proper shadow study, you need to see where the shadows fall on the longest and shortest days of the year. In the Northern Hemisphere, these days are June 21 and December 21, respectively. In the Southern Hemisphere, it's the opposite.

Remember that SketchUp does not support daylight saving time. When you do a shadow study over the course of a year, mentally adjust the shadows an hour forward if daylight saving time will be in effect.

Figure 9-12

Scene tab   Add button

Click the Add button to add a scene to your model.

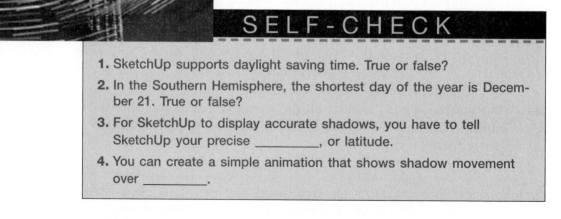

SELF-CHECK

1. SketchUp supports daylight saving time. True or false?
2. In the Southern Hemisphere, the shortest day of the year is December 21. True or false?
3. For SketchUp to display accurate shadows, you have to tell SketchUp your precise _____, or latitude.
4. You can create a simple animation that shows shadow movement over _____.

SUMMARY

Light and shadows affect how objects appear to us. By adding shadows to your models, you make them appear more realistic. In this chapter, you evaluated why shadows and light are necessary in many models. You also assessed the tools available to you, such as the Shadows dialog box. You created and displayed accurate shadows. You also created a simple shadow animation. All of these skills will help you with your model, whether you want to determine which flowers to plant, or whether you just want to add visual interest to your model.

KEY TERMS

Elevation	A straight-on, 2D view of the side of a building.
Geolocation	The process by which SketchUp sets the imported snapshot's latitude and longitude to match Google Earth, and it orients the snapshot in the right cardinal direction.
Latitude	Geographic location measured by the angular distance north or south from the earth's equator measured through 90 degrees.

ASSESS YOUR UNDERSTANDING

Go to www.wiley.com/college/chopra to evaluate your knowledge of working with light and shadows.

Measure your learning by comparing pre-test and post-test results.

Summary Questions

1. In architecture, an elevation is a straight-on, 2D view of the side of a building. True or false?
2. _____ in SketchUp are controlled by the changing position of the sun.
3. You can add light bulbs in SketchUp and make them a source of light in your models. True or false?
4. To decrease the darkness of shadows in SketchUp, you should slide the Dark slider:
   (a) left.
   (b) right.
   (c) up.
   (d) down.
5. Deselecting the _____ check box means that shadows will not be cast on faces in your model.
6. You can change your shadows in the _____ box.
7. _____ is the longest day of the year in the Southern Hemisphere.
8. To create accurate shadows in SketchUp, which of the following information is needed?
   (a) The time of day
   (b) The day of the year
   (c) The latitude of the building site
   (d) All of the above

Applying This Chapter

1. In your models, where can you display shadows?
2. What steps can you take to convey depth in 2D views?
3. Describe three reasons why you would want to display shadows accurately.

YOU TRY IT

Adding Shadows to Your Model House

Collect the information you need to create accurate shadows for your geographic location. Then use this information to add shadows to the model house you built in previous chapters.

Building a Sunroom

Either create a freestanding model of a sunroom or add a sunroom to the model house you created in previous chapters. Input the necessary information into SketchUp to create the shadows. Then create a simple shadow animation of your sunroom like the one that was presented in the last section of this chapter.

10

PRESENTING YOUR MODEL INSIDE SKETCHUP

Showing Off Your Model

Starting Point

Go to www.wiley.com/college/chopra to assess your knowledge of presenting your model inside SketchUp.
Determine where you need to concentrate your effort.

What You'll Learn in This Chapter

▲ The reasons why you would want to walk around inside your model
▲ How you can capture particular views
▲ Animating with scenes
▲ When to cut slices through your model with section planes
▲ The difference between plans and sections

After Studying This Chapter, You'll Be Able To

▲ Explore the inside of your model virtually
▲ Create scenes to capture particular views
▲ Create animations with scenes
▲ Create slices through your model with section planes
▲ Generate plans and sections

INTRODUCTION

After you've made a model, you're probably going to want to show it to someone. How you present your work depends on the idea you're trying to convey. The challenging part about using SketchUp to present a model isn't actually using the tools; it's choosing the *right* tools to get your idea across without distracting your audience with too much extra information. Most 3D models have so much to look at that the real challenge is to figure out a presentation method that helps you focus on the features that you want to talk about. You also will want to match the presentation style and method depending on the phase of the presentation you are in. It makes a difference if you are in a conceptual stage or in a final stage, as your goals at each stage will be different.

In this chapter, you'll learn three different ways to show off your models without ever leaving SketchUp. Specifically, if you've made a building, you can walk around inside it. You can even walk up and down stairs and ramps, just like in a video game. You can also create animated slide shows by setting up scenes with different camera views, times of day, and even visual styles. Also, if you want to talk about what's *inside* your model, you can cut sections through it without taking it apart. Thus, in this chapter, you'll learn how to create scenes, sections, and animations.

As you read this chapter, keep in mind what you want your model to communicate. Think about how you might use each method to make a different kind of point, and think about the order in which you'd like those points to be made. As with everything else in SketchUp, a little bit of planning goes a long way.

10.1 Exploring Your Creation on Foot

Few experiences in SketchUp are as satisfying as running around inside your model. After you've made a space, you can drop down into it and explore by walking around, going up and down stairs, bumping into walls, and even falling off ledges. You can check to make sure that the television is visible from the kitchen, for example, or experience what it would be like to wander down the hall. In a potentially confusing building (like an airport or a train station), you could even figure out where to put directional signs by allowing someone who's never seen your model to explore the space "on foot."

10.1.1 Using SketchUp's Tools

A couple of tools in SketchUp are dedicated to moving around your model as if you were actually inside it. The first step is to position yourself so that it seems like you're standing inside your model. This can be tricky with just the Orbit, Pan, and Zoom tools, so SketchUp provides a tool just for this purpose: Position Camera. Once you're standing in the right spot (and at the right height), you can then use the Walk tool to move around. It's as simple as that.

The Position Camera Tool

The essence of the Position Camera tool is its ability to precisely place your viewpoint in SketchUp in a particular spot. That's really all this tool does, but it works in two different ways:

▲ **If you want to be standing in a particular location:** Choose Camera⇨Position Camera from the menu bar and then single-click anywhere in the modeling window to automatically position your viewpoint 5 feet, 6 inches above wherever you clicked. Because this is the conventional *eye-height* of an adult human being, the result is that you are, for all intents and purposes, standing on the spot where you clicked (see Figure 10-1). After using Position Camera, SketchUp automatically switches to the Look Around tool, assuming that, now that you're where you want to be, you might want to have a look around. (The Look Around tool is described in the next section of this chapter.) Note that you're not stuck being five-and-a-half-feet tall forever, though. After you use Position Camera, type in the height you'd rather "be" and press Enter. For example, type **18"** to see a golden retriever's view of the world, or type **7'** to pretend you play for a pro basketball team. Keep in mind that the VCB (the spot in the lower-right corner where numbers appear) displays your eye height as a distance from the ground, and not from whatever surface you're "standing on." Thus, to set your eye height to be 5 feet above a platform that's 10 feet high, you'd type in **15'**.

▲ **If you want your eyes to be in a specific location while you're looking in a particular direction:** Select Position Camera, click the mouse button while in the spot where you want your eyes to be, drag over to the thing you want to be looking at (you'll see a dashed line connecting the two points), and release the mouse button (as shown in Figure 10-2). Try this a couple of times; it takes a bit of practice to master. You'd use Position Camera in this way if you wanted to be standing in a particular

Figure 10-1

Drop yourself into your model with the Position Camera tool.

Figure 10-2

"Aim" your view by using Position Camera another way.

spot *and* looking in a particular direction. This technique works great with scenes, which are explained later in this chapter.

The Walk Tool

After you've used Position Camera to place yourself in your model, use the Walk tool to move through it. To walk around, click and drag the mouse in the direction you want to move, keeping the following rules in mind:

▲ Straight up is forward.

▲ Straight down is backward.

▲ Anything to the left or right causes you to turn while you're walking.

The farther you move your cursor, the faster you walk. Release the mouse button to stop walking. If you've ever played video games, you'll get used to this quickly.

You can also use the Walk tool to walk up and down stairs and ramps. Keep in mind that the highest step you can "climb" is 22 inches—anything higher and you get the "bump" cursor, just as if you walked into a wall. Also, if you walk off a high surface, you'll fall to the surface below.

Using modifier keys in combination with the Walk tool makes SketchUp even more like a video game:

▲ Hold down Ctrl (Option on a Mac) to run instead of walking.

▲ Hold down Shift to move straight up (like you're growing), straight down (like you're shrinking), or sideways (like a crab).

▲ Hold down Alt (⌘ on a Mac) to disable collision detection, which allows you to walk through walls instead of bumping into them.

10.1.2 Stopping to Look Around

Look Around is the third tool in SketchUp that's dedicated to exploring your model from the inside. If using Position Camera is like swooping in to stand in a particular spot, and Walk is like moving around while maintaining a constant eye-height, Look Around is like turning your head while standing in one spot. It does exactly what it says. To use Look Around, follow these steps:

1. Choose Camera⇨Look Around from the menu bar to activate the Look Around tool.
2. Click and drag around in the modeling window to turn your virtual head.

While in any of the navigation tools, you can right-click to access any of the other navigation tools; this makes switching between them easier.

When you use Look Around with the field of view tool discussed in the next section, you get a fairly realistic simulation of what it would be like to be standing in your model.

10.1.3 Setting Your Field of View

Field of view is the amount of your model you're able to see in your modeling window at one time. Imagine your eyesight like a cone, with the pointed end at your eyes and the cone getting bigger as it gets farther away from you. Everything that falls inside the cone is visible to you, and everything outside the cone isn't.

If you increase the angle of the cone at the pointed end, the cone gets wider and you see more of what's in front of you. If you decrease the angle, the cone gets narrower and you see less (see Figure 10-3).

Figure 10-3

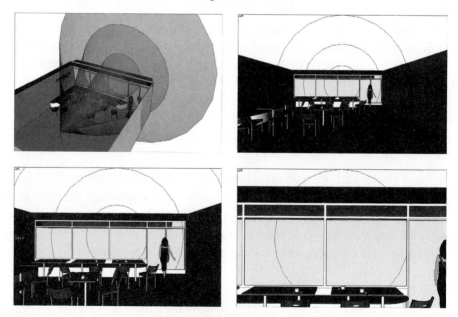

The wider your field of view, the more you can see.

Measured in degrees, a wide field of view means that you can see more of your model without having to move around. The bigger the angle, the more you can see. This comes in handy when you're inside a SketchUp model you're working on, because it's hard to work on things you can't see.

It's a good idea to adjust your field of view while walking around inside your model. Follow these steps to do so:

1. **Choose Camera⇨Field of View.** Notice that the Value Control Box in the lower-right corner of your modeling window says "Field of View" and that the default value is "35 deg." This means that you currently have a 35-degree cone of vision, which is somewhat narrow.

2. **Type 60 and press Enter.** Your field of view is increased, and you now have a wider view of your model. The downside is that you see more distortion at the edges of your modeling window as more information is being displayed in the same amount of space.

A good rule of thumb for setting your field of view is to strike a balance between quantity and quality; a wider view always means more distortion. For views of the *outside* of something you've built, you may want to use a field of view of 35 to 45 degrees. For interior views, you might use 60 or 70 degrees.

If you are familiar with photography, you can also express field of view in millimeters, just as if you're using a camera lens. Typing in **28mm** gives you a wide-angle view, just like you're looking through a 28-mm lens. For people who think about field of view in these terms, this can be more intuitive than trying to imagine cones of vision.

SELF-CHECK

1. If you wanted a view just like you would have if you were looking through a 35-mm lens, you would type in _____ mm.

2. _____ is the amount of your model you're able to see in your modeling window at one time.

3. You can use the Walk tool to move through your model. True or false?

4. Which tool would you use to place your viewpoint in SketchUp precisely in a particular spot?

   a. Pan

   b. Zoom

   c. Orbit

   d. Position camera

10.2 Taking the Scenic Route

With SketchUp, you can save a particular view of your model so that you can come back to that view whenever you want. That saved view can also save things like styles and shadow settings. Plus, you can come back to any saved view by clicking a button on your screen.

SketchUp **scenes** are saved views of your model. Scenes can be thought of as cameras, except that scenes can save much more than just camera positions. Although they don't get much space in this book, scenes are one of the most important features in SketchUp, for three reasons:

▲ **Scenes can save you hours of time.** It's not always easy to get back to exactly the right view by using Orbit, Zoom, and Pan. Sometimes a view involves shadows, styles, sections (you'll read about those later), and even hidden geometry. It can be frustrating to set up everything the way you need it, every time you need it. With SketchUp, you have a lot of different ways to view your model. Making a scene reduces the process of changing dozens of settings to a single click of your mouse.

▲ **Scenes are the most effective way of presenting your model.** Saving a scene for each point that you'd like to make in a presentation allows you to focus on what you're trying to say. Instead of fumbling around with the navigation tools, turning on shadows, and making the roof visible, you can click a button and SketchUp will automatically transition to the next scene (which you've already set up exactly the way you want it). Figure 10-4 illustrates a set of scenes to present a doghouse.

▲ **Scenes are the key to making animations.** You make animations by creating a series of scenes and telling SketchUp to figure out the transi-

Figure 10-4

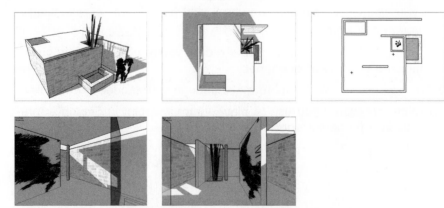

To be able to come back to very specific views, create scenes.

tions between them. The process, which is explained in later sections, is as simple as clicking a button.

After you get used to them, you'll find yourself using scenes all the time. Here are some of the most common uses for scenes:

▲ Showing shade conditions for the same area at different times of the day.

▲ Saving scenes for each floor plan, building section, and other important views of your model.

▲ Building a walk-through or flyover animation of your design.

▲ Creating scenes to show several views of the same thing with different options.

▲ Demonstrating change over time by showing or hiding a succession of components.

10.2.1 Creating Scenes

Making a scene in SketchUp is *not* like taking a snapshot of your model. If you create a scene to save a view, then do more modeling, and then return to that scene, your model will not go back to the way it was when you created the scene. The camera position will be the same and the settings will be the same, but your geometry won't be. This is an important concept, and one that makes using scenes so powerful.

A scene is simply a set of view settings, which means that they're automatically updated to reflect your changes every time you edit your model. You can make some scenes and use them all the way through your process, from when you start modeling to when you present your design.

Creating scenes is a simple process. The basic idea is that you add a scene to your SketchUp file whenever you have a view you want to return to later. You can always delete scenes, so there's no downside to using several of them. Follow these steps to make a new scene:

1. **Choose Window⊏▷Scenes to open the Scenes dialog box.** When it first opens, it doesn't look like there's much to the Scenes dialog box. Expanding it by clicking the expansion toggle in the upper-right corner reveals more options, which are covered in the next section.

2. **Set up your view however you want.** Navigate around until you're satisfied with your point of view. If you want, use the Shadows and Styles dialog boxes to change the way your model looks.

3. **Click the Add button to make a new scene with your current view settings.** At this point, a new scene is added to your SketchUp file. If

Figure 10-5

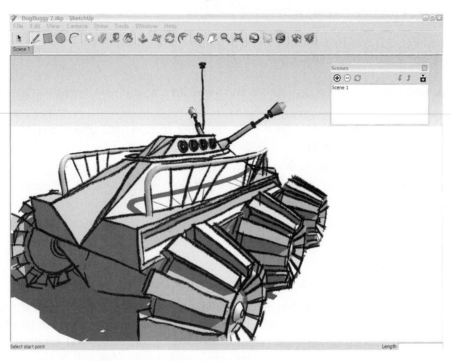

The scene you just added shows up in two places.

this is the first scene you've created, it will be called Scene 1 and will appear in two places (see Figure 10-5):

- As a list item in the Scenes dialog box, right underneath the Add button.
- As a tab at the top of your modeling window, labeled Scene 1.

Nothing is generated outside of SketchUp when you add a scene; it's not like exporting a JPEG or a TIFF. Scenes are just little bits of programming code that "remember" the view settings in effect when they were created. Scenes also don't add much to your file size, so you don't have to worry about using too many of them.

10.2.2 Moving from Scene to Scene

Activate a scene you've added earlier by doing one of three things:

1. Double-clicking the name of the scene in the Scenes dialog box.
2. Single-clicking the tab for that scene at the top of the modeling window.
3. Right-clicking any scene tab and choosing Play Animation to make SketchUp automatically flip through your scenes. (Choose Play Animation again to make the animation stop.) Only scenes that have "include in animation" checked will be in the animation.

Notice how the transition from one scene to the next is animated? You don't have to do anything special to make this happen; it's something SketchUp automatically does to make things look better.

You can adjust the way SketchUp transitions between scenes, which is handy for customizing your presentations. Follow these steps to access these settings:

1. **Choose Window⇨Model Info to open the Model Info dialog box.**

2. **On the left side of the Model Info dialog box, choose Animation.** The Animation settings panel in the Model Info dialog box (see Figure 10-6) isn't very complicated, but it can make a great difference in the appearance of your scene-related presentations.

3. **In the Scene Transitions area, set how SketchUp transitions from one scene to another.** These settings apply to both manual (clicking on a page tab) and automatic (playing an animation) scene transitions:

   • **Enable Scene Transitions:** Deselect this check box to make SketchUp change scenes without animating the transitions between them. You'll probably want to do this if your model is so complex (or your computer is so slow) that animated transitions don't look good.

   • **Seconds:** If you've selected the Enable Scene Transitions check box, the number of seconds you enter here will be the amount of time it takes SketchUp to transition from one scene to the next. If you're "moving the camera" very far between scenes, it's a good idea to increase the transition time. Three seconds is generally a good transition time.

If you're presenting an incomplete model (perhaps you've thought about the garage and the living room, but nothing in between), it can be helpful to turn off scene transitions. That way, your audience won't see the things you haven't worked on when you click a tab to change scenes.

Figure 10-6

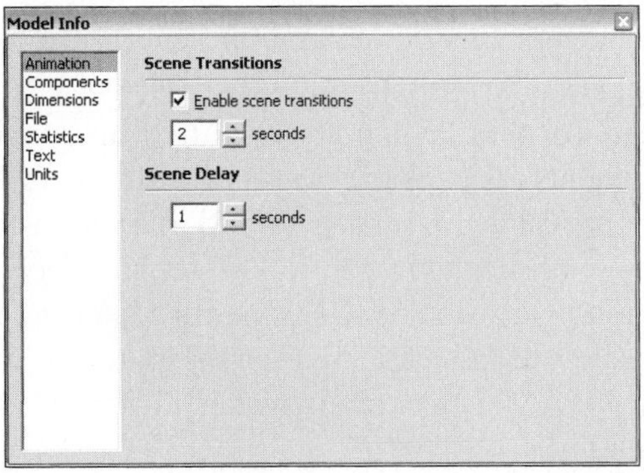

The Animation settings panel is helpful
in customizing your presentations.

4. **In the Scene Delay area, set the length of time SketchUp pauses on each slide before it moves to the next one.** If you want it to seem like you're walking or flying, set this to 0. If you want time to talk about each scene in your presentation, increase this a few seconds.

MAKING WALK-THROUGHS

A great way to use scenes is to pretend you're walking or flying through your model. By setting up your scenes sequentially, you can give a seamless tour without having to use the navigation tools. This is especially handy when you need to be able to "walk and talk" at the same time.

Here are some tips that can help you to simulate a person walking or flying through your model with scenes:

▲ **Adjust your field of view.** For interior animations, make your camera "see" a wider area by setting your field of view to 60 degrees. For exterior views, a field of view set between 30 and 45 degrees works well.

▲ **Make sure that your scenes aren't too far apart.** Instead of racing through a room, consider adding more scenes.

▲ **Add scenes at equal distance intervals.** Because SketchUp only lets you control the scene transition timing for all your scenes at once, it's best to make sure that your scenes are set up about the same distance apart. If you don't, your walk-through animations will be awkward.

▲ **Don't forget the animation settings in the Model Info dialog box.** Set the scene delay to 0 seconds so that your animation doesn't pause at every scene. For a normal walking speed, set your scene transitions so that you're moving about 5 feet per second. If your scenes are about 20 feet apart, set your scene transition time to 4 seconds. This gives your audience time to look around and notice things. For flying animations, pick a scene transition time that looks good.

▲ **Slide around corners.** When you're setting up a walking animation, you have an easy, reliable way to turn corners without seeming too robotic. Basically, the trick is to add a scene just short of where you want to turn—for example, a few feet ahead of a doorway. The key is to angle your view *into* the turn slightly. You should set up your next scene just past the turn, close to the inside and facing the new view. This technique makes it seem like you're turning corners naturally.

10.2.3 Modifying Scenes after You've Created Them

After you create several scenes, it's inevitable that you're going to need to adjust them in some way. After all, modifying something is almost always easier than making it all over again, and the same thing holds true for scenes. Because your SketchUp model will change many times, understanding how to make changes to your existing scenes can save you a lot of time.

Certain aspects of the scene-modification process can get a little complicated. Pay special attention to the section on updating scenes, and don't worry if it takes some time to figure things out.

Reordering, Renaming, and Removing Scenes

Making simple modifications to scenes, such as reordering, renaming, and removing them, is easy. You can accomplish each of these in two ways: You either use the Scenes dialog box, or you right-click the scene tabs at the top of your modeling window. Figure 10-7 is an illustration of this.

Figure 10-7

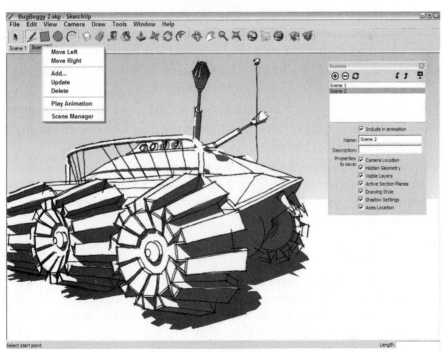

You can modify scenes by right-clicking scene tabs or by using
the Scenes dialog box.

To access the modification controls in the Scenes dialog box, click the arrow-shaped expansion button in the upper-right corner.

Here's how to reorder, rename, or remove scenes:

▲ **Reordering scenes:** You can change the order in which scenes play in a slide show. If you're using scenes, you'll need to do this often. Use one of the following methods:

- Right-click the tab of the scene you want to move (in the modeling window) and choose Move Right or Move Left.
- In the expanded Scenes dialog box, click the name of the scene you want to move to select it, and then click the up or down arrows to the right of the list to change the scene's position in the scene order.

▲ **Renaming scenes:** It's a good idea to give your scenes meaningful names: "Living Room," "Top View," and "Shadows at 5:00 p.m." are descriptive enough to be useful. "Scene 14" is not. Use one of the following methods to rename a scene:

- Right-click the scene tab and choose Rename.
- In the Scenes dialog box, select the scene you want to rename and type something into the Name field below the list. You may want to give it a description, too.

▲ **Removing scenes:** If you don't need a scene anymore, you can delete it. Use one of the following methods to remove a scene:

- Right-click the scene tab and choose Delete to remove it permanently.
- In the Scenes dialog box, select the scene you want to remove and click the Delete button.

However, if you have a scene that you don't want to appear in slide shows, you don't have to delete it. To exclude a scene from slide shows without getting rid of it, select its name in the list and deselect the Include in Animation check box.

Updating Scenes

The process of updating scenes isn't altogether straightforward. Basically, a scene is just a collection of saved viewing *properties*. Each of these properties has something to do with how your model looks. A scene can save one, some, or all of the following properties, depending on what you need to do:

▲ **Camera location:** Camera location properties include the position of the camera, or viewpoint, and the field of view. Field of view is discussed earlier in this chapter.

▲ **Hidden geometry:** Hidden geometry properties are simply what elements are hidden and what elements aren't. These properties keep track of the visibility of the lines, faces, groups, components, and axes in your model.

▲ **Visible layers:** Visible layer properties keep track of the visibility of the layers in your model.

▲ **Active section planes:** Active section plane properties include the visibility of section planes and whether they are active. Sections are discussed in the last part of this chapter.

▲ **Style and fog:** Style and fog properties are all the settings in the Styles and Fog dialog boxes, and there are several.

▲ **Shadow settings:** Shadow settings properties include whether shadows are turned on and the time and date for which the shadows are set. They also include all the other settings in the Shadow Settings dialog box.

▲ **Axes locations:** Axes location properties are very specific. They keep track of the visibility of the main SketchUp red, green, and blue axes in your modeling window. Because you'll often want to hide the axes when you're giving a presentation, these elements get their own properties.

Updating All the Scene Properties at Once

The simplest way to modify a scene is to not worry about individual properties. If all you want to do is update a scene after you've made an adjustment to the appearance of your model, follow these steps:

1. **Go to the scene you want to update by clicking its tab at the top of the modeling window.**

2. **Make whatever styles, shadows, camera, or other display changes you want to make to your model.**

3. **Right-click the current scene tab and choose Update.** Be careful not to accidentally double-click the tab or you'll reactivate the scene and lose all the changes you made. The old scene properties are replaced by the new ones.

After you update a scene, you can't use Undo to revert things back to the way they were. You may want to save your SketchUp file right before updating a scene, and choosing File⇨Revert from the File menu if you don't like how things turn out.

Updating Scene Properties Selectively

Here's where things get complicated. At times, you'll want to update a scene without updating all its properties.

Updating scenes selectively involves making changes that you won't be able to see immediately; whenever you do this, it's a good idea to make a copy of your SketchUp file before updating more than one scene at a time, just in case a mistake occurs.

Maybe you've used scenes to create a tour of the sunroom you're designing for a client, and you want to change the shadow settings to make your model look brighter. You have 30 scenes in your presentation, and your meeting is in 5 minutes. You don't have time to change and update all 30 scenes one at a time. What to do? Follow these steps (and see Figure 10-8):

1. **Adjust the shadow settings to where you want them to be for all the scenes you'd like to update.** While this example deals with shadows, this same method applies to any scene properties changes you'd like to make.

2. **In the Scenes dialog box, select all the scenes you'd like to update.** Hold down Shift to select more than one scene at a time.

3. **Click the Update button in the Scenes dialog box.** A Properties to Update dialog box appears.

4. **Select the Shadow Settings check box and click the Update button.** If all you want to update are the shadow settings, make sure that only that check box is selected. More generally, you would select the check box next to each of the properties you want to update. All the selected scenes are updated with those new properties, and all the properties left deselected remain unchanged.

Figure 10-8

Updating only certain scene properties
is a little more involved.

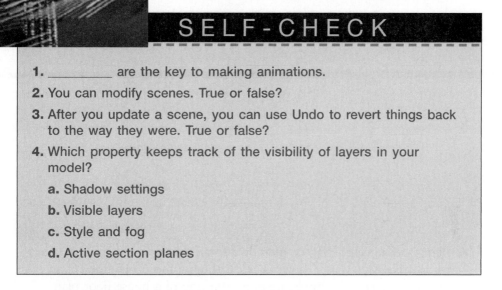

10.3 Mastering the Sectional Approach

Section planes are objects that let you cut away parts of your model to look inside. You place them wherever you need them, use them to create views you wouldn't otherwise be able to get, and then delete them when you're done. When you move a section plane, you get instant feedback; the "cut" view of your model moves, too. If you want, you can embed them in scenes and even use them in animations. Sections are easy to use, incredibly important, and impressive. People use sections in many ways:

▲ To create standard orthographic views (like plans and sections) of buildings and other objects

▲ To make cutaway views of complex models so these models are easier to understand

▲ To work on the interiors of buildings without having to move or hide geometry

▲ To generate sectional animations with scenes

10.3.1 Cutting Plans and Sections

The most common use for sections is to create straight-on, cut-through views of a model. These are some of the views that often include dimensions, and they are typical of the kinds of drawings that architects make to design and explain space. They're useful because they're easy to read, you can take measurements from them (if they're printed to scale), and they provide information that no other drawing type can. The following terms (which are illustrated

Figure 10-9

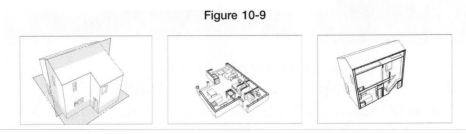

A plan is a horizontal cut, while a section is a vertical one.

in Figure 10-9) can help you more easily create different views of your model:

▲ **Plan:** A *planimetric view*, or **plan**, is a top-down, two-dimensional, non-perspectival view (also known as an **orthographic projection**) of an object or space. Put simply, it's every drawing of a house floor plan you've ever seen. You generate a plan by cutting an imaginary *horizontal* slice through your model. Everything below the slice is visible, and everything above it isn't.

▲ **Section:** Not to be confused with sections (the SketchUp feature about which this section of the book is written), a *sectional view*, or **section**, is a from-the-side, two-dimensional, nonperspectival view of an object or space. You would make a section by cutting an imaginary *vertical* slice through your model. Just like in a plan view, everything on one side of the slice is visible, and everything on the other side is hidden.

You cut plans and sections by adding section planes to your model. These are a little abstract, because nothing like them exists in real life. In SketchUp, section planes are objects that affect the visibility of certain parts of your model. When a section plane is active, everything in front of it is visible and everything behind is hidden. Everywhere your model is "cut" by a section plane, a slightly thicker "section cut" line appears.

If you're using Windows, now would be a good time to open the Sections toolbar by choosing View⇨Toolbars⇨Sections. If you're on a Mac, the Section Plane tool is in the Large Tool Set, which you can activate by choosing View⇨Tool Palettes⇨Large Tool Set in the menu bar. On both platforms, Section Plane looks like a white circle with letters and numbers in it.

To add a section plane, follow these steps:

1. **Choose Tools⇨Section Plane to activate the Section Plane tool.** You can also activate Section Plane by choosing its icon from the Large Tool Set (Mac) or the Sections toolbar (Windows), if you have it open.

Figure 10-10

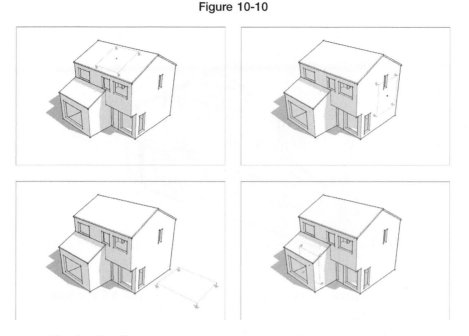

The Section Plane tool changes as you move it around your model.

2. **Move the Section Plane tool around your model.** Notice how the orientation of the Section Plane cursor (which is quite large) changes to be coplanar to whatever surface you're hovering over. Figure 10-10 shows this in action.

3. **When you've decided where you want it, click once to add a section plane.** To create a plan view, add a horizontal section plane by clicking a horizontal plane like a floor. For a sectional view, add a vertical section plane by clicking a wall or other vertical surface. You can, of course, add section planes wherever you want; they don't have to be aligned to horizontal or vertical planes. Figure 10-11 shows a section plane added to a model of a house.

4. **Choose the Move tool.**

5. **Move the section plane you just added by clicking it once to pick it up and again to drop it.** You can only slide your section plane back and forth in two directions; SketchUp only allows section planes to move perpendicular to their cutting planes. After you've added a section plane and moved it to the desired location, you can rotate and even copy it, just like any other object in your model. It will never affect your geometry—just the way you view it.

6. **If you need to rotate your section plane, select it and use the Rotate tool (which you can read more about in Chapter 6).** Why

Figure 10-11

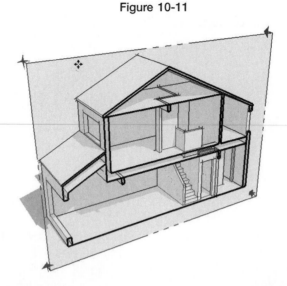

Add a section plane wherever you want one, and then move it into position.

rotate a section plane? In certain circumstances, rotating a section plane (instead of creating a new one) can help explain a complex interior space. Showing a plan view *becoming* a sectional one is a powerful way to explain architectural drawings to an audience that doesn't understand them.

7. **To make a new section plane by copying an existing one, use the Move or Rotate tool to do it the same way you would make a copy of any other SketchUp object.** Chapter 2 explains these basic actions in detail. Copying section planes is a great way to space them a known distance apart; this can be trickier if you use the Section Plane tool to keep adding new ones instead. Figure 10-12 shows moving, rotating, and copying a section plane.

Figure 10-12

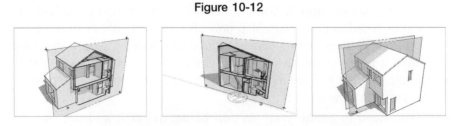

Moving, rotating, and copying a section plane.

When the section plane you've added is in position, you're ready to control how it impacts visibility in a number of other ways. See the following sections for details.

10.3.2 Controlling Individual Section Planes

You can control the way section planes behave by right-clicking them to bring up a context menu that looks like the one shown in Figure 10-13. Examples of what the following options do are shown in the same illustration:

▲ **Reverse:** This option flips the "direction" of the section plane, hiding everything that was previously visible, and revealing everything that used to be "behind" the cut. Use this when you need to see inside the rest of your model.

▲ **Active Cut:** Although you can have multiple section planes in your model, only one of them can be "active" at a time. The **active cut** is the section plane that is actually cutting through your model; others are considered "inactive." If you have more than one section plane, use Active Cut to tell SketchUp which one should be active. You *can* have more than one active section plane in your model at a time, but doing so requires that you **nest**, or embed, each section plane in a separate group or component. It's possible to achieve some fairly elaborate effects with this technique. You can read all about groups and components in Chapter 5.

Figure 10-13

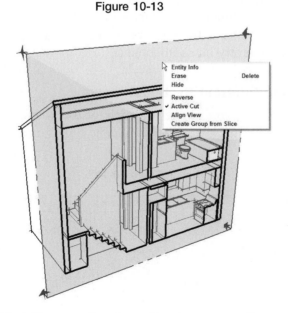

Right-clicking a section plane gives you some options.

▲ **Align View:** When you choose Align View, your view changes so that you're looking straight on at the section plane. You can use this option to produce views like the ones described in the section "Getting Different Sectional Views," later in this chapter.

▲ **Create Group from Slice:** This option doesn't have much to do with the other choices in this context menu; it's really a modeling tool. You can use this to do exactly what it says: create a group from the active slice, or section plane. This comes in handy for creating filled-in section cuts for final presentations.

10.3.3 Setting Section-Plane Visibility

If you want to control the visibility of all your section planes at once, a couple of menu options can help. You use both of these toggles in combination to control how section cuts appear in your model. These two options, shown on the View menu, are illustrated in Figure 10-14:

▲ **Section Planes:** This choice toggles the visibility of section-plane objects without affecting the section cuts they produce. More simply, deselecting Section Planes hides all the section planes in your model, but doesn't turn off the section cut effect, as shown in the middle image in Figure 10-14. This is how you'll probably want to show most of your sectional views, so this is an important toggle.

▲ **Section Cut:** Deselecting this option toggles the section cut effect on and off without affecting the visibility of the section-plane objects in your model. This choice is the opposite of Section Planes, in the previous point, but it's every bit as important.

10.3.4 Getting Different Sectional Views

Using section planes, you can get a couple of useful and impressive views of your model without much trouble. The second builds on the first, and both are

Figure 10-14

Control section plane visibility with Section Planes and Section Cut.

Figure 10-15

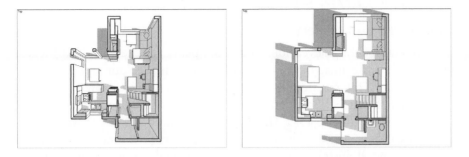

Turn Perspective on for a section perspective; choose Parallel Projection
to produce an orthographic view.

shown in Figure 10-15. A section perspective (left) is a special kind of way to view a three-dimensional space. The second type, an orthographic view (right), is straight on, doesn't use perspective, and is often used by interior designers.

10.3.5 Making a Section Perspective

If you imagine cutting a building in half and then looking at the cut surface straight on while looking inside, you have a **section perspective**. The *section* part of the term refers to the fact that the building has been cut away. The *perspective* part indicates that objects seen inside the space appear to get smaller as they get farther away.

Section perspectives are a great way of showing interior space in a way that's understandable to most people. To create a section perspective using the Section Plane tool in SketchUp, follow these steps:

1. **Select the section plane you'd like to use to make a section perspective by clicking it with the Select tool.** When it's selected, your section plane turns blue, assuming that you haven't changed any of the default colors in the Styles dialog box.
2. **If the selected section plane isn't active, right-click and choose Active Cut from the context menu.** Active section planes cut through their surrounding geometry. If your section plane is visible but isn't cutting through anything, it isn't active.
3. **Right-click the selected section plane and choose Align View from the context menu.** This aligns your view so that it's straight on (perpendicular) to your section plane.
4. **If you can't see your model properly, choose Camera⇨Zoom Extents.** This zooms your view so that you can see your whole model in the modeling window.

FOR EXAMPLE

Cutting Like an Architect

In architecture, the convention is to "cut" plans at a height of 48 inches, meaning that the imaginary horizontal slice is made four feet above the floor surface. This ensures that doors and most windows are shown cut through by the slice, while counters, tables, and other furniture are below it, and thus are fully visible. These things are important when you're trying to explain a space to someone. After all, architectural drawings are two-dimensional abstractions of three-dimensional space, and every bit of clarity helps.

When it comes to architectural sections (as opposed to sections, the SketchUp feature), there's no convention for where to cut them, but you should follow a couple of rules:

▲ **Never cut through columns.** If you show a column in section, it looks like a wall. This is bad, because sections are supposed to show the degree to which a space is open or closed. You can walk around a column, but you can't walk through a wall.

▲ **Try to cut through stairs, elevators, and other "vertical circulation."** Showing how people move up and down through your building makes your drawings more readable and interesting.

10.3.6 Generating an Orthographic Section

Ever seen a technical drawing that included top, front, rear, and side views of the same object? Chances are that was an orthographic projection, which is a common way for three-dimensional objects to be drawn so that they can be built and also measured.

Producing an orthographic section of your model is pretty easy; it's only one extra step beyond making a section perspective. Here's how to do it:

1. **Follow steps 1–3 in the preceding section, as if you're making a section perspective.**
2. **Choose Camera⇨Parallel Projection.** This switches off Perspective, turning your view into a true orthographic representation of your model. If you printed it at a specific scale, you could take measurements from the printout.

To print a plan or section view of your model at a particular scale, have a look at Chapter 12, which explains the whole process.

10.3.7 Creating Section Animations with Scenes

This is probably one of the most useful and impressive things you can do with this software, but some people who have been using SketchUp for years don't know about it. The basic idea is that you can use scenes to create animations where your section planes move inside your model. Here are a few reasons you might want to use this technique:

▲ If you have a building with several levels, you can create an animated presentation that shows a cutaway plan view of each level.

▲ Using an animated section plane to "get inside" your model is a much classier transition than simply hiding certain parts of it.

▲ When you need to show the relationship between the plan and section views for a project, using an animated section plane helps to explain the concept of different architectural views to 3D beginners. This also helps you sell projects to clients who do not understand technical drawings.

Follow these steps to create a basic section animation (a simple example is illustrated in Figure 10-16):

1. **Add a section plane to your model.** A complete explanation of how to create section planes can be found in the section "Cutting Plans and Sections" earlier in this chapter.
2. **Add a scene to your model.** Check out the section "Creating Scenes," earlier in this chapter, for a complete rundown on adding scenes.
3. **Add another section plane to your model.** You can add another section plane in one of two ways:
   - **Use the Section Plane tool to create a brand new one.** This is probably the easiest option, especially if you're just starting out.

Figure 10-16

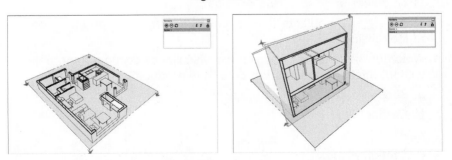

Making a section animation is a fairly straightforward process.

- **Use the Move tool to copy an existing section plane.** Copying section planes is discussed in the section "Cutting Plans and Sections," earlier in this chapter.

  Make sure that your new section plane is active; if it is, it'll be cutting through your model. If it isn't, right-click the section plane and choose Active Cut from the context menu.

4. **Add another scene to your model.** This new scene "remembers" which is the active section plane.

5. **Click through the scenes you added to view your animation.** You should see an animated section cut as SketchUp transitions from one scene to the next. If you don't, make sure that you have scene transitions enabled. You can verify this by choosing Window⇨Model Info and then choosing the Animations panel in the Model Info dialog box. The Scene Transitions check box should be selected.

If you don't like being able to see the section-plane objects (the boxy things with arrows on their corners) in your animation, switch them off by deselecting Section Planes on the View menu. You should still be able to see your section cuts, but you won't see the gray rectangles.

The hardest thing to remember about using scenes and section planes to make section animations is this: You need a separate section plane for each scene that you create. That is to say, SketchUp animates the transition from one active section plane to another active section plane. If all you do is move the same section plane to another spot and add a scene, this technique won't work.

SELF-CHECK

1. A(n) _____ projection is a common way for three-dimensional objects to be drawn so that they can be built.

2. A planimetric view, or plan, is a top-down, three-dimensional, view of an object or space. True or false?

3. _____ are objects that let you cut away parts of your model to look inside.

4. Which of the following toggles the visibility of section-plane objects without affecting the section cuts they produce?

   a. Section cuts

   b. Section view

   c. Plan

   d. Section planes

SUMMARY

Showing your model to others should give you a lot of pride and satisfaction. Although it isn't difficult to show your model to others, it is important to select the right tools. In this chapter, you assessed the correct tools to use when showing your model to an audience. Specifically, you explored your model virtually, creating scenes, sections, and animations. These skills will serve you well when presenting ideas and concepts to an audience.

KEY TERMS

Active cut	The section plane that is actually cutting through your model; others section planes are considered "inactive."
Field of view	The amount of your model you're able to see in your modeling window at one time.
Nest	To embed an object in a separate group or component.
Orthographic projection	A common way for three-dimensional objects to be drawn so that they can be built.
Plan	A top-down, two-dimensional, nonperspectival view of an object or space. Also referred to as a planimetric view.
Scenes	Saved views of a model.
Section	A from-the-side, two-dimensional, nonperspectival view of an object or space. Also referred to as a sectional view.
Section perspective	The view of a cut building where objects seen inside the space appear to get smaller as they get farther away.
Section planes	Objects that let you cut away parts of your model to look inside.

ASSESS YOUR UNDERSTANDING

Go to www.wiley.com/college/chopra to evaluate your knowledge of presenting your model inside of SketchUp.

Measure your learning by comparing pre-test and post-test results.

Summary Questions

1. With the Walk Tool, moving your cursor straight up causes you to walk forward. True or false?

2. When setting your field of view, you should strike a balance between _____ and _____.

3. _____ are a great way of showing interior space in a way that's understandable to most people.

4. Saving a scene for each point that you'd like to make in a presentation is tedious and wastes time in the long run. True or false?

5. If you have more than one section plane, use Passive Cut to tell SketchUp which one should be active. True or false?

6. Which properties keep track of the visibility of the lines, faces, groups, components, and axes in your model?

    (a) Hidden geometry

    (b) Hidden layers

    (c) Axes

    (d) Visible layers

7. Camera location properties include the position of the camera, or _____, and the field of view.

8. You can use scenes to create animations where your section planes move inside your model. True or false?

9. Saved views of your model are:

    (a) plans.

    (b) sections.

    (c) placemarks.

    (d) scenes.

10. Which term refers to the amount of your model that you're able to see in your modeling window at one time?

    (a) Plan

    (b) Section

    (c) Orthographic projection

    (d) Field of view

Applying This Chapter

1. Why would you want to create scenes from your model? List and describe two reasons.

2. You have created a model of a house and you want to present it to your class. How do you use SketchUp's tools to explore the model and present the scenes to your class?

3. You created scenes for presenting your model to the class. How do you modify these scenes?

4. Although the presentation of your model looks great, you want to create a section animation with scenes. Write down the steps needed to do this.

YOU TRY IT

Create Scenes

Using the model of your house, create four scenes:

1. From outside the house
2. From inside the living room
3. From inside the bathroom
4. From inside the bedroom

Modify Scenes

Take the scenes you have already created and put them in the opposite order that you originally had them. Also add shadows to your scenes if you do not already have shadows present.

Create Animations

Using the model of your house, create three section animations using scenes. Play your animations as a presentation for your class.

11

WORKING WITH GOOGLE EARTH AND THE 3D WAREHOUSE
Tying Together All of Google's 3D Software

Starting Point

Go to www.wiley.com/college/chopra to assess your knowledge of Google Earth and the 3D Warehouse.
Determine where you need to concentrate your effort.

What You'll Learn in This Chapter

▲ The relationship between SketchUp, Google Earth, and the 3D Warehouse
▲ The capabilities of Google Earth
▲ The process for building SketchUp models for Google Earth
▲ How to use the 3D Warehouse

After Studying This Chapter, You'll Be Able To

▲ Evaluate how to best use SketchUp, Google Earth, and the 3D Warehouse to serve your modeling needs
▲ Navigate in Google Earth
▲ Build a model in SketchUp for Google Earth
▲ Contribute to the 3D Warehouse

INTRODUCTION

If you've ever used Google Earth, you know what it's like to spend several hours traveling to Paris, Cairo, and the South Pole while checking out the peak of Mount Everest and looking at your old elementary school along the way.

What if you could see 3D models of buildings and other man-made structures in Google Earth the same way that you can see aerial images and 3D topography? You can. What if you could build your own models in SketchUp and see them in Google Earth? You can do that, too. What if you could allow *everyone* who uses Google Earth—there are hundreds of millions of them—to see your models in *their* copies of Google Earth, no matter where they are? That, too, is possible.

This chapter focuses on making SketchUp models that you and (if you'd like) anyone else can see on Google Earth. In this chapter, you will evaluate how to best use SketchUp, Google Earth, and the 3D Warehouse. You will learn how to navigate in Google Earth and how to build a model in SketchUp for Google Earth. Finally, you will learn how to contribute to the 3D Warehouse, a large online repository of free 3D models that anyone can contribute to or borrow from.

11.1 Getting the Big (3D) Picture

SketchUp, Google Earth, and the 3D Warehouse have a relationship that allows them to function together:

▲ **Google SketchUp:** Because SketchUp is especially good for architecture, you can use it to make buildings that you can later view in Google Earth. If you want, you can also upload (send) what you make to the 3D Warehouse, where anyone who finds it can download (borrow) your model and use it in his or her own copy of SketchUp.

▲ **Google Earth:** Google Earth (http://earth.google.com) is a software program that lets you explore the world by "flying" around, zooming in on things that interest you. The more you zoom, the better the detail is; in some places, you can see things as small as coffee cups. The imagery in Google Earth is anywhere from a couple of weeks to 4 years old, but it gets updated all the time. If you want, you can build models in SketchUp and view them in Google Earth. You can also see models that other people have made. Eventually, Google Earth will include entire 3D cities, built in SketchUp by people all over the world.

▲ **Google 3D Warehouse:** The Google 3D Warehouse (http://sketchup. google.com/3dwarehouse) is a collection of 3D models that is found on Google's servers. Anyone can contribute models, and anyone can use

Figure 11-1

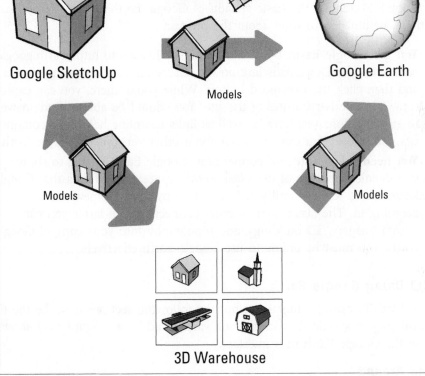

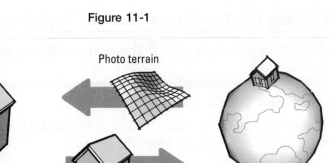

SketchUp, Google Earth, and the 3D Warehouse are all related.

Warehouse are used in a special layer where anyone can see them while they're flying around in Google Earth.

Figure 11-1 shows the SketchUp/Google Earth/3D Warehouse workflow in a diagram.

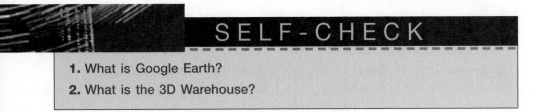

SELF-CHECK

1. What is Google Earth?
2. What is the 3D Warehouse?

11.2 Taking the Ten-Minute Tour of Google Earth

Google Earth can do many things. This section will help get you started using this dynamic tool.

11.2.1 Getting Google Earth

Like Google SketchUp, the basic version of Google Earth is free. Here is some additional helpful information about the program:

▲ **You get Google Earth by downloading it.** Just go to http://earth.google.com, click the Downloads link on the left, select your operating system, and then click the Download button. While you're there, you can explore some of the other features of the site. You should be able to find answers to any questions you have, as well as links to online help, user communities, and more. You can also learn about other versions of Google Earth.

▲ **You need a fast Internet connection.** Google Earth is able to show you detailed imagery of the *whole world*—quite a bit of data that Google keeps on its servers until you "request" it by flying somewhere and zooming in. The faster your Internet connection, the faster you can stream imagery, 3D buildings, and topography into your copy of Google Earth. You must be online to use Google Earth effectively.

11.2.2 Using Google Earth

Google Earth has several functions, but the following sections describe the first three things you should do with the software. In addition, Figure 11-2 shows a view of the Google Earth user interface.

Flying Around

On the upper-right corner of the screen, you'll find the navigation controls for Google Earth conveniently grouped together. Notice how they appear when you hover over them? Go ahead and experiment to figure out what they do. In the meantime, here's some help:

▲ **Zoom:** Move this slider back and forth to zoom in and out on whatever's in the center of your screen. You can also use the scroll wheel on your mouse to zoom, just like in SketchUp.

▲ **Pan:** You can move around by clicking the arrow buttons, but the easier way is to use your mouse. Just click and drag to "spin" the world in whatever direction you want.

▲ **Rotate:** Turn the wheel to spin yourself around without moving. This works like the Look Around tool in SketchUp. Click the N button to reorient the world so that north is up.

Figure 11-2

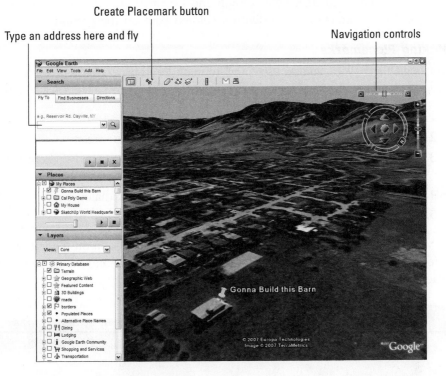

The Google Earth user interface makes navigation easy.

▲ **Tilt:** Google Earth is 3D. Move the Tilt slider back and forth to tilt your view. If you're looking at an area with mountains, they should resemble a 3D image (if they don't, make sure that the Terrain layer is enabled in the lower-left corner). You can also tilt by holding down your scroll wheel button, just as you do to orbit in SketchUp. (See Chapter 2 for more on orbiting.)

Going Someplace Specific

In the blank field in the upper-left corner that says "Fly To," you can type in an address anywhere in the world, and Google Earth will fly you directly there. However, this feature works better for some places than for others. Here are some tips for using "Fly To":

▲ **Use the right format.** If you're entering an address in the United States or Canada, use this format: Street Number Street Name, Zip (Postal) Code. Here's an example: 1234 Cherry Blvd, 64254. If it doesn't work the first time, try a few variations.

▲ **Type in landmarks.** Try typing "Eiffel Tower" or "Statue of Liberty," for instance.

▲ **Get directions.** Click the Directions tab (also in the upper-left corner of the screen), and then enter Origin and Destination addresses to see a list of driving directions along with a colored path on the ground.

Making Placemarks

In Google Earth, you can also use "pins" to mark locations you'd like to come back to later; these are called **placemarks**. Follow these steps to create a placemark:

1. Fly to where you want to create a placemark.
2. Click the Create Placemark button at the top of the screen.
3. Move your placemark (it looks like a thumbtack) to exactly where you want it (on top of your house, for instance).
4. Give your placemark a name in the Edit Placemark dialog box.
5. Click the OK button.

Your new placemark should show up in the Places section on the left of your screen. No matter where you are in the world, double-clicking the name of your placemark in the Places list will fly you right there.

SELF-CHECK

1. Google Earth is:
   a. free to everyone and 3D.
   b. free to students and 3D.
   c. free to everyone and 2D.
   d. not free to anyone and 3D.
2. To get the most out of Google Earth, you need a _____ Internet connection.
3. You can pan in Google Earth by using the onscreen arrow buttons or your _____.
4. You can use placemarks in Google Earth to mark where you would like to come back later. True or false?

11.3 Building Models for Google Earth

With SketchUp, you can build a model of a building (maybe your house) and see it in Google Earth. After you've done that, you can email the model to your friends (or clients) so that they can see it in Google Earth, too. And if you'd like, you can upload it to the 3D Warehouse so that the whole world can see it as well.

Figure 11-3

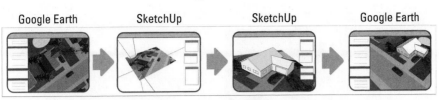

Making a SketchUp model for Google Earth is a four-step process.

This section deals with the basic procedure for making a model in SketchUp and viewing it in Google Earth. It also provides some tips for making buildings that are optimized for Google Earth.

11.3.1 Understanding the Process

Very simply, building SketchUp models for Google Earth involves the following steps:

1. Choose a site in Google Earth.
2. Import the view into SketchUp.
3. Build a model using the imported view as a guide.
4. Export your model to Google Earth.

Figure 11-3 is an illustration of these steps.

11.3.2 Finding a Site and Bringing It into SketchUp

Follow these steps to import a building site into SketchUp from Google Earth:

1. **Launch Google Earth.** Make sure that you're online when you launch Google Earth; if you aren't, you won't be able to see much.
2. **In Google Earth, navigate to the area where you want to place a model.** The important thing is to fill your Google Earth window with the area that you want to import into SketchUp. Take a look at Figure 11-4 to see an example of this.
3. **Launch SketchUp and open a new file.** SketchUp opens a new file every time you launch it, so this step should be easy.
4. **Choose Tools⇨Google Earth⇨Get Current View from the menu bar.** When you do this, SketchUp imports a "snapshot" of whatever is currently visible in your Google Earth screen.

You can also access SketchUp's Google Earth commands by opening the Google Earth toolbar. Simply choose View⇨Toolbars⇨Google Earth to make this toolbar visible.

Figure 11-4

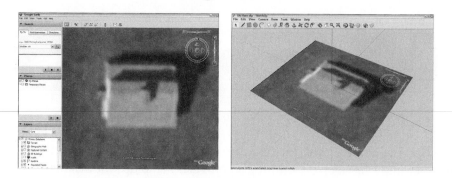

Whatever you can see in Google Earth (left) is what gets imported
into your SketchUp modeling window (right).

If you want to import additional snapshots from Google Earth into SketchUp, you can. SketchUp automatically tiles together all the snapshots you "take" (by choosing Get Current View) in your modeling window to form a kind of patchwork. This is especially helpful if you find that you didn't get everything you needed the first time.

You need to wait until your Google Earth view is at least 95 percent loaded before you can capture a snapshot in SketchUp. The "Streaming" readout at the bottom of your Google Earth window shows when you've waited long enough.

11.3.3 Modeling on a Google Earth Snapshot

Now that you've imported a snapshot from Google Earth into SketchUp, you can build a model on the snapshot. To do this, simply use SketchUp the way you always do—everything about SketchUp stays exactly the same, even after you import a snapshot. Of course, you first need to know how to do some SketchUp basics, such as how to use the Line tool to trace a building's footprint, work with the drawing axes, and more. These basics are discussed in detail in Chapter 2.

Building on Top of a Snapshot

Here are the basic steps for building a model on top of your Google Earth snapshot:

1. **Make sure that you have a flat view of your terrain.** Choose Tools⇨Google Earth⇨Toggle Terrain a couple of times to figure out which is the flat view, and then start from there.

2. **Trace the footprint of the building you want to model on the imported black-and-white image (see image A in Figure 11-5).** Of course, you can also model something that doesn't exist yet. If the building you're trying to make doesn't line up perfectly with the colored axes,

Figure 11-5

A   B

C   D

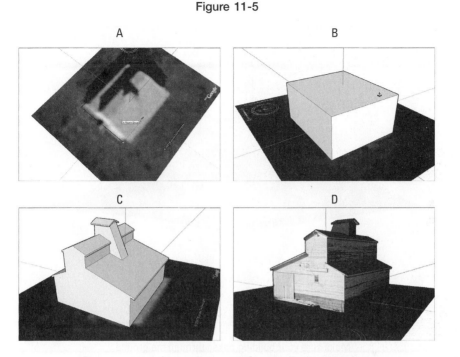

Draw on top of your flattened Google Earth snapshot.

using the Line and Rectangle tools can be difficult. To fix this problem, reposition your main drawing axes by choosing Tools⇨Axes. Click once to set your origin, again to establish the direction of your red axis (parallel to one of the edges in your photo), and a third time to establish your green axis. It may be helpful to set your origin at the corner of the building you're trying to make.

3. **Use Push/Pull to extrude the footprint to the correct height (see image B in Figure 11-5).**

4. **Keep modeling until you're satisfied with what you have.**

5. **Flip to a 3D view of your terrain (by choosing Tools⇨Google Earth⇨Toggle Terrain in the menu bar), and then move your building up or down until it's sitting properly (see Figure 11-6).** Select everything you want to move, and then use the Move tool to move it up or down. You can press the up- or down-arrow key to constrain your move to the blue axis if you so choose.

If you have a SketchUp model that you've already built and you'd like to export it to Google Earth, just import it into the same file as your snapshot. To do this, choose File⇨Import from the menu bar, find the model on your computer, and bring it in.

Figure 11-6

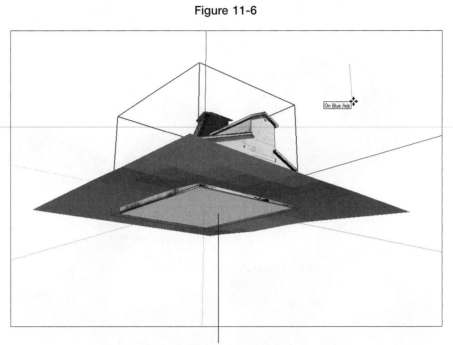

Make sure your building pokes through the ground

Move your model up or down until it's sitting properly on the terrain.

Letting SketchUp Take Care of the Details

The Google Earth import process saves time. Much of the information that you need is already in Google Earth, and SketchUp takes advantage of it as follows:

▲ **SketchUp geolocates your position automatically.** When SketchUp engages in **geolocation,** it sets your latitude and longitude to match Google Earth, and it orients your snapshot in the right cardinal direction. This means that any shadow studies you do with the Shadows feature will automatically be accurate for wherever you were in Google Earth when you took your snapshot.

▲ **Everything's already the right size.** Perhaps you take a snapshot of a football field in Google Earth; when you measure that football field in SketchUp, it will be exactly 100 yards long. That's because SketchUp scales your snapshot to the correct size as part of the import process.

▲ **There's more to snapshots than meets the eye.** The snapshot that SketchUp imports from Google Earth is more than just a black-and-white aerial photo—it also includes a section of topography called terrain. The terrain is flat when you first import it because it's easier to build on it that way, but you can toggle between flat and 3D (not flat) views by

choosing Tools⇨Google Earth⇨Toggle Terrain. If you don't see any difference when you flip between the views, you probably just chose a flat
site. Figure 11-7 shows the same snapshot with terrain toggled off (top)
and on (bottom).

Figure 11-7

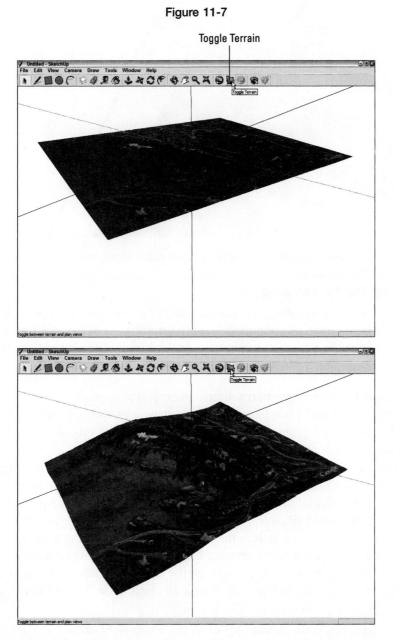

Use Toggle Terrain to switch between flat and 3D views of your Google Earth snapshot.

Figure 11-8

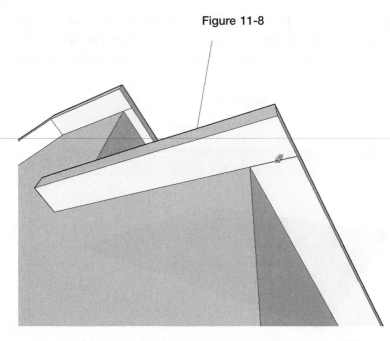

Take a couple of minutes to erase extra edges and faces.

Thinking Big by Thinking Small

When it comes to modeling for Google Earth, lightness is desirable. **Lightness** refers to the file size of your model, or the number of faces and textures you use to build it. The more complicated your model is, the slower Google Earth will run. To do the most with the least geometry, follow these tips:

▲ **Get rid of extra geometry.** Often when you're modeling, you end up with edges (and even faces) that don't have a purpose. Figure 11-8 shows a prime example of the kinds of little edges you can erase to drastically reduce the number of faces in your model.

▲ **Reduce the number of sides in your extruded arcs and circles.** Sketch-Up's default number of sides for circles is 24. This means that every time you use Push/Pull to extrude a circle into a cylinder, you end up with 25 faces: 24 around the sides, and the original face on top. Instead of using circles with 24 sides, reduce the number of sides by typing a number followed by the letter s and pressing Enter right after you draw a circle. The same thing goes for arcs; you change the number of sides in them in exactly the same way. For example, to draw a 10-sided circle, follow these steps:

1. Draw a circle with the Circle tool.

2. Type **10s** (this should appear in the lower-right corner of your modeling window), and then press Enter.

Figure 11-9

24-sided circle   10-sided circle

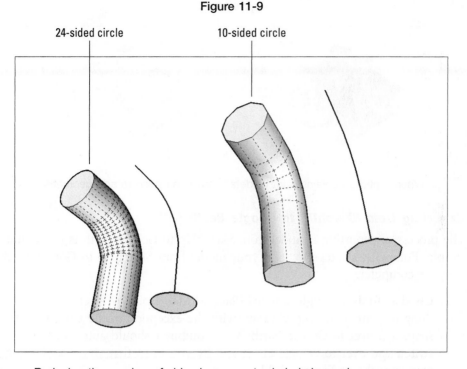

Reducing the number of sides in your extruded circles and arcs can save
hundreds of faces, and the object looks just as good.

Figure 11-9 illustrates the same pipe constructed by using Follow Me on
two circles: one with 24 sides and one with only 10. Note the difference
in the number of faces in each version.

▲ **When you can, use photo detail instead of geometry.** This really only
applies if you're mapping photos (or using Photo Match) on the model
you're making for Google Earth. If you are, it's a good idea to make as
basic a model as you can, and let the detail in the photo do the work.
Resist the temptation to model windows and doors. Figure 11-10
shows a model of a barn. The view on the left shows it with photo
textures visible; the version on the right is just the simple geometry.
You can read about how to use photos to add detail to your models in
Chapter 7.

11.3.4 Viewing Your Model in Google Earth

After you've made a model on top of a snapshot, it's a simple operation to send
it over to your copy of Google Earth. And after you've done that, you can save
it as a Google Earth KMZ file and email it to anyone you choose!

Figure 11-10

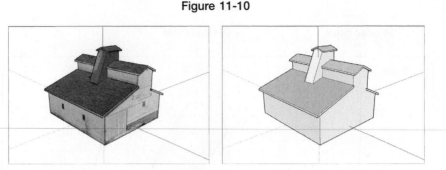

When a photo contains a lot of detail, you don't need to add geometry.

Exporting from SketchUp to Google Earth

The process of exporting a model from SketchUp to Google Earth is really quite simple. Follow these steps to send your model from SketchUp to Google Earth on your computer:

1. **Choose Tools⇨Google Earth⇨Place Model.** Doing this sends everything in your modeling window (with the exception of the Google Earth snapshot) over to Google Earth. Your computer should automatically switch you over to Google Earth and fly you in so that you're looking at your model (see Figure 11-11).

2. **If you decide you want to make changes to your model, go back to SketchUp, make your changes, and then choose Place Model again.** Google Earth pops up a dialog box that asks you whether you want to overwrite the old version of the model you placed the first time.

3. **Click the Yes button if you're sure that's what you want to do.**

4. **Continue to go back and forth between SketchUp and Google Earth until your model looks exactly the way you want it to.**

Saving Your Model as a Google Earth KMZ File

You can save your SketchUp model as a Google Earth KMZ file that you can send to anyone. When someone opens the KMZ file, Google Earth opens on his or her computer (if he or she has Google Earth), and he or she is "flown in" to look at the model you made. Follow these steps to save your model as a KMZ file:

1. **In Google Earth, select your model by clicking it in the Temporary Places list on the left of the screen.** Unless you've renamed it yourself, your model will be called *SUPreview1*. Click it once to select it.

2. **Choose File⇨Save⇨Save Place As.** The Save File dialog box opens.

3. **Give your file a name and figure out where to put it on your hard drive.**

4. **Click the Save button to save your model as a KMZ file.**

Figure 11-11

It's easy to view a SketchUp model in Google Earth.

SELF-CHECK

1. You can save your SketchUp model in a Google Earth XYZ file that you can send to anyone. True or false?

2. You need to wait until your Google Earth view is at least _____ percent loaded before you can capture a snapshot in SketchUp.

3. When SketchUp geolocates your position, it:

   a. sets your latitude.

   b. sets your longitude.

   c. orients your snapshot in the right cardinal direction.

   d. sets your latitude and longitude to match Google Earth, and it orients your snapshot in the right cardinal direction.

4. SketchUp scales your snapshot to the correct size as part of the import process. True or false?

11.4 Using the 3D Warehouse

Google gets most of the realistic buildings that show up by default on the 3D Buildings layer in Google Earth from SketchUp users. Google's strategy for building the whole man-made world in 3D is to rely on SketchUp users everywhere to model their local context. That's the main reason that SketchUp is a free program, and it's a fairly revolutionary way to think about tackling a massive project: millions of people working together to provide accurate, current information that can be used by anyone.

11.4.1 Getting to the Google 3D Warehouse

So how can you get your models into Google Earth so that everyone can see them? To do that, you need to upload your work into the 3D Warehouse. The 3D Warehouse is a huge collection of 3D models that is searchable and, most importantly, free for everyone to use.

The 3D Warehouse is basically a website; it exists online, and you need an Internet connection to access it. You can get there in two different ways:

▲ **From SketchUp:** Choose File⇨3D Warehouse⇨Get Models; when you do this, a mini web browser opens right in front of your modeling window.

▲ **From the web:** Browse to http://sketchup.google.com/3dwarehouse. This is a great way to hunt for 3D models without having to open SketchUp first.

Go ahead and explore the 3D Warehouse. It's amazing what you'll find; after all, thousands of people are adding new content every day. Most of this content isn't very useful, but you'll still find plenty of interesting things to download and look at. If you need more information, check out the online Help—it's in the lower-right corner of your browser window when you're in the 3D Warehouse. You can also build interior design models using the 3D Warehouse. You can also buy 3D replicas for interiors and other models on sites such as www.formfonts .com. Other sites and their SketchUp products are mentioned in Chapter 16.

11.4.2 Uploading Your Models

Before you upload your model to the 3D Warehouse, you need to understand which of the following broad categories it falls into:

▲ **Geolocated objects:** Things like buildings, monuments, bridges, and dams exist in a specific geographic location; they never move around. In other words, these are **geolocated objects.** These are the kinds of models that show up on the 3D Buildings layer in Google Earth, and the 3D Warehouse is where they come from. To upload your own geolocated models, you need to start with a Google Earth snapshot; this provides the geolocation information that Google needs to put your model in the right place. Check out the section "Building Models for Google Earth," earlier in this chapter, for a full account of how to build geolocated models that you can upload to the 3D Warehouse.

▲ **Nongeolocated objects:** Objects like toasters, SUVs, wheelchairs, and sofas aren't unique, and they don't exist in any one geographic location. Such items can be thought of as **nongeolocated objects.** For example, no physical address is associated with a model of a Honda Accord because millions of them exist, and because Honda Accords move around. Such objects never show up in Google Earth. That doesn't mean they don't belong in the 3D Warehouse, though; models of nongeolocated objects are incredibly valuable for people who are making their own SketchUp models.

Once you've determined what type of object you're working with, follow these steps to upload your own model to the Google 3D Warehouse:

1. **Open the model you want to upload in SketchUp.**
2. **Adjust your view until you like what you see.** When you upload a model to the 3D Warehouse, SketchUp automatically creates a preview image that's a snapshot of your modeling window.
3. **Choose File⇨3D Warehouse⇨Share Model.** A mini-browser window opens, and it shows the logon screen for the 3D Warehouse. If you want to upload models, you need a Google account. An account is free; you just need a valid email address to get one. If you don't already have one, follow the on-screen instructions to sign up. When you're creating your Google account, be sure to type something in where the system asks for a "nickname." If you don't, everything you upload will be attributed to "Anonymous."
4. **Enter your Google account information and click the Sign In button.**
5. **Fill out the Upload to 3D Warehouse form as completely as you can:**
   - **Title:** Enter a title for your model. If it's a public building, you might enter its name. Something like "Royal West Academy" would do nicely.
   - **Description:** Models with complete descriptions are very popular with people who are searching the Warehouse. Try to use complete sentences here; the more you write, the better.
   - **Address:** This field only appears if your model is geolocated, meaning that you started with a Google Earth snapshot. If you know the physical address of the thing you made, type it in.
   - **Google Earth Ready:** You only get this option if your model is geolocated. If your model is accurate, correctly sized, and in the right location, and if you want it to be considered for inclusion on the default 3D Buildings layer of Google Earth, select this check box. If you do, Google will consider adding it to Google Earth.

FOR EXAMPLE

Minding Your Modeling Manners

People sometimes wonder if anyone at Google is paying attention to what gets uploaded to the 3D Warehouse. The answer to that question is slightly complicated. For instance, nobody at Google minds if you refer to a website or enter tags that don't have anything to do with the model you upload.

On the other hand, it's frowned upon when people go anywhere near the usual taboo subjects for public, G-rated websites; pornography and/or foul language will get your model removed from the 3D Warehouse. Thousands of impressionable young people peruse Google's websites every day, so Google tries to keep its sites clean.

- **Website:** If you have a web address that you'd like people who view your model to visit, enter it here. For example, if your model is of a historic building, you might include the address of a website that provides more information about that building.
- **Tags:** Type in a string of words that describe the thing you modeled. Whatever you enter here will be used by the 3D Warehouse search engine to help people find your model. To increase the number of people who see what you made, add several tags. For example, to upload a modern coffee table, you might enter the following tags: coffee table, table, coffee, modern, living room, furniture, glass, chrome, metal, steel. Be exhaustive.

6. **Click the Upload button to add your model to the 3D Warehouse.** If everything works properly, you should get a page with your model on it, along with all the information you just entered. The words "Model has been uploaded successfully" will be highlighted in yellow at the top of your browser window.

SELF-CHECK

1. How do you place your models in Google Earth so everyone can use them?
2. Buildings, monuments, bridges, and dams are _____ objects.
3. _____ objects are invaluable in the 3D Warehouse.
4. Thousands of people add new content to the 3D Warehouse everyday. True or false?

SUMMARY

Google Earth allows you to visit the most beautiful places in the world without leaving your chair. This powerful program also interacts with SketchUp and the 3D Warehouse to enable you to create all types of models and share them with the world. In this chapter, you assessed how these programs work together to enable you and others to build creative and accurate models and to share these models. You navigated around Google Earth, built models, and contributed your models to the 3D Warehouse. These skills will help you become a vital part of the virtual modeling community.

KEY TERMS

Geolocated objects	Objects that never move and have a fixed position, such as buildings and monuments.
Geolocation	The process by which SketchUp sets the imported snapshot's latitude and longitude to match Google Earth, and it orients the snapshot in the right cardinal direction.
Lightness	The file size of a model, or the number of faces and textures used to build it.
Nongeolocated objects	Objects that do not have a fixed position, such as furniture and cars.
Placemarks	Pins in Google Earth that mark locations the user would like to visit again.

ASSESS YOUR UNDERSTANDING

Go to www.wiley.com/college/chopra to evaluate your knowledge of Google Earth and the 3D Warehouse.
Measure your learning by comparing pre-test and post-test results.

Summary Questions

1. The basic versions of SketchUp and Google Earth are both free. True or false?

2. You can _____ Google Earth at http://earth.google.com.

3. The Fly To feature in Google Earth works well for all addresses in the world. True or false?

4. You can place a _____ in the places you would like to visit later in Google Earth.

5. You don't have to worry about the size of your snapshots when importing them into SketchUp because SketchUp _____ your snapshots to the correct size as part of the import process.

6. Lightness refers to the contrast of colors in your model. True or false?

7. When you're modeling, you may end up with edges and faces that don't have a _____.

8. SketchUp's default number of sides for circles is:

    (a) 6.

    (b) 12.

    (c) 24.

    (d) 48.

9. The snapshot that SketchUp imports from Google Earth includes terrain, which is:

    (a) a nongeolocated object.

    (b) topography that is always flat.

    (c) topography that can be flat or 3D.

    (d) topography that is always 3D.

10. How do you rotate in Google Earth?

    (a) Move the slider back and forth.

    (b) Click the arrow buttons.

    (c) Use your mouse.

    (d) Turn the wheel and spin yourself without moving.

Applying This Chapter

1. You have a very complex model of a house that is causing Google Earth to run slowly. What steps can you take to simplify your model?

2. You want to build a model of your favorite downtown building and view it in Google Earth. What steps do you take to do this?

3. How does using the Google Earth import process save you time?

YOU TRY IT

Visit America's Landmarks

Download Google Earth onto your computer and take some time to tour the program. Using the Fly To feature, tour Mount Rushmore, the White House, and the Golden Gate Bridge.

Model and Upload Your Home or School

Go to Google Earth and see if your home is visible. If it is, import a snapshot from Google Earth into SketchUp. If your house isn't visible, import a snapshot of your school instead. Build a simple model of the building in your snapshot and upload it to the 3D Warehouse. Next, e-mail a link to your model to a classmate.

12

PRINTING YOUR WORK

With a Windows PC and a Mac

Starting Point

Go to www.wiley.com/college/chopra to assess your knowledge of printing your work.
Determine where you need to concentrate your effort.

What You'll Learn in This Chapter

▲ The differences in printing your model on a Windows PC versus a Mac
▲ The printing options available to you
▲ Under what circumstances you would want to print to scale or change the scale

After Studying This Chapter, You'll Be Able To

▲ Print views of your model on either a Windows PC or a Mac
▲ Evaluate the options available in the printing dialog boxes
▲ Print your model to scale

INTRODUCTION

As much as it seems we live in an all-digital world, the truth is that we don't. People use more paper now than they ever have.

This chapter explains how to print views of your SketchUp model. Because the Windows and Mac versions of this procedure are different, a section is dedicated to each platform. The last part of this chapter is devoted to scaled printing—a topic that can sometimes intimidate even experienced architects. SketchUp makes printing to scale slightly more difficult than it could be, but it's still easier than drawing things by hand.

12.1 Printing from a Windows Computer

It's very easy to print from SketchUp, as long as you're not trying to do anything too complicated, such as printing to a particular scale, which can be a harrowing experience the first few times you attempt it. Instructions for how to do so can be found at the end of this chapter.

12.1.1 Making a Basic Print (Windows)

Most of the time, all you need to do is to print exactly what you see on your screen. Follow these steps to do that on a Windows machine:

1. **Make sure that you have the view you want to print in your modeling window.** Unless you're printing to scale, SketchUp prints exactly what you see in your modeling window.
2. **Choose File⇨Print Setup.** This opens the Print Setup dialog box, which is where you make choices about what printer and paper you want to print to.
3. **In the Print Setup dialog box (see Figure 12-1), do the following:**
   • Choose the printer you'd like to use.
   • Choose a paper size for your print.
   • Choose an orientation for your print; most of the time, you'll want to use Landscape, because your screen is usually wider than it is tall.
4. **Click the OK button to close the Print Setup dialog box.**
5. **Choose File⇨Print Preview.** This opens the Print Preview dialog box, which lets you see an image of what your print will look like before you send it to a printer.
6. **In the Print Preview dialog box, do the following:**
   • In the Tabbed Scene Print Range area, choose which scenes you'd like to print, if you have more than one. If you need to, you can read about scenes in Chapter 10.

Figure 12-1

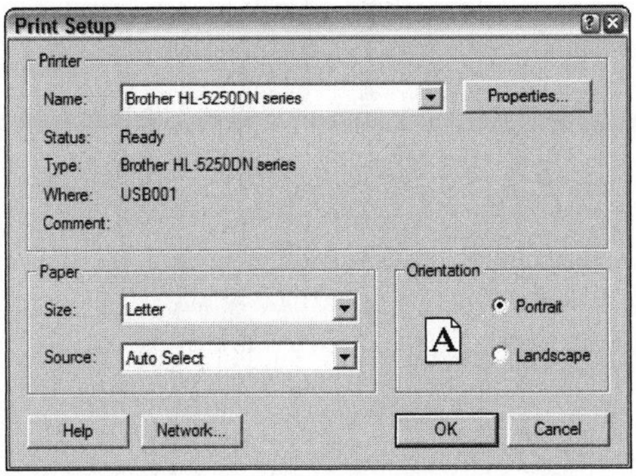

The Print Setup dialog box in Windows asks you
to choose a printer, paper size, and orientation.

- Tell SketchUp how many copies of each scene you need.
- Make sure that the Fit to Page check box is selected.
- Make sure that the Use Model Extents check box *isn't* selected.
- Choose a print quality for your printout (High Definition is best for most jobs).

7. **Click the OK button to close the Print Preview dialog box and generate an on-screen preview of what your print will look like.**

8. **If you are satisfied with what you see, click the Print button in the upper-left corner of the Print Preview window to open the Print dialog box.** If you *don't* like what you're about to print, click the Close button (at the top of the screen) and go back to step 1.

9. **In the Print dialog box (which should look exactly like the Print Preview dialog box), click the OK button to send your job to the printer.**

12.1.2 Decoding the Windows Print Dialog Box

The Print Preview and Print dialog boxes in SketchUp are exactly the same. Figure 12-2 shows the former, but the descriptions in this section apply to both.

Printer

If you used the Print Setup dialog box first, you shouldn't need to change any of the settings in this section. If you want, you can choose which printer to print to from the drop-down list. You can also click the Properties button to make adjustments to your printer settings. (Because these are different for every printer, you may need to consult your printer's user manual.)

Figure 12-2

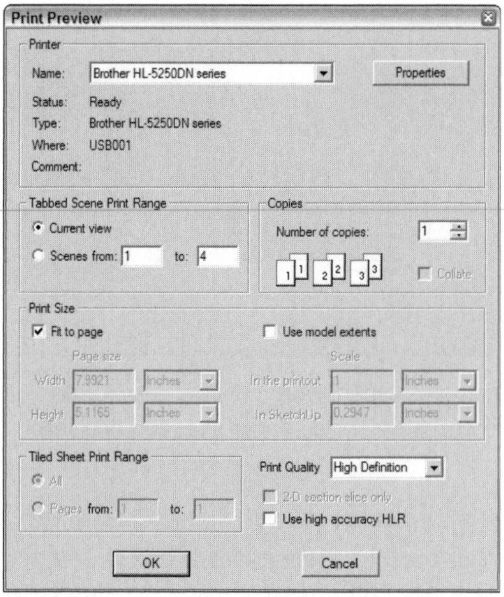

The Print Preview dialog box in Windows looks exactly the same as the Print dialog box.

Tabbed Scene Print Range

Use this area to tell SketchUp which of your scenes you'd like to print, if you have more than one. This is handy for quickly printing all your scenes. Select the Current View option to print only what is currently in your modeling window.

Copies

This step is fairly basic: Choose how many copies of each view you'd like to print. If you're printing multiple copies of multiple scenes, select the Collate check box to print "packets," which can save you from having to assemble them yourself. Here's what happens when you're printing three copies of four scenes:

▲ Selecting the Collate check box prints the pages in the following order: 123412341234.

▲ Deselecting the Collate check box prints the pages like this: 111222333444.

Print Size

This is the most complicated part of this dialog box; you use the Print Size controls to determine how your model will look on the printed page. Figure 12-3 shows the effect of some of these settings on a final print.

Figure 12-3

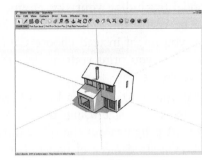

My SketchUp screen

Fit to Page

Fit to Page and Use Model Extents

Different Print Size settings have different results
when applied to the same view in SketchUp.

The Print Size controls are as follows:

▲ **Fit to Page:** Selecting this check box tells SketchUp to make your
printed page look like your Modeling Window. As long as the Use Model
Extents check box isn't selected, you should be able to see exactly what
you see on your screen.

▲ **Use Model Extents:** All this option does is instruct SketchUp to zoom in to make your model (excluding your sky, ground, watermark, and whatever else might be visible on your screen) fit the printed page. If you want this effect, you might instead choose Camera⇨Zoom Extents from the menu bar before you print your model; it's easier, and you know exactly what you're getting.

▲ **Page Size:** As long as you don't have the Fit to Page check box selected, you can manually enter a page size using these controls. If you type in a width or height, SketchUp figures out the other dimension and pretends it's printing on a different-sized piece of paper. This option is especially useful if you want to make a big print by tiling together lots of smaller pages. See the next section in this chapter for more details.

▲ **Scale:** This step is slightly complicated. To print to scale, you have to do two things before you use the Print or Print Preview dialog boxes:

• Switch to Parallel Projection mode.

• Make sure that you're using one of the Standard views.

Take a look at the section "Printing to Scale (Windows and Mac)," later in this chapter, for a complete rundown on printing to scale in SketchUp.

Tiled Sheet Print Range

Perhaps you're printing at a scale that won't fit on a single page, or you've entered a print size that's bigger than the paper size you chose in the Print Setup dialog box. The Tiled Sheet Print Range area lets you print your image on multiple sheets and then attach them all together later. In this way, you are able to create posters using your small-format printer.

Print Quality

When selecting a print quality for your image, the result of each setting depends on your model, so you should probably try a few different settings if you have time. Draft and Standard are really only useful for making your model appear the way you want it to on the printed page; you may want to use High Definition first, then increase to Ultra High Definition if your computer/printer setup can manage it.

Other Settings

You can control the following settings in the Print Preview dialog box, too:

▲ **2-D Section Slice Only:** If you have a visible section cut in your model view, selecting this check box tells SketchUp to only print the section cut edges. Figure 12-4 shows what the same model view would look like without (on the left) and with (right) this option selected. This can be used to produce simple plan and section views that you can sketch on by hand.

Figure 12-4

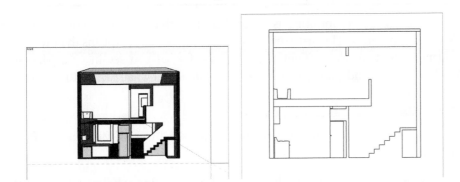

Printing only the 2-D section slice yields a simple drawing that's easy to sketch over.

▲ **Use High Accuracy HLR:** Selecting this check box tells SketchUp to send vector information to the printer instead of the usual raster data. **Vector** images consist of instructions written in computer code, whereas **raster** images are composed of pixels. Vector lines look much smoother and cleaner when printed, so your whole model will look better—with one exception: Gradients (especially the smooth shadows on rounded surfaces) don't print well as vectors. If you have a lot of rounded or curvy surfaces in your model view, you probably don't want to choose this option. Also, if your model view includes a sketchy edges style, don't use high accuracy HLR; you won't see any of the sketchy effects in your final print.

SELF-CHECK

1. If you want to print ordered packets of material, what check box do you need to select?
2. Print Size is the most complicated section of the Print dialog box. True or false?
3. _____ images are composed of pixels.
4. The Print Setup dialog box in Windows asks you to choose a:
    a. printer.
    b. paper size.
    c. paper orientation.
    d. printer, paper size, and paper orientation.

12.2 Printing from a Mac

If you're using a Mac, printing is slightly simpler than it is for people who use Windows computers. The first part of the following sections explains the procedure for generating a simple, straightforward print of what you see in your Modeling Window. The second part goes into some detail about what each setting does.

12.2.1 Making a Basic Print (Mac)

Follow these steps to print exactly what you see in your Modeling Window on a Mac:

1. **Make sure that your modeling window contains whatever you want to print.** SketchUp prints exactly what you see in your Modeling Window, unless you're printing to scale. This is considerably more complicated, and it is explained in a section at the end of this chapter.
2. **Choose File⇨Page Setup.** This opens the Page Setup dialog box, where you decide what printer and paper size to use.
3. **In the Page Setup dialog box (see Figure 12-5), do the following:**
   • Choose the printer you'd like to use from the Format For drop-down list.
   • Choose a paper size for your print.
   • Choose an orientation for your print.
4. **Click the OK button to close the Page Setup dialog box.**
5. **Choose File⇨Document Setup.** This opens the Document Setup dialog box.
6. **In the Document Setup dialog box, make sure that the Fit View to Page check box is selected.** See the next section in this chapter for a full description of what everything does.

Figure 12-5

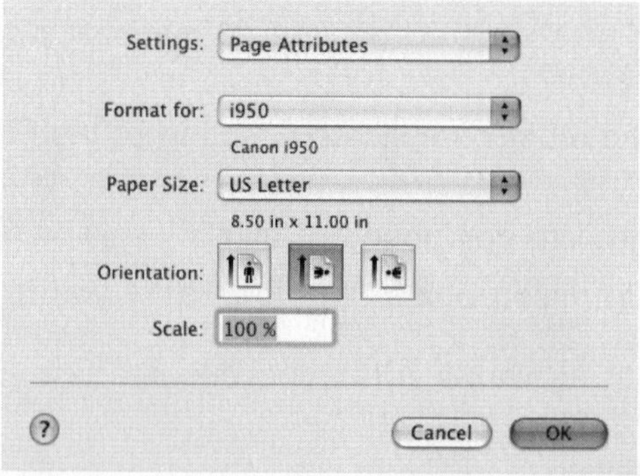

The Page Setup dialog box on a Mac lets you select
a printer, a paper size, and a page orientation.

7. Click the OK button to close the Document Setup dialog box.

8. Choose File⇨Print to open the Print dialog box.

9. **In the Print dialog box, click the Preview button.** This generates an on-screen preview of what your print will look like on paper.

10. **If you are satisfied with the preview, click the Print button to send your print job to the printer.** If you're not satisfied with the preview, click the Cancel button and start again at step 1.

12.2.2 Deciphering the Mac Printing Dialog Boxes

Because printing from SketchUp on a Mac involves two separate dialog boxes, both are described in the following sections.

The Document Setup Dialog Box

You use the settings in the Document Setup dialog box (see Figure 12-6) to control how big your model prints.

Here's what everything in the Document Setup dialog box does:

▲ **Print Size:** This one's fairly self-explanatory, but here are some details:

 • **Fit View to Page:** Selecting this check box tells SketchUp to make your printed page look just like your Modeling Window on-screen.

 • **Width and Height:** If the Fit View to Page check box is deselected, you can type in either a width or a height for your final print. This is what you should do if you want to print a tiled poster out of several sheets of paper; simply enter a final size.

▲ **Print Scale:** Use these settings to control the scale of your printed drawing, if that's the kind of print you're trying to make. Because printing to

Figure 12-6

Print Size		
	☑ Fit View to Page	
Width:	10 11/16"	
Height:	7 9/16"	
Print Scale		
	1"	In Drawing
	2' 9 5/16	In Model
Pages Required		
	1 Page	
	Cancel	OK

The Mac Document Setup dialog box controls
how big your model will be when printed.

scale is somewhat difficult, the last section of this chapter is devoted to the topic. Refer to that section for a description of what these settings do.

▲ **Pages Required:** This is simply a readout of the number of pages you need to print. If you have selected the Fit View to Page check box, this should read 1. If your print won't fit on one sheet, it will be tiled onto the number of sheets displayed in this section of the dialog box.

The Print Dialog Box

The Print dialog box on the Mac contains several more panels in the Copies & Pages drop-down list. You only need to use two. Both are pictured in Figure 12-7 and described in the following list:

▲ **Copies & Pages panel:** The controls in this part of the Print dialog box are fairly straightforward; use them to tell SketchUp how many copies and pages you want to print:

• **Copies:** If you're printing more than one copy of a print that includes multiple pages, select the Collated check box to tell

Figure 12-7

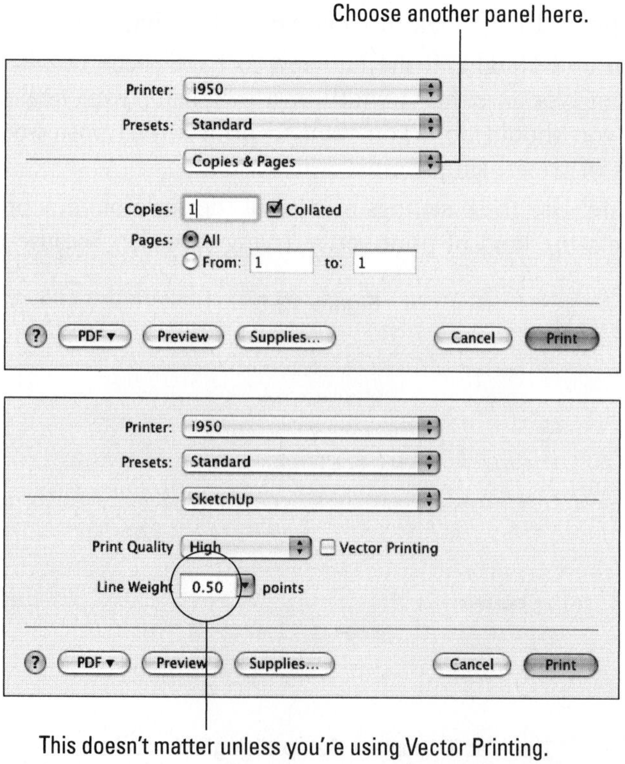

Choose another panel here.

This doesn't matter unless you're using Vector Printing.

The Copies & Pages and SketchUp panels of the Print dialog box.

SketchUp to print "packets," which can save you from having to collate them yourself.

- **Pages:** If the Pages Required readout at the bottom of the Document Setup dialog box said that you need more than one sheet to print your image, you can choose to print all or some of those pages here.

▲ **SketchUp panel:** You use the settings in this panel to control the final appearance of your print:

- **Print Quality:** The results you get with this setting depend on your printer model. In general, Draft or Standard shouldn't be used unless you're simply making sure your page will look the way you want it to. If you have time, try both High and Extra High and see which one looks better.

- **Vector Printing:** When you select this option, SketchUp sends vector (instead of raster) information to the printer. Vector printing makes edges look smoother and cleaner, but it does poorly with gradients. Use vector printing if your model view is made up of mostly flat faces, but try printing both ways (with vector printing on and off) to see which looks better. If your model view includes a sketchy edges style, don't choose Vector Printing; you won't see any of the sketchy effects in your final print.

- **Line Weight:** This option only works if you've selected the Vector Printing check box. The number in this box represents the thickness of edges in your print; any edges that are 1 pixel thick in your model view will be drawn with a line as thick as what you choose for this option. The default is 0.50 points, but you can experiment to see what looks best for your model.

SELF-CHECK

1. The Line Weight option only works if you've selected the _____ check box.
2. To print on a Mac, you must first make sure that your modeling window contains whatever you want to print. True or false?
3. The Mac Document Control dialog box controls how big your model will be when printed. True or false?
4. _____ printing makes edges look smoother.

12.3 Printing to a Particular Scale

Sometimes, instead of printing exactly what you see on your screen so that it fits on a sheet of paper, you might need to print a drawing to scale. The following sections provide more detail on printing to scale.

12.3.1 Printing to Scale (Windows and Mac)

Before you can print a view of your model to a particular scale, you have to set things up properly. Here are some things to keep in mind:

▲ **Perspective views can't be printed to scale.** In perspectival views, all lines appear to "go back" into the distance, which means that they look shorter than they really are. Because the point of a scaled drawing is to be able to take accurate measurements directly off your printout, views with perspective don't work.

▲ **Switch to Parallel Projection if you want to print to scale.** To change your viewing mode from Perspective to Parallel Projection, choose Camera⇨Parallel Projection.

▲ **You must use the Standard views.** SketchUp allows you to quickly look at your model from the top, bottom, and sides by switching to one of the Standard views. Choose Camera⇨Standard and pick any of the views except Iso.

12.3.2 Producing a Scaled Print

The steps in this section allow you to produce a scaled print from SketchUp; Windows instructions are presented first, and then Mac instructions. When the user-interface elements are different for the two platforms, the ones for Mac are shown in parentheses. Figure 12-8 shows the relevant dialog boxes for printing to scale in Windows and on a Mac.

Before you begin, check that you've switched to Parallel Projection and that your view is lined up the right way. See the previous section of this chapter for information on what you need to do to prepare your model view for scaled printing. Follow these steps to produce a scaled print:

1. Choose File⇨Print Setup (Page Setup).
2. **Select a printer, paper size, and paper orientation, and then click the OK button.**
3. **Choose File⇨Print Preview (Document Setup).**
4. **Deselect the Fit to Page (Fit View to Page) check box.**
5. **Make sure that the Use Model Extents check box is deselected.** Mac users don't have this option.
6. **Enter the scale at which you'd like to print your model view.** If you wanted to print a drawing at 1/4-inch scale, you would enter the following:
   - **1 Inches** into the In the Printout (In Drawing) box.
   - **4 Feet** into the In SketchUp (In Model) box.

Figure 12-8

When printing to scale, don't worry about these numbers.

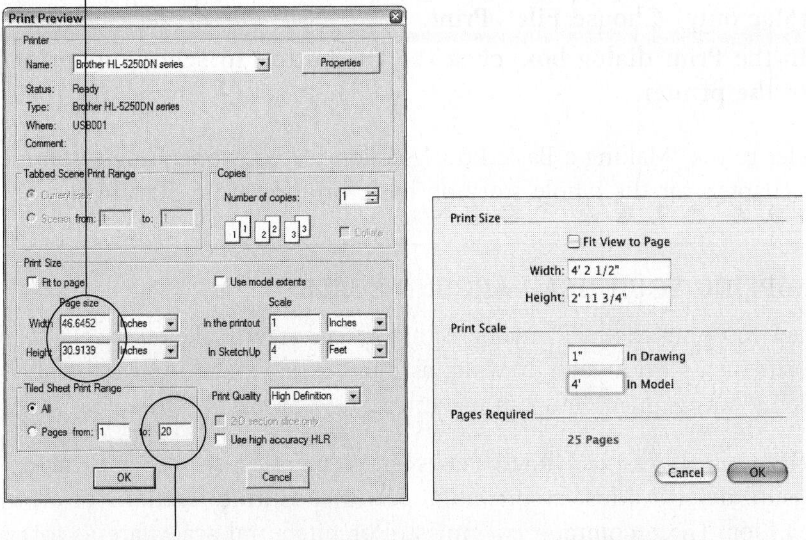

To print at 1 inch = 4 feet, you'll need 20 pages

Setting up to print at 1 inch = 4 foot (1/4 inch = 1 foot) scale.

Similarly, if you wanted to produce a print at 1:100 scale, you would enter the following:

- **1 m** into the In the Printout (In Drawing) box.
- **100 m** into the In SketchUp (In Model) box.

7. **Take note of how may pages you'll need to print your drawing.** If you're using Windows, you can check this in the Tiled Sheet Print Range area of the dialog box. On a Mac, the number of pages you'll need appears in the Pages Required section of the Document Setup dialog box. If you want to print on a different-sized piece of paper, change the setting in the Print Setup (Page Setup) dialog box.

8. **If you want to print your drawing on a single sheet and it won't fit, try using a smaller scale.** Using the 1/4 inch = 1 foot example, try shrinking the drawing to 3/16 inch = 1 foot scale. To do this, you would enter the following:

- **3 Inches** into the In the Printout (In Drawing) box.
- **16 Feet** into the In SketchUp (In Model) box.

9. **When you're satisfied with how your drawing will print, click the OK button.**

10. **(Windows only) If you're satisfied with what you see in the Print Preview window, click the Print button (in the upper-left corner) to open the Print dialog box.**

11. **(Mac only) Choose File⇨Print.**

12. **In the Print dialog box, click the OK button to send your print job to the printer.**

Refer to the "Making a Basic Print" section for your operating system, earlier in the chapter, for the whole story on basic printing from SketchUp.

WRAPPING YOUR HEAD AROUND SCALE

When you print to scale, anyone with a special ruler (called a *scale*) can take measurements from your drawing, as long as he or she knows the scale at which it was printed. You can use three different kinds of drawing scales:

Architectural: In the United States, most people use feet and inches to measure objects. Most architectural scales substitute fractions of an inch for a foot. Three common examples of architectural scales are as follows:

▲ 1/2 inch = 1 foot (1 inch = 2 feet)
▲ 1/4 inch = 1 foot (1 inch = 4 feet)
▲ 1/8 inch = 1 foot (1 inch = 8 feet)

Engineering: When it comes to measuring large things like parcels of land and college campuses, U.S. architects, engineers, industrial designers, and surveyors still use feet, but they use engineering scales instead of architectural ones. Three common engineering scales include the following:

▲ 1 inch = 20 feet
▲ 1 inch = 50 feet
▲ 1 inch = 100 feet

Metric: Outside of the United States, most people use the metric system. Because all measurement is based on the number 10, metric scales can be applied to everything from very small things (such as blood cells) to very large things (such as countries). This is called the DIN system. Metric scales use ratios instead of units of measure; here are three examples:

▲ 1:10 (the objects in the drawing are 10 times bigger in real life)
▲ 1:100 (the objects in the drawing are 100 times bigger in real life)
▲ 10:1 (the objects in the drawing are 10 times smaller in real life)

SELF-CHECK

1. What does it mean to print to scale?
2. Perspective views can be printed to scale. True or false?
3. If you want to print to scale, you'll need to switch to _____ Projection.
4. If you wanted to print at 1:200 scale, you would enter the following numbers in the In Drawing and In Model box respectively:

   a. 1:2   **b.** 1:200
   c. 1:20   **d.** 10:20

SUMMARY

In addition to sharing your models virtually, you can also share them the old-fashioned way by printing them out on paper and showing your friends and colleagues. In addition to being an avenue for sharing your models, printing them often helps you see flaws that your eyes do not catch on screen. In this chapter, you learned how to print your models both on a Windows PC and a Mac. You also evaluated what it means to print to scale and you learned how to print to scale. These steps will help you in your creative endeavors, both in sharing with others and in enabling you to clearly see what improvements you would like to make to your model.

KEY TERMS

Raster	Term describing images that are composed of pixels.
Vector	Term describing images that consist of instructions written in computer code.

ASSESS YOUR UNDERSTANDING

Go to www.wiley.com/college/chopra to evaluate your knowledge of printing your work.

Measure your learning by comparing pre-test and post-test result

Summary Questions

1. The smooth shadows on rounded surfaces are examples of _____.
2. Deselecting the Collate check box prints pages like this: 123412341234. True or false?
3. What type of images consist of instructions written in computer code?
   (a) Raster
   (b) Gradient
   (c) Vector
   (d) Scaled
4. To print at 1:500 m scale, you would type 1 m into the _____ box.
5. To print at 1:500 m scale, you would type 500 m into the _____ box.
6. If you want to print your model on a single sheet of paper and it won't fit, you should try using a _____ scale.
7. You can use the Tabbed Scene Print Range to tell SketchUp which of your scenes you would like to print. True or false?
8. You select the High Accuracy HLR box to send raster information to the printer instead of vector data. True or false?

Applying This Chapter

1. What does printing to scale mean, and why would you want to have scaled printouts?
2. List and describe three settings in the SketchUp print panel and when you would use them.

YOU TRY IT

Print Your House Model to Scale

Taking your print it at the following scales:

- 1 inch = 2 feet
- 1 inch = 16 feet
- 1 inch = 100 feet

Which option is best and why?

13

EXPORTING IMAGES AND ANIMATIONS
Making Image Files and Movies

Starting Point

Go to www.wiley.com/college/chopra to assess your knowledge of exporting images and animations.
Determine where you need to concentrate your effort.

What You'll Learn in This Chapter

▲ The difference between TIFFs, JPEGs, and PNGs
▲ Qualities of raster images
▲ How to export your animation
▲ Animation export options settings

After Studying This Chapter, You'll Be Able To

▲ Create 2D views of your model as TIFFs, JPEGs, and PNGs
▲ Evaluate pixels and resolution
▲ Assess different types of images and ensure that you export the right kind of image
▲ Export the kind of movie file you need

INTRODUCTION

Want to email a JPEG of your new patio to your parents? How about a movie that shows what it's like to walk out onto that new patio? If you need an image or a movie of your model, forget about viewing or printing within SketchUp. Exporting is the way to go.

SketchUp can export both still images and animations in most of the major graphics and movie formats. Here's the part that's a bit confusing: Which file formats you can export depend on the version of SketchUp you have. If you have regular Google SketchUp (the free one), you can create *raster* image files as well as movies. If you have Google SketchUp Pro, you can also export *vector* files and a lot of 3D formats; all of them are discussed in Chapter 14.

This chapter focuses on the export file formats that are common to both versions of Google SketchUp. Thus, the 2D raster image formats that you can create with SketchUp are explained. More specifically, in this chapter, you will create 2D views of your models as TIFFS, JPEGS, and PNGs. You will also evaluate pixels and resolution. Then, in the final part of this chapter, you will learn how to export animations as movie files that anyone can open and view.

13.1 Exporting 2D Images of Your Model

Even though the free version of SketchUp can only export 2D views of your model as *raster* images, it's helpful to know about graphics file formats in general.

Pictures on your computer are divided into two basic types: *raster* and *vector*. The difference between these two categories of file types has to do with how they store image information:

▲ **Raster:** Raster images are made up of dots. (Technically, these dots are called pixels, just like the pixels that make up the images you take with a digital camera.) Raster file formats consist of information about the location and color of each dot. When you export a raster, you decide how many dots (pixels) it should include, which directly affects how big it can be displayed. SketchUp exports TIFF, JPEG, and PNG raster images; the Windows version also exports BMPs.

▲ **Vector:** Vector images consist of instructions written in computer code. This code describes *how* to draw the image to whatever software is trying to open it. The major advantage of using vector imagery (as opposed to raster) lies in its scalability—vectors can be resized larger or smaller without affecting their image quality, while rasters lose quality if you enlarge them too much. The free version of SketchUp can only export raster images, but SketchUp Pro can export vectors in both PDF and EPS file formats; you can read about it in Chapter 14.

13.1.1 Exporting a Raster Image from SketchUp

The process of exporting a view of your SketchUp model is fairly straightforward. Depending on which format you choose, the export options are slightly different, but all of them are addressed in this section.

Follow these steps to export a raster image from SketchUp:

1. **Adjust your model view until you see exactly what you'd like to export as an image file.** With SketchUp's raster image export, your entire modeling window view is exported as an image, so use the navigation tools or click on a scene to set up your view. Use styles, shadows, and fog to make your model look exactly the way you want it to. To change the proportions of your image, resize your SketchUp window. Follow these steps to do so:

   • If your SketchUp window is full-screen (Windows only), click the Minimize button in its upper-right corner.

   • Drag the Resize tab in the lower-right corner of your SketchUp window until the modeling window is the right proportion.

   Figure 13-1 shows adjustment to the proportions of a modeling window in order to export a wide view of a modeled house. You might be wondering whether everything in your modeling window shows up in an

Figure 13-1

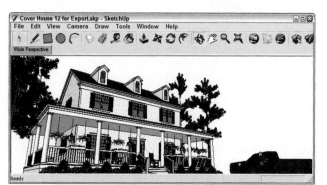

SketchUp Modeling Window

Exported Image

Adjust your view and your modeling window until things look the way you want them to in your exported image.

exported raster image. The red, green, and blue axes don't, but guides do. If you don't want your guides to be visible in your exported image, deselect Guides in the View menu.

2. **Choose File⇨Export⇨2D Graphic.** This opens the File Export dialog box.

3. **Choose the file format you'd like to use from the Format drop-down list.** Before you choose JPEG by default, you should know that this file type isn't always the best choice. For a complete description of each format (as well as recommendations for when to choose each), see the section "Looking at SketchUp's Raster Formats," later in this chapter.

4. **Choose a name and a location on your computer for your exported image.**

5. **Click the Options button.** This opens the Export Options dialog box, where you can control how your image is exported. Figure 13-2 shows what this dialog box looks like for each of SketchUp's raster file formats.

6. **Adjust the settings in the Export Options dialog box.** Here's a description of what the settings do:

   • **Use View Size:** Selecting this check box tells SketchUp to export an image file that contains the same number of pixels as are currently being used to display your model on-screen. If you're just planning to use your exported image in an email or in an on-screen presentation (like PowerPoint), you select Use View Size, but it's still better to manually control the pixel size of your exported image. If you're planning to print your exported image, don't select this check box.

   • **Width and Height:** When you don't select the Use View Size check box, you can manually enter the size of your exported image. Because this process requires a fair amount of figuring, a whole section is

Figure 13-2

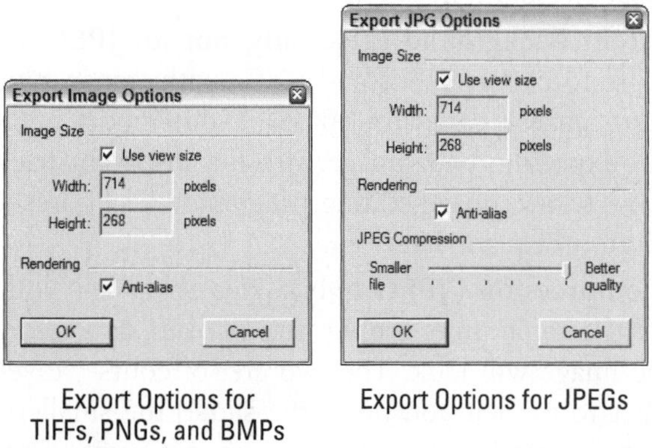

Export Options for   Export Options for JPEGs
TIFFs, PNGs, and BMPs

The Export Options dialog boxes for TIFFs, PNGs, and BMPs (left) and JPEGs (right).

Figure 13-3

No anti-aliasing   With anti-aliasing

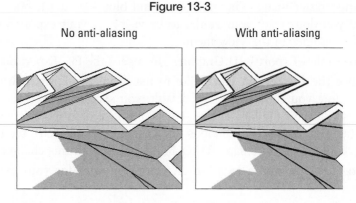

A view of the same image with anti-aliasing off (left) and on (right).

devoted to it; take a look at "Making Sure That You're Exporting Enough Pixels," later in this chapter, to find out what to type into the Width and Height boxes.

- **Anti-alias:** Because raster images use grids of colored squares to draw pictures, diagonal lines and edges can sometimes look jagged. **Anti-aliasing** is a process that fills in the gaps around pixels with similar-colored pixels so that things look smooth. Figure 13-3 illustrates the concept. In general, you want to leave anti-aliasing on.

- **Resolution (Mac only):** This is where you tell SketchUp how big each pixel should be, and therefore how big (in inches or centimeters) your exported image should be. Pixel size is expressed in terms of pixels per inch/centimeter. This option is only available when the Use View Size check box isn't selected. Just like with the Width and Height boxes, the next section of this chapter goes into a lot of detail about image resolution.

- **Transparent Background (Mac only, not for JPEGs):** Mac users can choose to export TIFFs and PNGs with transparent backgrounds, which can make it easier to "cut out" your model in another piece of software. Exporting your image with a transparent background is also a nice way to use image-editing programs like Photoshop to drop in a sky and ground plane later on.

- **JPEG Compression (JPEG only):** This slider lets you decide two things at the same time: the file size of your exported image and how good the image will look. The two are, of course, inversely related; the farther to the left you move the slider, the smaller your file will be, but the worse it will look. You may not want to set JPEG compression any lower than 8.

7. **Click the OK button to close the Export Options dialog box.**
8. **Back in the File Export dialog box, click the Export button to export your raster image file.** You can find your exported file in whatever location on your computer you specified in step 4. What you do with it is entirely up to you—you can email it, print it, or use it in another software program to create a presentation. The export process may take longer than you think it should. If you're exporting a large image (one with lots of pixels), the export will take a while.

UNDERSTANDING RASTERS

When you look at a photograph on your computer, you're really looking at a lot of tiny dots of color called pixels. These are arranged in a rectangular grid called a raster. Digital images that are composed of pixels arranged in a raster grid are called raster images, or rasters for short. Have a look at the first image in the figure below for a close-up view of a raster image. Here are some things to keep in mind about rasters:

▲ **Rasters are everywhere.** Almost every digital image you've ever seen is a raster. TIFF, JPEG, and PNG are three of the most common raster file formats, and SketchUp exports all three of them.

▲ **Rasters are flexible.** Every two-dimensional image can be displayed as a raster; a grid of colored squares is an incredibly effective way of saving and sharing picture information. As long as you have enough pixels, any image can look good as a raster.

▲ **Rasters take up a lot of space.** If you think about how raster images work, it takes a lot of information to describe a picture. Digital images are made up of anywhere from thousands to millions of pixels, and each pixel can be any one of millions of colors. To store a whole picture, a raster image file needs to include the location and color of *each* pixel; the bigger the picture, the more pixels it takes to describe it, and the bigger the file size gets.

▲ **Rasters are measured in pixels.** Because every raster image is made up of a specific number of pixels, you use a raster's *pixel dimensions* to describe its size. If you were told that you'd been emailed a photograph that was 800 × 600, you could expect to receive a picture that is 800 pixels wide by 600 pixels tall (see the figure below). Pixels don't have a physical size of their own—they're just dots of color. You determine a picture's physical size by deciding how big its pixels should be; this is referred to as *resolution,* and is generally expressed in terms of *pixels per inch* (ppi).

Why use pixels instead of inches or centimeters to describe the size of a digital image? It all has to do with how computer screens work. Because not all screens display things at the same size, it's impossible to predict how *big* an image will look when it shows up on someone's computer. Depending on the person's display settings, an 800-×-600-pixel image might be a few inches across, or it might take up the whole screen. Giving a digital image's dimensions in pixels is the only accurate way of describing how "big" it is.

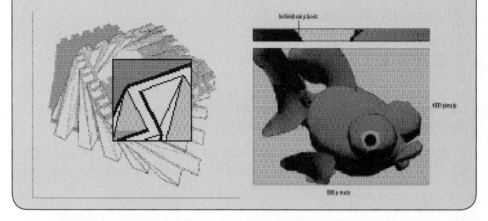

13.1.2 Looking at SketchUp's Raster Formats

So you know you need to export a raster image from SketchUp, but which one do you choose? You have four choices in Windows; three of them are available on a Mac. The following sections give you the details.

When you export a raster image, you're saving your current view in SketchUp to a separate file somewhere on your computer. As a raster image, that file consists of tiny, colored dots called pixels. When you look at all the pixels together, they form an image.

Tagged Image File (TIFF or TIF)

TIFFs are the stalwarts of the raster image file format world; everyone can read them and just about everyone can create them. TIFF stands for Tagged Image File Format. Here's everything you need to know about TIFFs:

▲ **When image quality is important, choose TIFF.** Unless file size is a concern (because, for example, you need to send an image by email), always export a TIFF if you need a raster image. For everything from working in Photoshop to creating a layout in InDesign or QuarkXPress, a TIFF can provide the image quality you need.

▲ **TIFFs don't compress your image data.** That means they don't introduce any unwanted elements like JPEGs do, but it also means that they're especially big files.

▲ **Pay attention to your pixel count.** If you're exporting a TIFF, you're probably looking for the best image quality you can get. And if that's the case, you need to make sure that your TIFF is "big" enough—that it includes enough pixels—to display at the size you need. See the next section in this chapter for more information.

JPEG (or JPG)

JPEG stands for Joint Photographic Experts Group. Almost every digital image you've ever seen was a JPEG (pronounced *JAY-peg*); it's the standard file format for images on the web. Below are a few details about JPEGs:

▲ **When file size is a concern, choose JPEG.** The whole point of the JPEG file format is to compress raster images to manageable file sizes so that they can be emailed and put on websites. A JPEG is a fraction of the size of a TIFF file with the same number of pixels, so JPEG is a great choice if file size is more important to you than image quality.

▲ **JPEGs compress file size by degrading image quality.** This is known as **lossy** compression; JPEG technology basically works by removing a lot of the pixels in your image. JPEGs also introduce a fair amount of pixel garbage; these smudges are called **artifacts**. Refer to Figure 13-4 to see what this looks like.

▲ **JPEG and SketchUp are a dangerous combination.** Because of the way the JPEG file format works, JPEG exports from SketchUp are particularly

Figure 13-4

TIFF   JPEG

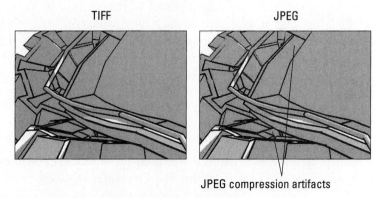

JPEG compression artifacts

A TIFF, on the left, and a JPEG, on the right; JPEGs compress
file size by reducing image quality.

susceptible to looking terrible. Images from SketchUp usually include straight lines and broad areas of color, both of which JPEGs have a hard time handling. If you're going to export a JPEG from SketchUp, make sure that the JPEG Compression slider is never set below 8. For more details, see the section "Exporting a Raster Image from SketchUp," earlier in this chapter.

Portable Network Graphics (PNG)

Pronounced *ping,* PNG is a graphics file format. Unfortunately, it isn't as widely used as many other formats. As far as SketchUp is concerned, PNG combines all the best features of TIFF and JPEG. PNG details are as follows:

▲ **PNGs compress image data without affecting image quality.** As a lossless compression technology, PNGs are smaller files than TIFFs (just like JPEGs), but they don't mess up any pixels (unlike JPEGs). PNGs aren't as small as JPEGs, but the difference in image quality is worth a few extra bits.

▲ **If you're exporting an image for someone who knows about computers, choose PNG.** Some software doesn't know what to do with a PNG, so there's a risk in using it. If you plan to send your exported image to someone who knows what she is doing, go ahead and send a PNG. If the recipient of your export is less technologically sophisticated, stick with a JPEG or TIFF file; it's the safe choice.

The PNG file format wasn't developed to replace JPEG or TIFF; it was supposed to stand in for GIF (Graphics Interchange Format), which is a file type that SketchUp doesn't export. Without going into too much detail, people use JPEG for images like photographs and GIF for things like logos. Because exported SketchUp views usually have more in common with the latter, PNG (the replacement for GIF) is the better choice. So why can't PNG replace JPEG and TIFF? For most photographs (which are the majority of images on the web), JPEG is better than PNG because it produces smaller files, which in turn yields faster load times when you're surfing the Internet. TIFF is more versatile than PNG because it supports different *color spaces,* which are important to people in the printing industry. For reasons that are beyond the scope of this book, that isn't relevant to exports from SketchUp; PNG is still the best—if not the safest—choice.

Windows Bitmap (BMP)

Windows Bitmap, or BMP, files can only be used on Windows, and they're big. BMPs should rarely be used for anything, with a couple of exceptions:

▲ **To send your exported file to someone with a late model Windows computer:** If the person to whom you're sending an exported image has a Windows computer that's more than about five years old, you may want to send a BMP.

▲ **To place an image in an old Windows version of layout software:** If your layout person is using a copy of Word or PageMaker that's a few years old, he might need a BMP file.

13.1.3 Making Sure You're Exporting Enough Pixels

When it comes to raster images, it's all about pixels. The more pixels your image has, the more detailed it is, and the bigger it can be displayed or printed. Figure 13-5 shows the same image three times. The first image is 150 × 50, meaning that it's 150 pixels wide by 50 pixels high. The second image is 300 × 100, and the third is 900 × 300. Notice that the more pixels an image has, the better it looks.

Why not always export as many pixels as possible, just in case you need them? There are two reasons:

▲ Image exports with lots of pixels take a long time to process.

▲ Raster images are very big files.

How many pixels you need to export depends on what you're going to use the image *for*. Very broadly, you can do two things with your image:

▲ Display or project it on a screen, digitally.

▲ Print it.

The next two sections discuss each of these possibilities in detail.

Figure 13-5

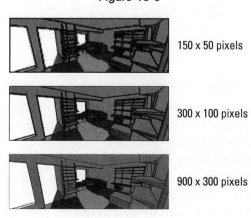

150 x 50 pixels

300 x 100 pixels

900 x 300 pixels

More pixels yield a much more detailed image.

Table 13-1: Suggested Image Sizes for On-screen Use

How the Image Will Be Used	Image Width (Pixels)
Email	400 to 800
Website, large image	600
Website, small image	200
PowerPoint presentation (full-screen)	800 or 1024 (depends on projector)
PowerPoint presentation (floating image)	400

Exporting Enough Pixels for a Digital Presentation

If you plan to use your exported image as part of an on-screen presentation, it's helpful to know what computer monitors and digital projectors can display:

▲ The smallest, oldest devices currently in use have images that are 800 pixels wide by 600 pixels high.

▲ At the other end of the spectrum, high-end, 30-inch LCD monitors display 2560 × 1600 pixels.

So it stands to reason that if you're exporting an image that will be viewed on-screen only, you need to create an image that's somewhere between 800 and 2500 pixels wide. Table 13-1 provides some guidelines on image sizes for different digital applications.

For images that will be shown digitally, leave the Resolution setting (in the Export Options dialog box) at 72 pixels per inch. For computer monitors and digital projectors, the image resolution is meaningless because the pixels in your image correspond directly to the pixels on your screen; inches and centimeters don't even come into play.

Understanding Resolution: Exporting Images for Print

Images that you want to print need to have more pixels than ones that are only going to be displayed on-screen. That's because printers—inkjet, laser, and offset—all operate very differently than computer monitors and digital projectors. When you print something, the pixels in your image turn into microscopic specks of ink or toner, and these specks are smaller than the pixels on your computer screen. To make a decent-sized print of your exported image, it needs to contain enough *pixels per inch* of image. An image's pixel density, expressed in pixels per inch (ppi), is its **resolution**.

What kind of resolution you need depends on three things:

▲ **The kind of device you'll be printing to:** For home inkjet printers, you can have a resolution of as little as 150 ppi. If your image will be appearing in a commercially produced book, you need a resolution of at least 300 ppi.

▲ **How far away the image will be from the audience:** There's a big difference between a magazine page and a trade-show banner. For close-up applications, a resolution of 200 to 300 ppi is appropriate. Large graphics that will be viewed from several feet away can be as low as 60 ppi.

▲ **The subject matter of the image itself:** Photographic images tend to consist of areas of color that blur together a bit; these kinds of images can tolerate being printed at lower resolutions than drawings with lots of intricate detail. For images with lots of lines (like SketchUp models), it's best to work with very high resolutions—300 to 600 ppi—especially if the image will be viewed close-up.

Table 13-2 provides some guidelines for exporting images that will be printed. Keep in mind that the biggest raster image that SketchUp can export is 10,000 pixels wide or tall (whichever is greater). This means that the largest banner image, printed at 100 ppi, that SketchUp can create is about 100 inches wide. To make larger images, you need to export a vector file; find the details on exporting to vector formats with SketchUp Pro in Chapter 14.

Follow these steps to make sure that you're exporting enough pixels to be able to print your image properly:

1. **In the Export Options dialog box, make sure that the Use View Size check box is deselected.** To get to the Export Options dialog box,

Table 13-2: Recommended Resolutions for Prints

How the Image Will Be Used	Image Width (Pixels)	Image Resolution (pixels/cm)
8.5 × 11 or 11 × 17 inkjet or laser print	200 to 300	80 to 120
Color brochure or pamphlet	300	120
Magazine or book (color and shadows)	300	120
Magazine or book (linework only)	450 to 600	180 to 240
Presentation board	150 to 200	60 to 80
Banner	60 to 100	24 to 40

follow steps 1 through 6 in the section "Exporting a Raster Image from SketchUp," earlier in this chapter.

2. **Decide on the resolution that you need for your exported image. (Refer to Table 13-2.)** Remember the resolution or record it.

3. **Decide how big your exported image will be printed, in inches or centimeters.** Note your desired physical image size, just like you did with the resolution in the previous step.

4. **Multiply your resolution from step 2 by your image size from step 3 to get the number of pixels you need to export.** In other words, if you know what resolution you need to export, and you know how big your image will be printed, you can multiply the two numbers to get the number of pixels you need. Here's an example:

$$300 \text{ pixels/inch} \times 8 \text{ inches wide} = 2,400 \text{ pixels wide}$$

To export an image that can be printed 8 inches wide at 300 ppi, you need to export an image that's 2,400 pixels wide. Figure 13-6 illustrates this example.

Figure 13-6

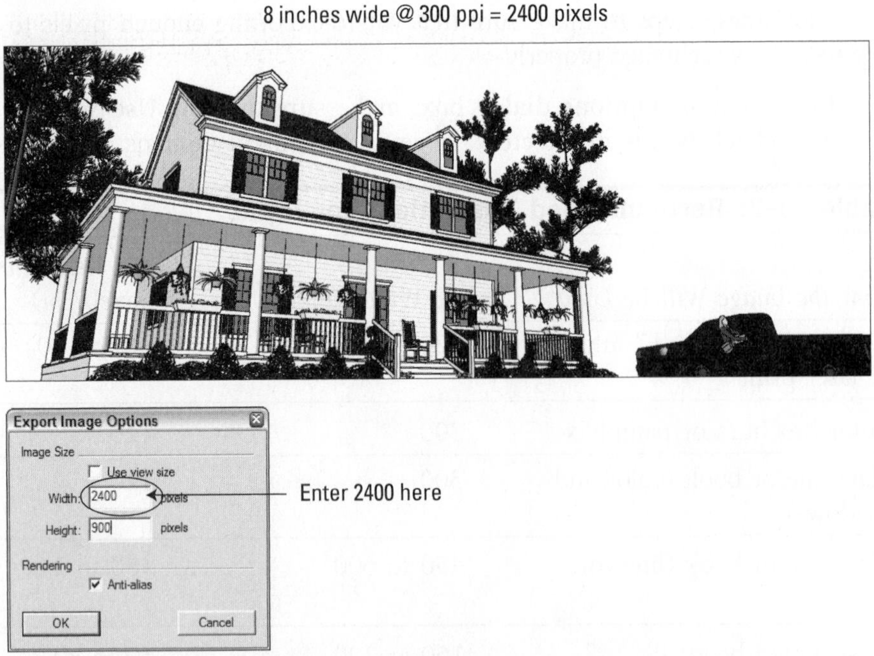

8 inches wide @ 300 ppi = 2400 pixels

Enter 2400 here

To figure out how many pixels you need to export, multiply the resolution by the physical size.

SketchUp's default setting is to make your exported image match the proportions of your modeling window; that is, you can only type in a width *or* a height, but not both. If you're on a Mac, you can manually enter both dimensions, by clicking the Unlink button (which looks like a chain). You can always click it again to relink the width and height dimensions later.

5. **Type in the width *or* height of the image you'd like to export, in pixels.** It's usually difficult to know *exactly* how big your image will be when it's printed, and even if you do, you probably want to leave some room for cropping. For these reasons, you may want to add 15–25 percent to the number of pixels you think you'll need. If your image calls for 2,400 pixels, export 3,000 pixels, just to be safe.

If you're on a Mac, things are a little easier, because SketchUp's designers built a pixel calculator right into the Export Options dialog box. Just enter your desired resolution in the appropriate spot, change the width and height units from pixels to inches or centimeters, and type in your desired image size. SketchUp does the arithmetic for you.

6. **Click the OK button to close the Export Options dialog box.**

SELF-CHECK

1. _____ can be resized larger or smaller without affecting their image quality, while rasters lose quality if you enlarge them too much.

2. Almost every digital image you have ever seen is a vector. True or false?

3. When file size is a concern, you should choose:
   a. JPEG.
   b. TIFF.
   c. BMP.
   d. PNG.

4. When image quality is important, you should choose:
   a. JPEG.
   b. TIFF.
   c. BMP.
   d. PNG.

13.2 Making Movies with Animation Export

What's so great about animation export is how *easy* it is to do. That's not to say that animation and digital video are simple topics—they're not. If you are primarily interested in 3D modeling, what you'll find in the following sections are instructions for doing what you need to do.

13.2.1 Getting Ready for Prime Time

The key to exporting animations of your SketchUp models is using scenes; see Chapter 10 for information on scenes. Scenes are saved views of your model that you can arrange in any order you want. When you export an animation, SketchUp strings together the scenes in your model to create a movie file that can be played on just about any computer made in the last several years.

Follow these steps to get your model ready to export as an animation:

1. **Create scenes to build the "skeleton" of your animation.**

2. **To adjust the animation settings in the Model Info dialog box, choose Window⇨Model Info and then select the Animation panel.** All the controls are explained in the section about moving from scene to scene in Chapter 10.

3. **Click the Enable Scene Transitions check box to tell SketchUp to move smoothly from one scene to the next.**

4. **Enter a transition time to tell SketchUp how long to spend moving between scenes.** If your Scene Delay is 0 (see below), you can multiply your transition time by your number of scenes to figure out how long your exported animation will be.

5. **Enter a scene delay time to pause at each scene before moving on to the next one.** If you plan to talk about each scene, use this feature. If your animation is supposed to be a smooth walk-through or flyover, set the scene delay time to 0.

6. **Adjust the proportions of your modeling window to approximate the proportions of your movie.** Unlike SketchUp's 2D export formats, the proportions of your exported movie don't depend on those of your modeling window; that is to say, making your modeling window long and narrow won't result in a long and narrow movie. You choose how many pixels wide and tall you want your movie to be, so to get an idea of how much you'll be able to see, make your modeling window match the proportions of your exported file (4:3 is common for video formats). See step 1 in the section "Exporting a Raster Image from SketchUp," earlier in this chapter, for guidance on adjusting your modeling window.

7. **When your project is ready to go, move on to the next section to export your animation.**

13.2.2 Exporting a Movie

Fortunately, you have only one choice if you want to export a movie from SketchUp. If you're using Windows, you create an AVI file; Mac users create QuickTime MOVs.

If you're paying close attention to the available file formats for exporting movies, you'll probably notice three more choices in the drop-down menu: TIF, JPG, and PNG. You probably won't need these formats for animation (movie) export in SketchUp; choosing to export in any of these formats will give you a set of image files that each represents one frame in your animation. People who want to include their SketchUp animation in a Flash file should take advantage of this option, but explaining how to do so is beyond the scope of this book.

While exporting animations in SketchUp is a pretty simple operation, figuring out how to set all the animation export controls can be intimidating. What follows are step-by-step instructions for generating a movie file; settings recommendations are in the next section.

Follow these steps to export a movie file from SketchUp:

1. **Prepare your model for export as an animation.** See the section "Getting Ready for Prime Time," earlier in this chapter, for a list of things you need to do before you export an animation.
2. **Choose File⇨Export⇨Animation.** This opens the Animation Export dialog box.
3. **Give your movie file a name, and choose where it should be saved on your computer system.**
4. **Make sure that the correct file format is selected.** In the Format drop-down menu, choose AVI if you're using Windows and QuickTime if you're on a Mac.
5. **Click the Options button to open the Animation Export Options dialog box (see Figure 13-7).**

Figure 13-7

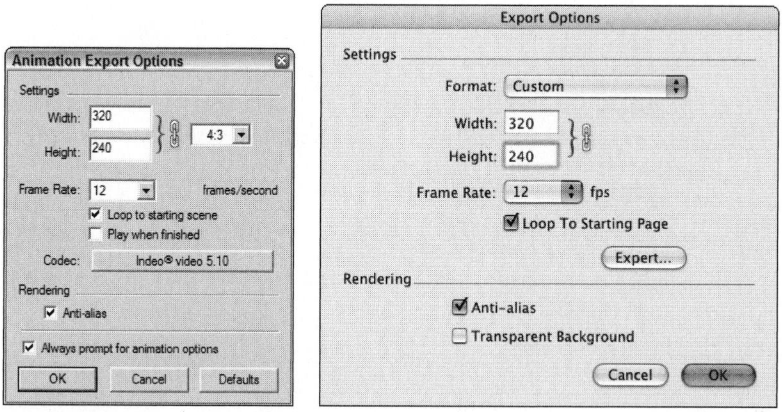

The Windows (left) and Mac (right) versions of the Animation Export Options dialog box.

6. **Adjust the settings for the type of animation you want to export.** How you set everything up in this dialog box depends on how you plan to use the animation you end up creating. See the next section in this chapter for recommended settings for different applications.

   If you're working on a Mac, there's an extra drop-down menu that you might find helpful: Format includes a short list of uses for your animation. Choosing one automatically sets most of the controls for you, though (as you'll see in the next section) you can improve things a bit by making some of your own selections.

7. **Select the Anti-alias check box, if it isn't already selected.** Choosing this doubles the amount of time it takes for your animation to export, but it makes your edges look much better in the final movie.

8. **Click the Codec button (Windows) or the Expert button (Mac).** This opens the Video Compression (Compression Settings on a Mac) dialog box (see Figure 13-8). Choose the correct settings for the type of animation you want to export, again referring to the next section of this chapter for details about what the options mean.

Figure 13-8

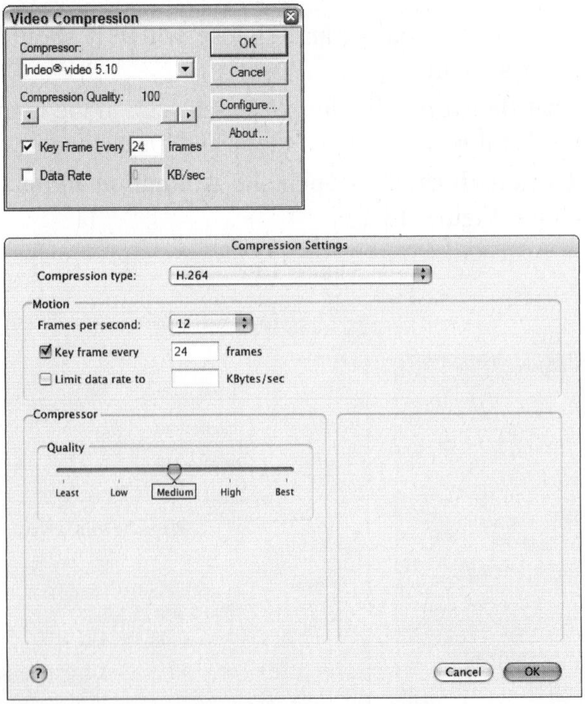

The Video Compression dialog box for Windows (left) and Mac (right).

9. **Click the OK button in the compression dialog box, and then the OK button again in the Export Options dialog box.** This returns you to the Animation Export dialog box.

10. **Check to make sure that everything looks right, and then click the Export button.** Because exporting an animation takes a while, it pays to double-check your settings before you click the Export button. When the export is complete, you can find your animation file in the location you specified in step 3. Double-clicking it should cause it to open in whatever movie-playing software you have that can read it. On Windows computers, this is usually Windows Media Player; on Macs, it's QuickTime.

13.2.3 Figuring Out the Animation Export Options Settings

Digital video is complicated. Luckily, you don't have to know what everything means to export the right kind of movie; you just have to know how to set up everything.

What follows are a number of different things you might want to do with your animation, and recommended settings for getting good results. Feel free to experiment, but the following sections are a good place to start.

For Sending in an Email

If you're going to email someone an animation file, you have to make the file as small as you can. These settings can help you do just that:

▲ **Width and Height:** 160 × 120
▲ **Frame Rate:** 10 fps
▲ **Codec (Windows):** Indeo Video 5.10
▲ **Compression Type (Mac):** H.264
▲ **Key Frame Every:** 24 frames
▲ **Compression Quality (Windows):** 50
▲ **Quality (Mac):** Medium

For Posting on the Web

When you're creating a movie that will be placed on a website, you need to make sure that it's small enough to load quickly but big enough to look good. Try these settings:

▲ **Width and Height:** 320 × 240
▲ **Frame Rate:** 12 fps
▲ **Codec (Windows):** Indeo Video 5.10
▲ **Compression Type (Mac):** H.264

▲ **Key Frame Every:** 24 frames

▲ **Compression Quality (Windows):** 50

▲ **Quality (Mac):** Medium

For Viewing On-Screen (Computer or Projector)

If you plan to use your animation as part of an on-screen presentation (such as with PowerPoint or Keynote), you probably want it to look good full-screen. You'll probably be using a digital projector to present, and these days, most digital projectors come in two resolutions: 800 × 600 and 1024 × 768. You may know the resolution of the projector you'll be using, but if not, export at the lower pixel count, just to be safe:

▲ **Width and Height:** 800 × 600 or 1024 × 768

▲ **Frame Rate:** 15 fps

▲ **Codec (Windows):** Indeo Video 5.10

▲ **Compression Type (Mac):** H.264

▲ **Key Frame Every:** 24 frames

▲ **Compression Quality (Windows):** 100

▲ **Quality (Mac):** Best

You want your exported animations to look smooth—the transitions from one frame to the next shouldn't be jumpy or awkward. If your camera is covering a lot of ground (in other words, moving a large distance between scenes) in a very short time, you might want to experiment with increasing your frame rate to smooth things out. Doing so adds more frames between transitions, which means the camera isn't traveling as far between frames.

For Exporting to DV (To Be Viewed on a TV with a DVD Player)

If you need to export an animation that will be burned onto a DVD that will (in turn) be played in a DVD player, you should do everything you can for quality and file size. The export process will take a long time, but you'll get the best-looking movie you can get. Try these settings first:

▲ **Width and Height:** 720 × 480

▲ **Frame Rate:** 29.97 fps

▲ **Codec (Windows):** Full Frame

▲ **Compression Type (Mac):** DV/DVCPRO

▲ **Compression Quality (Windows):** 100

▲ **Quality (Mac):** Best

▲ **Scan Mode (Mac):** Interlaced

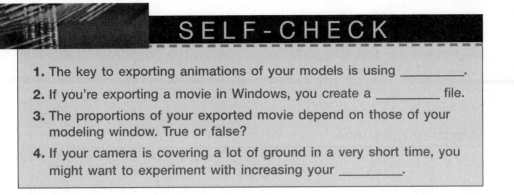

SELF-CHECK

1. The key to exporting animations of your models is using _____.
2. If you're exporting a movie in Windows, you create a _____ file.
3. The proportions of your exported movie depend on those of your modeling window. True or false?
4. If your camera is covering a lot of ground in a very short time, you might want to experiment with increasing your _____.

SUMMARY

SketchUp allows you to do much more than create a static image; you can use different views of your model to make animations, and you can share these "virtual tours" with anyone in the world.

In this chapter, you assessed the pros and cons of various image file formats such as JPEGs, TIFFs, and PNGs. You created 2D views of your model in these file formats. You evaluated pixels and resolution. Finally, you exported a movie file and optimized its settings for different uses, such as for distribution on email, the web, and DVD. These skills will serve you well as you seek to share your models with your colleagues.

KEY TERMS

Anti-aliasing	A process that fills in the gaps around pixels with similar-colored pixels so that things look smooth.
Artifacts	Smudges and other image degradation introduced by file compression; common in JPEGs.
Lossy	Type of compression that occurs with JPEGs. JPEGs compress file size by degrading image quality.
Resolution	An image's pixel density.

ASSESS YOUR UNDERSTANDING

Go to www.wiley.com/college/chopra to evaluate your knowledge of exporting images and animations.

Measure your learning by comparing pre-test and post-test results.

Summary Questions

1. Rasters take up a lot of space. True or false?
2. Which format compresses image data without affecting image quality?
   (a) TIFF
   (b) JPEG
   (c) PNG
   (d) BMP
3. Which files can only be used with Windows?
   (a) TIFF
   (b) JPEG
   (c) PNG
   (d) BMP
4. What type of movie file must Mac users export from SketchUp?
   (a) AVI
   (b) QuickTime MOVs
   (c) JPEG
   (d) TIFF
5. When you export an animation, SketchUp strings together the scenes in your model to create a movie file. True or false?
6. Choosing _____ doubles the amount of time it takes for your animation to export, but it makes your edges look much better in the final movie.

Applying This Chapter

1. You want to export your animation to a DVD so you can send it in to a design competition. How do you do this, and what settings do you use?
2. When should you use PNGs, TIFFs, and JPEGs?

YOU TRY IT

Exporting a High-Resolution Image

Choose a view of your model house, and export it as a TIFF that can be printed at least 14 inches wide at a good resolution.

Posting Your Animation on the Web

Create an animation of your model house, and post it on the web for your classmates and colleagues to view. Be sure to use settings that will optimize the quality of your animation for the web.

Emailing Your Animation

Create an animation of your model house, and email it to yourself and others. Be sure to use settings that will optimize the quality of your illlustration for email.

14

EXPORTING TO CAD, ILLUSTRATION, AND OTHER MODELING SOFTWARE

Using SketchUp Pro

Starting Point

Go to www.wiley.com/college/chopra to assess your knowledge of exporting to CAD, illustration, and other modeling software.
Determine where you need to concentrate your effort.

What You'll Learn in This Chapter

▲ Different export formats
▲ How to use the PDF/EPS Options dialog box
▲ 3D file format options
▲ Useful plugins

After Studying This Chapter, You'll Be Able To

▲ Generate 2D files for CAD and illustration software
▲ Evaluate PDF and EPS formats and their uses
▲ Export your model to other 3D software
▲ Evaluate the DWG and DXF 3D formats

INTRODUCTION

If you don't have the Pro version of SketchUp, you may not want to bother reading this chapter (or the next one, either). The material in these chapters only applies to those who have SketchUp Pro. However, if you're using Google SketchUp (free), and you're wondering what's in Pro, you might find it useful to peruse these pages to see what you're missing.

SketchUp Pro users have access to a few file export formats that aren't available in the free version of SketchUp. These file formats let you share your work with other "pro-grade" software programs like Illustrator, AutoCAD, and 3D Studio MAX. Most people who design things for a living use a number of different pieces of software to get their work done, and they need the ability to move their data between them. That's where SketchUp Pro's exporters come in.

This chapter is divided into two halves: The first part talks about SketchUp's 2D export formats, and the second part deals with the 3D ones. Thus, as you work through this chapter, you will generate 2D files for CAD and illustration software. You will also export your model to other 3D software. You will additionally evaluate PDF and EPS formats and their uses. For each file format that SketchUp exports, this chapter includes a description of what the settings do, and in some cases, why you might need them. Which format (or formats) you choose depends entirely on what other software you're using.

14.1 Exporting Drawings in 2D

Most people who design 3D objects eventually need to create 2D views of their designs. Sometimes these views are for presentations, and sometimes you need to import a 2D view into other software programs, where you can continue to work on it. You can use SketchUp Pro's 2D export formats to do both.

14.1.1 Sizing Up the Export Formats

You can find a lot of other software out there, and luckily, SketchUp Pro provides enough export formats that you can interact with most of it. On the 2D export side, here's a brief rundown on what SketchUp Pro has to offer:

▲ **PDF:** Lately, Portable Document Format (PDF) files have become more and more common. On top of the fact that almost anyone can read them, PDF files are great for sending information to vector-illustration programs like Illustrator and FreeHand.

▲ **EPS:** Encapsulated Postscript (EPS) files are what people *used* to use to transfer vector information, but these days, more and more people are using PDFs.

▲ **DWG:** This is AutoCAD's native file format, and it's the best one to use for transferring information to that program and other pieces of CAD software. DWGs can also contain 3D information, so they are discussed in the second part of this chapter, too.

▲ **DXF:** Document Exchange Format (DXF) is another type of DWG. It was developed by Autodesk to be the file format that other pieces of software use to transfer data into AutoCAD, because they weren't supposed to be able to create DWGs. The trouble is, DWG has been *reverse-engineered* (taken apart, figured out, unlocked, and put back together again), so now most CAD programs can exchange both DXF and DWG files.

▲ **EPIX:** You may have never heard of Piranesi, but you should know about it. It's a piece of software that lets you "paint" on top of 2D views of your model. EPIX lets you open 2D views of your SketchUp model in Piranesi, if you have it.

The sections that follow discuss each of the formats in more detail.

14.1.2 Exporting a 2D Drawing in Any Format

Regardless of which 2D format you choose to export, the procedure is always the same. Follow these steps to export a 2D image from SketchUp Pro:

1. **Adjust your model view until you have the view you want to export.**
2. **Choose File⇨Export⇨2D Graphic.** This opens the File Export dialog box.
3. **Choose the file format you'd like to use from the Format drop-down list.** Each format is described in a fair amount of detail later in this chapter.
4. **Choose a name and a location on your computer for your exported image.**
5. **Click the Options button.** This opens the Export Options dialog box for the file format you chose in step 3. The options are unique to each file format, so see the section on the one you're using for details on that particular format.
6. **Adjust the settings in the Export Options dialog box, and click the OK button.** This closes the Export Options dialog box.
7. **Click the Export button to export your 2D image file.**

14.1.3 Getting to Know PDF

You've probably already heard of PDF files. In the past (a few years ago), it was hard to send someone a digital graphics file because so many different kinds were available, and because the person to whom you were sending the file had to have the right kind of software to be able to open it. For example, if you made a brochure in QuarkXPress and wanted to send it to someone to review, that person had to have QuarkXPress, too—and chances were, that person didn't.

Adobe developed PDF to solve this problem, and it's been quite successful. Because PDF reader software is already installed on tens of millions of computers, anyone can open and view a PDF file created by anyone else. Lots of programs (including SketchUp Pro) can export PDFs, so now there's an easy way for people to share graphics files.

Here are some things to consider about PDF and SketchUp:

▲ **PDF is universal.** Anyone with Adobe Reader (which is free from Adobe's website, www.adobe.com) can open and view a PDF you create with SketchUp. In fact, anyone with a Mac can open a PDF just by double-clicking it; the picture-viewing software that comes with the Mac operating system uses PDF as its native format.

▲ **PDF is consistent.** When you send someone a PDF file, you can be 99 percent sure that it will look just like it looks on your computer. The colors, line weights, and text will all stay the same, which is important if you're showing someone a design.

▲ **When you need to send a vector graphic file, use PDF unless someone specifically requests an EPS file.** Just about every piece of software handles PDFs with no problem. If you or someone else needs a vector export from SketchUp, PDF works just about every time.

14.1.4 Getting to Know EPS

Postscript is a computer language that was developed to describe graphical objects. An EPS is an *encapsulated* Postscript file, meaning that it's a self-contained bundle of instructions for how to draw an image. Back before PDFs existed, this was the best way to move vector information around. Today, you don't have much reason to use EPS when you could export a PDF file instead. In any case, here are some things you should know about the EPS file format:

▲ **EPS is complicated.** EPS files are different depending on what software and what operating system made them. What's more, you won't find any free, commonly used programs that can open them. You need something like Illustrator or a layout program like InDesign, which most people don't have. Also, EPS files are larger in size.

▲ **Use EPS if your other graphics software is more than a couple of versions old.** PDF support has only been widely incorporated in the last few years, so if you're using older image-editing, illustration, or layout software, you might need to use EPS.

▲ **If someone you're working with insists on EPS, go ahead and send an EPS file.** Some workflows have been designed with EPS files in mind, which is why SketchUp exports EPS in the first place. It's good to know that EPS is there if you need it.

VECTORS: PICTURES MADE OF MATH

Remembering the location and color of millions of tiny dots isn't the only way that computers save images; it just happens to be the most common. The alternative to raster imaging is *vector graphics,* or *vectors* for short. In a vector, lines, shapes, and colors are described by mathematical functions. You don't need to do any math to create a vector. Your hardware and software do it for you. Here are some things to think about when it comes to vectors:

▲ **Vectors don't take up much space.** Imagine a straight line drawn using pixels. In order to draw the line, your computer has to be told where to put each and every pixel. In a vector image (which doesn't use pixels), a mathematical function is used to tell your computer how to draw that same line. Instead of having to provide details for every single pixel, only two instructions are needed: the function that defines the line and its color. Of course, actual vector graphics programming is more complicated than this, but you get the general idea. Thus, vector files are much smaller than raster files.

▲ **Vectors are scalable.** With a raster, you're limited by the number of pixels you have in your image. If you don't have enough, you might not be able to print or otherwise display your image very big. If you have a large number of pixels, your image might look terrific, but your file might be too large to work with. Because vectors are math-based instructions that tell your software how to draw an image, there's no size limit to how big—or small—your image can be. With the same vector file, you could print your company logo on your business card and on the side of a blimp, and they would both look great. The figure that follows shows what this means.

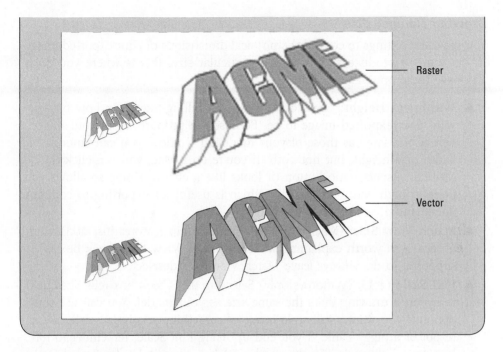

14.1.5 Navigating the PDF/EPS Options Dialog Box

Figure 14-1 shows what this dialog box looks like. It's the same for both PDF and EPS exports.

In Windows, the name of this dialog box, as written in its title bar, is PDF (or EPS) Hidden Line Options.

Figure 14-1

The PDF/EPS Options dialog box for Windows (left) and the Mac (right).

Drawing (Image) Size

You use these settings to control the physical dimensions of your exported image. If you want to produce a PDF that's a particular size, this is where you do it. You have these options:

▲ **Width and Height:** These controls are for telling SketchUp how big you want your exported image to be. Because the proportions of your image will be the same as those of your modeling window, you can enter a width or a height, but not both. If you're on a Mac, you can click the Maintain Aspect Ratio button (it looks like a chain). Doing so allows you to enter both width and height, which is useful for exporting to common document sizes like letter and tabloid.

▲ **Match View Size:** (Mac only) Sometimes certain features just don't work; it's not even worth explaining what the Match View Size check box is supposed to do. *Always* leave Match View Size deselected.

▲ **Full Scale (1:1):** (Windows only) Selecting this check box tells SketchUp to export a drawing that's the same size as your model. You can use this option if you want a full-scale image of something relatively small, like a teapot or a piggy bank. If you end up using Full Scale, remember to follow steps 1 through 3 in the nearby sidebar, "Setting Up for Scaled Drawings," to make sure that your drawing exports the way you want it to.

SETTING UP FOR SCALED DRAWINGS

To export a scaled drawing from SketchUp Pro, you have to set up your model view properly. It's pretty simple—just follow these steps:

1. Before you go anywhere near the 2D Graphic dialog box, switch from Perspective to Parallel Projection view. You do this by choosing Camera⇨Parallel Projection. It's impossible to make a scaled perspective view—drawings just don't work that way.

2. Switch to one of the standard views. Choose Camera⇨Standard and pick a view from the submenu to see a straight-on top, side, or other view of your model.

3. Use the Pan and Zoom tools to make sure that you can see everything you want to export. Whatever you do, don't orbit. If you do, you can always repeat step 2.

Drawing (Image) Scale

Perhaps you're designing a deck for your neighbor's house, and you want to export a scaled PDF file so that the lumberyard can take measurements right off the printed drawing. You want your drawing scale to be 1/8 inch = 1 foot, and this is how you would specify that:

1. Enter 1" into the In Hidden Line Output (In Image) box.
2. Enter 8' into the In SketchUp (In Model) box.

If you want to export a scaled drawing from SketchUp Pro, you have to set up your model view a certain way. If you're not set up properly, the Scale controls are grayed out.

You can choose to set the Drawing (Image) Size or Scale, but not both. You can't, for instance, tell SketchUp to export a 1/8-inch drawing as an 8 1/2-×-11-inch PDF file.

Profile Lines (Windows only)

Profiles don't export very well to PDF and EPS, so you may only want to use this option if you're going to be tweaking your image in a vector drawing program like Illustrator or Freehand. You have the following options:

▲ **Show Profiles:** Select this check box to export profile lines in your image, assuming that you're using them in your model.

▲ **Match Screen Display (Auto Width):** Selecting this check box tells SketchUp to make the exported profiles look as thick, relative to other edges, as they do in your modeling window. If this check box isn't selected, you can type in a line width (thickness).

FOR EXAMPLE

What You See Isn't Always What You Get

With their ability to scale without losing detail and their (relatively) tiny file sizes, vector images seem ideal, but unfortunately, they're not perfect. Whereas exported raster images look just like they do on-screen, vector images don't. Most of SketchUp's graphic effects can't be exported as vector information. Here's a list of what you give up with PDF and EPS:

▲ Photo textures and transparency on faces
▲ Edge effects like depth cue, endpoints, and jitter
▲ NPR (Sketchy Edge) styles
▲ Shadows and fog
▲ Background, ground, and sky colors
▲ Watermarks

Section Lines (Windows Only)

If you have section cut lines in your model view, these options become available:

▲ **Specify Section Line Width:** *Not* selecting this option is the same as choosing Match Screen Display (see the next point).

▲ **Match Screen Display (Auto Width):** Select this check box to export section cut lines that look like they do on your screen. If you have another thickness in mind, don't select this check box; just enter a width right beside it.

Extension Lines (Windows Only)

As the only edge-rendering effect (besides profiles) that SketchUp can export to PDF and EPS, extensions are important; this is where you control them. You have the following options:

▲ **Extend Edges:** Even if you have edge extensions turned on in your model, you can choose not to export them by deselecting this check box.

▲ **Match Screen Display (Auto Length):** Select this check box to let SketchUp make your extensions look like they do on your computer screen. To put in a custom length, type one into the box on the right.

Line Quality (Mac Only)

Whereas Windows users get to be very specific if they want to, Mac users only have one point of control over exported line thickness, or weight. For very detailed models, turn the Line Weight setting down to 0.5 or 0.75 points; otherwise, leave it at 1.00 and see whether you like it. This setting depends on the complexity of your model and on your personal taste.

Other Windows-Only Controls

You have a couple of other options in this dialog box; both can be very helpful:

▲ **Always Prompt for Hidden Line Options:** Do yourself a favor and select this check box; it never hurts to look over your options before you do an export.

▲ **Map Windows Fonts to PDF Base Fonts:** Even though PDF almost always preserves the original appearance of your image, fonts are tricky. For this reason, the PDF file format comes with a set of "safe" fonts that will work on any computer, anywhere. Choosing this option tells SketchUp to "map"—substitute—PDF-safe fonts for the ones in your SketchUp file. Unless you're completely satisfied with the fonts you originally chose, it's not a bad idea to select this check box.

14.1.6 DXF and DWG (in 2D)

DXF and DWG are the only 2D CAD formats that SketchUp can export. Just about every CAD program in existence can do *something* with either DXF or

DWG, so your bases should be covered, no matter what you're using. Here are some things to keep in mind:

▲ **DWG is more capable than DXF.** Because the former is AutoCAD's *native* (private) file format, and DXF was developed by Autodesk to be an *exchange* (public) file format, DWG has more features. Thus, for exporting 2D drawings from SketchUp to use in other CAD applications, using DWG usually yields better results.

▲ **Don't be afraid to experiment.** Data export from *any* program is a somewhat uncertain endeavor, and you never know what you're going to get until you try. Whenever you send your information from one piece of software to another, you may want to leave yourself an extra hour for troubleshooting. You can adjust settings until things work.

▲ **Don't get confused by all the version numbers.** Which version of DWG or DXF you decide to export depends on what CAD software you're using. In general, it's a good idea to use the most recent version available, which is DWG/DXF 2004 in SketchUp Pro 6. If your CAD program is older than that, try exporting an earlier version.

The most recent version of DXF or DWG that SketchUp Pro 6 can *import* is 2004. If you're working in AutoCAD 2007, you'll need to save your file as version 2004 to bring it into SketchUp.

Figure 14-2 shows what the DWG/DXF Hidden Line Options dialog box looks like, which contains your export options. The options are the same for both DWG and DXF, and the following explanation (the figure and the text), apply to both.

Drawing Scale & Size

These settings let you control the final physical size of your exported drawing. If you're in Parallel Projection view, you can assign a scale; if you're in Perspective view, scale doesn't apply. You have the following options:

▲ **Full Scale (1:1):** Most people use SketchUp Pro's DXF/DWG Export feature to produce nonperspectival, orthographic views of their models that they can use in their CAD programs. If that's what you're trying to do, you should select this check box; it'll make opening your exported file in another program that much easier.

To export a scaled view of your model, you need to set things up properly in your modeling window before you begin the export process. You need to be in Parallel Projection view, and you have to be using one of the standard views from the Camera menu. This is discussed in the sidebar "Setting Up for Scaled Drawings," earlier in this chapter. Keep in mind that unless you're set up properly, this option will be grayed out.

▲ **In Drawing and In Model:** If you're exporting a scaled drawing, and you haven't chosen the Full Scale option (see the previous point), you

Figure 14-2

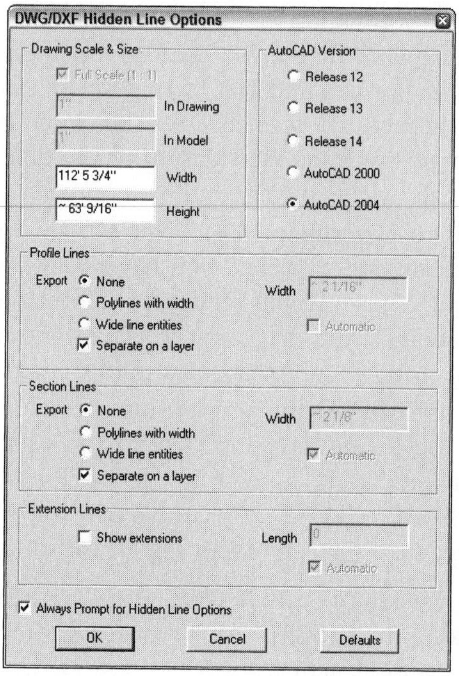

DWG/DXF Hidden Line Options

Drawing Scale & Size
- ☑ Full Scale (1 : 1)
- 1"   In Drawing
- 1"   In Model
- 112' 5 3/4"   Width
- ~ 63' 9/16"   Height

AutoCAD Version
- ○ Release 12
- ○ Release 13
- ○ Release 14
- ○ AutoCAD 2000
- ● AutoCAD 2004

Profile Lines
Export ● None
        ○ Polylines with width   Width   2 1/16"
        ○ Wide line entities   ☐ Automatic
        ☑ Separate on a layer

Section Lines
Export ● None
        ○ Polylines with width   Width   2 1/8"
        ○ Wide line entities   ☑ Automatic
        ☑ Separate on a layer

Extension Lines
        ☐ Show extensions   Length   0
                                      ☑ Automatic

☑ Always Prompt for Hidden Line Options

[OK]   [Cancel]   [Defaults]

The DWG/DXF Hidden Line Options dialog box.

can set your drawing's scale using these controls. If you're not set up to export at scale, these settings won't be available. As an example, for a drawing at 1/16-inch scale, you would do the following:

- Enter **1"** in the In Drawing box.
- Enter **16'** in the In Model box.

▲ **Width and Height:** You can use these settings to determine the dimensions of your exported drawing, as long as you're not printing to scale.

Profile Lines

This is where you control how profile lines in your SketchUp model view are exported. You have the following options:

▲ **None:** Exports profiles the same thickness as all your other edges.

▲ **Polylines with Width:** Exports profiles as polylines, which are a different kind of line object in CAD programs.

▲ **Wide Line Entities:** Exports profiles as thicker lines.

▲ **Width:** You can enter your own line thickness for exported profiles, or you can select the Automatic check box to tell SketchUp to match what you see in your modeling window.

▲ **Separate on a Layer:** Puts your profiles on a separate layer in the exported file. This is handy for being able to quickly select all your profiles and give them a line weight when you open your exported file in a CAD program.

Section Lines

Section lines occur where section planes create section cuts in your model. Traditionally, these lines are thick, which is why SketchUp gives you control over how they export. The options in this section are identical to those for exporting section lines in the PDF/EPS Export Options dialog box. See the section "Section Lines (Windows only)," earlier in this chapter, for information on what everything in this part of the dialog box means.

Extension Lines

Extensions are the little line overruns you can choose to display in the Styles dialog box. If you want to include them in your exported file, you can. Just select the Show Extensions check box, and then either enter a length or select the Automatic check box to let SketchUp try to match how they look on your screen. Extension lines are exported as several tiny, individual edge segments.

If you're using the Windows version of SketchUp, you have an extra option in this dialog box: Always Prompt for Hidden Line Options. This simply means "Do you always want to see this dialog box when you're exporting to DXF or DWG?" Selecting this check box reminds you to look at these settings every time you export.

IT SLICES, IT DICES...

SketchUp's Section Plane tool is quite helpful. See Chapter 10 for more information on this tool. If you have a section cut in your model that you'd like to export to a CAD program, follow these steps:

1. Make sure that the section cut you'd like to export is active.
2. Choose File⇨Export⇨Section Slice.
3. Click the Options button to open the Section Slice Export Options dialog box.
4. Set the export options the way you want them, and then click the OK button.
5. Click the Export button.

The most important part of the Export Options dialog box is right at the top: You need to choose either True Section or Screen Projection. See the following figure to see what happens when you choose each. Chances are, you'll want to pick True Section; it yields the most useful information. The top image is a screen shot of a modeling window in SketchUp. The lower-left image shows what a file export as a true section looks like in AutoCAD. The lower-right image is an AutoCAD view of the same file exported as a screen projection. For a description of the controls in the rest of this dialog box, see the section "DXF and DWG (in 2D)," earlier in this chapter.

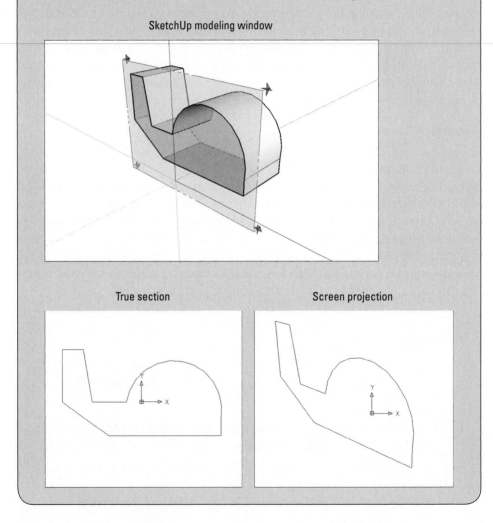

SketchUp modeling window

True section

Screen projection

14.1.7 Peeking at EPIX

You only need to use the EPIX file format if you're using Piranesi, a great artistic rendering program that you can buy. Basically, EPIX is kind of a hybrid raster format that keeps track of pixels, just like other raster formats. But it also remembers another piece of information: the depth of each pixel in your scene. If you have a tree in the foreground, the pixels that make up that tree "know" they're, three feet away, for example.

Figure 14-3

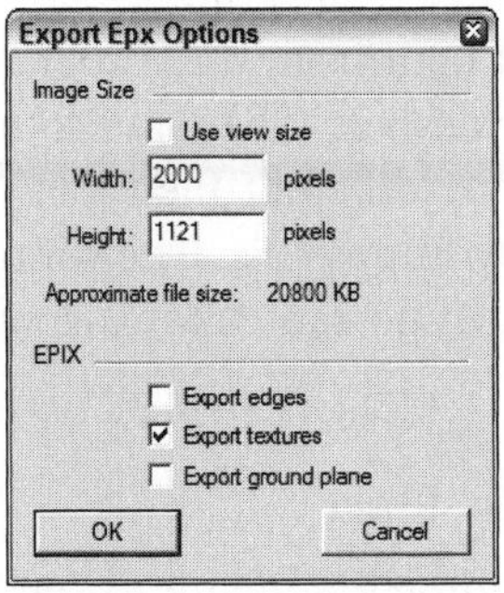

Width: 2000 pixels

Height: 1121 pixels

Approximate file size: 20800 KB

The Export Epx Options dialog box.

Figure 14-3 shows the Export Epx Options dialog box. (Note that Epx and EPIX are the same thing.) Here's what all the options do:

▲ **Image Size:** This part of the Export Epx Options dialog box is just like the Export Options dialog boxes you use for exporting 2D raster images (like JPEG, TIFF, and PNG). Chapter 13 includes an explanation of what everything means, and how to set things up properly.

▲ **Export Edges check box:** Choose this option to export the edge-rendering settings you currently have applied to your model.

▲ **Export Textures check box:** Piranesi can do some remarkable things with the textures you apply in SketchUp; select this check box to export those textures as part of your EPIX file. Just a note: You need to have a style applied to your model that displays textures for those textures to be exported properly.

▲ **Export Ground Plane check box:** Exports a ground plane in your model view, regardless of whether a ground plane is in your currently applied style.

SELF-CHECK

1. What is AutoCAD's native file format?
   a. PDF   b. EPIX
   c. EPS   d. DWG

2. The procedure for exporting a file depends on the 2D format you choose to export. True or false?

3. When you need to send a vector file, you should use PDF unless someone specifically requests an EPS file. True or false?

4. You only need to use the EPIX file format if you're using Piranesi. True or false?

14.2 Exporting 3D Data for Other Software

The process of exporting 3D data from *any* program to *any* program is fraught with equal parts mystery and despair. There are so many pieces of software, with so many versions, and so many different file types, that finding a "step-by-step" recipe for success is practically impossible. The simple truth is that 3D file export from SketchUp Pro is about 50 percent knowing where to start and 90 percent trial and error after that.

14.2.1 Knowing Where to Start

This section focuses on the "knowing where to start" part. First, a list of 3D file types that you can export with SketchUp Pro is provided so you can make some decisions about which format you should use. Second, a general procedure for how to export a 3D model from SketchUp Pro is provided.

Examining Your 3D File Format Options

Here's a bit of information about the 3D file formats that SketchUp Pro 6 can export:

▲ **DAE (Collada):** Every couple of years or so, a new 3D file format comes out. More capable than 3DS, DAE (Collada) is being adopted everywhere by 3D software and gaming companies; Google has even chosen Collada as the file format for the 3D buildings in Google Earth. If you're using a recent version of any of the most popular 3D modeling programs, you might well be able to deal with Collada files; you should try it and find out.

▲ **DWG/DXF:** These are 2D formats. Ever since AutoCAD went 3D a few versions ago, its formats have gone 3D, too. These are a good choice for most of the CAD-type programs out there, but not as good a choice as 3DS. You need to know that, given the choice between the DXF and DWG, you should usually pick the latter.

▲ **3DS:** This has become one of the few standard 3D file formats in the industry. When in doubt, export a 3DS file and see whether your program can open it. SketchUp Pro's options for 3DS export are kind of complicated, so be sure to read the section about this later in the chapter.

▲ **OBJ:** OBJ is probably your best option for sending your data to Maya, which is now owned by Autodesk. While it doesn't offer some important things that 3DS does, it's still a pretty common 3D format.

▲ **XSI:** The folks at SketchUp built XSI export into SketchUp Pro so that it would be more useful to people who use Softimage, a modeling/rendering/animation program from Canada.

▲ **VRML:** Though it's older, several people still use VRML to exchange 3D information.

FOR EXAMPLE

Keep an Eye Out for Plugins

Sometimes, two software companies figure out that they have a large number of users in common, and they set out to make it easier for these users to transfer files back and forth between their products. These file-exchanging solutions are usually called *plugins,* because they're little pieces of software code that you can download and install (plug in) separately. Some handy plugins are available for SketchUp Pro. If you're using ArchiCAD, MicroStation, VectorWorks, Architectural Desktop, or ESRI ArcGIS, you should check out Google's SketchUp Plugins webpage—they're all there, and they're free. It's worth visiting just to see what's available. Go to www.sketchup.com/downloads and click the SketchUp Plugins link at the top of the page.

- ▲ **FBX:** The FBX format is used primarily by people in the entertainment industry who use Maya, 3DS Max, or Autodesk VIZ. Depending on what you're doing, you might want to use it instead of DAE (Collada), 3DS, or OBJ; try it and see whether you like it.
- ▲ **KMZ:** This is the Google Earth file format. Technically, the ability to export KMZ files isn't restricted to the Pro version of SketchUp; anyone with regular, free SketchUp can export them, too.

A great place to go for help with exporting 3D files is the SketchUp Pro Forum. Consulting with the experts there can save you hours of frustration. Check out Chapter 16 for more information on this (and other) forms of further SketchUp edification.

Exporting Your 3D Model

The process of exporting your 3D data from SketchUp Pro is the same no matter what file format you choose. Follow these steps to export a 3D model from SketchUp Pro:

1. **Choose File⇨Export⇨3D Model.** This opens the File Export dialog box.
2. **Choose the file format you'd like to use from the Format drop-down list.**
3. **Choose a name and a location on your computer for your exported image.** Whenever you're exporting a 3D model from SketchUp, it's a *very good* idea to create a new folder for your exported file. A lot of the file formats that SketchUp Pro exports save the textures in your model as separate files alongside your model. You'll want to have everything in a single folder.

4. **Click the Options button.** This opens the Export Options dialog box for the file format you chose in step 2. Check out the sections in the rest of this chapter for more information about all the controls in the Export Options dialog box—they're anything but intuitive.

5. **Adjust the settings in the Options dialog box, and then click the OK button.** This closes the Export Options dialog box.

6. **Click the Export button to export your 3D model file.**

14.2.2 Getting a Handle on OBJ, FBX, XSI, and DAE (Collada)

The Export Options dialog boxes for each of the aforementioned file formats are almost identical, even if the file formats themselves aren't, which is why they are dealt with together in this section. Here are a few reminders about using OBJ, FBX, XSI, and DAE (Collada):

▲ **Try using Collada first.** Because it's relatively new, not all 3D programs support it yet, but your software might.

▲ **If Collada doesn't work, use OBJ for Maya, XSI for Softimage, and FBX if someone tells you to.** The sheer number of programs and versions out there means that it's impossible to give hard-and-fast rules.

▲ **Experiment.** Leave yourself some time to try exporting your model in more than one format. Then open each one in your other piece of software and see what works best.

Figure 14-4 illustrates the Export Options dialog boxes for all four file formats. Here's some help with what everything does:

▲ **Export Only Current Selection:** Tells SketchUp Pro to only export the geometry you currently have selected in your model.

▲ **Triangulate All Faces:** Some programs don't support faces with cutouts in them, so selecting this check box carves things into triangles so that you don't end up with any holes. Experimentation will tell you whether you need to use this; don't choose this option if you don't have to.

▲ **Export Two-Sided Faces:** SketchUp's faces are two-sided, but not all 3D programs' faces are. Choose this option if you've spent a lot of time **texture-mapping** (painting with textures) your model in SketchUp and you want it to look the same in the program you're sending it to. If you plan to use another piece of software to add textures to your model, don't select this check box.

▲ **Export Edges:** SketchUp models *must* include edges and faces, but some programs' models only support the latter. Select this check box if you want to export the edges in your model; leave it deselected if you don't.

Figure 14-4

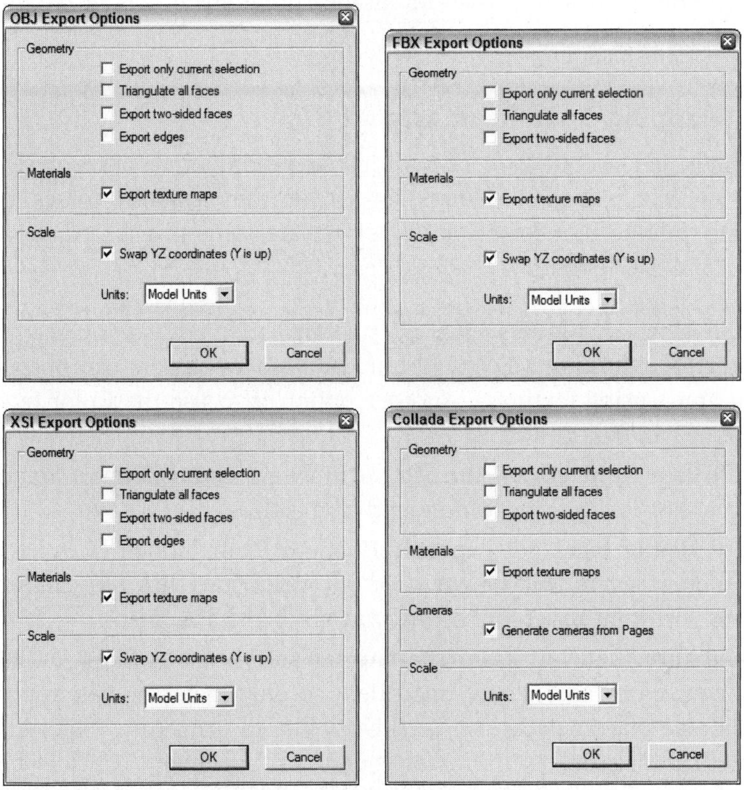

The Export Options dialog boxes for OBJ, FBX, XSI, and DAE (Collada).

Programs that don't support edges (and that includes most of them) will leave them out, anyway. The Export Edges option isn't available for FBX files.

▲ **Export Texture Maps:** This option includes the textures you used in your SketchUp model in the exported file. If you plan to "paint" your model in another program, deselect this check box.

▲ **Generate Cameras from Pages (Scenes):** The Collada file format can store information about different views of your model. Selecting this check box exports each of your scenes (if you have any) as a separate camera object. Note that this option doesn't exist for OBJ, FBX, or XSI.

▲ **Swap YZ Coordinates (Y Is Up):** If your model ends up oriented the wrong way when you open it in another piece of software, try selecting this check box and exporting it again. Some programs set up their axes differently. This option isn't available for Collada.

▲ **Units:** Leave this option on Model Units unless something is wrong when you open your model in another program. If it is, make an adjustment and export again.

14.2.3 Wrapping Your Head around 3DS

3DS is almost guaranteed to work with just about any other piece of 3D software you're using, which is good. What's bad is that this flexibility comes at a price: a seemingly infinite number of options. Here are some things you should know about the 3DS file format:

▲ **You'll lose your layers.** 3DS doesn't support them, so you might be better off exporting a DWG file (if your other software can open it and if you aren't using textures). Another option is to use the Color by Layers option, which is described later.

▲ **You'll lose your edges, too.** You can always choose Export Stand Alone Edges, but few people recommend doing that.

▲ **Only visible faces get exported.** None of your hidden faces, or faces on hidden layers, will be exported, so make sure that you can see everything you want to export before you go to the File menu.

▲ **Make sure that you paint the correct side of your faces.** Faces (or the equivalent) in 3DS are one-sided, so only materials you apply to the front side of your faces in SketchUp will end up getting exported. If you have materials on both sides of your faces, you might consider choosing the Export Two-Sided Faces option, described later in this section.

Figure 14-5 shows the 3DS Export Options dialog box. Your options are as follows:

▲ **Export:** You have four choices here:
   • **Full Hierarchy:** This option tells the 3DS exporter to make separate **meshes** (surfaces made out of triangles) for each "chunk" of geometry in your SketchUp model. Chunks are things like groups, components, and groupings of connected faces.
   • **By Layer:** This option tells the exporter to create separate meshes based on two things: chunks of geometry, and what layer things are on. If several faces are connected and they're on the same layer, they get exported as a single unit.
   • **By Material:** When you choose this option, you get a separate set for each grouping of connected geometry that shares the same material.
   • **Single Object:** Choosing this option exports all your geometry as one big 3DS unit.

Figure 14-5

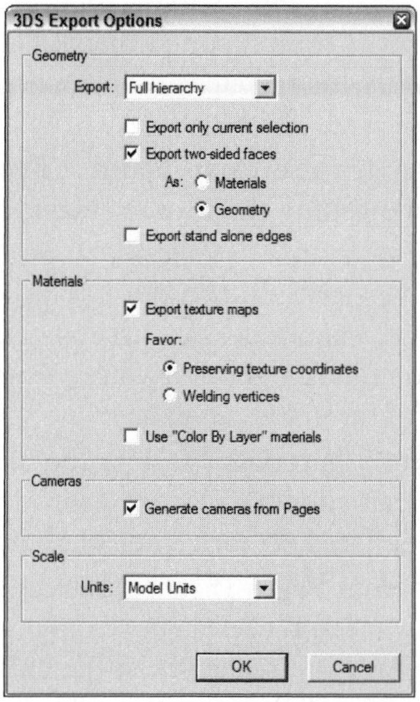

The 3DS Export Options dialog box.

▲ **Export Only Current Selection:** This option only exports the geometry you've selected in your SketchUp model.

▲ **Export Two-Sided Faces:** Selecting this check box exports two faces (back to back) for every face you have in your SketchUp model. Because 3DS supports only single-sided faces, this is necessary to preserve the appearance of your textures in your exported model. If you don't care about preserving your SketchUp textures, or if you didn't apply any in the first place, don't bother choosing this option:

• **As Materials:** Choose this option to export your back-side materials as 3DS materials without corresponding geometry.

• **As Geometry:** Choose this option to export your extra set of faces as actual geometry. You should choose this option if you're wondering what to do.

▲ **Export Stand Alone Edges:** 3DS doesn't support edges the way SketchUp does—you don't have a good way to export edges as "lines" to 3DS. When you select this check box, the exporter substitutes a long, thin rectangle for every edge in your model. The appearance is almost the same, but this can cause major problems in your file. You should not select this check box. If you really need to be able to see your edges, you should probably try another export format altogether.

▲ **Export Texture Maps:** If you have photo textures in your model (this includes the photo textures from the Materials dialog box), you might want to include them in your exported model file. 3DS handles these textures very differently than SketchUp does, so you have to decide on an export method:

- **Favor Preserving Texture Coordinates:** Choose this option if you've spent a lot of time getting the texture "maps" right in your SketchUp model.
- **Favor Welding Vertices:** Choose this option if it's more important that your geometry export as accurately as possible. In some cases, your textures won't look right, but your geometry will be correctly welded (stuck together) and smoothed.

▲ **Use "Color by Layer" Materials:** Because the 3DS file format doesn't support layers, you can choose to export your model with different colors assigned to the faces on each layer in SketchUp.

▲ **Generate Cameras from Pages (Scenes):** Select this check box to export your file with a different camera position saved for each scene in your SketchUp file. An extra scene (called Default Scene) is also exported to reflect your current model view.

▲ **Units:** If you leave this set to Model Units, most other 3D programs will understand what you mean—your geometry will appear the right size when you open your exported 3DS file. In some cases, it won't, and the best thing to do is to manually choose the units that you'll be using in the other program. Sometimes this doesn't work either, and you'll just have to experiment until something works.

14.2.4 Dealing with VRML

The VRML file format is pronounced *vermal*. Virtual Reality Modeling Language is used by a large number of people around the world. There are newer, arguably better, formats out there, but VRML's been around long enough that it's tightly integrated into lots of professional workflows.

Figure 14-6 shows the VRML Export Options dialog box; what follows is some help with all the controls:

▲ **Output Texture Maps:** If you don't select this check box, you'll get colors instead of textures in your exported VRML file.

▲ **Ignore Back of Face Material:** Go ahead and select this check box unless your faces have different materials painted on either side of them.

▲ **Output Edges:** VRML supports edges, so select this check box if you want to export your edges (along with your faces) as part of your VRML file.

Figure 14-6

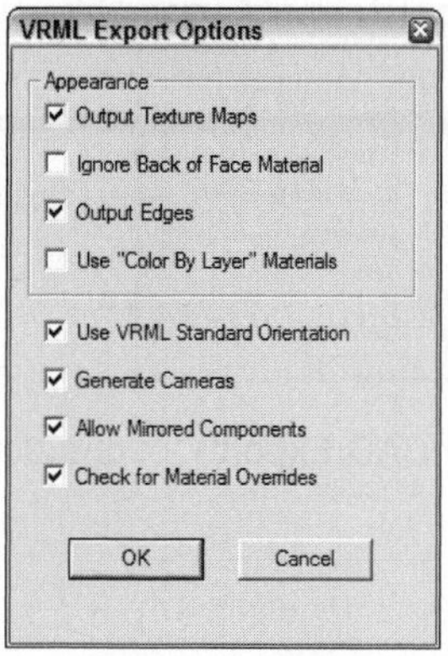

The VRML Export Options dialog box.

▲ **Use "Color by Layer" Materials:** VRML doesn't do layers, so if your layers are important to you, you should consider selecting this check box. All the faces in your exported model will be painted with the colors in the Layers dialog box (Chapter 5 has more information on assigning colors to layers).

▲ **Use VRML Standard Orientation:** You should select this check box to convert your model's "up" axis to match VRML's "up" axis.

▲ **Generate Cameras:** If you have scenes in your SketchUp model, you might want to select this check box. It tells the exporter to create a separate camera view for every one of your scenes, and an extra one for your current view.

▲ **Allow Mirrored Components:** If you have components in your model whose instances you've mirrored (flipped over), you should select this check box. Because this is a standard technique for building symmetrical things like vehicles (as discussed in Chapter 6), this might apply to your model.

▲ **Check for Material Overrides:** This option makes sure that the materials in your exported model end up looking like they do in your SketchUp model.

14.2.5 Handling DWG and DXF (in 3D)

You should use these two 3D file formats if you need to export your 3D data to AutoCAD, but for other programs, you're probably better off getting the right plugin. Here is some information about DXF and DWG:

▲ **You'll lose your materials.** Your materials won't export to DXF/DWG, so pick another format if they're important to you.

Figure 14-7

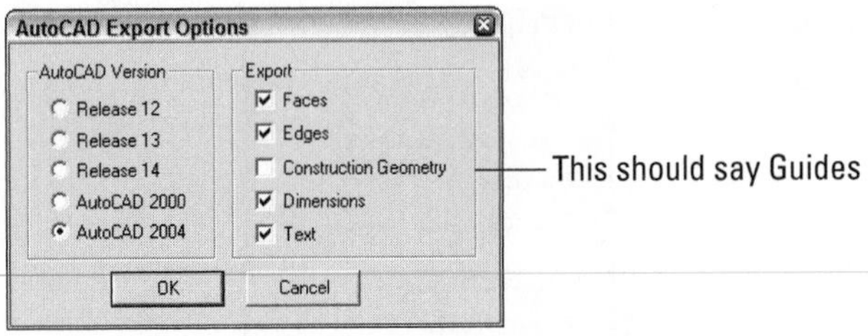

The AutoCAD Export Options dialog box.

▲ **You'll keep your layers.** The one great thing about exporting to DXF/ DWG is that you get to keep your layers.

▲ **Go with DWG.** If you can, pick DWG instead of DXF; it's more robust, which means that it saves more of your data.

Figure 14-7 is a screen shot of the AutoCAD Export Options dialog box; it's quite simple compared to the one for 3DS. Just select the kinds of things you want to export, and then click the OK button.

SELF-CHECK

1. SketchUp's faces are two-sided, but not all 3D programs' faces are. True or false?

2. If your model ends up oriented the wrong way when you open it in another piece of software, try selecting the _____ check box and exporting it again.

3. 3DS is almost guaranteed to work with just about any other piece of 3D software you're using. True or false?

4. When exporting a 3DS file, you lose everything but which of the following?

   a. Layers

   b. Edges

   c. Visible faces

   d. Hidden faces

SUMMARY

If you're a SketchUp Pro user you have many more tools at your disposal as you create your models. If you are not a SketchUp Pro user, then perhaps this chapter showed you what you are missing and the additional capabilities you could have if you upgraded to the Pro version of SketchUp.

In this chapter, you evaluated many file formats and when to use each one. You generated 2D files for CAD and illustration software. You evaluated PDF and EPS formats and their uses. Finally, you exported your model to other 3D software. These skills will serve you well as you continue your SketchUp modeling. You now have a whole new world open to you.

KEY TERMS

3DS	One of the few standard 3D file formats.
DAE (Collada)	A new 3D file format that is gaining acceptance with a large number of gaming and animation programs.
DWG	AutoCAD's native file format and the best one to use for transferring information to that program and other pieces of CAD software.
DXF	Document Exchange Format, a type of DWG that was developed by Autodesk to be the file format that other pieces of software use to transfer data into AutoCAD.
EPIX	A file format that lets you open 2D views of your SketchUp model in Piranesi.
EPS	Encapsulated Postscript, a file format that some people still use to transfer vector information.
Extensions	The line overruns that you can choose to display in the Styles dialog box.
FBX	A 3D file format used primarily by people in the entertainment industry who use Maya, 3DS Max, or Autodesk VIZ.
KMZ	The Google Earth 3D file format.
Meshes	Surfaces made out of triangles.
OBJ	A 3D file format that can be used to send data to Maya.
PDF	Portable Document Format, a file format that can be read by almost anyone and that is great for sending information to vector-illustration programs.

Section lines	Lines that occur where section planes create section cuts in a model.
Texture-mapping	Painting with textures.
VRML	An older 3D file format that is still used by some programs.
XSI	A 3D file format for people who use Softimage.

ASSESS YOUR UNDERSTANDING

Go to www.wiley.com/college/chopra to evaluate your knowledge of exporting to CAD, illustration, and other modeling software.

Measure your learning by comparing pre-test and post-test results.

Summary Questions

1. What type of files did people used to use to transfer vector information?
   (a) PDF   (b) EPS
   (c) DXF   (d) EPIX

2. Use _____ if your other graphics software is more than a couple of versions old or if someone you're working with insists on it.

3. DXF is more capable than DWG, and for exporting 2D drawings from SketchUp to use in other CAD applications, using DXF usually yields better results. True or false?

4. Data export from any program is a somewhat uncertain endeavor, so you should experiment and allow extra time for troubleshooting. True or false?

5. The most recent version of DXF or DWG that SketchUp Pro 6 can import is _____.

6. DWG and DXF are 2D formats that are a good choice for most of the CAD-type programs out there, but not as good a choice as 3DS. True or false?

7. When in doubt, export a _____ file and see whether your program can open it.

8. A great place to go for help with exporting 3D files is the _____.

9. The process of exporting your 3D data from SketchUp Pro is the same no matter what file format you choose. True or false?

10. Most of the file formats that SketchUp Pro exports do not save the textures in your model as separate files alongside your model, so you needn't create a new folder for your exported 3D file. True or false?

Applying This Chapter

1. You create a model of a new art institute that you need to email to the institute's architecture committee. How do you go about deciding which file format to export out of SketchUp?

2. List the steps that you would follow to export a 2D vector image from SketchUp Pro.

3. List three 3D file formats and the differences between them.

4. What are the differences between DWG and DXF?

Exporting a 2D SketchUp Pro Image

Choose a view of your model and export it both as a PDF and as a TIFF. Make note of the differences in the resulting images.

15

CREATING PRESENTATION DOCUMENTS WITH LAYOUT
Presenting 3D SketchUp Models on Paper and On Screen

Starting Point

Go to www.wiley.com/college/chopra to assess your knowledge of creating presentation documents with LayOut.
Determine where you need to concentrate your effort.

What You'll Learn in This Chapter

▲ What LayOut is
▲ The difference between layers and master layers
▲ How to use templates with LayOut
▲ How to bring raster images and SketchUp models into LayOut
▲ The different uses for your LayOut documents

After Studying This Chapter, You'll Be Able To

▲ Assess when you would use LayOut
▲ Assess how to simplify LayOut with layers and master layers
▲ Evaluate the qualities that make LayOut unique
▲ Build a simple presentation document from scratch
▲ Print and export your work

INTRODUCTION

People who design things in 3D have to present their ideas to other people, and most of the time, they have to present in a 2D format. Creating these presentations almost always involves the use of layout or illustration software like InDesign, Illustrator, or QuarkXPress; these programs are great, but they can be expensive and tricky to get the hang of, especially if you're not a graphic designer.

If you're lucky enough to have the Pro version of Google SketchUp 6, you have access to a whole separate piece of software called Google SketchUp LayOut, or LayOut for short.

LayOut is a program that lets you create documents for presenting your 3D SketchUp models, both on paper and on-screen. LayOut was designed to be easy to use, quick to learn, and tightly integrated with SketchUp. The people who built it want you to use LayOut to create all your design presentations; here are some examples of what you can make with this software:

▲ Information sheets
▲ Storyboards
▲ Design packs
▲ Presentation boards and posters
▲ Banners
▲ On-screen, PowerPoint-style slide shows

LayOut gives you the tools to create cover pages, title blocks, callouts, and symbols—whatever you need to accompany views of your model. You can create presentations that are just about any physical size, and you can export them as PDF files to send to other people. Best of all, when your design changes in SketchUp, you can easily update your model views in LayOut to reflect the changes. If you make your living designing and presenting ideas in 3D, LayOut can save you valuable time.

This chapter gives a fairly high-level overview of what you can do with LayOut. First it discusses the different things you can use LayOut to accomplish, followed by a quick tour of the LayOut user interface, explaining where everything is and what it's supposed to do. Next, the chapter discusses the process of creating a simple presentation drawing set from one of your SketchUp models—not exhaustively, but it should be enough to see you through a tight deadline.

15.1 Getting Your Bearings

Even though LayOut comes with SketchUp Pro, it's not just a SketchUp feature—LayOut is its own program. As such, LayOut has its own menus, tools, dialog boxes, and Drawing Window.

Figure 15-1

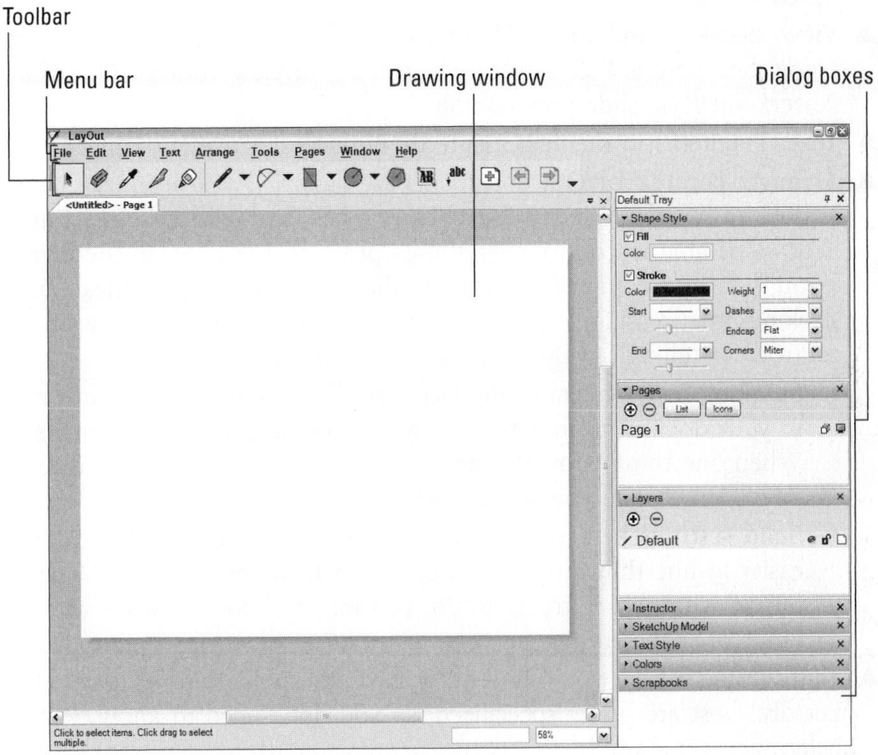

Toolbar

Menu bar   Drawing window   Dialog boxes

The LayOut user interface.

Even though LayOut's user interface is pretty standard, this section provides a quick overview of the different elements. Knowing that LayOut is a lot like other software you've used (including SketchUp) should help you come up to speed quickly. Figure 15-1 shows the LayOut user interface.

15.1.1 Some Menu Bar Minutiae

Just like almost every other piece of software, LayOut has a menu bar. And just like SketchUp, you can use LayOut's menu bar to access the vast majority of its tools, commands, settings, and dialog boxes. Here's a brief description of each of LayOut's nine menus:

▲ **File:** You use the items in the File menu to create new LayOut files, save and adjust settings for the document you're working on, and insert SketchUp and other graphics files.

▲ **Edit:** You use the items in the Edit menu to copy and paste, work with clipping masks (LayOut's version of cropping), and control object grouping.

In the Windows version of LayOut, the Edit menu includes Preferences, which is where you can do some things to customize LayOut.

▲ **View:** Besides standard items like controls for zooming, the most interesting item here is Full Screen, which lets you view your LayOut as a PowerPoint-style slide presentation.

▲ **Text:** The items in the Text menu are nothing out of the ordinary.

▲ **Arrange:** Because LayOut documents are basically well-organized collections of images, inserted SketchUp models, text, and callouts, you need to be able to control everything's place on the page. In the Arrange menu, you find commands for controlling the horizontal, vertical, and stacking-order position of every element in your document, as well as controls for telling LayOut what snap settings to use.

• **Stacking order** refers to the fact that all elements on the same layer in your document are either in front of or behind other elements. When one thing is overlapping another, their stacking order determines which one you see and which one is hidden.

• **Snap settings** help you position elements on your page by making it easier to line things up with a grid or with other elements. Depending on what you're trying to do, you might choose to work with both kinds of snap settings, just one, or none at all.

▲ **Tools:** Here's where you'll find all of LayOut's tools; there are several. Luckily, most are pretty specialized, so you don't need to know them all before you get started.

▲ **Pages:** There are few items in the Pages menu. Your LayOut presentation can have many pages, and here's where you add, delete, duplicate, and move among them.

▲ **Window:** In the Window menu, you find links to all of LayOut's dialog boxes; see the next section in this chapter for a rundown on all of them.

▲ **Help:** Just like in SketchUp, the Help menu should be the first and last place you go when you're stuck. It's a great place to look for resources that can help you get started; the video tutorials are also helpful.

▲ **LayOut (Mac only):** The Mac version of LayOut includes a LayOut menu, which is standard operating procedure for Mac applications. The important thing in this menu is Preferences, which lets you set up the program the way you want it.

15.1.2 A Dialog Box Discourse

You can find most of LayOut's knobs and switches in its eight dialog boxes. In Windows, most of LayOut's dialog boxes are contained in a "tray" that appears on the right side of your screen by default. On the Mac, your dialog boxes float around, but you can "snap" them together if you want.

Here's a description of each:

▲ **Colors:** Just about all your LayOut documents will use color in some way, so you'll need this dialog box most of the time. The nice thing about Color is that it appears when you need it; clicking any color well in LayOut opens it (if it isn't already open).

▲ **Shape Style:** A lot of the graphic elements in your presentation can have color fills and strokes (outlines). The Shape Style dialog box is where you control the appearance of those fills and strokes. Check out the options in the Start and End drop-down menus—you won't find callout styles like these in most other layout programs.

▲ **SketchUp Model:** The greatest thing about LayOut (at least with respect to other software like it) is its ability to include 2D views of your SketchUp models. In the SketchUp Model dialog box, you can control all sorts of things about the way your "placed" SketchUp model looks, including camera views, scenes, styles, shadows, and fog. For those who spend a lot of time laying out presentation drawings that include SketchUp models, the SketchUp Model dialog box is especially helpful.

▲ **Text Style:** If you've ever used another piece of page layout or illustration software, you should be pretty familiar with what the Text Style dialog box lets you do. You use it to control the font, size, style, color, and alignment of text in your document.

▲ **Pages:** You use the Pages dialog box to manage the pages in your document. You can add, delete, and rearrange them as much as you like. The List and Icon buttons at the top let you toggle between views of your pages; you may prefer to use the former and give your pages meaningful names as you work. The little icons on the right control visibility for shared layers and full-screen presentations. **Shared layers** are somewhat unique to LayOut; they let you automatically place elements on more than one page. For more detail, see the section "Simplifying LayOut with Layers and Master Layers," later in this chapter.

▲ **Layers:** You can have multiple layers of content in every LayOut document you create. You may prefer to work with at least four layers, organizing content on each as follows:

  • Elements that should appear in the same place on almost every page, like logos and project titles

  • Things that appear in the same place on most pages, but that change from page to page, like numbers and page titles

  • Content (like images and SketchUp model views) that only appears on a single page

  • Unused stuff that you're not sure you want, but that you don't want to delete

Use the Layers dialog box to add, delete, and rearrange layers in your document. The icons on the right let you hide (and show), lock, and share individual layers.

▲ **Scrapbooks:** This one's a little more difficult to explain; scrapbooks are unique to LayOut, so you probably haven't worked with anything like them before. Scrapbooks are LayOut files that exist in a special folder on your computer system. They contain colors, text styles, and graphic elements (like scale cars, trees, and people) that you might need to use in more than one of your LayOut documents. To use something you see in a scrapbook, just click it, and then click again in your Drawing Window to "stamp" it in (if it's a graphic element), or to apply it to something (if it's a color or a text style). You can also create your own scrapbooks if you want. Just choose File⇨Save as Scrapbook from the menu bar to save any LayOut file as a scrapbook that will show up in your Scrapbooks dialog box.

▲ **Instructor:** The Instructor dialog box works just like it does in SketchUp; it shows information on whichever tool you happen to be using. If you're just starting out with LayOut, make sure that this dialog box is open.

15.1.3 Setting Up LayOut Preferences

In LayOut, as in SketchUp, you have two kinds of preferences to consider: those that apply to *every* LayOut document you work on and those that only apply to the document you happen to be working on at the moment. Settings for the former are made in the Preferences dialog box; controls for the latter reside in Document Setup. The following sections explain.

Preferences

The LayOut Preferences dialog box is made up of six panels. You open it by choosing Edit⇨Preferences in Windows or LayOut⇨Preferences on the Mac. Here's what you'll find on each panel:

▲ **Applications:** Here, you tell LayOut what programs you want to use to edit image and text files when you right-click them (in LayOut) and choose Open with Image (or Text) Editor from the context menu.

▲ **Backup:** You can work smart by letting LayOut auto-save and create automatic backups of your file. Here's where you tell it how often to do so.

▲ **Folders:** Here, you let LayOut know where to look for templates and scrapbooks on your computer. Templates show up when you start LayOut or open a new document; scrapbooks appear in the Scrapbook dialog box.

▲ **Scales:** This is a list of scales you can choose from for a SketchUp model view you've placed in your LayOut document. If you want to use a certain drawing scale and it doesn't show up in the Scales pane of the SketchUp Model dialog box, you can add it here. This is *not* the drawing scale for the document you're currently working on.

▲ **Shortcuts:** Just like SketchUp, you use this panel to define a keyboard shortcut for any tool or command in LayOut.

▲ **Startup:** In this panel, tell LayOut how to behave every time you launch it (or just start a new file).

Document Setup

The Document Setup dialog box includes five panels. You open it by choosing FileDocument Setup in the menu bar. Here's information on each panel:

▲ **General:** You can enter information about yourself and your document; this might be important if you're working on a team.

▲ **Grid:** Grids help line up elements in your presentations. Use the options in this panel to control the visibility and size of the grid in your document, if you want one. For Major Grid, type in an interval for the darker grid lines. For Minor Grid, enter the number of divisions between dark lines you'd like to have. For 1/4-inch squares, you would enter 1 inch for the former and 4 for the latter.

▲ **Paper:** Here's where you tell LayOut the size and color of the sheet of paper you'd like to use for your document. You can also control the width of your margins and the resolution at which you'd like your SketchUp model views to print. See the section "Creating a New, Blank Document," later in this chapter, for a list of recommended resolutions.

▲ **References:** When you insert a SketchUp model or an image in your LayOut document, LayOut creates a file reference that keeps track of where it came from. If you edit the original file (which you probably will), this panel lets you know whether LayOut is showing the most currently saved version. For people who go back and forth between design and presentation documents often, the References panel is very helpful.

▲ **Units:** Depending on where you live and work, you might use a different system of measurement. Use the Units panel to pick the right one for your workflow.

15.1.4 Tooling Around

LayOut has lots of tools, but as with most software, you spend most of your time with only a handful of them. You can find the complete list in the Tools menu, but it's easier to get at them on the toolbar. This strip, across the top of

Figure 15-2

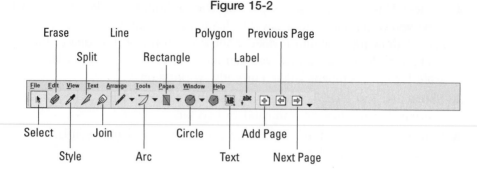

The default toolbar in LayOut. You can customize it if you want to.

your Drawing Window, includes icons for the most commonly used tools (and commands), but you can easily add others if you want to. Here's a bullet point on each of the tools in the LayOut toolbar's default set (see Figure 15-2, which shows the toolbar for the Windows version of LayOut):

▲ **Select:** This tool lets you select, rotate, move, copy, and scale elements in your document. Using this tool, you can also double-click to edit text and SketchUp model views.

▲ **Erase:** With this tool, you can click or drag over any unlocked elements to erase them.

▲ **Style:** Here, you can click any element to **sample** (soak up) its fill, stroke, and other attributes. Doing so turns the tool into the Bucket, which you use to apply those attributes to other elements in your document by clicking them.

▲ **Split:** Use Split to cut one line segment (whether curved or straight) into two by clicking where you want the split to occur. Turning Object Snap on (in the Arrange menu) is very helpful for splitting shapes at their corners.

▲ **Join:** This tool lets you turn two line segments (curved or straight) into a single one by clicking each in turn. Both are highlighted blue when they're joined.

▲ **Line:** With this tool, you can draw a straight line by clicking to define start points and endpoints. Press Esc to stop drawing a line.

▲ **Arc:** With this tool, you can draw an arc by clicking once to define the arc's center point, again to start the arc (which defines its radius), and a third time to end the arc. You can draw an arc in four ways; check out the Tools menu to see all of them.

▲ **Rectangle:** With this tool, you can draw a rectangle by clicking to define opposite corners.

▲ **Circle:** This tool lets you draw a circle by clicking once to define a center and again to define a radius.

▲ **Polygon:** Using this device, you can draw polygons by first entering a side count and then using your mouse. Select the Polygon tool, type the number of sides followed by the letter *s* (*8s* for an octagon), and then press Enter. Now click once with your mouse to define a center point and again to draw the shape.

▲ **Text:** Use this tool to draw an empty text box into which you can enter text. If you need to edit text you've already typed, double-click it with the Select tool or the Text tool.

▲ **Label:** This tool lets you draw a text label with a leader line by clicking to define the end of the line (where it's pointing), clicking again to define the beginning, and then typing in some text.

▲ **Add Page:** Use this to add a page after the one you're on.

▲ **Previous Page:** This tool lets you view the previous page in your document.

▲ **Next Page:** Use this to view the next page in your document.

Adding more tool icons to your toolbar is easy; just right-click the toolbar and choose Customize to bring up the Customize dialog box. Now drag tool icons up into your toolbar (if you're on Windows, you'll have to select the Command tab first).

SWITCHING TO LAYOUT FROM SIMILAR SOFTWARE

If you're used to using other page-layout or illustration software, some things about LayOut are useful to know when you're just getting started. The people who designed LayOut did things a little differently on purpose, hoping to do for page layout in 2007 what they did for 3D design seven years earlier—make it easier for motivated people with no experience to produce good work, quickly.

Here are the five things you should keep in mind when you're exploring LayOut:

▲ LayOut includes templates that help you get started in no time. See the nearby section "Starting Out with Templates" for details.

▲ You can insert models from SketchUp, skipping the process of exporting your model as an image file. Importing has the added benefit of helping you automatically update model views in your presentation. See the section "Bringing In Everything You Need," later in this chapter, for details.

▲ The Layers feature in LayOut is a powerful tool for organizing your content. In particular, you can place content that appears on more than one of your pages on a master layer, so you only have to position it once. The section "Simplifying LayOut with Layers and Master Layers," later in this chapter, outlines just what you need to know.

▲ In LayOut, you have enormous flexibility to crop images, including model views, with ease using clipping masks. The section "Cropping with Clipping Masks," later in this chapter, explains how in four easy steps.

▲ When your presentation is ready to go, LayOut enables you to set up digital slide shows in full-screen mode, as well as to create printouts and PDF files.

SELF-CHECK

1. Which menu do you use to copy and paste, work with clipping masks, and control object grouping?

   a. View

   b. Edit

   c. Text

   d. Pages

2. LayOut has the ability to include 2D views of your SketchUp models. True or false?

3. _____, which are somewhat unique to LayOut, let you automatically place elements on more than one page.

4. When you insert a SketchUp model or an image in your LayOut document, LayOut creates a file reference that keeps track of where it came from. True or false?

Figure 15-3

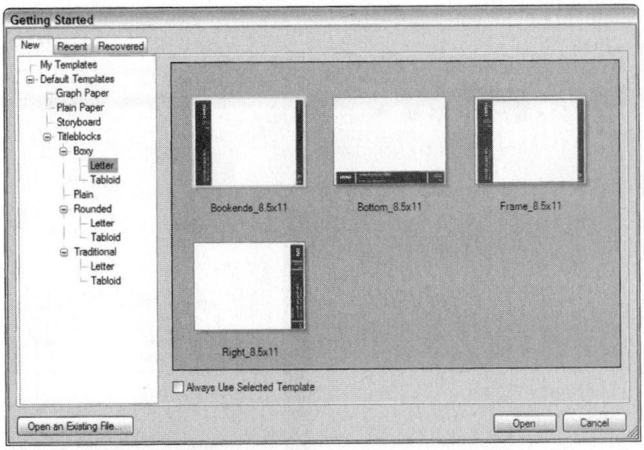

The Getting Started dialog box.

15.2 Getting Set Up

Every time you launch LayOut, and every time you choose File⇨New, you're presented with a dialog box that asks you how you want to start out (see Figure 15-3).

The theory is that when you open most programs, you usually want to do one of two things:

▲ **Start a new document:** The New tab at the top of the dialog box presents you with a list of templates that come preloaded in LayOut. There's nothing special about these templates—they're just ready-made LayOut files you can use as a starting point for your presentation. Expand the items in the list on the left to see the available templates broken down by category.

▲ **Open a document you've already started:** Click the Recent tab at the top of the dialog box to show a list of LayOut files you've worked on most recently. Select one and click the Open (Choose on the Mac) button to open it. To open an existing document that doesn't appear in the Recent list, click the Open an Existing File button to pop up the Open dialog box.

Sometimes you see a third tab in your Getting Started dialog box: Recovered. If LayOut has crashed on you, or if you ever had any LayOut files that weren't saved when things went awry, the document you were working on should show up in the Recovered tab. It's still a good idea to save often, though.

Figure 15-4

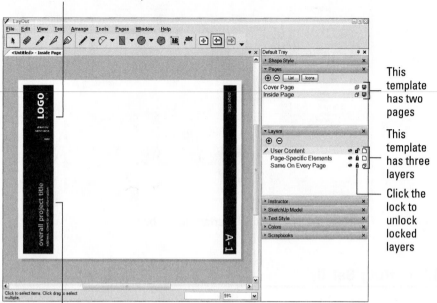

One of LayOut's fancier prebuilt templates.

15.2.1 Starting Out with Templates

More often than not, you can find a template to use as a starting point for your presentation. Browse the list, select one you like, and click the Open (Choose on the Mac) button to begin working with a template. You can also create a custom template, which is explained later. Usually, templates are the quickest way to get started with a new LayOut project.

Here are a few things you should know about templates; Figure 15-4 points them out in a screen shot:

▲ **Pay attention to the layers.** Many of the templates that come with LayOut have multiple layers, and some of these layers are locked by default. They're locked so that you can't accidentally move things around, but you can always unlock them if you need to. In the Layers dialog box, click the lock icon to lock or unlock a layer; knowing you need to unlock a layer is especially handy when you want to swap in your logo instead of using the generic "Logo Design" that comes preinstalled.

▲ **Have a look at the pages.** Most of the more interesting templates include at least two pages; the first one's a cover page. Don't forget to look at the all the pages when you're working with a template.

▲ **Double-click to edit text.** One of the nice things about LayOut is that you can edit text on locked layers. Using the Select tool, just double-click any text you want to edit (and in some templates, you'll want to edit all the text), type in new text, and then click once somewhere else to finish the edit.

▲ **You can change colors.** LayOut's templates are designed so that you can easily change the overall color scheme. Just unlock all the layers, open the Shape Styles dialog box, and proceed. For more information about changing colors, see the section "Drawing Something from Scratch," later in this chapter.

Most of the design presentations that you (or your firm) put together probably look a lot alike—after all, they're part of your brand identity. If the presentation documents you make are all variations on a couple of themes, why not build your own templates and use them every time you need to start a new project? You can set things up so that your templates appear in the Getting Started dialog box, making it easier to build consistent presentations quicker.

Follow these steps to turn any LayOut file into a template:

1. **Build a LayOut file that includes all the elements you want.** These elements might include a title block, a logo, a page number, and a cover page. Make sure that you're viewing the page you want to use as the thumbnail preview in the template list before you move on to step 2.

2. **Choose File⇨Save as Template.** The Save as Template dialog box opens.

3. **Type a name for your template.**

4. **Choose a location for your new template.** In the list at the bottom of the dialog box, click the folder (they're all folders) in which you want to include the template you're adding.

5. **Click the OK button. On a Mac, click Save.** The next time the Getting Started dialog box appears, your new template will be in it.

15.2.2 Creating a New, Blank Document

If you decide not to start with one of LayOut's templates, you'll need to set up a new document from scratch.

Follow these steps to create a new LayOut document:

1. **Launch LayOut.** Keep in mind that LayOut and SketchUp are separate software programs, so you need to launch them individually. If you've

already launched LayOut, choose File⇨New to open the Getting Started dialog box.

2. **In the Getting Started dialog box, click the New tab.** This shows a list of available templates on the left, with thumbnail previews of each template on the right.

3. **Click My Templates (All on the Mac) in the list on the left.**

4. **Select one of the Plain Paper Templates on the right, and click Open (Choose if you're on Mac).** The plain paper templates are easy to spot; they're completely white. When a new, blank document that you can set up however you like appears, you then need to set up your new document the way you want it.

5. **Choose File⇨Document Setup.** This opens the Document Setup dialog box.

6. **Click Units in the panel list on the left, and select the type of measurement units you prefer to use, as shown in Figure 15-5.** The Units panel lets you choose which units you'd like to use.

7. **Click Paper in the list on the left, and set your paper size and color.** If you know you'll be printing on paper that isn't white, you can simulate the color by choosing one here. You shouldn't try to print out a paper color; most printers don't print **full bleed** (right to the edges), so the effect really isn't that great.

8. **Set up some margins, if you want to.** Margins are useful if you know how close to the edge of your paper you can print.

Figure 15-5

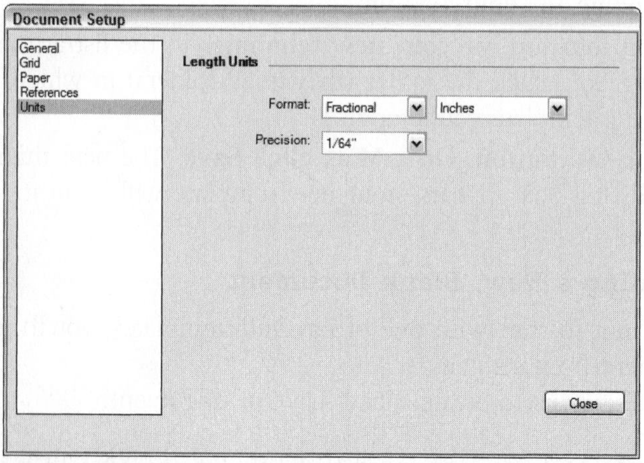

The Units panel in the Document Setup dialog box.

9. **Set the rendering resolution according to your document size.** Basically, the rendering resolution you choose depends on the physical size of your printed document. As long as your paper size isn't any bigger than 11 × 17 inches, you should probably choose 300 dpi. For bigger presentations (like boards and posters), use a setting of 100 or 150 dpi. The goal is to limit the size of the file (in megabytes) that gets sent to your printer—if it's too big, it can be a problem. For more information on image resolution, have a look at Chapter 13.

10. **Click Grid in the list of panels on the left, and set up your grid options the way you want them.** Now you're in the Grid panel. For more information about this section of the Document Setup dialog box, see the section "Getting Your Bearings," earlier in this chapter.

11. **Click the Close button to close the Document Setup dialog box.**

15.2.3 Adding Pages to Your Document

Follow these steps to add a few blank pages to your document:

1. **If your Pages dialog box isn't already open, choose Window⇨Pages to open it.**

2. **Choose Pages⇨Add.** This adds a page to your document. You can also add pages by clicking the little button that looks like a plus sign (in the upper-left corner of the Pages dialog box). Add as many pages as you want.

3. **In the Pages dialog box, double-click the name of your new page, and then type in a name for it.** Press Enter when you're done. Repeat to give all your pages meaningful names.

15.2.4 Moving Around Your Document

You move around on the pages in your document just like you do in SketchUp—except in 2D instead of 3D. Here's how to move around:

▲ **Panning:** Hold down your scroll wheel button while moving your mouse around to slide your page around in your Document Window. This is called panning.

▲ **Zooming:** Roll your scroll wheel back and forth to zoom in and out on your page. To fill your Document Window with the page you're viewing, choose Scale to Fit (Zoom to Fit on the Mac) from the Zoom drop-down list in your window's lower-right corner.

▲ **Moving from page to page:** Click the Next Page and the Previous Page buttons on your toolbar to move among the pages in your document. You can also click your pages' names in the Pages dialog box.

SELF-CHECK

1. Usually, custom templates are the quickest way to get started with a new LayOut project. True or false?

2. In LayOut, you can edit text on locked layers by double-clicking while using the Select tool. True or false?

3. The rendering resolution you choose depends on the physical size of your printed document, but as long as your paper size isn't any bigger than 11 × 17 inches, you should probably choose a setting of 100 or 150 dpi. True or false?

4. To move from page to page in your document, which of the following should you do?

   a. Hold down your scroll wheel button while moving your mouse around.

   b. Roll your scroll wheel back and forth.

   c. Click your pages' names in the Pages dialog box.

   d. Choose Zoom to Fit from the Zoom drop-down list in your window's lower-right corner.

15.3 Simplifying LayOut with Layers and Master Layers

You use layers to create multipage documents with elements that are consistent from page to page. You can have two different kinds of layers in LayOut:

▲ **Unshared: Unshared layers** are like layers in every other software program. Any element (text, graphic, or otherwise) that you put on an unshared layer exists only on one page: the page you're on when you put the element on the layer.

▲ **Shared (Master Layers):** LayOut introduces the notion of **master layers**; anything you put on a master layer appears on every page of your document, as long as those pages are set up to show master layers.

Here are a few quick tips about how you can organize content on layers—including master layers—as you create presentations in LayOut:

▲ **You can make an element (like a logo) appear in the same spot on more than one page by putting it on a master layer.** For example, if the logo and the project title need to appear in the same spot on every page, put these two elements on the master layer called "On Every Page." In Figure 15-6, note how the logo and project title appear in exactly the same place in the pages labeled B and C.

▲ **Put content that appears on only one page on an unshared layer.** Again, in the pages labeled B and C, the image boxes and page titles are different on each page, so put them on the unshared layer called "Unique."

Figure 15-6

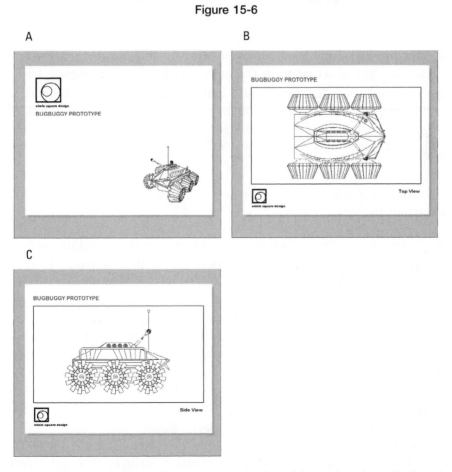

A simple document with two layers: one that's shared (master) and one that's not.

Figure 15-7

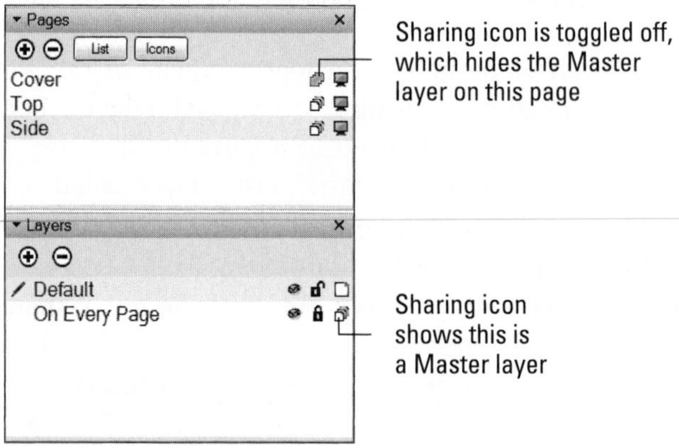

Sharing icon is toggled off, which hides the Master layer on this page

Sharing icon shows this is a Master layer

Click the Sharing icon to control master layers.

▲ **You can make any layer a master layer by clicking the Sharing icon to the right of its name in the Layers dialog box (see Figure 15-7).**

▲ **You decide which pages should display master layers by toggling the Sharing icon to the right of their names in the Pages dialog box.** For example, if you don't want the logo and the project title to be on the cover page (labeled A in Figure 15-6), toggle the Show Master Layers icon beside the cover page to Off, as shown in Figure 15-7.

When you're manipulating elements on individual layers in LayOut, keep these points in mind:

▲ **To add a new layer,** click the plus sign icon in the Layers dialog box.

▲ **To change which layer something's on,** select the destination layer in the Layers dialog box, right-click the element you want to move, and choose Move to Current Layer.

▲ **To see what layer an element is currently on,** select the element, then look for the tiny blue dot in the Layers dialog box. If you select two elements on two different layers, you see two blue dots.

▲ **To lock layers you're not using,** click the Lock icon. With this step, you avoid accidentally moving the wrong things around, or even deleting them.

▲ **To hide layers and improve your performance,** make liberal use of the Hide icon next to the name of each layer; this can really improve LayOut's performance, especially on slower computers. Hide any layers you're not working with, and you'll notice the difference.

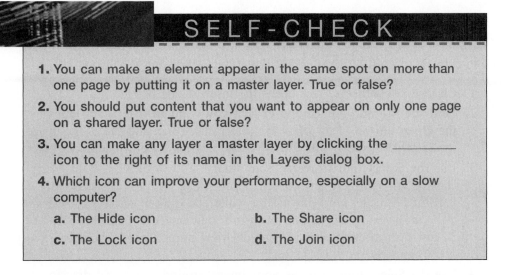

1. You can make an element appear in the same spot on more than one page by putting it on a master layer. True or false?

2. You should put content that you want to appear on only one page on a shared layer. True or false?

3. You can make any layer a master layer by clicking the _____ icon to the right of its name in the Layers dialog box.

4. Which icon can improve your performance, especially on a slow computer?

  a. The Hide icon   b. The Share icon

  c. The Lock icon   d. The Join icon

15.4 Bringing In Everything You Need

After you have your document set up the way you want it, you probably want to start bringing in images. Some programs call this *importing,* and others call it *placing.* LayOut calls it *inserting.*

You can insert two kinds of images into your LayOut documents:

▲ **Raster images:** This means TIFFs, JPEGs, GIFs, BMPs, and PNGs—these are all graphics file formats that save pictures as lots of tiny dots. Unfortunately, LayOut can't insert vector images in its first version. See Chapter 13 for a full description raster and vector images.

▲ **SketchUp models:** To get a SketchUp model view into your presentation, LayOut lets you insert SketchUp models directly into your document.

With every other page-layout program, the only way to include a view of a SketchUp model is to export that view from SketchUp as an image file, and then place it in the layout program. Changing the SketchUp file means having to go through the whole process again, and if your presentation includes lots of SketchUp model views, this can take hours.

Instead of exporting views from SketchUp to get them into LayOut, all you do is insert a SketchUp file. From within LayOut, you can pick the view you like best. You can also use as many views of the same model as you want. When your SketchUp file is modified, LayOut knows about it and (using the References panel in the Document Setup dialog box) lets you update all your views at once by clicking a single button.

In the sections that follow, you'll find the best tips and tricks for working with models, and you'll also learn how to insert other images and text.

15.4.1 Inserting Images and Model Views

Regardless of which kind of image you want to insert, the procedure is the same; follow these steps to bring an image into your LayOut document:

1. **Choose File⇨Insert.** This opens the Insert dialog box.

2. **Find the file on your computer that you want to insert, and click the Open button.** This closes the Insert dialog box and places the image (or SketchUp model) you chose on your current LayOut document page.

3. **Use the Select tool to resize your image.** You can resize an image by clicking and dragging any corner. If your image is a TIFF, JPEG, GIF, BMP, or PNG file, hold down Shift while you drag to resize *proportionally;* you probably don't want to distort your image by stretching it out. To resize an inserted SketchUp model view proportionally, hold down Alt (Command on the Mac).

4. **Use the Select tool to move your image around.** Click and drag to move any element in your document around on the page.

5. **Use the Select tool to rotate your image, if you want to.** This is probably best explained with a picture; Figure 15-8 shows the Rotate Circle (here called the Steering Wheel) that shows up in front of any element when you click to select it with the Select tool. You rotate an element by

Figure 15-8

The "Steering Wheel"

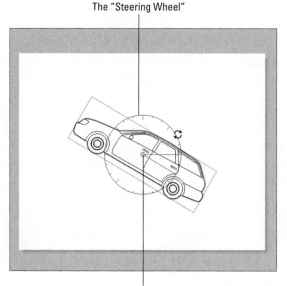

The center point

Use the Steering Wheel to rotate an element.

clicking and dragging its Steering Wheel. To rotate about a different point (a different center of rotation), just move the Steering Wheel by clicking its center point and dragging it around.

15.4.2 Working with Inserted Model Views

Figure 15-9 shows a view of a LayOut drawing window with a SketchUp model inserted. The following are some things you should know about working with inserted model views:

▲ **Double-click to change your view.** When you're using the Select tool, double-clicking a SketchUp model view allows you to orbit, pan, and zoom around your model. When you like what you see, click anywhere outside the view to exit.

▲ **Right-click.** The key to working with SketchUp models you've inserted into LayOut is to right-click them; this opens a context menu full of useful options.

▲ **Display your model views at scale.** One of the options in the context menu that pops up when you right-click on a model view is "Scale." Click on it, then choose a scale from the long list. Keep in mind that

Figure 15-9

Inserted SketchUp model

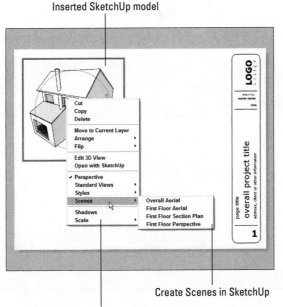

Create Scenes in SketchUp

Right-click to bring up the context menu

A SketchUp model view inserted in a LayOut document.

only *non-perspectival, orthographic* model views can be displayed at a true scale. See Chapter 12 for more information on this.

▲ **Do your dimensioning in SketchUp.** The first version of LayOut doesn't have a way to add dimensions to your drawings. Dimensions you add in SketchUp show up in LayOut, though, so you can add them there.

▲ **Create scenes in SketchUp to make work easier in LayOut.** In the context menu that appears when you right-click an inserted SketchUp model view, you can pick a scene. This is incredibly convenient, because getting just the right view is easier in SketchUp than it is in LayOut. If you know which views you need, create scenes in SketchUp and then choose them in LayOut. See Chapter 10 for details about creating scenes.

▲ **Tweak your line weights.** In the Styles pane of the SketchUp Model dialog box, you find a setting at the bottom called Line Weights. Reduce that number from 1.00 to 0.25 and your inserted SketchUp models will look a whole lot better.

▲ **Don't forget to check the document setup.** When a SketchUp model you've inserted is modified, LayOut knows about it—but it doesn't automatically update your views to reflect the changes. You have to do it yourself: Choose File⇨Document Setup and then click to open the References panel (see Figure 15-10). Select each model view you want

Figure 15-10

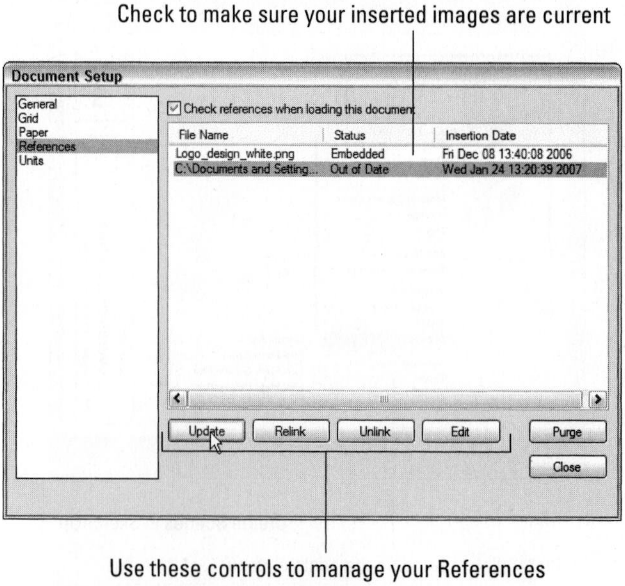

Check to make sure your inserted images are current

Use these controls to manage your References

The References panel, inside the Document Setup dialog box.

to update, and then click the Update button. Click the Purge button to dump references to external files you're not using anymore. It can't hurt anything to click it, and doing so reduces the size of your LayOut file and keeps it from getting corrupted.

▲ **Choose Open with SketchUp to avoid the Document Setup dialog box.** Choosing Open with SketchUp from the right-click context menu opens your model in SketchUp, where you can make any edits you want. When you're done, save your SketchUp file, and then come back to LayOut; your view will have changed to reflect the edits you made in SketchUp.

15.4.3 Inserting Text

You can insert a third type of content into LayOut documents: text. This is useful if the text you want to use is already typed, spell-checked, proofread, and ready to present.

Insert a text file the same way you do an image, but keep in mind that it has to be an RTF or a TXT file. Luckily, any text editor (like Word or TextEdit) can save to these formats.

SELF-CHECK

1. The first version of LayOut doesn't allow you to add dimensions to your drawings, but you can add dimensions in SketchUp that will show up in LayOut. True or false?

2. Getting just the right view is easier in LayOut than it is in SketchUp. True or false?

3. When a SketchUp model you've inserted is modified, LayOut knows about it, but it doesn't automatically update your views to reflect the changes. True or false?

4. You can insert text into LayOut documents. True or false?

15.5 Presentation-Perfect Images

After you import content, it's generally not quite presentation-ready. You may want to crop images or use the drawing tools to create a professional-looking, well-organized layout. The following sections show you how.

Figure 15-11

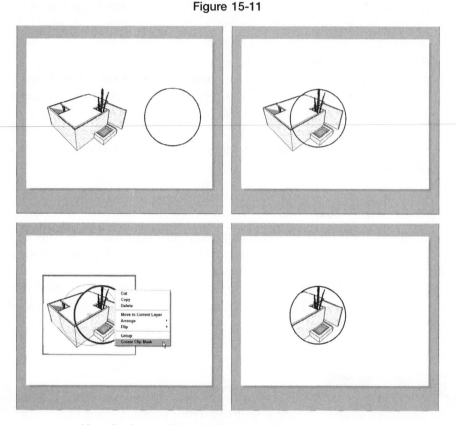

Use clipping masks to hide parts of images you insert.

15.5.1 Cropping with Clipping Masks

Cropping an image means reframing it so that you can only see part of it; every page-layout program allows you to crop images, and each one insists that you do it a little differently. LayOut is no exception.

In LayOut, you use **clipping masks** to hide the parts of images that you don't want to see. Follow these steps to use a shape as a clipping mask (see Figure 15-11):

1. **Draw the shape you want to use as a clipping mask.**

2. **Make sure that it's positioned properly over the image you want to crop.**

3. **Use the Select tool to select both the clipping mask object and the image you want to crop.** Hold down Shift while clicking to select more than one object.

4. **Right-click the selected elements and choose Create Clip Mask from the context menu.**

Here are some facts about clipping masks in LayOut:

▲ **Clipping masks work on inserted images.** These include pictures and SketchUp models that you place in your LayOut document.

▲ **Deleting clipping masks is easy.** To see a whole image again, you need to "release" its clipping mask. Select the image and then choose Edit⇨Remove Clipping Mask.

▲ **Edit clipping masks by double-clicking them.** When you double-click a clipping mask, you can see the whole image and the shape you used to create the mask. Now you can modify the shape, the image, or both. Clicking somewhere else on your page exits the edit mode.

15.5.2 Drawing Something from Scratch

LayOut includes a full slate of drawing tools that you can use to create logos, title bars, north arrows, graphic scales—anything you want. The drawings you create are vectors, meaning that you can do the following:

▲ Scale them without losing quality.

▲ Change their fill and stroke (outline) colors.

▲ Split lines and then rejoin them to make new shapes.

Here are a few pointers to get you started:

▲ **Use the right kind of snaps.** It's easier to draw exactly what you want if you let the software help a bit. Just like SketchUp, LayOut includes an elaborate (but easy-to-use) inference system of red and green dots and lines to help you line things up. LayOut also allows you to use a grid (that you define) to help you keep things straight:

• **Snap to objects:** Choose Arrange⇨Object Snap to turn on object snapping; this gives you colored "hints" to help you draw.

• **Snap to grid:** Choose Arrange⇨Grid Snap to turn on grid snapping. Now your cursor automatically *snaps* to (is attracted to) the intersection of grid lines in your document—whether your grid is visible or not. See the section "Getting Your Bearings," earlier in this chapter, for more information on using grids in LayOut.

You can use any combination of snapping systems (Object or Grid) while you're working, but you may prefer to use one or the other—it depends on what you're trying to do. To save time, you can assign a keyboard shortcut that toggles each system on and off. (To do that, use the Shortcuts panel in the Preferences dialog box, which you can find in the Edit menu—on a Mac, it's in the LayOut menu.)

▲ **Build complex shapes out of simpler ones.** Figure 15-12 shows how to draw a simple arrow. You can follow these steps:

1. Make sure that Grid Snap is turned off and Object Snap is turned on.

2. Draw a rectangle with the Rectangle tool.

3. Draw a triangle with the Polygon tool (Type in **3s** and press Enter before you start drawing to make sure that you're drawing a triangle). Hold down Shift to make sure that the bottom of the triangle is a horizontal line.

4. Use the Select tool to select both shapes by holding down Shift as you click them.

5. Choose Arrange⇨Align⇨Vertically to line up the rectangle and the triangle vertically.

6. Deselect both shapes by clicking once somewhere else on your page.

7. Select one of the shapes and move it up or down on the page (by pressing the up- and down-arrow keys) until the two shapes overlap.

8. Use the Arc tool to draw a half-circle at the bottom of the rectangle.

9. Using the Split tool, click and *hold down* each of the points of intersection in the figure; don't let go until all the lines stop flashing blue. Do this for all four intersection points to split the shapes into a series of line segments.

10. Use the Join tool (it looks like a bottle of glue) to connect all the line segments by clicking once on the "arrowhead" part, once on each half of the "stem" part, and once on the half-circle. Now you have one shape instead of three; verify this by clicking the shape once with the Select tool. You should see one red "selected" rectangle around your new shape. If you don't have one shape, try using the Join tool again; sometimes it takes a couple of tries to get things to work.

11. Move your new shape somewhere else, and then delete the leftover lines segments you don't need.

▲ **Open the Shape Style dialog box.** You use the Shape Style dialog box to change the fill and stroke characteristics of elements in your document (see Figure 15-13). This is where you pick colors for the things you draw. The controls are fairly straightforward; just experiment and see what happens.

Figure 15-12

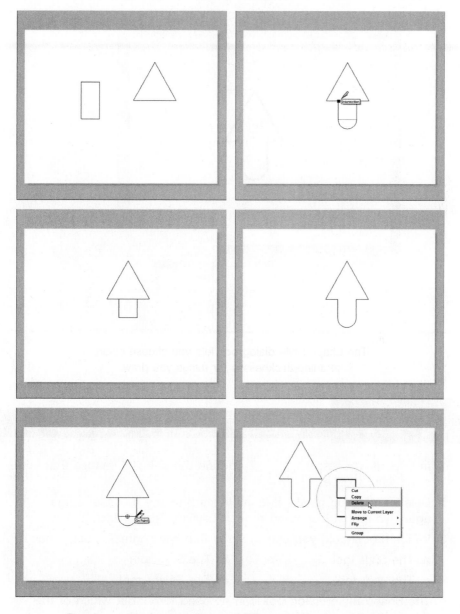

Drawing a simple arrow by combining a rectangle, a triangle,
and an arc.

Figure 15-13

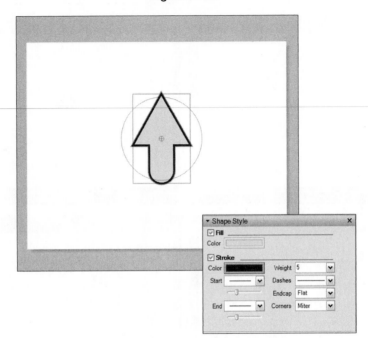

The Shape Style dialog box lets you choose colors
and line thicknesses for things you draw.

SELF-CHECK

1. In LayOut, you use _____ to hide the parts of images that you don't want to see.

2. Deleting clipping masks is complicated; to see a whole image again, you must close and reopen LayOut. True or false?

3. Which tool should you use to verify that line segments are joined?
   - **a.** The Shift tool
   - **b.** The Split tool
   - **c.** The Join tool
   - **d.** The Select tool

4. The Shape Style dialog box can be used for all but which of the following?
   - **a.** To change the fill characteristics of elements in your document
   - **b.** To change the stroke characteristics of elements in your document
   - **c.** To split lines and then rejoin them to make new shapes
   - **d.** To pick colors for the things you've drawn

15.6 Life After LayOut

After you've created your LayOut document, you can do the following three things:

1. Print it
2. Export it as a PDF file
3. View it as a full-screen presentation

The next three sections provide more detail on each of these options.

15.6.1 Printing Your Work

Follow these steps to print your LayOut document:

1. **Choose File⇨Page Setup.** In the Page Setup dialog box, choose a printer and a paper size and orientation.
2. **Click the OK button to close the Page Setup dialog box.**
3. **Choose File⇨Print.** In the Print dialog box, choose which pages to print and how many copies you want.
4. **Click the OK button to send your document to the printer you chose in Page Setup.**

15.6.2 Exporting a PDF File

Anyone with Adobe Reader software (which is free and is already loaded on most computers) can look at a PDF document you create; all you have to do is email it to him or her. Follow these steps to export your LayOut document as a PDF file:

1. **Choose File⇨Export PDF (it's just Export on the Mac).** This opens the Export dialog box.
2. **Give your PDF file a name, and figure out where to save it on your computer.**
3. **Click the Save button (in Windows) to open the PDF Export Options dialog box (see Figure 15-14); click the Options button if you're on a Mac.**
4. **Set the PDF options the way you want them.** Here's what everything means:
   - **Pages:** Choose which pages you want to export.
   - **Resolution:** See the section "Creating a New, Blank Document," earlier in this chapter, for a brief discussion of resolution. Here's a good rule of thumb: For documents that are small enough to be hand-held, use setting of 300 dpi. For anything bigger, go with 150 dpi.

Figure 15-14

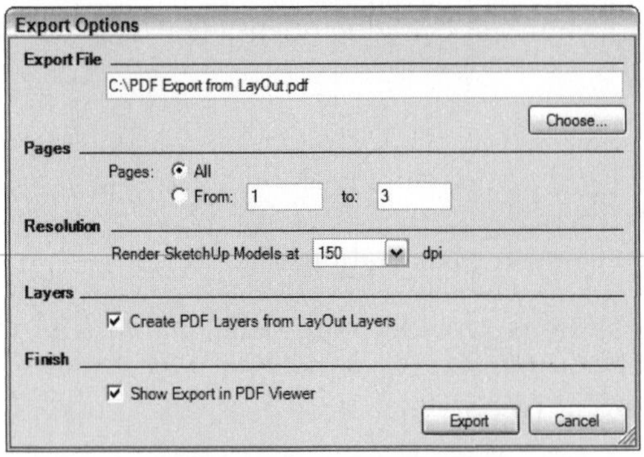

LayOut's PDF Export Options dialog box.

- **Layers:** PDFs can have layers, just like LayOut documents do. If it makes sense to do so, you can export a layered PDF so that people who view it can turn the layers on and off.
- **Finish:** Select this check box to view your PDF after it's exported.

5. **Click the OK button to close the PDF Options dialog box (Mac only).**

6. **Click the Export button (Save button on a Mac) to export your document as a PDF file.**

15.6.3 Going Full-Screen

Many times, design presentations for clients go beyond printed boards and booklets; they include a digital slide show that usually involves a few hours of work in a program like PowerPoint or Keynote (if you're on a Mac).

LayOut was designed to help you skip the PowerPoint step by letting you display your presentation in a full-screen view. You can move back and forth between pages with the arrow keys on your computer, and you can even double-click SketchUp model views to orbit them around. Follow these tips:

▲ **Switching to full-screen mode takes less than a second.** Choose View⇨Full Screen to view your presentation full-screen. Press Esc to exit full-screen mode.

▲ **Move from page to page.** Use the left- and right-arrow keys to flip through pages.

▲ **Choose which pages to show full-screen.** You can decide not to show certain pages in full-screen mode by toggling the Show in Presentations icon to the right of those page names in the Pages dialog box (make sure that you're in List view to be able to do this).

▲ **Double-click to change your view of a SketchUp model.** When you're in full-screen mode, you can double-click any SketchUp model view to orbit and zoom around inside it. Just use your mouse's scroll wheel button the same way you do in SketchUp. Click anywhere outside the view to exit.

▲ **Draw while you're in full-screen mode.** Try clicking and dragging while you're in full-screen mode; doing so lets you make red annotations right on your presentation. For example, if a client doesn't like the porch you designed, you can scrawl a big, red X over it to let him know you understand.

▲ **Play scene animations right in full-screen mode.** You can double-click, then right-click on a model view with scenes that you've set up in SketchUp and choose Play Animation. LayOut will transition from scene to scene, just like SketchUp does. You can read more about scenes in Chapter 10.

SELF-CHECK

1. After you've created your LayOut document, you can print it, export it as a PDF file, or view it as a full-screen presentation. True or false?

2. Anyone with _____ can look at a PDF document you create.

3. PDFs, unlike LayOut documents, cannot have layers. True or false?

4. What kind of view must you be in to choose which pages to show full-screen?

SUMMARY

If you have the Pro version of Google SketchUp 6, then you have access to a separate piece of software: LayOut. LayOut enables you to create documents for presenting your 3D SketchUp models both on paper and on-screen. In this chapter, you assessed when you would use LayOut and how to simplify your use with layers and master layers. You evaluated LayOut and the qualities that make it unique. You built a simple presentation document from scratch, and you printed and exported your work. Your LayOut skills will prove to be invaluable.

KEY TERMS

Bulge	The curvature of an arc.
Clipping masks	Used in LayOut to hide the parts of images that you don't want to see.
Full bleed	Printing that extends to the edges of the paper.
Master layers	Shared layers, containing anything you want to appear on every page of your document.
Sample	To "soak up" an element's fill, stroke, and other attributes.
Shared layers	Layers that let you automatically place elements on more than one page.
Snap settings	Help you line up elements on your page with a grid or with other elements.
Stacking order	The arrangement of all elements on the same layer in a document, determining which elements appear to be in front of which.
Unshared layers	Layers containing elements that exist only on one page.

ASSESS YOUR UNDERSTANDING

Go to www.wiley.com/college/chopra to evaluate your knowledge of creating presentation documents with LayOut.
Measure your learning by comparing pre-test and post-test results.

Summary Questions

1. When you insert a SketchUp model or an image in your LayOut document, LayOut creates a file reference that keeps track of where it came from. True or false?

2. What is the first thing you should do to change the overall color scheme of a LayOut template?

    (a) Unlock all the layers.

    (b) Open the Shape Styles dialog box.

    (c) Insert a SketchUp file.

    (d) Click the New tab.

3. Many of the templates that come with LayOut have multiple layers, and some of these layers are locked by default so that you can't accidentally move things around. True or false?

4. When your design changes in SketchUp, the views you've placed in LayOut update automatically to reflect the changes. True or false?

5. You can have two different kinds of layers in LayOut: _____ and _____.

6. You should hide the layers you aren't using to avoid accidentally moving the wrong things around, or even deleting them. True or false?

7. You can insert two kinds of images into your LayOut documents: _____ and _____.

8. Which of the following must you do to include a view of a SketchUp model in LayOut?

    (a) Export the view from SketchUp as an image file.

    (b) Place the view in a layout program.

    (c) Export the view every time you change the SketchUp file.

    (d) Simply insert the SketchUp file.

9. The key to working with SketchUp models you've inserted into LayOut is to right-click them; this opens a context menu full of useful options. True or false?

10. Clicking the Purge button does all but which of the following?

    (a) Dumps references to external files you're not using anymore.

(b) Reduces the size of your LayOut file.

(c) Poses a threat to your LayOut file.

(d) Keeps your LayOut file from getting corrupted.

11. When you _____ a clipping mask, you can see the whole image and the shape you used to create the mask.

12. LayOut was designed to help you skip the _____ step by letting you display your presentation in a full-screen view.

Applying This Chapter

1. Name and describe three of LayOut's nine menus.

2. Why would you use a template to begin your presentation? Name three things that you should know about using templates.

3. What is the difference between the two different kinds of layers in LayOut?

4. You want to insert an image into your LayOut document. How do you do this?

5. You want to export your LayOut document as a PDF file. How do you do this?

YOU TRY IT

Drawing from Scratch

In LayOut, draw a rectangle, a triangle, a square, and an ellipse. Then move them so that they overlap, and combine them into a single shape using the Split and Join tools.

Create a Template

Create a simple LayOut file with a title block. Then take this LayOut file and turn it into a template.

16

TROUBLESHOOTING AND USING ADDITIONAL RESOURCES
Fixing Problems and Enhancing Your Model

Starting Point

Go to www.wiley.com/college/chopra to assess your knowledge of troubleshooting and using additional resources.
Determine where you need to concentrate your effort.

What You'll Learn in This Chapter

▲ How to persuade components to budge
▲ Places to find more components
▲ Scripts that make your life easier
▲ Some great, free resources for finding out more about SketchUp

After Studying This Chapter, You'll Be Able To

▲ Evaluate how to fix a slow or crashing SketchUp
▲ Evaluate why faces, colors, and edges are not working the way you would like them to
▲ Assess the purpose of various plugins and how you can use them to improve your model
▲ Access other helpful resources

INTRODUCTION

We've all had an experience where we are working in a program and something goes wrong. It doesn't work the way it is supposed to, or it gives an indecipherable error message, or it just completely crashes. In this chapter, you will evaluate what steps to take when this happens to you as you are working in SketchUp. Not only will you assess what to do when SketchUp is slow or crashes, but you will also assess what to do when faces, colors, and edges are not working the way they should.

However, this chapter is not only about troubleshooting. This chapter is also about plugins that might enhance your SketchUp experience, as well as resources that can help you take your SketchUp skills to the next level. Thus, in this chapter, you will assess plugins that have specific purposes, and you will also assess various resources available to you.

16.1 Ten SketchUp Traps and Their Solutions

The bad news is that every single new SketchUp user runs into certain problems, usually in his or her first couple of hours with the software. The good news is that such predictability means that you can anticipate a great deal of the traps you'll encounter. Here are some of those traps, as well as methods that will help you make sense of what's going on so that you can get on with your life as quickly as possible.

16.1.1 SketchUp Won't Create a Face Where You Want It To

Say that you've dutifully traced all around the boundary of where you'd like SketchUp to create a face, but nothing's happening. To remedy the problem, try checking whether your edges aren't all on the same plane or whether one edge is part of a separate group or component.

To check whether you have a component problem, try hiding groups or components and checking the edges to make sure that they're all in the group or component you think they're in. See Chapter 5 for details.

However, 90 percent of the time, when SketchUp won't create a face where you think it should, an edge isn't on the *plane* you think it's on. To check whether your edges are coplanar, draw an edge that cuts diagonally across the area where you want a face to appear. If a face appears now, all your edges are not on the same plane. To fix the problem, you have to figure out which edge is the culprit. Try doing this by using the method illustrated in Color Plate 20 and described below:

1. **In the Styles dialog box, change your edge color from All Same to By Axis.** See Chapter 8 for details. Doing this step tells SketchUp to draw the edges in your model the color of the axis to which they're parallel; edges parallel to the red axis will be red, and so on.

2. **Look carefully at the edges you were hoping would define a face.**
Are all the edges the color they're supposed to be? If they're not all supposed to be parallel to the drawing axes, this technique doesn't do much
good. But if they are, and one (or more) of them is black (instead of red
or green or blue), that edge (or edges) is your problem. Fix it and switch
back to All Same when you're done.

16.1.2 Your Faces Are Two Different Colors

In SketchUp, faces have two sides: a front and a back. By default, these two
sides are different colors. When you do certain things like use Push/Pull or Follow Me on a face, sometimes the faces on the resulting geometry are "inside out."
If it bothers you to have a two-tone model, just right-click the faces you want
to flip over and choose Reverse Faces from the context menu. If you have lots
of them, you can select them all and then choose Reverse Faces to flip them all
at once.

16.1.3 Edges on a Face Won't Sink In

This tends to happen when you're trying to draw a rectangle (or another geometric figure) on a face with one of SketchUp's shape-drawing tools. Ordinarily,
the Rectangle tool creates a new face on top of any face you use it on; after that,
you can use Push/Pull to create a hole, if you want. If your shape's edges look
thick instead of thin, they're not cutting through the face they're drawn on.
When that happens, try these approaches:

▲ **Retrace one of the edges.** This simple method works often.

▲ **Select Hidden Geometry on the View menu.** Here, you're checking
to make sure that the face you just drew isn't crossing any hidden or
smoothed edges; if it is, the face you thought was flat might not be.

▲ **Make sure that the face you drew on isn't part of a group or
component.** If it is, undo a few steps and then redraw your shape
while you're editing the group or component.

16.1.4 SketchUp Crashed, and You Lost Your Model

Unfortunately, SketchUp crashes happen sometimes. The good news is that
SketchUp automatically saves a copy of your file every five minutes. The file that
SketchUp autosaves is actually a *separate* file, which it calls *AutoSave_your
filename.skp*. So if your file ever gets corrupted in a crash, there's an intact one,
ready for you to find and continue working on. The problem is that most people don't even know it's there. So where is it?

▲ If you've ever saved your file, it's in the same folder as the original.

▲ If you've never saved your file, it's in your My Documents folder—unless you're on a Mac, in which case it's here: *User folder/Library/Application Support/Google SketchUp 6/SketchUp/Autosave.*

Keep in mind that normally, SketchUp cleans up after itself by deleting the autosaved file when you close your model, and nothing untoward happens.

To minimize the amount of work you lose when software (or hardware) goes south, you should always do two things: save often (compulsively, even), and save numbered copies as you're working. Consider using Save As to create a new copy of your work every half-hour or so.

16.1.5 SketchUp Is Slow

The bigger your model gets, the worse your performance gets, too. What makes a model big? In a nutshell, faces. You should do everything in your power to keep your model as small as you can. Here are some tips for doing that:

▲ **Reduce the number of sides on your extruded circles and arcs.** See the sidebar in Chapter 6 for instructions on how to do this.

▲ **Use 2D people and trees instead of 3D ones.** 3D plants and people have *hundreds* of faces each. Consider using 2D ones instead, especially if your model won't be seen much from overhead.

Some models are just big, and you can't do much about it. Here are some tricks for working with very large SketchUp models:

▲ **Make liberal use of the Outliner and layers.** Explained in detail in Chapter 5, these SketchUp features were specifically designed to let you organize your model into manageable chunks. Hide everything you're not working on at the moment—doing so gives your computer a fighting chance.

▲ **Use substitution for large numbers of complex components.** For example, insert sticks as placeholders for large sets of 3D trees, cars, and other big components. See the tips for replacing components in Chapter 5 for details.

▲ **Turn off shadows and switch to a simple style.** It takes a lot of computer power to display shadows, edge effects, and textures in real time on your monitor. When you're working, turn off these elements.

▲ **Use scenes to navigate between views.** Scenes aren't just for presenting your model—they're also great for working with it. Creating scenes for the different views you commonly use, and with different combinations of hidden geometry, means that you don't have to orbit, pan, and zoom around your gigantic model. Better yet, deselect Enable Scene Transitions (in the Animation panel of the Model Info dialog box) to speed things up even more.

16.1.6 You Can't Get a Good View of the Inside of Your Model

It's not always easy to work on the inside of something in SketchUp. You can do these things to make it easier, though:

▲ **Cut into it with sections:** SketchUp's Sections feature lets you cut away parts of your model—temporarily, of course—so that you can get a better view of what's inside. Take a look at Chapter 10 for the entire story on sections.

▲ **Widen your field of view:** Field of view is basically the amount of your model you can see on the screen at one time. A wider field of view is like having better peripheral vision. You can read all about it in Chapter 10.

16.1.7 A Face Flashes When You Orbit

If you have two faces in the same spot—maybe one is in a separate group or component—you see an effect called **Z-fighting**. What you're witnessing is SketchUp trying to decide which face to display by switching back and forth between them. It's not a good solution, but certainly a logical one, at least for a piece of software. The only way to get rid of Z-fighting is to delete or hide one of the faces.

16.1.8 You Can't Move a Component the Way You Want

Some components are set up to automatically *glue* to faces when you insert them into your model. A glued component instance isn't actually glued in one place. Instead, it's glued to the plane of the face you originally placed (or created) it on. For example, if you place a sofa component on the floor of your living room, you can only move it around on that plane, not up and down. This behavior comes in handy when you're dealing with things like furniture. It allows you to use the Move tool to rearrange things without having to worry about accidentally picking them up.

If you can't move your component the way you want to, right-click it and check to see whether Unglue is an option. If it is, choose it. Now you can move your component around however you want.

16.1.9 Every Time You Use the Eraser, You Accidentally Delete Something

It's pretty easy to delete things accidentally with the Eraser tool. Basically, just because you can't see an edge (for instance, because it's behind something else) doesn't mean that you can't erase it. Worse yet, you usually don't notice what's missing until it's too late. Here are some tips for erasing more accurately:

▲ **Orbit around.** Try to make sure that nothing is behind whatever it is you're erasing; use SketchUp's navigation tools to get a view of your model that puts you out of danger.

▲ **Switch to Wireframe mode.** Choose View⇨Face Style⇨Wireframe when you're going to be using the Eraser heavily. That way, you won't have any faces to obstruct your view, and you'll be less likely to erase the wrong edges.

▲ **Double-check.** Get into the habit of giving your model a quick once-over with the Orbit tool after you do a lot of erasing, just to make sure that you didn't get rid of anything important.

16.1.10 All Your Edges and Faces Are on Different Layers

Using Layers in SketchUp is a dangerous business. Chapter 5 has tips you should follow when using layers, but here's the short version: You should always build everything on Layer0, and only put whole groups or components on other layers if you really need to.

If you used layers and things are now messed up, here's what you can do to recover:

1. **Make sure that everything is visible.** Select Hidden Geometry on the View menu, then (in the Layers dialog box) make all your layers visible. Just make sure that you can see everything in your model.
2. **Choose Edit⇨Select All to select everything.**
3. **In the Entity Info dialog box, move everything to Layer0.**
4. **In the Layers dialog box, delete your other layers, telling SketchUp to move anything remaining on them to Layer0.**
5. **Create new layers, and follow the rules in Chapter 5.**

SELF-CHECK

1. How many sides do faces have?
   a. 1
   b. 2
   c. 3
   d. 4
2. How can you keep your SketchUp model small?
3. When SketchUp switches back and forth between coplanar, overlapping faces, it is called Z-fighting. True or false?
4. When edges on a face won't sink in, you can often remedy this by _____ one of the edges.

16.2 Ten Plugins, Extensions, and Resources Worth Getting

The great thing about SketchUp's price is how much room it frees up in your budget for add-ons. This section is a list of ten such add-ons, along with a little bit of information about them, and where you can go to find them. These add-ons have been split into four categories, just to make things clearer: components, Ruby scripts, renderers, and hardware.

16.2.1 Components

If you do any amount of modeling with SketchUp, you'll quickly realize how much time you can save by having the right components to "populate" your work with people, cars, trees, furniture, and similar objects. Why make your own sofa when you can grab one from somewhere else? If the components that you can download from SketchUp's website aren't enough for you (see Chapter 5 for more information about this), the following are some additional websites where you can buy what you need.

Form Fonts

Form Fonts (www.formfonts.com) is a website that sells components for a flat monthly fee. You simply pay a (surprisingly low) monthly fee, and you have access to thousands of high-quality models of just about anything you can think of. Form Fonts' international team of modelers even takes requests—if you need something that they don't have, they can probably make it for you! In addition to components, Form Fonts also has tons of extra materials you can apply to your work, as well as a growing library of styles. Even if you're not interested in signing up, it's worth checking out the website just to see the beautiful models Form Fonts makes.

Sketchupmodels.com

Along the same lines as Form Fonts, Sketchupmodels.com (www.sketchupmodels .com) is a site where you can buy SketchUp components, although here, you buy them *à la carte*. Some of this site's models might seem a little expensive, but when you consider how much time it would take you to make them yourself, it might be worth it to buy them—especially if you use SketchUp for work.

16.2.2 Ruby Scripts

What's a **Ruby script**? Basically, Google provides a way for people to make their own plugins for SketchUp. These plugins are just mini-programs (scripts) written in a computer programming language called Ruby. The best thing about

Ruby scripts (Rubies, for short) is that you don't have to know anything about Ruby, or programming in general, to use ones that other people have created. To install Rubies, you just drop them into a special folder on your computer:

▲ **Windows:** C:/Program Files/Google/Google SketchUp 6/Plugins.

▲ **Mac:** Hard Drive/Library/Application Support/Google SketchUp 6/SketchUp/Plugins.

The next time you launch SketchUp, Rubies you put in the preceding location become available for you to use. How you use them depends on what they do. They might show up on one of the toolbar menus or on your right-click context menu. The more complex ones even come with their own toolbars. Most Rubies also come with a set of instructions that tells you how to use them.

Luckily for those of you who aren't programmers, plenty of people develop and (in some cases) sell Rubies that anyone can use. Smustard.com (www.smustard .com) is a website run by a few of these individuals. You can choose from dozens of helpful Rubies that add functionality to SketchUp, and best of all, they're *very* inexpensive. Here are some of the most useful:

▲ **Weld:** This Ruby takes edges you've selected and "welds" them together to make a single edge that you can select with a single click. This is especially handy when you're using Follow Me.

▲ **PresentationBundle:** This is a package of five Rubies that help you use scenes to create better presentations. You can customize the transition time between individual scenes, for instance, and even create really elaborate fly-by animations.

▲ **CAD cleanup scripts:** If you routinely import 2D CAD drawings to use as a starting point for SketchUp models, you need these scripts. Cleaning up imported CAD drawings is a drag, but the following Rubies make the whole process immeasurably easier:

▲ **StrayLines:** Run this script to figure out how much work you'll have to do to a CAD file after you've imported it—it goes through and labels items you'll probably have to fix.

▲ **CloseOpens:** Imported CAD drawings almost always have one glaring problem: Their edges don't meet precisely, which means that you can't create faces. You end up hunting around with the Zoom tool, looking for all the tiny gaps and filling them in. This script does that for you, which makes it worth a lot more than Smustard charges for it.

▲ **MakeFaces:** When you import a 2D CAD drawing, you get edges but not faces. Trouble is, you need faces for working in SketchUp, so you end up retracing lots of little lines to make faces appear. Run this Ruby, and you don't have to.

▲ **IntersectOverlaps:** You know how edges that cross don't automatically cut each other? If you use this script they will. Be careful to read the instructions (on the website); this Ruby can cause some unexpected results.

▲ **Flatten:** Sometimes, imported CAD lines don't all come in lying on the ground. You probably want them to be (so that they're all coplanar), and this Ruby makes sure that they are.

▲ **DeleteShortLines:** When people make CAD drawings, they often accidentally overshoot their targets, creating hundreds of tiny edge segments that you need to get rid of in SketchUp. This Ruby will do that for you.

16.2.3 Renderers

One thing SketchUp does not do is create photorealistic renderings. Its styles are great for making your models look hand-drawn, but none of them can make your work look like a photograph. Most SketchUp users are okay with that, but for those who aren't, you can find some nice solutions out there.

Of course, SketchUp Pro's 3D export formats make it possible to render SKP files with just about any of the dozens of powerful renderers on the market, but the ones described in the following list have three important things in common: They work with the free version of SketchUp, they were developed with SketchUp in mind, and you don't have to be a computer expert to figure them out. Here's the list:

▲ **SU Podium (www.suplugins.com):** If you're using a Windows computer, you should probably check out Podium first. It's a plugin that lets you create photorealistic views right inside SketchUp. It's really too bad that Podium isn't available for the Mac, but it might be sometime in the future. Regardless of which platform you're on, it's definitely worth checking out.

▲ **TurboSketch (www.turbosketch.net):** The good news about TurboSketch is that it's available for both Windows and the Mac, and that it (like Podium) also runs as a plugin inside SketchUp. The bad thing is that users think Podium's a bit better. You should try both (if you can) and make up your own mind.

▲ **Artlantis R (www.artlantis.com):** If you're really serious about making images that look like photographs, take a good look at Artlantis R. Instead of running as a plugin inside SketchUp, it's a fully functional, separate piece of software that works with lots of other 3D modeling programs. The results it produces are out of this world.

Again, lots of rendering applications are out there, and depending on what you want to do, different ones might work better than others. If photo rendering is your thing, try plugging these names into your favorite search engine: Kirkithea, Maxwell, Cheetah3D, and Vue. They're hard-core, but they all work well.

16.2.4 Hardware

All you really need to use SketchUp is a computer with a decent video card, a keyboard, and a mouse. On the other hand, having specialized hardware can come in handy—especially if you find yourself using SketchUp all the time:

▲ **A second monitor:** Having a dual-monitor setup makes using SketchUp a lot easier. All of a sudden, you have space for all your dialog boxes and toolbars on one side of your setup, and you still have a whole screen just for your SketchUp modeling window.

▲ **SpaceNavigator from 3Dconnexion:** Using a scroll-wheel mouse to fly around in three-dimensional space works well for most people, but many SketchUp power users swear by dedicated 3D navigation tools like the **SpaceNavigator.** It looks a little like an enormous button that sits on your desk, connected to your computer via a USB cable. You use it with whichever hand you aren't using for your mouse; it's an add-on (and not a replacement) for any of the other peripherals in your system. Basically, the SpaceNavigator enables you orbit, pan, and zoom with subtle movements of your hand; it really is a much more natural way to interact with a 3D model. You'll find a bit of a learning curve, but that's nothing for serious SketchUp users. Anything that makes software easier and more fun to use is worth the time it takes to master it.

SELF-CHECK

1. _____ is a website that sells components for a flat monthly fee.
2. You must have a second monitor to work on SketchUp. True or false?
3. Ruby is a computer _____ language.
4. SketchUp creates photorealistic renderings. True or false?

16.3 Ten Ways to Discover Even More

In addition to this book, there are many great resources out there that will help you learn even more about SketchUp. Thus, the first part of this section is devoted to free resources, all of which are available online to anyone who wants them. The second part of the section describes some other resources that are available for purchase.

Figure 16-1

The SketchUp Help menu directs
you to a variety of free resources.

16.3.1 Free Resources

Everything in this section requires that you have an Internet connection, so make sure that your computer's online before you try any of these. Also note that you can access many of these resources via SketchUp's Help menu. Here's what's available through the various options on that menu (Figure 16-1):

▲ **Video Tutorials:** When SketchUp was first launched in 2000, it became known for its excellent video tutorials. There's nothing like *seeing* SketchUp in action!

▲ **Self-Paced Tutorials:** These are SketchUp files that use scenes to teach different aspects of the program in a "follow along with me" style. If this is how you like to figure things out, have a look.

▲ **Online Help Center:** Google maintains extensive help centers (websites, basically) for all its products. These include hundreds of articles in question-and-answer format, created specifically to help new users along. The SketchUp one is terrific.

▲ **SketchUp Community:** This consists of two online "places." Though they're intended for different kinds of SketchUp users, you'll find valuable resources in each of them:

  • **Google SketchUp User Groups:** This option uses Google's Groups feature to let SketchUp users from all over the world get help, ask questions, and show off their work.

  • **Google SketchUp Pro User Forums:** Plenty of people out there use SketchUp to make a living, and many of them hang out in the SketchUp forums. These are a lot like the groups (in the previous point), but they're for people who use SketchUp *often*. Sketch-Up's forum users are legendary for their generosity. Post a question (remember to be polite), and you'll see for yourself.

In addition, here are a couple of great online destinations for people (like yourself) who are SketchUp beginners:

▲ **School Podcasts (www.go-2-school.com):** This is a terrific website. Check out the Podcasts area for a list of free online videos. There's also a learning DVD you can buy, which is described in the next part of this section.

▲ **SU Wiki (www.suwiki.org):** This is a website built by SketchUp users, for SketchUp users. It's a goldmine of tutorials, tips and tricks, plugins, and other resources you'll find useful.

16.3.2 Resources You Can Purchase

These resources cost a bit of money, but they're worth every penny:

▲ **Bonnie Roskes' books:** Bonnie Roskes' *The SketchUp Book* was the first such product available, and now she has two new titles. If you think you'd like to get another, bigger book about SketchUp (written with architects and other design pros in mind), check out these books at www.f1help.biz. (Notice the .biz suffix.)

▲ **School DVD:** School's videos are mentioned in the previous section, but School's designers have also produced the world's first SketchUp educational/training DVD, which you can order from the company's website (www.go-2-school.com). The production quality on this video is outstanding, and the DVD does an amazing job of teaching SketchUp for both Windows and the Mac.

▲ **Dennis Fukai's books:** These books are hard to describe. Dennis Fukai has written three of them; each is fully illustrated in SketchUp, and each teaches a different subject. If you want to discover more about using SketchUp in building construction or more about construction itself, or if you just want to be completely inspired by what you can do with SketchUp, have a look at these books. Search for Fukai's name on Amazon (www.amazon.com) or go to his company's website, www.insitebuilders.com.

▲ **SketchUp Pro training:** If you think you might benefit from being able to spend a few hours with a real-live trainer and a handful of other SketchUp students, Google's SketchUp training might be for you. Its trainers travel to different cities, giving training seminars that you can sign up to attend. Check out the following website for more information: www.sketchup.com/training.

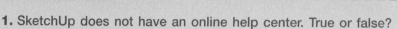

SELF-CHECK

1. SketchUp does not have an online help center. True or false?
2. SketchUp and Google offer many free resources for SketchUp users. True or false?
3. SketchUp offers many _____ tutorials that enable you to see the program in action.
4. Professional SketchUp trainers tour the country and offer training sessions for a fee. True or false?

SUMMARY

Congratulations! You are at the end of the first phase of your SketchUp journey. You can now model with the best of them. In this chapter, you evaluated what to do when things go wrong—and it's inevitable that something will go wrong sometime. You also evaluated different components, plugins, and websites that can help improve your model. Finally, you assessed the resources that are available to you and how to best use them to your advantage. Knowing how to troubleshoot, where to go for help, and what additional plugins you can use will enhance your SketchUp experience.

KEY TERMS

Ruby scripts	Mini-programs (scripts) written in a computer programming language called Ruby.
SpaceNavigator	A 3D navigation tool that looks a little like an enormous button that is connected to the computer via a USB cable. It enables the user to orbit, pan, and zoom with subtle movements of his or her hand.
Z-fighting	The effect resulting from SketchUp trying to decide which face to display by switching back and forth between two faces.

ASSESS YOUR UNDERSTANDING

Go to www.wiley.com/college/chopra to evaluate your knowledge of trouble-shooting and using additional resources.

Measure your learning by comparing pre-test and post-test results.

Summary Questions

1. By default, the two sides of faces in SketchUp are two different colors. True or false?

2. SketchUp automatically saves a copy of your file every _____ minutes.

3. 3D plants and people have _____ of faces each.

4. The Google SketchUp Pro User Forum is for people who use SketchUp often. True or false?

5. There are free components on the SketchUp website that you can download. True or false?

6. SketchUp files that use scenes to teach different aspects of the program in a "follow along with me" style are:

    (a) video tutorials.

    (b) self-paced tutorials.

    (c) school podcasts.

    (d) in the books by Bonnie Roskes.

7. In imported CAD drawings, the _____ don't meet precisely.

8. If you want to make images that look like photographs, consider using:

    (a) SU Podium.

    (b) Form Fonts.

    (c) TurboSketch.

    (d) Atlantis R.

Applying This Chapter

1. You're working on a complex model of a building when SketchUp crashes. Where can you find a copy of your model, and how much work have you lost?

2. If you find yourself using SketchUp all the time, what additional hardware might you want to purchase to become more efficient and productive?

3. You are good at using SketchUp, but you want to get better. What free resources are available to you to help you take your skills to the next level?

Rubies

Download and install the Presentation Bundle of Ruby scripts, which is mentioned earlier in this chapter. Use one or more of these scripts to create an animation with the model of the house you've built while working through this book.

GLOSSARY

3DS One of the few standard 3D file formats.

Active cut The section plane that is actually cutting through your model; others section planes are considered "inactive."

Anti-aliasing A process that fills in the gaps around pixels with similar-colored pixels so that things look smooth.

Array A series of copies that are equally spaced apart.

Artifacts Smudges and other image degradation introduced by file compression; common in JPEGs.

As-built A drawing of an existing building.

Bilateral symmetry Mirrored halves.

Building Information Modeling (BIM) Software that enables users to make models that automatically keep track of things such as quantities, and that automatically generate standard drawing views (plans and sections) from the model.

Bulge The curvature of an arc.

Clipping masks Used in LayOut to hide the parts of images that you don't want to see.

Components Edges and faces grouped together into objects that display certain useful properties.

Coplanar On the same plane.

Curves-based modelers Modeling programs that use curves to define lines and surfaces.

DAE (Collada) A new 3D file format that is gaining acceptance with a large number of gaming and animation programs.

Dormer A structure above a roof surface that serves to make attic space more usable.

Drawing axes   Three colored lines visible in the SketchUp modeling window that enable users to work in three-dimensional space.

DWG   AutoCAD's native file format and the best one to use for transferring information to that program and other pieces of CAD software.

DXF   Document Exchange Format, a type of DWG that was developed by Autodesk to be the file format that other pieces of software use to transfer data into AutoCAD.

Eave   A part of a roof that overhangs the building.

Edges   In SketchUp, straight lines.

Elevation   A straight-on, 2D view of the side of a building.

EPIX   A file format that lets you open 2D views of your SketchUp model in Piranesi.

EPS   Encapsulated Postscript, a file format that some people still use to transfer vector information.

Extensions   The line overruns that you can choose to display in the Styles dialog box.

Exterior model   A model of the outside of a building, which does not include interior walls, rooms, or furniture.

Faces   In SketchUp, infinitely thin surfaces.

Fascia   The trim around the edge of a roof's eaves where gutters are sometimes attached.

FBX   A 3D file format used primarily by people in the entertainment industry who use Maya, 3DS Max, or Autodesk VIZ.

Field of view   The amount of your model you're able to see in your modeling window at one time.

Fillet   A thin narrow strip of material.

Flat roof   A roof that appears flat but is sloped very slightly.

Folds   Edges and faces that are created in place of a single face.

Full bleed   Printing that extends to the edges of the paper.

Gable   The pointed section of wall that sits under the peak of a pitched roof.

Gabled roof   A roof with two planes that slope away from a central ridge.

Geolocated objects   Objects that never move and have a fixed position, such as buildings and monuments.

Geolocation   The process by which SketchUp sets the imported snapshot's latitude and longitude to match Google Earth, and it orients the snapshot in the right cardinal direction.

Geometry   Edges and faces in SketchUp models.

Gradient   A gradual change in color over a given distance. For instance, in SketchUp, the sky is rendered as a gradient that gets lighter as it gets closer to the horizon.

Group   Collection of edges and faces that are grouped together and act like a mini-model within the main model.

Guides   Temporary lines that users can create to work more accurately in SketchUp.

Hip roof   A roof where the sides and ends all slope together.

Inference engine   Objects such as colored squares, dotted lines, yellow tags, and other similar objects that appear as the user moves his or her cursor around the SketchUp modeling window.

Interior model   A model of the inside of a building, which must take into account interior wall thicknesses, floor heights, ceilings, and furnishings.

Isometric view   A kind of three-dimensional view of a model.

Iteration   The process of doing multiple versions of the same thing.

JPEG   A compressed file type for digital images.

KMZ   The Google Earth 3D file format.

Landing   A platform somewhere around the middle of a set of stairs.

Lathed form   3D form created by spinning a 2D shape around a central axis.

Latitude   Geographic location measured by the angular distance north or south from the earth's equator measured through 90 degrees.

Layers   A collection of geometry (including groups and components) that can be made visible or invisible all at once.

Lightness   The file size of a model, or the number of faces and textures used to build it.

Linear array   Several copies at regular intervals and in the same direction.

Linear inferences   Helper lines that allow a user to work more accurately.

Lossy   Type of compression that occurs with JPEGs. JPEGs compress file size by degrading image quality.

Mapping   Painting surfaces with pictures using 3D software.

Master layers   Shared layers, containing anything you want to appear on every page of your document.

Materials   The colors and textures in SketchUp models.

Meshes   Surfaces made out of triangles.

Modifier key   A button on the keyboard that users can push to take a different action than what they are currently doing.

Move/Scale/Rotate/Shear/Distort Texture mode   Mode to use when manipulating textures in SketchUp; also called Fixed Pin Mode.

Nest   To embed an object in a separate group or component.

Nongeolocated objects   Objects that do not have a fixed position, such as furniture and cars.

Nonphotorealistic rendering (NPR)   Technology that makes objects look hand-drawn or otherwise not like a photograph. SketchUp is a nonphotorealistic rendering program.

Nosing   A bump at the leading edge of a tread on a stair.

OBJ   A 3D file format that can be used to send data to Maya.

Orbit   Ability to look at a SketchUp model from every angle; this is accomplished with the Orbit tool.

Orthographic projection   A common way for three-dimensional objects to be drawn so that they can be built.

Outliner   A dialog box that lists all of the groups and components in a model.

Pan   Sliding the model view around the modeling window; this is accomplished by using the Pan tool.

Parapet   The extension of a building's walls that go up a few feet past the roof.

PDF   Portable Document Format, a file format that can be read by almost anyone and that is great for sending information to vector-illustration programs.

Pitch   The angle of a roof surface.

Pitched roof   A roof that isn't flat.

Placemarks   Pins in Google Earth that mark locations the user would like to visit again.

Plan   A top-down, two-dimensional, nonperspectival view of an object or space. Also referred to as a planimetric view.

Point inferences   Small colored squares that appear when a SketchUp user moves the cursor over specific parts of their model.

Polygonal modelers   Modeling programs that use straight lines and flat surfaces to define everything; within these modelers, even things that look curvy aren't actually curvy.

Radial symmetry   Having similar parts arranged around a central point.

Rake   The part of a gabled roof that overhangs the gable.

Raster   Term describing images that are composed of pixels.

Resolution   An image's pixel density.

Rise   The total vertical distance a staircase climbs.

Riser   The part of a step that connects each tread in the vertical direction.

Rubber banding   Drawing edge segments, automatically starting each new one at the end of the previous one.

Ruby scripts   Mini-programs (scripts) written in a computer programming language called Ruby.

Run   The total horizontal distance a staircase takes up.

Sample   To "soak up" an element's fill, stroke, and other attributes.

Scenes   Saved views of a model.

Section   A from-the-side, two-dimensional, nonperspectival view of an object or space. Also referred to as a sectional view.

Section lines   Lines that occur where section planes create section cuts in a model.

Section perspective   The view of a cut building where objects seen inside the space appear to get smaller as they get farther away.

Section planes   Objects that let you cut away parts of your model to look inside.

Shared layers   Layers that let you automatically place elements on more than one page.

Shearing   Action that keeps the top and bottom edges of an image parallel while making the image lean to the left or right.

Shed roof   A roof that slopes from one side to the other.

Snap settings   Help you line up elements on your page with a grid or with other elements.

Soffit   The underside of an overhanging eave.

Solid models   Models that are not hollow but are dense throughout.

SpaceNavigator   A 3D navigation tool that looks a little like an enormous button that is connected to the computer via a USB cable. It enables the user to orbit, pan, and zoom with subtle movements of his or her hand.

Stacking order   The arrangement of all elements on the same layer in a document, determining which elements appear to be in front of which.

Stretch Texture mode   Mode to use to edit a texture by stretching it to fit the face it is painted on. Also known as Free Pin Mode.

Stringer   A diagonal piece of structure that supports all the steps in a staircase.

Style   A collection of settings that determines how the geometry appears in a given SketchUp model.

Surface models   Models that are hollow.

Texture-mapping   Painting with textures.

Tread   An individual step, or the part of a staircase that you step on.

Unshared layers   Layers containing elements that exist only on one page.

User interface   The visual elements in a software program that the user uses to interact with the software, such as dialog boxes and buttons.

Valley   The place where the bottoms of two roof slopes come together.

Vector   Term describing images that consist of instructions written in computer code.

Vertices   The endpoints of edges.

VRML   An older 3D file format that is still used by some programs.

Watermark   A graphic element that can be applied either behind or in front of a model to produce certain effects.

XSI   A 3D file format for people who use Softimage.

Z-fighting   The effect resulting from SketchUp trying to decide which face to display by switching back and forth between two faces.

Zoom   Getting closer or further away from the model; this is accomplished by using the Zoom tool.

INDEX